◤ KENT Series in Management

Barnett/Wilsted, *Cases for Strategic Management*

Barnett/Wilsted, *Strategic Management: Concepts and Cases*

Barnett/Wilsted, *Strategic Management: Text and Concepts*

Berkman/Neider, *The Human Relations of Organizations*

Carland/Carland, *Small Business Management: Tools for Success*

Davis/Cosenza, *Business Research for Decision Making*, Second Edition

Duncan/Ginter/Swayne, *Strategic Management of Health Care Organizations*

Finley, *Entrepreneurial Strategies: Text and Cases*

Kemper/Yehudai, *Experiencing Operations Management: A Walk-Through*

Kirkpatrick, *Supervision: A Situational Approach*

Lane/DiStefano, *International Management Behavior*, Second Edition

Mendenhall/Oddou, *Readings and Cases in International Human Resource Management*

Mitchell, *Human Resource Management: An Economic Approach*

Nkomo/Fottler/McAfee, *Applications in Personnel/Human Resource Management: Cases, Exercises, and Skill Builders*, Second Edition

Plunkett/Attner, *Introduction to Management*, Fourth Edition

Puffer, *Managerial Insights from Literature*

Punnett, *Experiencing International Management*

Punnett/Ricks, *International Business*

Roberts/Hunt, *Organizational Behavior*

Scarpello/Ledvinka, *Personnel/Human Resource Management: Environments and Functions*, Second Edition

Singer, *Human Resource Management*

Stahl/Grigsby, *Strategic Management for Decision Making*

Starling, *The Changing Environment of Business*, Third Edition

Steers/Ungson/Mowday, *Managing Effective Organizations: An Introduction*

Tate/Hoy/Stewart/Cox/Scarpello, *Small Business Management and Entrepreneurship*

Tosi, *Organizational Behavior and Management: A Contingency Approach*

KENT Series in International Dimensions of Business

Series Consulting Editor, David A. Ricks

Adler, *International Dimensions of Organizational Behavior*, Second Edition

AlHashim/Arpan, *International Dimensions of Accounting*, Third Edition

Daniels/Radebaugh, *International Dimensions of Contemporary Business*

Deans/Kane, *International Dimensions of Information Systems and Technology*

Dowling/Schuler, *International Dimensions of Human Resource Management*

Folks/Aggarwal, *International Dimensions of Financial Management*

Garland/Farmer/Taylor, *International Dimensions of Business Policy and Strategy*, Second Edition

Litka, *International Dimensions of the Legal Environment of Business*, Second Edition

Phatak, *International Dimensions of Management*, Third Edition

Terpstra, *International Dimensions of Marketing*, Second Edition

 KENT Series in Human Resource Management

Series Consulting Editor, Richard W. Beatty

Bernardin/Beatty, *Performance Appraisal: Assessing Human Behavior at Work*

Breaugh, *Recruitment Science and Practice*

Cascio, *Costing Human Resources: The Financial Impact of Behavior in Organizations*, Third Edition

Kavanagh/Gueutal/Tannenbaum, *Human Resource Information Systems: Development and Application*

Ledvinka/Scarpello, *Federal Regulation of Personnel and Human Resource Management*, Second Edition

McCaffery, *Employee Benefit Programs: A Total Compensation Perspective*, Second Edition

Wallace/Fay, *Compensation Theory and Practice*, Second Edition

*M*anagerial
*I*nsights <small>FROM</small>
*L*iterature

SHEILA M. PUFFER
Northeastern University

PWS-KENT PUBLISHING COMPANY
Boston

PWS–KENT
Publishing Company

For Hugh,
a connoisseur of business and literature

Sponsoring Editor: Rolf A. Janke
Assistant Editor: Kathleen M. Tibbetts
Production Editor: Laura Mosberg/Chris Crochetière
Manufacturing Coordinator: Lisa Flanagan
Interior Designer: Laura Mosberg
Cover Designer: Diane Levy
Typesetter: Modern Graphics, Inc.
Printer/Binder: The Maple-Vail Book Manufacturing Group
Cover Printer: Henry N. Sawyer Co., Inc.

PWS-KENT Publishing Company is a division of Wadsworth, Inc.

Printed in the United States of America.

2 3 4 5 6 7 8 9 - 95 94 93 92

Library of Congress Cataloging-in-Publication Data

Managerial insights from literature
 / [selected by] Sheila M. Puffer.
  p. cm.
  ISBN 0-534-92481-6
  1. Industrial management—Psychological aspects. 2. Work—
Psychological aspects. I. Puffer, Sheila M.
  HD38.M31873 1991
  658—dc20   91-21834
                                               CIP

Foreword

The publication of this book represents the culmination of a project that I first heard about several years ago when its initiator, Professor Puffer, was beginning to think seriously about the possibility of bringing together a collection of short works of fiction that related to the field of management. The idea excited me then, as it does now, and therefore it is a pleasure to see it come to fruition in the form of this volume. The reason why I lent my encouragement to the book's development can be summed up in my view that—to borrow a phrasing used in other contexts—writing about managerial issues is too important to be left (only) to management scholars. Just because O'Henry or Maugham or Kafka or Melville or de Saint Exupéry or other authors represented here never had a course in Management 100, and never carried out a meta analysis of findings from leadership studies, does not mean that they have nothing to say to us on some of the most critical and important managerial issues of our time. Those of us who study and conduct research on organizational and managerial phenomena need to have our thinking stimulated and deepened by writers of fiction who are insightful observers and interpreters of everyday life. This unique volume serves admirably to fulfill that need.

From my experience, and from conversations with many thoughtful executives over a number of years, it seems clear that those who advance to the highest levels of responsibilities in our organizations—whether they be business, governmental, educational or other types of enterprises—are most often those who are able to grasp the subtleties and complexities of managerial problems. To me, this implies that management education must be broad rather than narrow and overly specialized. Thus, a challenge for students of management is to be able to develop the capacity to relate issues and problems from one realm of activity to those from another realm even though the connections may not always be obvious. The present volume, drawing on fictional accounts of "life," illustrates this kind of challenge that is worth taking on. Fictional literature, by definition, involves imaginary characters and events, but it is precisely such imagination that can be a great teacher—if we accept the challenge to learn from it.

Lyman W. Porter

Preface

◆ *ORGANIZATION OF THE VOLUME*

This volume contains short stories, management readings, and discussion questions. The book is divided into four parts. The first three deal with three levels of organizational phenomena: the individual, groups, and the organization. Each part is subdivided into several topics. For example, the topics at the individual level are: life and career choices, stress and coping, perception, and motivation. Part Four is devoted to cross-cutting issues that arise at the individual, group, and organizational levels. These are: leadership, ethics in decision making, encountering other cultures, and change.

In many cases the stories span several topics. *Mayhew*, for instance, could just as easily have been included in the section, "Stress and Coping," as in "Life and Career Choices." This overlap should be seen as an advantage rather than as a blurring of topics. It attests to the richness of the stories. Each story is followed by a set of discussion questions that highlight the major issues in the stories and draw upon the concepts presented in the management readings. The management readings are clustered at the end of each of the four parts of the book because they frequently relate to several stories in the section.

And now a few words about the stories' length, setting, time period, and representative culture. Most are written in the traditional short-story format and are typically a few pages long. However, also included are a story of two pages *(The Seamstress)* and a story of almost 30 pages *(Bartleby the Scrivener)*. Not all the stories take place in work settings. In *Sunday in the Park* you'll be in— where else?—a city park, and in *The King of Jazz* you'll go to—naturally—a jazz club. Nevertheless, I think you'll find that the themes apply to many contexts including the workplace. After all, people who take part in the work world are also members of the nonwork world. The stories span many time periods. You'll go back to the 16th century in *An Interview with Niccolo Machiavelli* (but you don't need to know renaissance Italian, since his descendant speaks 1990s American English). You'll find out what it was like to be an auto worker on the assembly line in the 1930s in *Ex-Champion Nailer*. And you'll learn about the pressures of creating the personal computer in the '80s in *The Inner Circle*. The stories take place in different cultures. Most are set in the United States, but

you'll also learn how the customer is treated (or rather, mistreated) in Russia in *A New Customer,* how the night airmail service got started between South America and Europe in *Night Flight,* and how elephants can wreak havoc in Burma in *Shooting an Elephant.*

You'll also find that a few of the stories are nonfiction. They are essays or excerpts from books about contemporary corporations. The reason is that some topics, such as job design, organizational structure, and culture, are not commonly featured in short stories. Or if they are, they are often depicted in a negative or tragic light. To fill in these gaps and to balance the positive with the negative, I have added several real-life pieces. *Confessions of a Working Stiff* is a first-person account by a former cargo handler at Seaboard World Airlines. *The Inner Circle* is a description of the organizational structure created to develop the IBM personal computer. *Memoirs of a Cub* is a retrospective view of the culture at *The Boston Globe* in the 1950s.

I included the management readings in the hope that you will find them a useful door opener to analyzing the stories (of course, they make good reading in their own right). The management selections are written in a lively style and are often rich in anecdotes and examples from real organizations. Most of them were published in the last several years and reflect the latest thinking. For example, the 1990 article, *Managing Diversity,* addresses an important topic that organizations are beginning to deal with in preparation for the changing composition of the workforce. A few selections, such as *On the Folly of Rewarding for A, While Hoping for B,* were published a number of years ago. They are considered classics whose message and insights are still fresh and relevant today.

♦ ACKNOWLEDGEMENTS

The authors of the literary and management selections collected in this volume may consider themselves strange bedfellows. It might come as a surprise to them to be paired with members of a different discipline. I hope they do not consider it a marriage of convenience, but one of mutual respect that affords opportunities to readers for growth and discovery. I am grateful that these authors have granted permission to reproduce their work. Their talents are to be applauded.

The people at PWS-KENT were instrumental in making this volume possible. I am indebted to Rolf Janke, Managing Editor, for believing in the project and putting the full support of PWS-KENT behind it. Rolf also came up with the clever idea of including management readings to complement the short stories. I want to thank Kathleen Tibbetts, Assistant Editor, for her professionalism and good humor. She was the nerve center of the project and kept the complexities of the review process and copyright permissions under control. The expertise of Laura Mosberg and the other members of the production staff ensured an attractive end product.

Many people offered their suggestions and encouragement. Among them

are the pioneers who have been using literature and other material from the
humanities in their management courses over the past few years. My colleague
at Northeastern University, Edward Wertheim, was very gracious in critiquing
my initial selection of short stories and suggesting management readings. He
anticipated many of the criticisms that later came from reviewers. The reviewers
themselves were of enormous help to me. They gave moral support along with
valuable concrete suggestions that make the book, I think, more useful and appealing. I extend my thanks to all of them, with special recognition of Craig
Lundberg's prodigious efforts.

Dr. Charles Burden
Georgia State University

Prof. William P. Ferris
Western New England College

Prof. Craig C. Lundberg
Cornell University

Prof. Monty L. Lynn
Abilene Christian University

I am also grateful to Stephen Robbins of San Diego State University for his
comments at the final editing stage.

On the literature side, I appreciate the guidance of Richard Fly, professor
of English at the State University of New York at Buffalo. He blessed the project
and assured me I was not a "pseudo-defender of the humanities," a term he
has coined for people who, perhaps unintentionally, misuse literature for other
purposes.

Students at Northeastern University and SUNY Buffalo who have taken
my courses over the past few years were a good sounding board and a true test
of how the selections work in the classroom. In addition, MBA student and
research assistant, Beth Donnelly, collected and evaluated some of the stories.

I would also like to acknowledge the support of several institutions. I am
grateful to the Lilly Endowment for awarding me a teaching fellowship in 1987
to develop materials for a course in management and the humanities. Some of
the materials were the precursor to this book. At the State University of New
York at Buffalo, Joseph Alutto and Raymond Hunt, formerly dean and department chair, respectively, made it possible for me to offer the course as an elective
in the School of Management in 1987 and 1988. The College of Business Administration at Northeastern University awarded me release time, which I used to
work on this book.

Finally, thanks are due to my family. It expanded along with the book. In
their typical style, Hugh and Douglas had more than enough patience to welcome
both a new baby and a new book.

Contents

Introduction

When was the last time you relaxed with a good story? If you're a typical student, practitioner, or teacher of management, you may find that a tough question to answer. The pressures of keeping up with the latest publications in business leave little time for pleasure reading.

Well, all that is about to change. This volume will allow you to enjoy a good story, without the guilt. The short stories collected here are not only entertaining in their own right, but they offer insights into organizational life and the issues that managers deal with on a regular basis.

What do short stories have to offer to the study of organizations and management that isn't found in conventional business cases? These stories are not meant to replace business cases, but to provide a different perspective. Short story writers are good at playing on our emotions: they can get us to feel joy, sadness, humor and frustration. Fiction gives an appreciation of issues that span time and settings, lending itself to interpretation at many levels—literal and symbolic. Fiction provides richness in the description of feelings, people and places, and presents issues in an entertaining and memorable way. All of these reasons suggest that the humanities, as exemplified by literature, can play a valuable role in educating people to be effective in organizational life.

Business leaders have long recognized the value that a background in the humanities can bring to the workplace. In the book, *Educating Managers: Executive Effectiveness Through Liberal Learning*, executives from various industries discussed how their liberal arts education has helped them in their jobs. Some of the comments by Nancy Zimmerman, John Gidding, Charlotte Kuenan, and Patrick Coady are presented below. According to these executives, the benefits of a liberal arts education include adaptability, appreciation of diverse cultures, the development of thought processes, and personal growth [1].

Nancy Zimmerman is President and Chief Executive Officer of Zimmerman Associates, Inc., a 150-employee firm that she founded. Ms. Zimmerman says that the liberal arts degree is especially helpful in developing adaptability, which is a critical skill at the executive level:

> The liberal arts degree, I believe, keeps your mind open to change. Most
> CEOs are probably spending a great deal of their time, as I am, in planning,

which is focusing on the near-term changes as well as the future and being flexible enough to move with change, what you anticipate, or expect. Adaptability is important because servicing a Department of Defense contract that is directly responsible either to an air force or navy customer is very different from servicing an individual, a law firm, or a small business who comes to us for some type of management help.

John Gidding is President of Ex Cellars, Ltd., a wine importing firm involved in buying, financing, shipping, and selling wine from around the world. Mr. Gidding has discovered that a liberal arts education helps him appreciate the historical and cultural contexts of the wines he trades:

> European history is terribly important in terms of understanding how the product is traded. A lot of people get out of the business because they're not really interested in these things. Wine is traded in a peculiar way in Europe and in a very peculiar way in America. They're not rational ways, they're historical ways. There's a reason to be Protestant in Bordeaux, there's a reason to be Catholic in Burgundy. It's not obvious, so the education that I received didn't close down any of these doors. It opened them. It opened up the particular aims of studying, so that in that sense, it was very valuable. What's interesting in the wine business are these historical models and how they are related to one another. I think that's the most interesting thing, other than sipping vintage champagne, if you want to know the truth.

Charlotte Kuenan is Director of Database Publishing at the Bureau of National Affairs, Inc., a company that provides reference information services to businesses and professionals. Ms. Kuenan agrees with the two previous executives about the relevance of a liberal arts education in the business world. Her degree in philosophy gives her the adaptability that Nancy Zimmerman mentioned, and the appreciation of diverse cultures that John Gidding described:

> If you have enough background from a liberal [arts] education to borrow approaches from other cultures and other times and other disciplines, then I think you have gained some of the flexibility that you need, certainly in business, to be able to look at things in different ways, and not to get tunnel vision about a particular project or problem.
>
> As a manager, you have a staff that you are responsible for hiring and developing. Seeing how you can bring the expertise of various people together on a project and have this confluence of different backgrounds bring a project to fruition—that's invaluable.

Patrick Coady is Chief Financial Officer at Acacia Mutual Life Insurance Company. During the early stages of his career in investment banking, he relied largely on his technical education. However, when he rose to the executive ranks, he found that his liberal arts background became more valuable:

> It is when you get into areas of leadership that you begin to truly appreciate a liberal [arts] education. You get to wrestle with issues that no longer have automatic answers. Until you start getting to positions of responsibility that deal with human issues, judgment issues—things that cause you to take a

look at why you do what you do—you probably don't appreciate a liberal [arts] education. Especially if you never thought it was worth anything to begin with.

As you go up an organization, the issues just aren't answered by more facts. You make judgments based upon something that you think is going to happen in the future or happen a certain way or happen just because you say it's going to happen. You know that you're playing a role in creating the consequences. You start looking at facts, and then you begin to discover what shaky ground you're on. What is your goal? What is your willingness to be right or wrong? What do you want out of a decision for yourself? You become better grounded in the diversity of human experience.

The fact [is] that I can sit down and talk intelligently about the history of architecture or the social sciences or the Russian revolution and that such material can give me a new perspective on things—there was a time I didn't think it was worth anything. To me, the beauty of a liberal [arts] education is its value as a thought process, a development process, a growth process.

◆   SUGGESTIONS FOR APPROACHING THE SELECTIONS

My intention is that the works of fiction collected in this volume will serve two purposes. One, to entertain you—to bring a smile to your lips or a tear to your eye. After all, that is why they were written in the first place, and we must never lose sight of this. And two, to help you learn—to help you gain an understanding of organizational and managerial issues. With these two purposes in mind, I recommend that you read each selection at least twice. The first time, read it purely as it was meant to be read—as a story to be enjoyed. In preparation for the second reading, read the discussion questions that follow the story, as well as the management selections at the end of the section. Then, reread the story taking an analytical approach. As with all good literature, the more you read these stories, the more meaning and the more questions you will find in them. It also doesn't hurt to broaden your vocabulary by looking up the unusual words that crop up.

With regard to the management readings, you may find it helpful to refer to the sources where the readings were originally published. The original, unexcerpted versions contain more examples, references, and other material that could not be included in this volume due to space restrictions.

It has been a gratifying experience compiling this collection, and a great excuse to curl up with volumes of short stories and savor them. Therefore, a word of caution: these stories are like chocolates. You sit down to eat just one, and before you know it, you've devoured the whole box.

◆   REFERENCES

1. Kantrow, A.M., and Burns, S.T. 1986. "Conversations with Five Managers" (Chapter 3). In J.S. Johnston, Jr., and Associates (eds.), *Educating Managers: Executive Effectiveness Through Liberal Learning*. San Francisco: Jossey-Bass.

PART 1

Individual Attitudes and Behaviors

Class Notes

Lucas Cooper

In this selection the secretary of the Class of 1966 reports on the activities of classmates some 13 years after graduation. The information in these class notes is not typically included in alumni newsletters, but that is not to say it is any less true. These notes cause us to reflect about the life and career choices we make and how they translate into success and failure.

Lucas Cooper is the pseudonym of Barry Lopez (b. 1945). He was born in Port Chester, New York, grew up in southern California, and attended the University of Notre Dame. Since 1970 he has lived in rural Oregon. Mr. Lopez has written extensively about the relationship between people and the environment in such works as the award-winning nonfiction book, *Arctic Dreams*.

TED MECHAM may be the first member of the Class of '66 to retire. I met him and his beautiful wife Kathy at a Buccaneers game in Tampa Bay in October. His investments in sugar refining and South American cattle have paid off handsomely. Any secret? "Yes," says Ted. "In and out, that's the key." Also in Florida, I saw JIM HASLEK and BILL STEBBINS. They left their families behind in Columbus and Decatur, respectively, to tune up a 1300-h.p. open-class, ocean racing boat, Miss Ohio, for trial runs near Miami. The racing season is set to open there in December, and Jim and Bill (famous for their Indy 500 pilgrimages) are among the favorites. JOHN PESKIN writes to say, sad to relay, that he has been sued by BILL TESKER. Bill, general manager at the Dayton office of TelDyne Industries, claims he gave John the idea for a sit-com episode that John subsequently sold to NBC. It all took place 16 years ago and is more than I can believe. RALPH FENTIL, handling the case for Bill, made it clearer. Ralph is

Source: "Class Notes," by Lucas Cooper, published in *The North American Review,* © 1984 by the University of Northern Iowa.

director of Penalty, Inc., a franchised California paralegal service, which helps clients develop lawsuits. "This is a growing and legitimate consumer-interest area. We encourage people to come in, we go over their past. It's a potential source of income for the client. We let the courts decide what's right and wrong." Hmmm. RICHARD ENDERGEL phoned a few weeks ago from Houston, under arrest for possession of cocaine—third time since 1974. Richard thinks this is it. Unless a miracle happens he is looking at 15 years or more for dealing in a controlled substance. STANFORD CRIBBS, mangled practically beyond recognition in an automobile accident in 1979, took his own life on March 19, according to a clipping from the Kansas City *Star*. His former roommate, BRISTOL LANSFORD, has fared no better. Bristol was shot in the head by his wife's lover at the Lansfords' vacation home outside Traverse City. ROBERT DARKO of Palo Alto (where else?) sends word he is moving up very quickly at Mastuchi Electronics, and to thank DAVID WHITMAN. David, of Shoremann, Polcher & Edders, Los Angeles, specializes in celebrity and personality contracts. Bob Darko is the sixth middle-management executive hired in David's Free Corporate Agent draft. "Corporate loyalty is something from the fifties," says David. "I want to market people on a competitively-bid, short-term contract basis, with incentive and bonus clauses." Tell that to STEVEN PARKMAN. He has been living on unemployment benefits and his wife's income from a hairdressing concern since April of last year—with four kids. FRANK VESTA is certainly glad his job (in aerospace planning with General Dynamics of St. Louis) is holding up—he and wife Shirley had their ninth—a boy—in July. GREG OUTKIRK has grim news—daughter Michelle rode her thoroughbred Arabian, Botell III, off the boat dock in front of their Waukegan home in an effort to make the animal swim. It drowned almost immediately. DENNIS MITFORD, owner of a well-known Nevada wh---house (no class discounts, he jokes), reports an unruly customer was shot on the premises in October by his bodyguard, LAWRENCE ADENSON. Larry, who served in Vietnam, says the publicity is awful. He may go back to New York—after Denny officially fires him for the violence. Violence is no stranger to BILL NAST. His wife turned up in terrible shape at Detroit General Hospital two months ago, the victim of Bill's hot temper. Fifth time in memory. Four hours in surgery? JACK ZIMMERMAN'S second wife and two children by his first wife visited over Easter. SUE ZIMMERMAN was a 1978 Penthouse Pet. Jack is managing her modeling career, his entertainment career, *and* raising the kids. Kudos, Jack. TIM GRAYBULL is dead (of alcohol abuse) in Vermillion, South Dakota, where he taught English at the university. (Please let the editor of *Alumnus* know you want to see Tim's poems in a future issue.) ALEX ROBINSON won't say what films he distributes, but hints broadly that "beauty is in the eye of the beholder," even in *that* area. The profit margin, he claims, is not to be believed. I'm reminded of KEVIN MITCHELL, who embezzled $3.2 million from Sperry Tool in 1971. He periodically calls from I-know-not-where. Kevin was home free in 1982, with the expiration of the case. DONALD OVERBROOK—more bad news—is in trouble with the police again for unrequited interest in young ladies, this time in Seattle. JAMES COLEMAN called to say so. Jim and his wife Nancy are quitting their jobs to sail around the world in their 32' ferroconcrete boat. Nancy's parents died and left them well-off. "We were smart *not* to have kids," Jim commented. HAROLD DECKER writes from Arkansas that he is angry about Alumni Association fund-raising letters that follow him everywhere he goes. "I haven't got s---, and wouldn't give it if I did." Wow. NORMAN BELLOWS has been named managing editor of *Attitude*. He says the magazine's 380,000 readers will see a different magazine under his tutelage—"aimed at aggressive, professional people. No tedious essays." Norm's erstwhile literary companion in New York, GEORGE PHILMAN (Betsy BELLOWS and George are living together, sorely testing that close friendship from *Spectator* days) reports *Pounce* is doing very well. George's "funny but vicious" anecdotes about celebrities appear bi-weekly in the fledgling, nationally-syndicated column. "At first the humor went right by everyone," says George, feigning disbelief. "George is an a--h---," was GLEN GREEN's observation when I phoned. Glen opens a five-week show in Reno in January (and *he* will see to it that you get a free drink *and* best seats in the house). Another class celebrity, actor BOYD DAVIDSON, has entered Mt. Sinai, Los Angeles, for treatment of cocaine and Percodan addiction. Dr. CARNEY OLIN, who broke a morphine habit at Mt. Sinai in 1979, thinks it's the best program in the country. Carney says he's fully recovered and back in surgery in the Phoenix area. THOMAS GREENVILLE's business brochure arrived in the mail last week. He has opened his fifteenth *Total Review* salon. Tom combines a revitalizing physical-fitness program with various types of modern therapy, like est, to provide clients with brand-new life-paths. Some sort of survival prize should go to DEAN FRANCIS. MBA Harvard 1968. Stanford Law 1970. Elected to the California State Assembly in 1974, after managing Sen. Edward Eaton's successful '72 election campaign. In 1978, elected to Congress from California's 43rd District. It all but collapsed like a house of cards last fall. A jealous brother-in-law, and heir to the Greer fortune, instigated a series of nasty suits, publicly denounced Dean as a fraud, and allegedly paid a woman to sexually embarrass him. Dean won re-election, but the word is his marriage is over—and Phyllis Greer FRANCIS will go to court to recover damages from her brother. A sadder story came to light when I met DOUGLAS BRAND for drinks after the Oklahoma game last fall. Doug's wife Linda went berserk in August and killed their three children. She's in prison. Doug said he used to bait her to a fury with tales of his adulteries and feels great remorse. BENJAMIN TROPPE has been named vice-president for marketing for Temple Industries of Philadelphia. BERNARD HANNAH is new corporate counsel in Conrad Communications, Atlantic City. HENRY CHURCH was killed by police in Newark for unspecified reasons. Well-known painter DAVID WHITCOMB moved to Guatemala and left no forwarding address (Dave?). FREDERICK MANDELL weeps uncontrollably in his crowded apartment in Miami Beach. JOEL REEDE lives in self-destructive hatred in Rye, New York. JAY LOGAN has joined insurgency forces in Angola. ADRIAN BYRD travels to the Netherlands in the spring to cover proceedings against the Federal Government at The Hague for *Dispatch*. GORDON HAS-

KINS has quit the priesthood in Serape, a violent New Mexican border town, to seek political office. ANTHONY CREST succeeds father Luther (Class of '36) as chairman of Fabré. DANIEL REDDLEMAN continues to compose classical music for the cello in Hesterman, Tennessee. ODELL MASTERS cries out in his dreams for love of his wife and children. PAUL GREEN, who never married, farms 1200 acres in eastern Oregon with his father. ROGER BOLTON, who played professional baseball for nine years, lost his family in flooding outside New Orleans and has entered a Benedictine monastery. (Paul Jeffries, 1340 North Michigan, Chicago, IL 60602.)

◆   *DISCUSSION QUESTIONS*

1. What is your reaction to the way the people are described in *Class Notes?* What is your opinion of the class secretary, Paul Jeffries? What do you think of the tone of his reporting style and his choice of material?

2. What does this selection suggest about what we value in people and how we judge them in our society?

3. What motives and values do these people have? What were the influences in their lives? How much do you attribute their fate to their own beliefs and actions, to others, to their jobs and life situations? How will these people fill out the rest of their lives?

4. Compare *Class Notes* with an actual copy of class notes from an alumni newsletter. What are the similarities and differences? Which version do you prefer? How does each of them compare to the real lives people lead?

5. Imagine yourself and your classmates 20 years after graduation. How would you want to be described in the class notes? What criteria would you use to judge whether you had been a success?

6. Have you ever attended a class reunion? Explain why you would or would not attend. What would the interpersonal dynamics be like, and what would people talk about at the fifth, tenth, and twentieth reunions?

Mayhew

Somerset Maugham

Mayhew is an individual who abandons a successful career as an urban lawyer for the life of a writer of classical history on a tranquil island. This vignette leads us to question whether a dramatic change of lifestyle is necessary to cope with the stresses of modern life and to achieve self-actualization.

W. Somerset Maugham (1874–1965) had planned to be a physician, but his early literary success led him to change his career plans. He enjoyed fame as a prolific short-story writer, playwright, and novelist. His works frequently take place in exotic settings in Europe and the former British colonies in the Far East.

The lives of most men are determined by their environment. They accept the circumstances amid which fate has thrown them not only with resignation but even with good will. They are like streetcars running contentedly on their rails and they despise the sprightly flivver that dashes in and out of the traffic and speeds so jauntily across the open country. I respect them; they are good citizens, good husbands, and good fathers, and of course somebody has to pay the taxes; but I do not find them exciting. I am fascinated by the men, few enough in all conscience, who take life in their own hands and seem to mould it to their own liking. It may be that we have no such thing as free will, but at all events we have the illusion of it. At a cross-road it does seem to us that we might go either to the right or the left and, the choice once made, it is difficult to see that the whole course of the world's history obliged us to take the turning we did.

I never met a more interesting man than Mayhew. He was a lawyer in Detroit. He was an able and a successful one. By the time he was thirty-five he had a large and a lucrative practice, he had amassed a competence, and he stood on the threshold of a distinguished career. He had an acute brain, an attractive personality, and uprightness. There was no reason why he should not become, financially or politically, a power in the land. One evening he was sitting in his club with a group of friends and they were perhaps a little worse (or the better) for liquor. One of them had recently come from Italy and he told them of a house he had seen at Capri, a house on the hill, overlooking the Bay of Naples, with a large and shady garden. He described to them the beauty of the most beautiful island in the Mediterranean.

'It sounds fine,' said Mayhew. 'Is that house for sale?'

Source: "Mayhew" from W. Somerset Maugham, *The Collected Short Stories of W. Somerset Maugham,* New York, Penguin Books, 1978, pp. 173–175. Reprinted by permission of A P Watt Limited on behalf of the Royal Literary Fund.

'Everything is for sale in Italy.'

'Let's send 'em a cable and make an offer for it.'

'What in heaven's name would you do with a house in Capri?'

'Live in it,' said Mayhew.

He sent for a cable form, wrote it out, and dispatched it. In a few hours the reply came back. The offer was accepted.

Mayhew was no hypocrite and he made no secret of the fact that he would never have done so wild a thing if he had been sober, but when he was he did not regret it. He was neither an impulsive nor an emotional man, but a very honest and sincere one. He would never have continued from bravado in a course that he had come to the conclusion was unwise. He made up his mind to do exactly as he had said. He did not care for wealth and he had enough money on which to live in Italy. He thought he could do more with life than spend it on composing the trivial quarrels of unimportant people. He had no definite plan. He merely wanted to get away from a life that had given him all it had to offer. I suppose his friends thought him crazy; some must have done all they could to dissuade him. He arranged his affairs, packed up his furniture, and started.

Capri is a gaunt rock of austere outline, bathed in a deep blue sea; but its vineyards, green and smiling, give it a soft and easy grace. It is friendly, remote, and debonair. I find it strange that Mayhew should have settled on this lovely island, for I never knew a man more insensible to beauty. I do not know what he sought there: happiness, freedom, or merely leisure; I know what he found. In this place which appeals so extravagantly to the senses he lived a life entirely of the spirit. For the island is rich with historic associations and over it broods always the enigmatic memory of Tiberius the Emperor. From his windows which overlooked the Bay of Naples, with the noble shape of Vesuvius changing colour with the changing light, Mayhew saw a hundred places that recalled the Romans and the Greeks. The past began to haunt him. All that he saw for the first time, for he had never been abroad before, excited his fancy; and in his soul stirred the creative imagination. He was a man of energy. Presently he made up his mind to write a history. For some time he looked about for a subject, and at last decided on the second century of the Roman Empire. It was little known and it seemed to him to offer problems analogous with those of our own day.

He began to collect books and soon he had an immense library. His legal training had taught him to read quickly. He settled down to work. At first he had been accustomed to foregather in the evening with the painters, writers, and suchlike who met in the little tavern near the Piazza, but presently he withdrew himself, for his absorption in his studies became more pressing. He had been accustomed to bathe in that bland sea and to take long walks among the pleasant vineyards, but little by little, grudging the time, he ceased to do so. He worked harder than he had ever worked in Detroit. He would start at noon and work all through the night till the whistle of the steamer that goes every morning from Capri to Naples told him that it was five o'clock and time to go to bed. His subject opened out before him, vaster and more significant, and he imagined a work that would put him for ever beside the great historians of the past. As the years went by he was to be found seldom in the ways of men. He could be tempted to come out of his house only by a game of chess or the chance of an argument. He loved to set his brain against another's. He was widely read now, not only in history, but in philosophy and science; and he was a skilful controversialist, quick, logical, and incisive. But he had good-humour and kindliness; though he took a very human pleasure in victory, he did not exult in it to your mortification.

When first he came to the island he was a big, brawny fellow, with thick black hair and a black beard, of a powerful physique; but gradually his skin became pale and waxy; he grew thin and frail. It was an odd contradiction in the most logical of men that, though a convinced and impetuous materialist, he despised the body; he looked upon it as a vile instrument which he could force to do the spirit's bidding. Neither illness nor lassitude prevented him from going on with his work. For fourteen years he toiled unremittingly. He made thousands and thousands of notes. He sorted and classified them. He had his subject at his finger ends, and at last was ready to begin. He sat down to write. He died.

The body that he, the materialist, had treated so contumeliously took its revenge on him.

That vast accumulation of knowledge is lost for ever. Vain was that ambition, surely not an ignoble one, to set his name beside those of Gibbon and Mommsen. His memory is treasured in the hearts of a few friends, fewer, alas! as the years pass on, and to the world he is unknown in death as he was in life.

And yet to me his life was a success. The pattern is good and complete. He did what he wanted, and he died when his goal was in sight and never knew the bitterness of an end achieved.

♦ *DISCUSSION QUESTIONS*

1. How do you feel about Mayhew and the choices he made in life? Do you admire him, feel sorry for him, dislike him?

2. What things could trigger such a dramatic change of lifestyle? What kind of person would make such a change? Think of contemporary examples of individuals who have made radical career and life changes. What were their reasons for making such changes? Do you see yourself doing so in the future?

3. Compare the way Mayhew approached his work as a lawyer with the way he worked on the island. Where would he fit in the surveys reported in reading 5.4, *Is The Work Ethic Dead?*

4. Review the opening paragraph. How does it fit with the concepts of internal and external locus of control? Which type is Mayhew? Do you agree with the opening sentence: "The lives of most men are determined by their environment"? Justify your answer.

5. Reread the last paragraph of the story: "And yet to me his life was a success. The pattern is good and complete. He did what he wanted, and he died when his goal was in sight and never knew the bitterness of an end achieved." Do you agree with the author's assessment of Mayhew's life? Discuss from the perspective of Maslow's hierarchy of needs [1] (especially the concept of self-actualization), and goal setting theory [2].

◆   REFERENCES

1. Maslow, A.H. 1954. *Motivation and Personality*. New York: Harper and Row.

2. Locke, E.A., and Latham, G.P. 1984. *Goal Setting: A Motivational Technique That Works!* Englewood Cliffs, NJ: Prenctice-Hall.

The Ambassador

Alan Ziegler

In *The Ambassador* we are privy to the thoughts of a diplomat who reflects on his long career and what it means to him. Since his career has been the focal point of his life, one wonders how the ambassador will adjust to his retirement.

Alan Ziegler (b. 1947) has spent much of his career as a professor of English.

The ambassador will admit, to close friends, after a couple of drinks, that he really does not understand the country he is in. But, he is quick to add, that is to everyone's advantage. "The last thing they need is someone who thinks he 'understands' them. Me, I am baffled. Sometimes I think they are ignoramuses, with their silly costumes and bizarre customs, their naive concerns. Other times they fascinate me, and I love to watch them, listen to the way they talk, observe their manners. But never, never, do I understand them."

The ambassador's college roommate and lifelong friend is in the hospital, which makes the ambassador feel nervous and alone. The friend, like the ambassador, is no longer a young man, nor even middle-aged, and there is a chance, although slight, that he will not leave the hospital alive. The ambassador wants to go home, to see him, but it is a sensitive time at his outpost and he cannot leave to visit a friend in the hospital. The ambassador has many friends who go into hospitals; two or three a year don't come out alive. He has often said after dinner, "This is one of the by-products of a long life." If a friend happens to be an important government official, past or present, or some other national figure, the ambassador is allowed to go home—if the friend dies. Sometimes he is specifically requested to do so.

This sick friend is not a particularly important person, and there is a good chance he will survive, but the ambassador finds it crucial to make contact. He is not a sentimental man, except when it comes to his college days.

The ambassador makes a transoceanic phone call, but the hospital switchboard says it is too late at night to ring a patient's room. The ambassador identifies himself, and although he doesn't claim it is state business, he gives the operator that impression. He is a seasoned professional at that sort of thing. The call is put through. The ambassador's college roommate is clutched from a deep, drugged sleep. He thinks the ambassador is in town, and the ambassador has to explain that he is not able to "come right over." When the friend is fully awake

Source: Published in *The Green Grass of Flatbush,* Tallahassee, Word Beat Press, 1986. Reprinted by permission of the author.

and realizes where the ambassador is calling from, he says anxiously, "Is there anything wrong?"

The ambassador has been involved with three wars. He served in Army Intelligence in one, and twice as a diplomat he was stationed in a country at war. Once, he felt partly responsible for the war, which was a natural outgrowth of his country's policy. But he did not, and does not, feel regret, for he is sure the policy was sound. He is not always sure of that, and as he once remarked over coffee, "My greatest attribute to the government is my lack of desire to write a book and go on talk shows."

The ambassador recalls the only fistfight he had as a youth. It was at summer camp; there was a boy, quite athletic, named Corky, who used to pick on him because he was overweight. On a picnic the two of them were left behind to clean up while the rest of the group went swimming. Corky called him fatso, pushed him, said, "What are you going to do about it now that the counselor isn't around?" To both Corky's and his surprise, the ambassador fought back. There was a brief opening and his fist found it, striking a solid blow, then another, on Corky's face. Corky fell, hitting his head against a metal garbage can, then lay motionless. The ambassador still recalls the sickening feeling in his stomach, and praying that he hadn't killed Corky. Corky rolled over, his body shaking. At first the ambassador thought Corky was having convulsions, but then he heard the soft, throbbing sobs. The ambassador walked away and joined the others at the lake. Not a word was every spoken of the fight. The ambassador never got into another one, preferring to be called chicken. Considering his involvement with wars, the word *irony* comes to mind. The ambassador recalls that in college he acquiesced to repeated requests to find irony in literature. Irony has always been moderately interesting to him, to be pointed out, nodded at. But he has never found it amusing.

It is six A.M. The ambassador is at his desk. For his whole life he has been a morning person. As a kid he was at play by eight A.M.; as a college student he got most of his work done before his roommate was awake. Throughout his long career, every newspaper and magazine article about him has pointed out that he is "at his desk and working by seven A.M." Lately, though, he has taken to spending a lot of early-morning time at his desk *not* working: He sits back, sips coffee, and occasionally shuffles through papers, but it is not like it used to be. The phone rarely rings before nine unless there is a crisis.

At first, these unproductive hours bothered him, but now he has come to look forward to this time. He enjoys looking out the window at the weak winter sun behind strangely shaped buildings. The early morning is an escape from the twilight of his career. Though he works less, his superiors tell him he is getting more and more valuable. Irony again. His college roommate sent him a custom-made T-shirt for Christmas which said "Elder Statesman."

He thinks about his college roommate, how he always used to sleep until eleven, never scheduling any classes before noon. He must hate it in the hospital, where they wake and poke you before you can remember why you are there. The ambassador smiles, thinking about the time his roommate came home from a date at seven A.M., and the ambassador was at his desk, writing a paper on Keynesian economics. The roommate said wearily, "You know, I think this is the way I'll remember you and the way you'll remember me, this moment, the one time when our borderlines met." As a result of this statement, that is indeed how he remembers his roommate.

Lately, the ambassador has also been remembering Corky, whom he never saw after that summer. But when the ambassador pictures Corky, it is not usually lying sobbing on the ground but rather hugging his father on visiting day. The ambassador's father is dead. He went into a hospital and never came out. His college roommate is in the hospital, thousands of miles away. Corky is among the legion of the missing, in a procession that marches deep in the ambassador's mind. The ambassador has seven appointments today, but no one will interrupt him for another half-hour. He looks out the window, where a woman in colorful clothes walks with a small, almost-naked child. The ambassador sighs, the sigh of a man awakening from a long, deep sleep, who looks at the clock and sees that the alarm has not yet rung.

◆ DISCUSSION QUESTIONS

1. How does this person fit your image of an ambassador? Discuss his possible strengths and weaknesses in that role, and whether you think he feels he made the right career and life choices. Think of some sacrifices he may have made that are obvious by the fact he makes no mention of them.

2. What is your reaction to the ambassador's opening statements? Evaluate his opinion about the citizens of the country where he is posted: "The last thing they need is someone who thinks he 'understands' them." Is this a "copout"? arrogance? truth?

3. The diplomatic service demands an almost total commitment of one's life. It dictates where to live, with whom to associate, and how to conduct oneself on and off the job. The boundaries between work life and home life are often blurred. What other professions or organizations make similar demands upon employees? Use reading 5.1, *Balancing Work Life and Home Life: What Can Organizations Do to Help?* to make suggestions for improving the transitions in such jobs.

4. One viewpoint featured toward the end of reading 5.2, *Does Your Job Make You Sick?* is "that 'stress' has simply become a fashionable buzzword, a kind of primal scream used to express discomfort of all kinds." What kinds of stressors or discomforts might the ambassador have experienced in his job? Suggest ways of coping with them.

5. How will the ambassador cope with "the twilight of his career" and retirement? Pay particular attention to the following two observations and interpret them:

(a) "Though he works less, his superiors tell him he is getting more and more valuable."

(b) The last sentence of the story: "The ambassador sighs, the sigh of a man awakening from a long, deep sleep, who looks at the clock and sees that the alarm has not yet rung."

SECTION 2
Stress and Coping

The Romance of a Busy Broker

O. Henry

In *The Romance of a Busy Broker* we meet a workaholic whose obsession with work causes him to lose touch with reality. Despite its humorous tone, the story sounds a warning about how the excessive preoccupation with work can create imbalances in one's life.

O. Henry, the pseudonym of William Sydney Porter (1862–1910), is one of America's most famous short-story writers. His stories often have a surprise ending. He had little formal education, and got ideas for his stories while working as a pharmacist, ranch hand, draftsperson, and bank teller. He was arrested for embezzlement in 1894 and fled to Honduras. While in prison, Porter gained prominence for his writing. Since 1919 a volume of each year's best short stories has been published annually in the series, The O. Henry Awards.

Pitcher, confidential clerk in the office of Harvey Maxwell, broker, allowed a look of mild interest and surprise to visit his usually expressionless countenance when his employer briskly entered at half-past nine in company with his young lady stenographer. With a snappy "Good-morning, Pitcher," Maxwell dashed at his desk as though he were intending to leap over it, and then plunged into the great heap of letters and telegrams waiting there for him.

The young lady had been Maxwell's stenographer for a year. She was beautiful in a way that was decidedly unstenographic. She forewent the pomp of the alluring pompadour. She wore no chains, bracelets, or lockets. She had not the air of being about to accept an invitation to luncheon. Her dress was gray and plain, but it fitted her figure with fidelity and discretion. In her neat black turban hat was the gold-green wing of a macaw. On this morning she was

Source: O. Henry, "The Romance of a Busy Broker," from B. Cerf and V.H. Cartmell eds., *Best Short Stories of O. Henry*, New York: Doubleday and Company, Inc., 1945, pp. 59–63.

softly and shyly radiant. Her eyes were dreamily bright, her cheeks genuine peach-glow, her expression a happy one, tinged with reminiscence.

Pitcher, still mildly curious, noticed a difference in her ways this morning. Instead of going straight into the adjoining room, where her desk was, she lingered, slightly irresolute, in the outer office. Once she moved over by Maxwell's desk, near enough for him to be aware of her presence.

The machine sitting at that desk was no longer a man; it was a busy New York broker, moved by buzzing wheels and uncoiling springs.

"Well—what is it? Anything?" asked Maxwell, sharply. His opened mail lay like a bank of stage snow on his crowded desk. His keen gray eye, impersonal and brusque, flashed upon her half impatiently.

"Nothing," answered the stenographer, moving away with a little smile.

"Mr. Pitcher," she said to the confidential clerk, "did Mr. Maxwell say anything yesterday about engaging another stenographer?"

"He did," answered Pitcher. "He told me to get another one. I notified the agency yesterday afternoon to send over a few samples this morning. It's 9.45 o'clock, and not a single picture hat or piece of pineapple chewing gum has showed up yet."

"I will do the work as usual, then," said the young lady, "until some one comes to fill the place." And she went to her desk at once and hung the black turban hat with the gold-green macaw wing in its accustomed place.

He who has been denied the spectacle of a busy Manhattan broker during a rush of business is handicapped for the profession of anthropology. The poet sings of the "crowded hour of glorious life." The broker's hour is not only crowded, but minutes and seconds are hanging to all the straps and packing both front and rear platforms.

And this day was Harvey Maxwell's busy day. The ticker began to reel out jerkily its fitful coils of tape, the desk telephone had a chronic attack of buzzing. Men began to throng into the office and call at him over the railing, jovially, sharply, viciously, excitedly. Messenger boys ran in and out with messages and telegrams. The clerks in the office jumped about like sailors during a storm. Even Pitcher's face relaxed into something resembling animation.

On the Exchange there were hurricanes and landslides and snowstorms and glaciers and volcanoes, and those elemental disturbances were reproduced in miniature in the broker's offices. Maxwell shoved his chair against the wall and transacted business after the manner of a toe dancer. He jumped from ticker to 'phone, from desk to door with the trained agility of a harlequin.

In the midst of this growing and important stress the broker became suddenly aware of a high-rolled fringe of golden hair under a nodding canopy of velvet and ostrich tips, an imitation sealskin sacque and a string of beads as large as hickory nuts, ending near the floor with a silver heart. There was a self-possessed young lady connected with these accessories; and Pitcher was there to construe her.

"Lady from the Stenographer's Agency to see about the position," said Pitcher.

Maxwell turned half around, with his hands full of papers and ticker tape.

"What position?" he asked, with a frown.

"Position of stenographer," said Pitcher. "You told me yesterday to call them up and have one sent over this morning."

"You are losing your mind, Pitcher," said Maxwell. "Why should I have given you any such instructions? Miss Leslie has given perfect satisfaction during the year she has been here. The place is hers as long as she chooses to retain it. There's no place open here, madam. Countermand that order with the agency, Pitcher, and don't bring any more of 'em in here."

The silver heart left the office, swinging and banging itself independently against the office furniture as it indignantly departed. Pitcher seized a moment to remark to the bookkeeper that the "old man" seemed to get more absent-minded and forgetful every day of the world.

The rush and pace of business grew fiercer and faster. On the floor they were pounding half a dozen stocks in which Maxwell's customers were heavy investors. Orders to buy and sell were coming and going as swift as the flight of swallows. Some of his own holdings were imperilled, and the man was working like some high-geared, delicate, strong machine—strung to full tension, going at full speed, accurate, never hesitating, with the proper word and decision and act ready and prompt as clockwork. Stocks and bonds, loans and mortgages, margins and securities—here was a world of finance, and there was no room in it for the human world or the world of nature.

When the luncheon hour drew near there came a slight lull in the uproar.

Maxwell stood by his desk with his hands full of telegrams and memoranda, with a fountain pen over his right ear and his hair hanging in disorderly strings over his forehead. His window was open, for the beloved janitress, Spring, had turned on a little warmth through the waking registers of the earth.

And through the window came a wandering—perhaps a lost—odor—a delicate, sweet odor of lilac that fixed the broker for a moment immovable. For this odor belonged to Miss Leslie; it was her own, and hers only.

The odor brought her vividly, almost tangibly before him. The world of finance dwindled suddenly to a speck. And she was in the next room—twenty steps away.

"By George, I'll do it now," said Maxwell, half aloud. "I'll ask her now. I wonder I didn't do it long ago."

He dashed into the inner office with the haste of a short trying to cover. He charged upon the desk of the stenographer.

She looked up at him with a smile. A soft pink crept over her cheek, and her eyes were kind and frank. Maxwell leaned one elbow on her desk. He still clutched fluttering papers with both hands and the pen was above his ear.

"Miss Leslie," he began, hurriedly, "I have but a moment to spare. I want to say something in that moment. Will you be my wife? I haven't had time to make love to you in the ordinary way, but I really do love you. Talk quick, please—those fellows are clubbing the stuffing out of Union Pacific."

"Oh, what are you talking about?" exclaimed the young lady. She rose to her feet and gazed upon him, round-eyed.

"Don't you understand?" said Maxwell, restively. "I want you to marry me. I love you, Miss Leslie. I wanted to tell you, and I snatched a minute when things had slackened up a bit. They're calling me for the 'phone now. Tell 'em to wait a minute, Pitcher. Won't you, Miss Leslie?"

The stenographer acted very queerly. At first she seemed overcome with amazement; then tears flowed from her wondering eyes; and then she smiled sunnily through them, and one of her arms slid tenderly about the broker's neck.

"I know now," she said, softly. "It's this old business that has driven every-thing else out of your head for the time. I was frightened at first. Don't you remember, Harvey? We were married last evening at 8 o'clock in the Little Church around the Corner."

♦   DISCUSSION QUESTIONS

1. Examine the descriptions of the office atmosphere in the story and how peo-ple behave in it. Would you like to work in such an environment? How could conditions be improved?

2. Describe Maxwell, the broker, from the perspective of stress and Type A/ Type B personality [1]. Does the broker enjoy his work? Will he continue to react this way to his work?

3. As farfetched as the story may seem, what parallels are there to real life where people become so absorbed in their work that they forget other important aspects of their lives?

4. As a concerned friend, what advice would you give to Maxwell? To his wife? Draw upon suggestions from readings 5.1, *Balancing Work Life and Home Life: What Can Organizations Do to Help?* and 5.2, *Does Your Job Make You Sick?*

5. Did the ending come as a surprise to you? Knowing the ending, go back over the story for clues about how the story would conclude.

6. Compare Maxwell with Mayhew in selection 1.2 by Somerset Maugham. Role play a meeting between the two characters. How would they get along? How would they influence each other? Compare and contrast their person-ality traits.

♦   REFERENCE

1. Friedman, M., and Rosenman, R.H. 1974. *Type A Behavior and Your Heart*. New York: Fawcett Crest.

Toughing It Out

Stephen Minot

Manley Thompson, a cost accountant, tries to keep up appearances as his way of coping with a stressful problem. He believes it is best to handle the problem on his own and to conceal it from his family to protect their happiness.

Stephen Minot (b. 1927) was a professor of English at several New England colleges for twenty-five years. After a ten-year period as a full-time writer, he returned to academia in 1990 as chair of the creative writing program at the University of California, Riverside. About this story Professor Minot says "the response to stress is autobiographical, even though the events are not."*

The first week wasn't as bad as he had expected. He began each morning just as he always had—shaving carefully, dressing meticulously, appearing for breakfast on time at 7:15, kissing his wife, Martha, and his daughter, Kim, and reading the front page of the paper while eating. If he allowed any variation in the familiar pattern, it was to be just a bit more considerate—telling Martha how good the eggs were one morning, asking Kim how her homework went the next. These were a calculated part of the plan too. Little shows of affection were not entirely out of character for him, and they would help hide the fact that his stomach was tight as a clenched fist.

Kim's departure for school was generally less hectic than most fifteen-year-old girls he had heard about. She almost always had her books and papers ready. She never forgot to kiss her parents good-bye just as the school bus rounded the corner. But this was not really surprising. Manley Thompson had spent much of his adult life as a cost systems manager, and order was important to him. He had married late and with prudence, making sure that the woman with whom he would share his life would share his values as well. Martha was tall, serene, and self-contained. So it was natural that their one child should be quieter and more sensible than the average teenager. He didn't have to worry about them.

Here it was Friday, the end of the first week, and everything had gone exactly as he had planned. Perhaps he shouldn't have worried so. But then, he had never faced anything quite like this.

Ten minutes after Kim had left on the school bus, Manley was on the road, taking the old, familiar route just as he had every morning that week—through the suburban Oakdale area in which they lived, down Washington Avenue, with its auto agencies and muffler shops, and finally to the business district. It was

Source: Published in *The Available Press, PEN Short Story Collection*, Ballantine, NY, 1985.
*Personal communication.

all unchanged, of course, the same as it had been for years; but at the same time it was strangely unfamiliar. It was like seeing a movie in which they had used his town for a set. Here was the very area in which he had lived and worked for twenty years, yet he seemed to be looking at it for the first time.

It unnerved him a bit, this strange sense of numbed suspension. It was as if all his emotions had been shut down. Could he have caught some kind of virus in addition to everything else?

He swerved suddenly, making a quick left turn without signaling. A truck blasted its horn. A stupid error. It was not like him to daydream while driving. Not like him at all. Amazing, the force of habit. Well, now he had a new habit to learn. As he headed for the west end of town, he realized that he would have to tighten up a bit, keep his mind on his business.

In fifteen minutes he was at a branch library he had found at the other end of town. It was too small to be used by anyone he knew. Often he was the only patron there. When there were others, they were seedy, unshaven types—retirees or even bums. How could anyone let himself get like that?

He slipped into his familiar seat, his back to the reference desk, and began studying the paper. The library subscribed to three, two of them from larger cities. It took him most of the morning to cover them carefully. The afternoons he reserved for *Time* and *Newsweek*.

"Can I help you with anything?"

Manley jumped. Until that day, neither of the librarians had said a word to him. He had assumed that they never would. Having to deal with them was not a part of his plan.

There were two of them, a woman who seemed to know what she was doing and an older man who was either new or stupid. The man often had to ask her where to file this or that. How did someone like that hang on to his job? And how come he was the one offering assistance? As if he could help anyone with anything.

"Just doing a little research," Manley said. He wasn't going to be lumped with those unshaven bums. But perhaps the librarian had noticed that Manley hadn't asked for a single book. Just the papers and the magazines. What kind of research did that look like? "Research," he repeated, struggling for some plausible way to finish the sentence, "on the employment situation. How it differs in these three cities."

"Sounds interesting," the man said. "If I can be of any help . . ."

Manley nodded and pretended to study the news item in front of him— something about a pedestrian who had been hit by a truck on East End Avenue. Had the librarian noticed? He would see at once that the article had nothing whatever to do with employment. Perhaps he would put all the pieces together, realize that Manley had been fired, that he would never find another position at his age, that he was nothing but a bum in disguise. What a story that would make! The man would blab it all over town. Manley stared at the photo of the accident victim. He was bleeding from the temple.

When the weekend came, Manley realized he would have to do something extra to assure his wife and daughter that their lives were in perfect order. Although he had no appetite, he invited them both to go out to dinner. He chose a little steak house they used for each birthday and anniversary. The girls, as he called them, were surprised—not knowing that he was celebrating, in a sense, his first week of endurance. But they were delighted. "You're loosening up in your old age," Martha said, smiling. He forced himself to smile back, rigid as a poker.

At the restaurant he did his best to keep the conversation humming right along. It helped to have read three newspapers a day for a week. He figured that world, national, and local events for each of five days should take him right through to dessert. But when Martha started looking at him oddly, he switched tactics and asked Kim to tell him about each of her courses. "I really want to know," he said, trying hard to make his voice sound perfectly sincere.

As she told him, course by course, he found himself recalling the little office in which he had spent so many years. No, he did not love it. But what had that space become without him? They had talked about reducing personnel, about eliminating his position and even his title. Perhaps they had taken the very room as well. His associates would walk down the hall and find the door missing. Just a blank wall. Would they even notice?

Kim had just stopped talking, so he said, "And what about the math class?"

She looked at him with amused astonishment. "I just this minute got through telling you about that."

The second week didn't go as well. He had planned to go on long walks to get in shape and to read the novels he had never had time for at college. But somehow this drab little branch library was draining all his energy. He couldn't even focus his mind enough to read fiction. Here he was, ten years from retirement, and feeling like an old man already!

To make matters worse, the nosy librarian would not leave him alone. Manley was tempted to be rude, but that was not his nature. Besides, wouldn't he get thrown out if they caught on? So he compounded his lie about the research project. He began looking up back copies of the papers, pretending to be interested in which occupations were hardest hit in the recessions of previous years. He even got back to the big Depression of the '30s. What an appalling catastrophe that was! He'd been born in the middle of it, but what does a kid know about those things?

Reading about that period reminded him of his parents. Somehow they had hung on to their corner grocery store through those terrible times, and only years later did he learn what a struggle it had been for them just to pay the rent. Not once in all that time did they share their troubles with their only son. They didn't even ask him to help out around the store. He always tried to admire them, telling Martha how courageous they had been. But privately he felt some kind of resentment he didn't understand.

As the weeks passed, the nosy librarian turned out to be not such a bad sort. His name was Max and his interest was genuine. Actually, he wasn't even a librarian. He'd been a machinist for thirty years and had been permanently laid off. "I never finished school as a kid because of the Depression, so volunteering here gives me something of what I missed."

"Volunteering?"

"Well, they've got a budget problem like everybody else."

Without quite planning to, they began to develop a research project that interested them both. There were some occupations in the area that had been hard hit with every recession, and then there were others that seemed impervious. Little was being done to retrain those in vulnerable areas. Max felt there was a newspaper or magazine article here, and his enthusiasm was infectious. Manley began to look forward to his work at the library. Occasionally, he almost slipped and revealed everything to Martha and Kim. He reminded himself that he must tighten up and watch his step. He had no right to get careless with their happiness.

In three weeks he and Max were well into the article. Max managed to dig up figures from his union hall records, and Manley applied his statistical abilities to the data they were gathering. When Friday came, they had a rough draft typed. He decided to invite "the girls" out to dinner again. It was an odd sensation, having something to celebrate and yet not being able to mention it. But he couldn't share the news about the report without revealing the rest, so this would have to do.

They were well into the meal and chatting almost as if everything were normal, when he heard a familiar voice:

"Well, Manley, how goes it?"

There was Max. And a woman. His wife? What on earth was he doing on this side of town?

"Well, what a surprise." Surprise? It was a disaster. Stumbling like a kid, he made introductions as best he could. The woman's name turned out to be Francine and was indeed Max's wife. She was outgoing, almost hearty. So much the worse.

"So I finally get to meet the fellow writer," she said. And to Martha, "They've really got something good going."

"All I hear is how busy he's been."

"Busy? That library hasn't been so well used since they built it."

"The company library," Manley said in a low voice to Martha, but not low enough.

"Company?" Max asked. "What company?"

Manley closed his eyes and ran his hand across his brow. It was damp with sweat. He wanted to smash Max against the wall and his wife, too, but Manley hadn't hit anyone since playing football in high school.

"Could you excuse us?" Martha said. "We're having a kind of family conference here. You know how it is. How about coming back to the house for coffee when you're through?" Before Manley could think of how to object, Martha had given them directions.

As soon as Max and Francine had left the table, Manley started to get up, muttering something about the men's room. He had some notion of telling Max that . . . what? That Kim was seriously ill and they really shouldn't have guests to the house, but that Martha didn't know and . . . It was all hopelessly out of hand.

But Martha put out her hand and stopped him. "Wait just a minute," she said, smiling. What could he do but sit down again? "You were going to tell us tonight, weren't you? Kim and I figured you were going to do it tonight."

"Do what?"

"It's really great," Kim said. "What you're doing with Max. But we wanted to hear all about it from you."

He looked from one to the other. "Max called on a Saturday," Martha said. "Three weeks ago. You weren't home. He wanted to give you a message about some more data he'd found. He so admires you. Did you know that? Well, we got to talking and, well, it all came out."

"About the job? Everything?"

"But you were going to tell us tonight, weren't you?"

He nodded tentatively. Then shook his head. "No, I wasn't. I wasn't ever going to tell you."

"Why on earth not?"

"Because . . ." Good God, did he have to say it out loud? Yes, he had to. "Because I was scared."

He reached out and held the hand of each of them. The faces of these two women, these two marvelous women, turned liquid in his vision, swimming, but what strength there was in their grasp!

◆   *DISCUSSION QUESTIONS*

1. Reading 5.2, *Does Your Job Make You Sick?* makes a strong case for work being a source of stress. However, this story deals with the stress of having no work. Identify the many stress symptoms evident in Manley Thompson's thoughts and actions.

2. Why did Manley Thompson handle the problem of being fired the way he did? Examine the reasons he gives, as well as the details of his personal background and upbringing.

3. Suggest other coping strategies Manley Thompson could have used and the likelihood of their effectiveness.

4. Reading 5.4, *Is the Work Ethic Dead?* reports that "workers say that work, rather than leisure, can give them what they're looking for: an outlet for self-expression as well as material rewards." How does this finding apply to Manley Thompson? What will his work ethic be like in his next job?

SECTION 3
Perception

Footfalls

Catherine Petroski

This is an amusing study of one man's stereotypes. The author tells us that "Winston lives by first impressions. He knows the first is always the strongest." While materially successful, Winston muses about why he has been less successful in interpersonal relationships. Perhaps his deep-seated stereotypes about people are part of the problem.

Catherine Petroski (b. 1939) is a freelance writer and lecturer who lives in North Carolina. She writes about various aspects of contemporary urban life. She got the idea for this story while observing joggers on her morning walks.*

Winston Wise regards himself, shaving. He puts down the razor, turns off the water. God, he says, what a handsome dog. He guesses it is so. That is what everyone says, has said as long as he can remember. He wonders will it never cease, even when he's old and gray and feeble. Possibly not. Will it ever do him any good? Will it ever mean anything?

Winston regards his handsome life, his considerable, measurable, verifiable accomplishment: D.D.S. private practice, phenomenal gross, and he's only thirty-two. Porsche 935, BMW 530i. A sound system no one can believe in an apartment everyone would give his eye teeth to have. Hartmann luggage, Club Med—for a while; now windjammers and Land's End. What the hell. Perennial tan. Fantastic health. His own curls in his own hair, his own beautiful straight white teeth.

Winston brushes his hair quickly, smiles at himself, and gets into his running clothes. Once everything would have been by Adidas, but now he is comfortable with a mongrel ensemble. He will probably do the five-mile loop

Source: Catherine Petroski, "Footfalls." Published in *The Available Press/PEN Short Story Collection.* New York: Available Press, 1985, pp. 321–325.

*Personal communication.

this morning. He'll see how the first three go, then decide. No. He tells himself that is no way for a serious runner to think. He tells himself one commits oneself first, then accomplishes. In running as in all things; otherwise, nothing. Five it will be. Winston will not slack off.

Winston sniffs. Hay fever season, already? The live oaks' leaves are falling, he notices. New leaves pushing the old ones off the bough. He thinks of things pushing other things out of the way, of territorial animals, of the neighborhood cats whose serenade woke him at three last night. All in the scheme, he thinks, the nature of nature. All things in their rightful place on the continuum. The universe seems as neat as his instrument cabinet. God would make a good dentist. He rounds the first corner.

Winston can practically run his route blindfolded. He closes his eyes. The morning air is soft as a woman's hand on his cheek, his arms, his legs. The morning is a woman, he thinks, and then he thinks he is a fool. No. He knows he is a fool, or else the whole rest of the world is. Where is this woman, the true morning of his life? Morning has never happened to Winston, and it is already early afternoon. He looks at his black running watch. 6:17:36. No morning. No one would believe it of this handsome dog. Handsome dog, maybe, was the real problem. He wonders if looking like a handsome dog makes women distrust him, fear him, suspect him, not take him seriously. Just another pretty face. No one would believe such a thing. People make themselves comfortable with their best-loved thoughts, however absurd they may be. Winston lengthens his stride and decides to think about his feet.

Winston reaches the country road, though it is definitely within the city limits. The man whose house is the only one on this road is a very powerful man, so powerful he's kept the city from paving the road and from cutting it through the woods to the next major thoroughfare. Now, *that's* power, Winston thinks. He recalls the one time, years ago, when he'd been invited to the house on the country road, a political fund-raiser. The candidate lost. Winston wonders what's the point.

Winston hears music. Debussy. *Images,* solo piano. The harmonies drift hypnotically through the morning's cool air, and Winston thinks of image and its basis in fact. Then he hears the record stick. The same set of notes play again and again and again, and he thinks perhaps no one will come and rescue the record. Finally someone does. With his left foot, Winston kicks a large piece of gravel. It scuds down the road ahead of him. He sees that somehow he is headed the wrong way, that he has been running aimlessly back and forth on this city-country road without realizing it. At this rate, he will never make the five-mile loop by 6:45. He is the stuck record, the perpetual bachelor, the perfect extra man, the eternally elusive good catch. Treading the mill.

Ahead of him on the road Winston sees another person running. The pines and aspens cling to either side of this path today. Whoever it is is too far away, and he thinks how odd that running people often seem genderless. The men are tan and lithe and many of them wear their hair longer; the women are sleek and slim-hipped, short-haired. They all wear the same asexual clothes, the same shoes, the same determined faces. He is gaining on the other runner. His sense of scale tells him: either a very tall woman or a good-sized man. He wonders, and he wonders why he wonders. What's the difference? He is close enough now to hear the other's footfalls, the crunchings in the country road's loose surface. He edges closer, very gradually, close enough to hear the breathing, the heavy exhalations. The length of leg tells Winston. This is a woman.

Winston never speaks when he runs. It is bad form, he believes. It makes one appear casual, half-assed, about the pursuit, when one should be dedicated, committed. Others greet him, or have in the past, and Winston looks through them, to a man, to a woman. This is no time to change. Runners like to be alone with the sound of their own running. If one takes the task at hand seriously, he reasons, others will take one seriously. There is a time and place for everything, and running is not the time for casual social intercourse. Perhaps this is the time to change.

Winston regards the running woman. Ironic, he thinks. The story of my life, he thinks. Jane run, Tarzan chase. He almost laughs, and manages to keep from doing so only with great effort, by shortening his stride. She would think him mad—and be right—running along, laughing at her derriere. Insulting, at the very least. Distance opens up between them. Winston sprints to make up the difference. She's married, he tells himself; she's got to be. Happily, monogamously. Or has a split end in the NFL for a boyfriend. Someone spectacularly fleet of foot. Nothing gross like a linebacker or offensive tackle. Or maybe she doesn't like men at all; that could be. What would he say? He can't think. What a body. With a body like that, she might be stupid. Boring, dull. Is that what people think about him? Winston begins to see the enormity of the problem.

And then Winston falls. "Oh, Jesus," he says, curling to his ankle. Will he one day learn to look where he is going, what he is doing with his feet? Will he one day learn to avoid the holes in the road of life that present no problem to all of those who seem so much less favored than he? Will he one day avoid making a total ass of himself? Why now, just as he's got it figured out? The words would have come. The woman turns and now she jogs up to him. "Are you okay?" she says, still jogging in place. The ankle hurts like hell. No, he is not okay. He will never be okay, not after this fall, this disaster. Ham, he thinks. He is overstating the difficulty, being overly dramatic. He will retain his composure, even if the ankle is killing him. This is it. God, she is beautiful. Tall, dark; intelligent eyes, and such gorgeous teeth.

Winston winces and sits up. "I wasn't watching where I was going," he says, and she smiles, still jogging, though more slowly now. Running is so sensual, he thinks, looking at her. Running is the next best thing to sex. So elemental. Does she know what he is thinking? He could sit here forever, ankle killing him and everything, if she would just stay there forever, jogging in place. He struggles to get to his feet. "Oh, Jesus," he says again. This isn't going to work. Has he broken something? "You can't put weight on it?" the running beauty asks. "It hurts like hell," he says. Manly, but vulnerable. Me Tarzan with soft heart. "I don't know what I was thinking of," he says, though of course he remembers very well what he was thinking of. "Quit trying to walk, then," she says to him rather sternly, "or you'll really mess things up. Sit back down." Who the hell does this woman think she is, the mother of the world? Me *Tarzan*, he wants to say. "Look," he says, "I'm Dr. Wise, and I know better than to . . . oh, shit." He sits back down. She is looking at him, all a question mark.

Winston lives by first impressions. He knows the first is always the strongest. *Dr. Wise.* It sounds so, well, reassuring. "Wise?" she says. "Did you say Wise?" What weird sense of humor does this woman have, making fun of names (which isn't polite) and making cracks about his lack of native intelligence. And at a time like this. Can't she see he's in pain? "I know it doesn't look that way," he says. "No—I didn't mean," she says, "I'm Dr. Chapple. Melissa. Orthopedics. Have we met at Memorial?" Oh, the luck of Winston Wise. "No. Private dentistry." That does it, he thinks. On her right hand is a star sapphire in an antique mounting. She wears no wedding ring. And now it's over. Not only gauche, falling over his own feet, but just a dentist. He won't even be able to run to forget about it.

But for the moment, Winston is in a fix. How will he ever get home? Maybe he could just die right here, put him down like a racehorse. This damned ankle. "I'm going to get stiff," Dr. Melissa Chapple says, and she does some cool-downs. "And you, too—what's your first name, Dr. Wise and Wonderful?" "Winston." She smiles. He loves her teeth. "Winston, we've got to get you home and then you ought to get an X-ray and have that taped." He nods. "Mmmm," he says. "Where do you live, Winston Wonderful?" Is she putting him on? He tells her. Is this her usual roadside manner? It's bad enough being patronized by a doctor, but by a beautiful, fast-running woman, it is excruciating. The hot pain in the ankle is killing him. "I can manage by myself, thanks," he says. He sounds like a fool; it's perfectly obvious he can't manage any such thing. "If you do, you'll be sorry," she says. No, there was no trace of coyness in her voice. Just concern, matter-of-fact concern. "Look, I left my car about a half mile from here. Let me run and get it. Now, will you promise to sit still?"

Winston promises. Nothing—not a Mack truck, not a bulldozer, not the bulls running in Pamplona or even wild horses could drag him from this spot. He will sit here forever. But it won't take that long. Melissa ought to be able to do a mile in six minutes, easy. So, three minutes. Plus a couple more to drive back. Get your head together, Winston. On your mark, Melissa. The fact of the matter is it won't take her long enough. Melissa Chapple will be back in a veritable flash. He will get her expert attention. That will be it with Melissa Chapple for all time. She will forget him, a passing of ships in the night, runners in the morning. Or maybe not. How much is real? How much is possible? Will he ever know before he commits himself?

Winston rests his head on his knees and thinks about that handsome dog in his bathroom mirror and this bumbling fool on the gravel road. Pride goeth before a fall. If Melissa Chapple thinks anything about Winston at this moment, it probably has nothing to do with handsome dogs and everything to do with malpractice suits and Good Samaritan laws. No. He can't believe that. He doesn't want to believe that. Whatever she is thinking of him, it can't be a very admiring thought, handsome dog or no. Winston's ankle feels numb, oddly, after all that pain. Where the hell is she? He checks his watch. She's had plenty of time to get back. Well, she's not coming, that's it. What a crummy trick, leaving him flat, and crippled at that. No. He is being silly. It is paranoid to think this way. Melissa Chapple will be back. People with teeth like that keep their word. She will be back.

Winston hears a runner and lifts his head. It is Melissa Chapple, on foot. What the hell is going on? Where the hell's the car? "You're not going to believe this," she says, "but I locked the damned keys in my car. I was going to get my medical bag out of the back, and I left the damned keys in the ignition. I don't know where my mind is—I never do things like that. God, what a flake!" His ankle is swelling, puffed up like a balloon, but Winston doesn't even notice. "God, that looks perfectly dreadful," she says. "Don't worry. I called a cab. They'll take us to the E.R. Okay?" Winston looks at beautiful, blushing Melissa, and he wants to cry. The ankle, he would say. The ankle has nothing to do with it. What is she thinking? Will women always be such a mystery to Winston Wise? Will he always be such a mystery to them? Melissa pats him reassuringly on the shoulder, then begins to jump up and down on both her feet. She is jogging in place when the cab crunches up the city-country road and stops. Melissa helps Winston up. He can feel that she is very strong. Her arm is around his waist, his arm is around her shoulder, so close. She feels cool and soothing, Winston thinks, very much like a perfect running morning. They get into the cab.

Winston settles back in the seat. He notices that the cabbie is peeking at them in his rearview mirror. Let him. A fare to talk about back at the garage, these two runners, see. Each to his own, according to his abilities. Winston has not caught sight of himself in the mirror and isn't trying to. Doesn't care. He looks at his left thigh, his right thigh. Then, just next to that, Melissa's left thigh, long and tan and very strong. He's forgotten the ankle. He looks up. Melissa smiles at him, and she pats him gently, so gently, on the leg. Winston closes his eyes and can hear footfalls, the beating of his heart.

◆   DISCUSSION QUESTIONS

1. In reading 5.3, *Self-fulfilling Stereotypes,* Mark Snyder says that "despite people's best intentions, their initial impressions of others are shaped by their assumptions about [highly visible and distinctive] characteristics." Identify the stereotypes Winston Wise holds about the runner from the moment he first sees her in the distance to how he relates to her at the end of the story. How do these stereotypes fit the research findings reported by Snyder?

2. Snyder's research also shows that individuals tend to behave in ways that conform to the stereotype others have of them. Select several of Dr. Chapple's behaviors and, using clues from the story, explain why this phenomenon does or does not occur.

3. This story is told from the perspective of Winston Wise. Retell the story from Melissa Chapple's perspective. What might she be thinking at each moment? What stereotypes might she harbor? Winston wonders whether she can read his thoughts. Can she? What signals might she be interpreting?

4. Imagine the two characters had met in a professional medical setting rather than on the running trail. How might they have perceived each other? What stereotypes might have come into play?

5. How sympathetic a character is Winston Wise? What do you like and dislike about him? Comment on his name, Winston Wise. Is he? What has he learned from this experience? Pay particular attention to Winston's reaction each time Dr. Chapple fails to conform to his stereotype of her.

The Seamstress

Wanda Coleman

This short piece is a sketch of a woman who sews in a factory by day and at home for her family by night. In relating the story, her young daughter gives a sensitive portrayal of the woman's burden and inner strength. She tries to make sense of what motivates her mother to carry on under such trying conditions.

Wanda Coleman (b. 1946) is well known in the Los Angeles area where she recites poetry and sings in rock music clubs, coffee houses, and schools. Her works, which focus on black urban life, include poems and short stories as well as the record album, *High Priestess of Word.* She has served in the Peace Corps and Vista in addition to her editorial and broadcasting work. Ms. Coleman was raised in Los Angeles, where her father worked in advertising and her mother was a seamstress.

Mama comes home tired from the sweatshops. She is so tired her body stoops—the weight of slaving on the double-needle power sewing machine from seven-thirty in the morning till four-twenty in the afternoon. So tired she can barely push open the door. So tired we are silenced by the impact of it on her face.

Mama comes home to the imperfect dinner almost ruined by the eleven-year-old anxious to please. To the petulent ten-year-old eager to play outside. To the five-year-old banging on his red fire engine. To the three-year-old crying for lack of attention.

Mama comes home to us so tired she must lie down awhile before she does anything.

So tired, baby, I could cry.

She goes into her room and collapses into the bed. I watch from the hallway. She cries for a few minutes—a soft plaintive whine. I go and set the table

Source: Published in *The Available Press/PEN Short Story Collection.* New York, Ballantine, 1985, in cooperation with the PEN Syndicated Fiction Project. Reprinted by permission of the author and publisher.

and serve the meal. I fix her a plate and take it to her on a tray. She is too tired to come to the table. *So tired, baby, I could die.*

We eat and my older brother and I do the dishes. Papa has not come home. He calls. I take the phone to her. Her side of the conversation is full of pain, anxiousness, and despair. So tired she sounds.

But it's the beginning of the school term. And we need clothes for school. We need. And I watch her rise.

"You know, it was hard today. The white man boss don't want to pay me what I make. I work fast. Faster than the other girls. They get jealous of me. They try and slow me down. My floor lady is an evil witch. She won't give me the good bundles. And she lets some girls take work home to make extra money. But not me.

"I don't care. I'm so fast I do it all right there. And those Mexican girls—they make me so angry. They all the time afraid. Won't speak up for their rights. Take anything they'll give 'em. Even work for less money, which weakens all our purses. We say, 'Hey—don't be afraid.' I don't understand them Mexican girls."

She fills my ears with her days when she comes home from work. I am the one she talks to. There is no one there to listen but me. Sometimes Papa is gone three or four days without word. And my brothers—little boys too impatient for such stuff as a woman's day is made of. And her few friends—she talks to them by phone now and then. She's too proud to tell them how hard it is for us. And since the hard times, few friends come by.

She goes into the bathroom, washes her face in cold water, and dries her eyes. She goes into the front room and sits at the coffee table and slowly, carefully, counts out the tickets that will determine her day's wage. I help her make the tally by reading off the numbers aloud. Her eyes are too tired to see them even with glasses. She marks them down on a sheet of paper and adds them up. Satisfied, she gathers them up and binds them with a rubber band.

I bring her fresh water from the kitchen. She drinks it in long slow swallows and then gets up slowly and goes over to her single-needle power machine, sits and picks up the pieces that will become my new dress. Within the hour I will try it on. She will pin up the hem and then sit in front of the television and stitch it in. And tomorrow the girls at school will again envy the one who always has new clothes.

But now I watch her back curve to the machine. She threads it with quick, dark cedar hands. She switches on the lights and the motor rumbles to life and then roars. Zip zip zip—the dress takes shape.

And this tired. I wonder as I watch her. What must it be like? And what makes her battle it so hard and never give in?

♦   *DISCUSSION QUESTIONS*

1. Analyze the following aspects of the vignette using the theories of motivation indicated:

(a) Use equity theory to account for the seamstress' view of how she is rewarded for her inputs [1]. Suggest ways the inequity could be reduced.

(b) Use expectancy theory to analyze how the seamstress might view the likely effect of exerting low, medium, and high levels of effort on the job [2].

(c) Use need theory to analyze the extent to which each of her needs is fulfilled [3].

(d) Use the concept of intrinsic and extrinsic motivation to compare how the seamstress may feel about doing the same task of sewing at work and at home [4].

2. Examine the stressors in the work life and home life of the seamstress.

(a) According to reading 5.2, *Does Your Job Make You Sick?* companies need to identify and eliminate sources of stress to avoid lawsuits from employees. Suggest ways the company can reduce stress for factory workers such as the seamstress.

(b) Use reading 5.1, *Balancing Work Life and Home Life: What Can Organizations Do to Help?* to develop a plan that the organization can use to ease the transitions for the seamstress.

(c) What impact are these changes likely to have on the seamstress' job satisfaction, life satisfaction, and productivity?

3. Review the last sentence in the vignette: "And what makes her battle it so hard and never give in?" Answer the question using your knowledge of motivation theories and the information presented in reading 5.4, *Is The Work Ethic Dead?* How can management improve the workplace to make it less of a battleground?

4. What are your feelings toward the seamstress and her daughter, who narrates the story?

♦   *REFERENCES*

1. Adams, J.S. 1965. Inequity in social exchange. *In* L. Berkowitz, ed. *Advances in Experimental Social Psychology.* New York: Academic Press 2:267–299.

2. Vroom, V.H. 1964. *Work and Motivation.* New York: Wiley.

3. Maslow, A.H. 1954. *Motivation and Personality.* New York: Harper and Row.

4. Staw, B.M. 1976. *Intrinsic and Extrinsic Motivation.* Morristown, NJ: General Learning Press.

A Hunger Artist

Franz Kafka

The main character in Kafka's *A Hunger Artist* has a passion for his work, but the source of his motivation is complex. The character's unconventional job of professional hunger striker ends with extreme consequences in this bizarre, symbolic story. Understanding the motives behind people's behavior can be difficult, since motives can only be inferred, not observed directly. Moreover, sometimes people have difficulty identifying their own motives. See if you can make sense of the motives of the hunger artist.

Franz Kafka (1883–1924) was educated in Czechoslovakia as a lawyer. He spent fourteen years at the Workers' Accident Insurance Office in Prague, where he rose to a senior position but disliked the work, preferring to write. While there, he invented a device to protect workers' fingers and hands from amputation by a power planing machine. Kafka requested that his unpublished manuscripts be burned upon his death; however his best friend, Max Brod, saw to it that they were preserved.

During these last decades the interest in professional fasting has markedly diminished. It used to pay very well to stage such great performances under one's own management, but today that is quite impossible. We live in a different world now. At one time the whole town took a lively interest in the hunger artist; from day to day of his fast the excitement mounted; everybody wanted to see him at least once a day; there were people who bought season tickets for the last few days and sat from morning till night in front of his small barred cage; even in the nighttime there were visiting hours, when the whole effect was heightened by torch flares; on fine days the cage was sent out in the open air, and then it was the children's special treat to see the hunger artist; for their elders he was often just a joke that happened to be in fashion, but the children stood open-mouthed, holding each other's hands for greater security, marveling at him as he sat there pallid in black tights, with his ribs sticking out so prominently, not even on a seat but down among straw on the ground, sometimes giving a courteous nod, answering questions with a constrained smile, or perhaps stretching an arm through the bars so that one might feel how thin it was, and then again withdrawing deep into himself, paying no attention to anyone or anything, not even to the all-important striking of the clock that was the only piece of furniture in his cage, but merely staring into vacancy with half-shut eyes, now and then taking a sip from a tiny glass of water to moisten his lips.

Source: From *The Metamorphosis, The Penal Colony, and Other Stories*, by Franz Kafka, translated by Willa and Edwin Muir. Reprinted by permission of Schocken Books. Published by Pantheon Books, a division of Random House, Inc. Copyright 1948 by Schocken Books Inc. Copyright renewed 1975 by Schocken Books Inc.

Besides casual onlookers there were also relays of permanent watchers selected by the public, usually butchers, strangely enough, and it was their task to watch the hunger artist day and night, three of them at a time, in case he should have some secret recourse to nourishment. This was nothing but a formality, instituted to reassure the masses, for the initiates knew well enough that during his fast the artist would never in any circumstances, not even under forcible compulsion, swallow the smallest morsel of food; the honor of his profession forbade it. Not every watcher, of course, was capable of understanding this, there were often groups of night watchers who were very lax in carrying out their duties and deliberately huddled together in a retired corner to play cards with great absorption, obviously intending to give the hunger artist the chance of a little refreshment, which they supposed he could draw from some private hoard. Nothing annoyed the artist more than such watchers; they made him miserable; they made his fast seem unendurable; sometimes he mastered his feebleness sufficiently to sing during their watch for as long as he could keep going, to show them how unjust their suspicions were. But that was of little use; they only wondered at his cleverness in being able to fill his mouth even while singing. Much more to his taste were the watchers who sat close up to the bars, who were not content with the dim night lighting of the hall but focused him in the full glare of the electric pocket torch given them by the impresario. The harsh light did not trouble him at all. In any case he could never sleep properly, and he could always drowse a little, whatever the light, at any hour, even when the hall was thronged with noisy onlookers. He was quite happy at the prospect of spending a sleepless night with such watchers; he was ready to exchange jokes with them, to tell them stories out of his nomadic life, anything at all to keep them awake and demonstrate to them again that he had no eatables in his cage and that he was fasting as not one of them could fast. But his happiest moment was when the morning came and an enormous breakfast was brought them, at his expense, on which they flung themselves with the keen appetite of healthy men after a weary night of wakefulness. Of course there were people who argued that this breakfast was an unfair attempt to bribe the watchers, but that was going rather too far, and when they were invited to take on a night's vigil without a breakfast, merely for the sake of the cause, they made themselves scarce, although they stuck stubbornly to their suspicions.

Such suspicions, anyhow, were a necessary accompaniment to the profession of fasting. No one could possibly watch the hunger artist continuously, day and night, and so no one could produce first-hand evidence that the fast had really been rigorous and continuous; only the artist himself could know that; he was therefore bound to be the sole completely satisfied spectator of his own fast. Yet for other reasons he was never satisfied; it was not perhaps mere fasting that had brought him to such skeleton thinness that many people had regretfully to keep away from his exhibitions, because the sight of him was too much for them, perhaps it was dissatisfaction with himself that had worn him down. For he alone knew, what no other initiate knew, how easy it was to fast. It was the easiest thing in the world. He made no secret of this, yet people did not believe him; at the best they set him down as modest, most of them, however, thought he was out for publicity or else was some kind of cheat who found it easy to fast because he had discovered a way of making it easy, and then had the impudence to admit the fact, more or less. He had to put up with all that, and in the course of time had got used to it, but his inner dissatisfaction always rankled, and never yet, after any term of fasting—this must be granted to his credit—had he left the cage of his own free will. The longest period of fasting was fixed by his impresario at forty days, beyond that term he was not allowed to go, not even in great cities, and there was good reason for it, too. Experience had proved that for about forty days the interest of the public could be stimulated by a steadily increasing pressure of advertisement, but after that the town began to lose interest, sympathetic support began notably to fall off; there were of course local variations as between one town and another or one country and another, but as a general rule forty days marked the limit. So on the fortieth day the flower-bedecked cage was opened, enthusiastic spectators filled the hall, a military band played, two doctors entered the cage to measure the results of the fast, which were announced through a megaphone, and finally two young ladies appeared, blissful at having been selected for the honor, to help the hunger artist down the few steps leading to a small table on which was spread a carefully chosen invalid repast. And at this very moment the artist always turned stubborn. True, he would entrust his bony arms to the outstretched helping hands of the ladies bending over him, but stand up he would not. Why stop fasting at this particular moment, after forty days of it? He had held out for a long time, an illimitably long time; why stop now, when he was in his best fasting form, or rather, not yet quite in his best fasting form? Why should he be cheated of the fame he would get for fasting longer, for being not only the record hunger artist of all time, which presumably he was already, but for beating his own record by a performance beyond human imagination, since he felt that there were no limits to his capacity for fasting? His public pretended to admire him so much, why should it have so little patience with him; he could endure fasting longer, why shouldn't the public endure it? Besides, he was tired, he was comfortable sitting in the straw, and now he was supposed to lift himself to his full height and go down to a meal the very thought of which gave him a nausea that only the presence of the ladies kept him from betraying, and even that with an effort. And he looked up into the eyes of the ladies who were apparently so friendly and in reality so cruel, and shook his head, which felt too heavy on its strengthless neck. But then there happened yet again what always happened. The impresario came forward, without a word—for the band made speech impossible—lifted his arms in the air above the artist, as if inviting Heaven to look down upon its creature here in the straw, this suffering martyr, which indeed he was, although in quite another sense, grasped him round the emaciated waist, with exaggerated caution, so that the frail condition he was in might be appreciated; and committed him to the care of the blenching ladies, not without secretly giving him a shaking so that his legs and body tottered and swayed. The artist now submitted completely; his head lolled on his breast as if it had landed there by chance; his body was hollowed out; his legs in a spasm of self-preservation clung close to each other at the knees, yet scraped on the ground as if it were not really solid ground, as if they were only trying to find solid ground; and the whole weight of his body, a feather-weight after all, relapsed onto one of the ladies, who, looking round for help and panting a little—this post of honor was not at all what she had expected it to be—first stretched her neck as far as she could to keep her face at least free from contact with the artist, then finding this impossible, and her more fortunate companion not coming to her aid but merely holding extended on his own trembling hand the little bunch of knucklebones that was the artist's, to the great delight of the spectators burst into tears and had to be replaced by an attendant who had long been stationed in readiness. Then came the food, a little of which the impresario managed to get between the artist's lips, while he sat in a kind of half-fainting trance, to the accompaniment of cheerful patter designed to distract the public's attention from the artist's condition; after that, a toast was drunk to the public, supposedly prompted by a whisper from the artist in the impresario's ear; the band confirmed it with a mighty flourish, the spectators melted away, and no one had any cause to be dissatisfied with the proceedings, no one except the hunger artist himself, he only, as always.

So he lived for many years, with small regular intervals of recuperation, in visible glory, honored by the world, yet in spite of that troubled in spirit, and all the more troubled because no one would take his trouble seriously. What comfort could he possibly need? What more could he possibly wish for? And if some good-natured person, feeling sorry for him, tried to console him by pointing out that his melancholy was probably caused by fasting, it could happen, especially when he had been fasting for some time, that he reacted with an outburst of fury and to the general alarm began to shake the bars of his cage like a wild animal. Yet the impresario had a way of punishing these outbreaks which he rather enjoyed putting into operation. He would apologize publicly for the artist's behavior, which was only to be excused, he admitted, because of the irritability caused by fasting; a condition hardly to be understood by well-fed people; then by natural transition he went on to mention the artist's equally incomprehensible boast that he could fast for much longer than he was doing; he praised the high ambition, the good will, the great self-denial undoubtedly implicit in such a statement; and then quite simply countered it by bringing out photographs, which were also on sale to the public, showing the artist on the fortieth day of a fast lying in bed almost dead from exhaustion. This perversion of the truth, familiar to the artist though it was, always unnerved him afresh and proved too much for him. What was a consequence of the premature ending of his fast was here presented as the cause of it! To fight against this lack of understanding, against a whole world of nonunderstanding, was impossible. Time and again in good faith he stood by the bars listening to the impresario, but as soon as the photographs appeared he always let go and sank with a groan back on to his straw, and the reassured public could once more come close and gaze at him.

A few years later when the witnesses of such scenes called them to mind, they often failed to understand themselves at all. For meanwhile the aforementioned change in public interest had set in; it seemed to happen almost overnight; there may have been profound causes for it, but who was going to bother about that; at any rate the pampered hunger artist suddenly found himself deserted one fine day by the amusement seekers, who went streaming past him to other more favored attractions. For the last time the impresario hurried him over half Europe to discover whether the old interest might still survive here and there; all in vain; everywhere, as if by secret agreement, a positive revulsion from professional fasting was in evidence. Of course it could not really have sprung up so suddenly as all that, and many premonitory symptoms which had not been sufficiently remarked or suppressed during the rush and glitter of success now came retrospectively to mind, but it was now too late to take any countermeasures. Fasting would surely come into fashion again at some future date, yet that was no comfort for those living in the present. What, then, was the hunger artist to do? He had been applauded by thousands in his time and could hardly come down to showing himself in a street booth at village fairs, and as for adopting another profession, he was not only too old for that but too fanatically devoted to fasting. So he took leave of the impresario, his partner in an unparalleled career, and hired himself to a large circus; in order to spare his own feelings he avoided reading the conditions of his contract.

A large circus with its enormous traffic in replacing and recruiting men, animals and apparatus can always find a use for people at any time, even for a hunger artist, provided of course that he does not ask too much, and in this particular case anyhow it was not only the artist who was taken on but his famous and long-known name as well; indeed considering the peculiar nature of his performance, which was not impaired by advancing age, it could not be objected that here was an artist past his prime, no longer at the height of his professional skill, seeking a refuge in some quiet corner of a circus; on the contrary, the hunger artist averred that he could fast as well as ever, which was entirely credible; he even alleged that if he were allowed to fast as he liked, and this was at once promised him without more ado, he could astound the world by establishing a record never yet achieved, a statement which certainly provoked a smile among the other professionals, since it left out of account the change in public opinion, which the hunger artist in his zeal conveniently forgot.

He had not, however, actually lost his sense of the real situation and took it as a matter of course that he and his cage should be stationed, not in the middle of the ring as a main attraction, but outside, near the animal cages, on a site that was after all easily accessible. Large and gaily painted placards made a frame for the cage and announced what was to be seen inside it. When the public came thronging out in the intervals to see the animals, they could hardly avoid passing the hunger artist's cage and stopping there for a moment, perhaps they might even have stayed longer had not those pressing behind them in the narrow gangway, who did not understand why they should be held up on their way towards the excitements of the menagerie, made it impossible for anyone to stand gazing quietly for any length of time. And that was the reason why the hunger artist, who had of course been looking forward to these visiting hours as the main achievement of his life, began instead to shrink from them. At first he could hardly wait for the intervals; it was exhilarating to watch the crowds come streaming his way, until only too soon—not even the most obstinate self-deception, clung to almost consciously, could hold out against the fact—the conviction was borne in upon him that these people, most of them, to judge from their actions, again and again, without exception, were all on their way to the menagerie. And the first sight of them from the distance remained the best. For when they reached his cage he was at once deafened by the storm of shouting and abuse that arose from the two contending factions, which renewed themselves continuously, of those who wanted to stop and stare at him—he soon began to dislike them more than the others—not out of real interest but only out of obstinate self-assertiveness, and those who wanted to go straight on to the animals. When the first great rush was past, the stragglers came along, and these, whom nothing could have prevented from stopping to look at him as long as they had breath, raced past with long strides, hardly even glancing at him, in their haste to get to the menagerie in time. And all too rarely did it happen that he had a stroke of luck, when some father of a family fetched up before him with his children, pointed a finger at the hunger artist and explained at length what the phenomenon meant, telling stories of earlier years when he himself had watched similar but much more thrilling performances, and the children, still rather uncomprehending, since neither inside nor outside school had they been sufficiently prepared for this lesson—what did they care about fasting?—yet showed by the brightness of their intent eyes that new and better times might be coming. Perhaps, said the hunger artist to himself many a time, things would be a little better if his cage were set not quite so near the menagerie. That made it too easy for people to make their choice, to say nothing of what he suffered from the stench of the menagerie, the animals' restlessness by night, the carrying past of raw lumps of flesh for the beasts of prey, the roaring at feeding times, which depressed him continually. But he did not dare to lodge a complaint with the management; after all, he had the animals to thank for the troops of people who passed his cage, among whom there might always be one here and there to take an interest in him, and who could tell where they might seclude him if he called attention to his existence and thereby to the fact that, strictly speaking, he was only an impediment on the way to the menagerie.

A small impediment, to be sure, one that grew steadily less. People grew familiar with the strange idea that they could be expected, in times like these, to take an interest in a hunger artist, and with this familiarity the verdict went out against him. He might fast as much as he could, and he did so; but nothing could save him now, people passed him by. Just try to explain to anyone the art of fasting! Anyone who has no feeling for it cannot be made to understand it. The fine placards grew dirty and illegible, they were torn down; the little notice board telling the number of fast days achieved, which at first was changed carefully every day, had long stayed at the same figure, for after the first few weeks even this small task seemed pointless to the staff; and so the artist simply fasted on and on, as he had once dreamed of doing, and it was no trouble to him, just as he had always foretold, but no one counted the days, no one, not even the artist himself, knew what records he was already breaking, and his heart grew heavy. And when once in a time some leisurely passer-by stopped, made merry over the old figure on the board and spoke of swindling, that was in its way the stupidest lie ever invented by indifference and inborn malice, since it was not the hunger artist who was cheating; he was working honestly, but the world was cheating him of his record.

Many more days went by, however, and that too came to an end. An overseer's eye fell on the cage one day and he asked the attendants why this perfectly good cage should be left standing there unused with dirty straw inside it; nobody knew, until one man, helped out by the notice board, remembered about the hunger artist. They poked into the straw with sticks and found him in it. "Are you still fasting?" asked the overseer. "When on earth do you mean to stop?" "Forgive me, everybody," whispered the hunger artist; only the overseer, who had his ear to the bars, understood him. "Of course," said the overseer, and tapped his forehead with a finger to let the attendants know what state the man was in, "we forgive you." "I always wanted you to admire my fasting," said the hunger artist. "We do admire it," said the overseer, affably. "But you shouldn't admire it," said the hunger artist. "Well, then we don't admire it," said the overseer, "but why shouldn't we admire it?" "Because I have to fast, I can't help it," said the hunger artist. "What a fellow you are," said the overseer, "and why can't you help it?" "Because," said the hunger artist, lifting his head a little and speaking, with his lips pursed, as if for a kiss, right into the overseer's ear, so that no syllable might be lost, "because I couldn't find the food I liked. If I had found it, believe me, I should have made no fuss and stuffed myself like you or anyone else." These were his last words, but in his dimming eyes remained the firm though no longer proud persuasion that he was still continuing to fast.

"Well, clear this out now!" said the overseer, and they buried the hunger artist, straw and all. Into the cage they put a young panther. Even the most insensitive felt it refreshing to see this wild creature leaping around the cage that had so long been dreary. The panther was all right. The food he liked was brought him without hesitation by the attendants; he seemed not even to miss his freedom; his noble body, furnished almost to the bursting point with all that it needed, seemed to carry freedom around with it too; somewhere in his jaws it seemed to lurk; and the joy of life streamed with such ardent passion from his throat that for the onlookers it was not easy to stand the shock of it. But they braced themselves, crowded round the cage, and did not want ever to move away.

♦ *DISCUSSION QUESTIONS*

1. Analyze the hunger artist's motives using need theory [1], expectancy theory [2], and goal setting [3].

2. Think of people who perform outrageous feats to get into the *Guinness Book of Records*. Do they have the same motives as the hunger artist?

3. Compare the hunger artist with the panther who replaced him. Why were the onlookers so entranced by the panther? Which do you prefer: the hunger artist or the panther?

4. Compare the hunger artist with Mayhew in selection 1.2 by Somerset Maugham. What are the similarities and differences in their motives?

5. What does the hunger artist symbolize? What other people do you know who could be considered hunger artists in their approach to life and work?

◆   *REFERENCES*

1. Maslow, A.H. 1954. *Motivation and Personality*. New York: Harper and Row.

2. Vroom, V.H. 1964. *Work and Motivation*. New York: Wiley.

3. Locke, E.A., and Latham, G.P. 1984. *Goal Setting: A Motivational Technique That Works!* Englewood Cliffs, NJ: Prentice-Hall.

SECTION 5

Management Readings

Balancing Work Life and Home Life: What Can Organizations Do to Help?

Douglas T. Hall ◆ *Judith Richter*

This reading introduces the concept of the daily transitions that people make between the boundaries of work and home, particularly at the beginning and the end of the day. The authors argue that psychological and physical boundaries need to be set to help people manage role conflict and overload. They evaluate options that organizations can consider to help employees ease the daily transition, taking into account such factors as gender and family status, job characteristics, and career stage.

Douglas Tim Hall is a professor of organizational behavior and associate dean of the School of Management at Boston University. He has served as a consultant to many large corporations including AT&T and Ford Motor Company. Judith Richter is a faculty member in the Graduate School of Business Administration at Tel Aviv University, Israel. She has been involved in human resources training programs for air crews in the Israeli air force.

The purpose of this article is to discuss what organizations can do to foster more effective management of professional and private lives. We will argue, for example, that organizations need to help employees define the boundaries between home and work, that these boundaries should be more flexible than they currently are, that the value of transition time between home and work should be recognized (as should the differences in employees' styles of making these daily transitions), and that the family should be more consciously integrated into career and human resource management.

Source: Excerpted from Douglas T. Hall and Judith Richter, "Balancing Work Life and Home Life: What Can Organizations Do to Help?" *Academy of Management EXECUTIVE*, 1988, Vol. II, No. 3, pp. 213–223. Reprinted by permission.

◆   *A NEW CONCEPT: DAILY TRANSITIONS*

We believe that the best way to study the work/home relationship is to look at people's actual behavior as they deal with the conflicts and other effects these two domains have on each other. (We will use the generic term "domain" to describe the areas represented by "home" and "work.")

The method we propose involves looking at the daily transitions that people make as they cross the boundaries between work and home. The idea is that the best way to understand how the two domains affect each other is to look at them in their interface; that is, as they come into contact with one another. The point at which home and work come into contact with one another is when the employee is moving, either physically or psychologically, from one to the other. We propose that the transitions between work and home capture the major issues in the general relationship between the two domains.

Transitions across the boundaries between work and home domains can occur either with the physical move from one domain to the other at the start or the end of the working day, or with the psychological shift that occurs when a person is physically in one domain and becomes mentally concerned with the other. The former are called planned transitions, while the latter are termed interposed transitions.

Interposed transitions can be either self-initiated or imposed by the actions of members of the other domain who intervene in one's current domain.

Domains are separated by boundaries, which are created by both the individual and by the work and home settings. Boundary demarcation may be physical, in which case the markers are time and location, or psychological, whereby in which what Kurt Lewin called the individual's "life space" (or view of the world) is separated into regions representing different roles or areas of activity.[1]

The boundaries are described by two dimensions: flexibility and permeability. Flexibility describes the extent to which the physical time and location markers, such as working hours and workplace, may be changed. Permeability describes the degree to which a person physically located in one domain may be psychologically concerned with the other.

Transition Styles

The process of crossing physical and psychological boundaries during scheduled transitions defines an individual's transition style. There are three basic styles: *anticipatory, discrete,* and *lagged.* By anticipatory we mean that concern with the domain of destination begins before the person physically leaves the current domain. In the discrete style the individual's concern with the domain of destination starts upon arrival there. In the lagged style, the person's concern with the newly entered domain does not start until he or she has been physically present for a period of time.

In the following sections we will discuss research findings related to the ways people cross the work/home boundaries on a daily basis and how they attempt to gain balance between the two domains. We will then consider steps that organizations can take to help employees manage work/home boundaries more effectively.

Differences Between Morning and Evening Transitions

We have found that people tend to use an anticipatory transition style in the move from home to work and a discrete transition style in the shift from work to home. In other words, in the morning, people begin thinking about work long before they leave home. In the afternoon, on the other hand, people do not start thinking about home until they leave work. In terms of boundary permeability, this indicates that the morning home boundaries tend to be permeable, while in the evening the work boundaries tend to be impermeable.

Our research also found that as people make daily transitions, they change their concepts of themselves; that is, the way they see themselves. In other words, there is a "work self" and a "home self." The process of changing self-image is asymmetrical, however. In the afternoon, people change to their "home self" only after leaving the office (discrete), while in the morning they change into their work self when they are still at home (anticipatory).

From the family's perspective, morning transitions are not experienced as an issue of conflict within the family, and most people are satisfied with the way they or their spouse leaves home in the morning. Conflict is more often associated with the way people reenter their home.

None of the organizations involved in our study seems to have any set rituals or procedures regarding entry into the workplace. The predominant organizational culture supports quick entry to work, and morning socializing is limited. This is especially true for younger, more junior employees, who need to be visibly hard-working and motivated. Similarly, in most cases concluding work is not associated with any organizational procedures or rituals. Organizations do, however, clearly convey the message that they expect time boundaries to be followed, and most employers set minimums—expecting workers to be available beyond them as well, at least occasionally. This expectation epitomizes a very clear conflict between the family and the organization, as an expansion of work hours has a direct effect on family time.

Gender Differences in Transition Styles

Evening transitions from work to home are experienced differently by the men and women in our sample. For women, the evening shift was considered highly stressful. The period of reentering their home was most often seen by women as the day's most hectic period, as they had to shift abruptly to their home roles and get immediately involved in their domestic chores. The men tended to leave the office later than the women; they were also more likely than their wives to go through an unwinding period (reading the newspaper, for example) before getting fully involved in their home activities. Thus, men experienced more flexible boundaries than women, both at work and at home. Spouses often seemed out of sync in the evening, as men tended to unwind from work rather slowly at home, while women became immediately involved in home tasks as soon as they arrived.

Interposed Transitions: The Management of Boundary Permeability

The research interviews consistently showed home boundaries to be more permeable than work boundaries, to both externally imposed and self-initiated penetrations. However, different patterns of work and home boundary permeability were found for men and women. Women's home boundaries were cognitively more permeable (that is, they thought about work at home more often than did men) while men's were behaviorally more permeable (that is, men did more actual job-related work in their homes than did women).

Many of the women we interviewed were pioneers in their respective careers and felt that they were "test cases." Their high work involvement might stem in part from strong motivation to establish their positions.

While women's level of involvement at work did not differ from men's, they admitted to a certain level of concern with home issues at work. As one of them put it, "There's always a low hum to cope with"—caused by the tendency of children to call their mothers more than their fathers at work, thereby forcing higher permeability of work boundaries on women.

Our findings suggest that different families have different norms about spouses bringing work home. Some encourage it, viewing it as a support for advancing the spouse's career or as a family endeavor ("What he/she does is for us"). Others discourage it, viewing it as a violation of the family's time.

Externally imposed penetration of work into the home (for example, a telephone call) is often perceived by the spouse as a matter of choice and control by his or her mate, thus potentially becoming an area of disagreement.

Overall, spouses tend to agree in their attitudes toward boundary permeability. Differences arise in men's greater conflict regarding activity and time-consuming home matters penetrating their work. Our research found that organizations did not have any specific structural regulations regarding this phenomenon.

◆ PERSONAL BOUNDARY MANAGEMENT

Need for Separation of Work/Home Boundaries

On the basis of our findings, two conclusions about boundaries can be drawn: First, that people have a preference for a psychological separation between work and home parallel to the physical separation and, second, interference can more easily be dealt with when home issues come to work than vice versa.

People have greater control over home interference at work and can handle it by simply asking that the interaction be delayed until a more favorable time. People are much less likely to consider making such a request when work penetrates the home, as unconditional availability is highly valued by individuals and their employers (though not always by the spouse). Moreover, people generally trust their relationships with their spouse and believe they can compensate for not being available while at work, but being unavailable to work at home is more risky.

Boundary permeability epitomizes role conflict, as a person engaged in a specific role is called on to operate in another role simultaneously. This might result in "role overload" and conflict between the expectations of the two domains.

◆ EFFECTS OF ORGANIZATIONAL LEVEL AND CAREER STAGE

While organizations often have no official policy regarding the permeability of home boundaries, it seems that the nature of the position one holds clearly relates to the extent of work penetration into the home. People in management positions mentioned that in earlier career stages, when they were more in "individual-contributor" positions (engineers, for example), their work inherently had more emergencies that required rapid action. Thus, junior employees had to be available to a greater extent than their seniors, and home boundaries were more permeable to work penetration, at least in regard to telephone calls. People in advanced career stages often noted that when lower on their career ladder they tended to carry work home more often. One of them, now in charge of his own company, said that once established in his business he tried to stop taking work home but hoped that his subordinates would continue and even commented, "They'd better do it."

On the basis of detailed calculations, Bartolemè has proposed that, in fact, after subtracting actual working hours from the day, managers could still spend more time with their families and that they tend to use their work as an "alibi" for their actual or psychological absence from home.[2] In our research we found home boundaries were frequently violated and were more permeable than work boundaries, as leaving the workplace did not necessarily mean reducing one's psychological work involvement. Participants reported that this continuous concern with work was even stronger early in their career.

◆ WHAT ORGANIZATIONS CAN DO

Helping Individuals Cope: Separating Work and Home

Many of the proposed remedies in the area of work/life conflicts, such as working at home and at-work child care, entail integration of work and home. Our findings, however, indicate a far greater need for separation of the two domains. For example, in a training seminar for district sales managers in a large corporation, an important issue that arose frequently was that of the boundary between work and home. Many managers felt that the boundaries were too "permeable" (as Richter also found was true for many people who work at home).[3] A district sales manager's work/home boundaries are quite permeable in that he or she is always "on call" vis-à-vis sales reps, often works at home, and has to travel to the field during personal time (evenings and weekends).

Legitimizing Boundaries

An important step in managing these work/home boundaries is legitimizing them. This entails a negotiation between the individual and the people involved in each of his or her domains so that they can agree on the limits of where work stops and home begins. For example, if a company has a policy that employees are not to be expected to travel on weekends, it should try to plan distant meetings so that they are not scheduled for Monday mornings or Friday afternoons.

Unfortunately, in many organizations, part of the current effort to enhance productivity—to do more with less staff—means the work day is spilling over into personal time, and work/home boundaries are becoming more blurred, not clarified. As a very concrete example, consider the breakfast meeting and the "power breakfast." As lunch schedules become more crowded, breakfast has become the new "free" time for work.

Breakfast meetings should be avoided as a frequent practice, and early morning time should be reserved for personal transitions. Managers should attempt to set priorities and plan work so that if a meeting is necessary it can be held during normal working hours.

Planning Personal Time

Another way to set boundaries is through advance personal planning. In the district seminars described earlier, there was a long discussion about simple ideas such as marking on one's new office calendar, at the beginning of each year, important family dates (birthdays, anniversaries, etc.), so that no business travel or dinner meetings would be scheduled at those times, and discussing with family members when peak times can be expected so that the family will be prepared for the individual's absence.

The critical point here is to make boundaries clear and discussable. What causes tension is boundaries becoming set through unspoken norms that develop over time and become undiscussable. This is an especially severe problem on the home side, since home life is usually affected more by work life than vice versa. Thus, unless explicit boundaries are set, home life can easily find itself at the mercy of work.

◆   CHANGING ORGANIZATIONS

Most of the suggestions so far have dealt with ways the organization can support individuals in managing work/home transitions. Now let us shift our focus and consider ways the organization itself might be changed to facilitate balance in daily transitions.

Recognizing the Value of the Transition

A critical first step is for organizations to recognize the value of the transition for the employee and the employer. The morning "fog period" mentioned earlier serves the important function of letting the employee disengage from unfinished tasks at home so that he or she can be fully available for work. If the individual's normal way of making the transition is interrupted, those home concerns may remain as unfinished business throughout the day, interfering with involvement in work tasks.

Similarly, the afternoon transition plays an important buffering role, letting the individual unwind from work before getting involved at home. Not only does this time increase the individual's availability to the family (and thus the quality of family life) but it also provides emotional rest from work, which improves the person's effectiveness the next day.

Making Boundaries More Flexible

In addition to flexibility in work arrangements, flexibility can take the form of staying late at work or coming in late. One of the most popular methods of adding flexibility at work is flextime, in which employees choose their own work hours surrounding certain core hours during which all employees work.

Another form of flexibility is flexplace, under which individuals are allowed to do certain work at home. An estimated 1.9 million Americans do paid work in their homes.[4] For example, Control Data has a Home-Work program, in which computer programmers work at home with computer terminals using a centrally located small office when they need meeting space or the use of support services, such as typing or photocopying.

A study by Honeywell Information Systems, cited by Kotlowitz, asked employees what they would prefer if given a choice between working at the office or at home by telecommunication. The preferences were as follows: continue to go to the office every day—56%; split time between home and office—36%; work at home—7%. Kotlowitz reports that results were found in a Wisconsin insurance firm where the majority of home-based clerical workers could not juggle work and child care in the same space and time; most quit within two years.

Kotlowitz reports that it is not impossible to combine work and home. Some people do make it work. It seems to become easier when the work is part-time and the children are past the toddler stage. These conditions make boundary-setting easier, as part-time work is more easily segmented and older children can be more understanding of work boundaries.

However, there are still risks, as the employee may be deprived of office social contact, and work demands might spill over too much into the territory of the home role. Thus, the greater flexibility permitted by arrangements such as flextime and flexplace is often at the expense of the greater permeability of the home domain: Work is literally moving into the home. Unless the employee can set clear boundaries, both physical and psychological, such arrangements can increase rather than decrease work and family stress.

Scheduling for Natural Working Day Rhythms

People develop natural rhythms as they make their daily transitions between work and home.[5] In the morning, some people start off in that "job fog" described earlier, while others arrive at work without any "leftovers" from home. In fact, many people are psychologically involved in work even before leaving home, so that once they enter the office they are already into their "work self" and available for almost any task. People tend to prefer to have that first half-hour or so unstructured to ease into work, go over their day's schedule, and plan the rest of the day.

In light of this, organizations considering flextime should be aware that it means employees may be out of sync with respect to where they are in their daily transitions. We suggest that the scheduling of formal work take into account a boundary zone that allows time for people to adjust to being at work. Specifically, this means that meetings should not be scheduled too close to the beginning or end of the day.

Understanding Employee Transition Styles

Not only should employees' needs for transition time be taken into account, but managers should be sensitive to individual differences among employees in their ways of making those transitions. Failure to do so could result in unnecessary group conflict and unfair "labeling" of peers. For example, what if one employee in a department tends to make discrete transitions, being immediately ready for work on arrival, while a co-worker makes more lagged transitions, taking more time to settle into work? And what if their manager regularly holds department meetings at the start of the work day? Chances are that those two employees are not going to be able to communicate too well with each other at that time of day.

We have already seen that there are male-female differences in transition styles, especially in the afternoon. Women tend to start thinking about home matters before they leave work, while men stay engaged in work until they arrive home. What if a particular meeting was always held in the afternoon, and one of its attendees was a woman who was perceived as "uninvolved" because she was thinking ahead to picking up her child at school? This would be a case of negative attribution, which could cause career damage, associated with gender, and would be completely unfair because the observed behaviors would be caused by a natural difference in transition style and not by a difference in work performance or dedication.

Managers should be able to construct a profile of the transition styles of their employees (or, better yet, have employees diagnose their own styles). What issues might a particular combination suggest? How should they be dealt with? A self-diagnosis by employees, followed by an open discussion, could be a useful form of team building. Our experience is that people can easily diagnose their own styles and are quite comfortable discussing them. It is a safe and usually lively way to discuss issues of work/home conflicts.

Optimal Commuting and Office Location

The daily commute to and from work plays an important psychological function in that it gives people a chance to get "into" work in the morning and to "unwind" in the afternoon. The commute serves as a buffer, an interface between professional and private life. Living too close shortens this crucial time. Some people who live near work schedule a transition period, such as walking around the block, before going home. According to our findings, a commuting time of about 30 minutes is ideal, as it allows time for gearing up in the morning and winding down in the evening. The use of car pools should be encouraged, not only because of energy conservation, but also because they free people to some extent psychologically from the strain of driving and allow them to put full energy into the transition to or from work.

Child Care at Work

Our study found that living too close to work put women under considerable pressure to be home more frequently, especially when they had young children, and thus increased the permeability of work and home boundaries. Accordingly, we would caution organizations about providing child care in the work setting because of its potential blurring of the work/family boundary. This does not necessarily mean that organizations should not provide child care benefits, but these benefits could be alternatives to on-site child care, such as child care vouchers and information about child care services. If an employer does provide child care, it should be located far enough away from the work setting that employees do not necessarily feel expected to go there during the day. We would caution employers that too permeable a boundary between work setting and a child care facility can lead employees to feel guilty if they are not there at lunch time and to feel not totally separate from their children during work hours. They could possibly feel too accessible, which could interfere with work concentration. We realize that this is a complex and controversial issue, but it does need to be taken into account as part of current policy discussions about on-site, employer-provided child care.

◆ INTEGRATING FAMILY INTO WORK

The Family and Career Discussions

Once the boundaries between work and home are clear, it is possible to cross them at specific times and for specific purposes. One of the most underutilized ways of doing so is involving the family in discussions and decisions regarding the employee's work and career at critical times. For example, when an employee is offered a transfer to a different city, the family certainly has a stake in the decision of whether or not to accept it. And the family will, in all probability, discuss with the employee at home the pros and cons of such a move. Why not do this more formally and bring the family into the work setting to discuss the matter with a manager or human resources professional, both to give the family realistic information about the new location and to help them think it through? Many companies are already doing this for major international transfers, such as to the Middle East, which are very expensive—especially if they don't work out—and which represent major adjustments for the family.

One of the reasons this approach is not taken more often is the concern that employees' spouses may not be open during such discussions out of fear of hurting the employee's career. These discussions would only have value if management were in fact truly open to the family concerns and were prepared to accept the employee's final decision. External third-party facilitators could be helpful in making these meetings problem-solving discussions and not just airings of employees' grievances.

Recruiting and Relocation

Today, more and more companies are offering spouse relocation assistance as an employee benefit. Companies that offer such assistance have found that it is a powerful aid in recruiting.

Recreation

Another way of integrating the family into work is providing company resources for family recreational and educational use. Many companies are now offering personal computers at a discount to employees, and these machines can be used both for the job and by the family. Employee country clubs, such as those at IBM and Bethlehem Steel, also foster family/work integration.

Family Days at Work

Other ways of linking work and family at clearly defined times includes company "family days" when family members are invited into work, taken on plant or office tours, wined and dined by management, and given a chance to see exactly what Mom or Dad does each day and how it fits into the company's overall activities. These are usually very popular events, cost very little, are a good source of information for family members, and increase the employee's pride in working for the organization.

◆   CONCLUSION

The most fruitful way to understand work/family interactions is to examine the transitions between the two domains. People tend to have consistent styles of dealing with home/work transitions, and these styles are affected by factors such as gender, type of work, and career stage.[6] As we have seen, organizations are becoming more active in helping employees manage their home and work boundaries more effectively.

A boundary does not necessarily mean a solid wall between the two areas, but something that helps define the separate entities while permitting interchange between them. A split-rail fence does not totally cut off two yards from each other, but it does demarcate private spaces while permitting visual contact and good neighborly conversation. As with fences and neighbors we conclude that good boundaries make for good employment relationships.

◆ ENDNOTES

This is a revised version of a paper, "Managing the Work/Home Interplay in the Organizational Context," presented at the Annual Meeting of the Academy of Management, New Orleans, April 11, 1987. This research was supported in part with funding from the Israel Institute of Business Research of Tel Aviv University's Faculty of Management and from the Human Resources Policy Institute at Boston University. The authors gratefully acknowledge the support of Fred Foulkes and the helpful comments of Kathy Kram on an earlier draft of this article.

1. See K. Lewin's *Field Theory in Social Science*, New York: McGraw-Hill, 1951.

2. See F. Bartolomè, "The Work Alibi: When It's Harder to Go Home," *Harvard Business Review,* Vol. 61, No. 2, 1982, 66–75.

3. Richter's work is described in more detail in J. Richter's *The Daily Transitions Between Professional and Private Life,* unpublished Ph.D. dissertation, Boston University, 1984.

4. See A. Kotlowitz, "Working at Home While Caring for a Child Sounds Fine—in Theory," *Wall Street Journal,* March 30, 1987, p. 21.

5. This research is reported in Richter (Endnote 3) and in J. Richter and D.T. Hall's "Psychological Availability and Daily Transitions: A New Way to Examine the Relationship Between Work Life and Personal Life," unpublished working paper, School of Management, Boston University, 1987.

6. See Richter and Hall, Endnote 5.

Does Your Job Make You Sick?

Randall Poe

This article warns employers to be mindful of the stressors they impose, wittingly or unwittingly, on their employees. There is a growing trend for organizations to be faced with lawsuits from employees demanding financial compensation for stress-induced illnesses.

Randall Poe is news director of the Conference Board.

A workaholic New York advertising executive, after being asked to take early retirement during a corporate restructuring, has a nervous breakdown. A Michigan auto worker, after watching his co-workers install defective parts in new cars, suffers disabling depression. A California cashier, alleging constant harassment by her boss, becomes psychotic and can no longer work.

Each of these employees recently filed a successful worker compensation claim. But they are only the tip of an accelerating national trend. Top managements have always known that their employees, like their most trusted machines, sometimes crack and break. Now they are learning something else: that they can be held legally responsible for the breakage.

The courts have steadily broadened the legal definition of "work stress." One example: Claims are increasingly being allowed for "repeated injury." Repeated, cumulative stress experienced during one's career can, under this doctrine, be held responsible for triggering heart attacks and other disabling illnesses.

Recent worker compensation awards have been granted for a bewildering variety of job-linked ailments, ranging from anxiety and nervous exhaustion to depression and schizophrenia. During the past four years, stress-related mental disorders have become this country's fastest-growing occupational disease. According to the National Council on Compensation Insurance, stress claims now account for nearly 14 percent of occupational disease claims, up from less than 5 percent only eight years ago.

The NCCI, which sets compensation rates in 32 states and advises in others, calls compensation for work-related stress ailments "the new legal right of the 1980s." A Los Angeles attorney, one of many now specializing in such cases, calls job stress "the psychological Agent Orange of the workplace."

While some 26 states now allow workers to file claims for job-related mental disorders, California has become this country's undisputed Stress Capital. More than 4,200 job-related stress claims were filed in California in 1984 (the

Source: Excerpted from Randall Poe, "Does Your Job Make You Sick?" *Across the Board,* The Conference Board, Inc., January, 1987, pp. 34–43. Reprinted by permission of the publisher.

latest year for which official data are available), up from fewer than 1,300 in 1980. Compensation experts say the actual number of stress-related claims is at least double that, since these figures do not include sharp claims increases over the past two years, and the official count includes only those cases that employers have acknowledged to be work related.

California is the only state with widely advertised 24-hour "work trauma hot lines," on which lawyers and psychologists counsel employees on their legal rights and ads constantly ask: "Does Your Job Make You Sick?" A recording played when calling one of these numbers tells employees: "Even if you have a preexisting problem which has been aggravated by the job, compensation is possible. If you have not gotten satisfaction from your employer, file an application for benefits with an attorney, who will send you to a medical expert. The case will be reviewed by the Workers' Compensation Appeal Board at no cost to you, since your employer is covered by insurance."

Some say that workers' attitudes are shifting faster than the law—one reason for the current turmoil. "The old saying, 'If you can't stand the heat, get out of the kitchen' is breaking down," says Dr. Martin Schaefer, director of the Stress Management Institute in San Francisco. "People are blaming the workplace for their problems, and they want to be compensated."

Last year, California's Division of Industrial Accidents hired a panel of health experts and psychiatrists to suggest ways to control the surge of stress claims in the state. In recent public hearings, the panel has been urging the establishment of new statewide medical standards on which competing psychiatric claims can be judged. Currently, courts must weigh evidence based on a variety of subjective and often conflicting medical criteria. "Methods of examination are too variable," says Allen Enelow, the psychiatrist who heads the panel. "As a result, some people who deserve compensation don't get it, and some people who have dubious claims get more than they deserve."

The courts are not finding it easy to decide cases, which are often based on raw emotion, contradictory medical testimony, and unprovable allegations. As a Rhode Island court lamented in examining a claim of job-caused neuroses: "It is all very well to say that the adversary system will expose the difference between the genuine neurotic and the malingerer. We have great fears that neither the science of psychiatry nor the adversary judicial process is equal to this task."

While it is hard to prove that one's job has caused a mental disorder, it is also hard to prove that it hasn't. The legal and medical battles have created a lucrative cash-for-stress industry consisting of lawyers and doctors. In fact, some observers blame attorneys and psychiatrists for the sharp rise in stress claims. "Attorneys have become very inventive in identifying the causes on which legal action can be based," says Alan Tebb, general manager of the California Workers' Compensation Institute. "But attorneys and doctors work closely together. In fact, it is often the attorney who makes the diagnosis and the doctor who determines the extent of liability. But there's another factor behind this increase. For many employees, psychiatric disorders don't carry the social stigma they once had, so many more people are willing to file a claim."

Most cases swing on the expert testimony of psychiatrists, who identify the basic sources of mental stress and describe the severity of the disability. More and more psychiatric claims are being challenged; nearly 80 percent in California are now contested. Challenging these claims is proving to be both difficult and expensive for companies, however, because firms are generally forced to conduct lengthy investigations into a plaintiff's personal life to prove that a mental malady was not job related.

"What makes all cases complex," says Philip Borba, director of economics and social research at the National Council on Compensation Insurance, "is that one person's stress is another person's job satisfaction." Indeed, a 1984 study conducted at Pennsylvania State University found a link between excellence in business and early, stress-related heart disease. It noted that most excellent managers are super-competitive, aggressive, and impatient, have difficulty delegating authority, and lack outside interests. All these traits are considered stressful.

Corporate fears have grown as a result of recent court decisions that some experts say could jeopardize the longstanding right of employers to fire employees. In an unprecedented decision in 1984, the highest court in Massachusetts upheld a compensation award granted to a training specialist named Helen Kelly, who had suffered an emotional breakdown after being told by the Raytheon Corporation that her department was being eliminated and that she was being laid off. The Supreme Judicial Court of Massachusetts held that she was entitled to a one-time award equal to two thirds of her annual salary, and payment of all her medical bills. In Oregon, a similar award was granted to a fired nurse who alleged that her demanding work schedule, coupled with constant harassment by her boss and co-workers, had triggered a mental breakdown.

Almost all of these cases involved legal and medical battles. As a New York-based compensation expert says: "You're seeing a kind of legal Super Bowl out there that's pitting lawyers against lawyers and shrinks against shrinks."

A claim filed by a computer programmer in California is typical. His legal and medical representatives presented evidence that a rapidly rising work load,

---

HIGHLIGHT

Stress indicators

Recent research findings underscore the growth and depth of the stress problem:

- Seventy-five percent to 90 percent of all doctors' visits are now for stress-related maladies, according to the American Institute of Stress.
- Seventy-eight percent of all Americans say their jobs cause them stress, with more than half saying their lives have turned more stressful during the past 10 years, according to a nationwide mid-1986 survey by D'Arcy, Masius, Benton & Bowles.
- Forty-five percent of the surveyed employees in both private and public sector organizations suffered psychological burnout, a University of Georgia study reveals.
- The National Institute of Mental Health reports that in any given six-month period, 19 percent of all adults are suffering from at least one psychiatric disorder.

a constantly changing schedule, and at least two abrasive bosses provoked chronic anxiety and then disabling paranoia. The employer, however, introduced evidence that the employee had spent two lengthy periods in a mental home before joining the company and was the sole supporter of an alcoholic mother, a major reason for his stress.

The programmer was awarded his claim. The rationale: His job stress was real and aggravated his previous mental condition.

But similar allegations can produce very dissimilar results, even in the same state. An Arizona insurance underwriter charged that increased work responsibility resulting from the expansion of his firm had caused a mental breakdown. His claim was upheld because "the stress was in excess of the usual stress encountered by employees performing the same kind of work." But in the same state, a highway patrolman claiming that he was mentally disabled because of overwork lost his case. His stress, the court found, was "merely the usual stress of employment."

Although a host of states have recently ruled against employees who were seeking damages for job stress, the overall trend suggests that companies may be losing some of their time-tested rights. "It can hardly be said that an employer has the right to fire an employee if he must pay damages (worker's compensation) caused by the firing," states a comprehensive study by the NCCI, published in 1985 and updated in 1986. "Just as the right to compensation for a work-related injury implies the right to a safe workplace, it seems that the right to compensation for an emotional disability caused by a firing implies a new right not to be fired."

The Massachusetts Legislature, after protests from employers, acted in 1985 to bar mental disability claims arising from "a bona fide personnel decision." But many say that the job-stress genie is now out of the bottle. "There is a growing legal concern that legislatures will soon act to establish standards in this area," says Philip Borba of the NCCI. "As it is, anybody can file a stress claim, but the problem is in defining what is and isn't a compensable claim."

The legislation in Massachusetts underscores a major problem nationwide: This country's state-run worker compensation system was built not to handle mental disorders, but to compensate workers for physical injuries suffered on the job.

If some firms seem confused as to what type of health program to adopt these days, it's partly because stress as a workplace problem is so complex and so new. Mental disability claims were almost unheard of 10 years ago. Nearly all of the major legal decisions have been handed down in the past decade.

The increase in claims for stress-related illness is simply one more force escalating the cost of worker's compensation, which is financed by employers. Benefits paid to workers under this state-run program, which totaled only $160 million in 1940, are well over $16 billion today. They've quadrupled since the late 70s.

Some influential observers are warning that stress has become too deadly and too costly to ignore. "Five years ago we were calculating that stress, in terms of such things as diminished productivity, absenteeism, and direct medical costs, was costing this country $50 billion to $75 billion a year," says Dr. Paul J. Rosch, president of the American Institute of Stress. "The figure is now estimated at $150 billion. Stress-related disorders are the major factor in escalating health-care costs, which exceed $1 billion a day."

Are new job pressures producing more stressed-out Americans? Or are modern workers simply becoming more aware of their legal options? Nobody knows for sure. But many experts on stress believe that the nation's turn from a goods-producing to a service-information society is a major factor in this trend. "In shifting from production to services, the loads we are putting on people are mental rather than physical," says Dr. Alex Cohen, a stress research specialist at the National Institute of Occupational Safety and Health. "While all of this is too new to determine cause-and-effect relationships, studies are showing strong associations between jobs and stress. Stress is now one of the 10 leading work-related problems."

NIOSH has included psychological disorders on its list of work-related injuries. One of its objectives for the next three years is to reduce stress levels in high-technology office jobs. The latest data show that a substantial number of job-stress insurance claims are coming from the service sector—especially from women. "Many women may be prone to job dissatisfaction where unequal job opportunities confine them to jobs with lower pay or less responsibility and independence than their similarly qualified male counterparts," says the NCCI study.

Alan Tebb of the California Workers' Compensation Institute echoes the

---

HIGHLIGHT

The twelve most stressful jobs

The National Institute for Occupational Safety and Health reports that 12 occupational groups are the most likely victims of severe stress. NIOSH studied hospital and clinic records in Tennessee and totted up the numbers treated for stress disorders in 130 job categories. The most frequent casualties were: (1) laborers, (2) secretaries, (3) inspectors, (4) clinical lab technicians, (5) office managers, (6) foremen, (7) managers and administrators, (8) waiters and waitresses, (9) machine operators, (10) farm owners, (11) miners, and (12) painters.

Health researchers have described a number of work situations that can cause stress. The consensus is that high levels are most prevalent in jobs that:

- Do not allow employees to participate in basic work decisions.
- Demand either more or fewer skills than employees actually have.
- Pit workers between often conflicting groups, such as management and customers or supervisors and shop-floor employees.
- Lack clearly defined standards and opportunities for advancement.
- Have been changed significantly through restructuring, staff cutbacks, or market shifts.
- Contain built-in conflict with co-workers or supervisors.

observation: "There are more women in the work force doing a greater variety of jobs than ever before. Like many men, a lot of these women, who must juggle families and homes, aren't coping so well. And unlike the old days, they are very much aware of their legal options."

The NCCI study emphasizes that managers and professionals, who once seemed immune, are becoming more susceptible to job stress. If this trend accelerates, it will mean a sharp rise in the cost of worker's compensation because insurance awards are based on earnings.

The study predicts that more stress claims are likely from: the white-collar and service industries, which employ large numbers of women; younger employees, who could either be "more prone to stress" or "more willing to view their emotional problems as compensable injuries"; and employees ousted as a result of mergers, plant closings, and relocations.

Stress experts tend to agree that competitive pressures almost guarantee more trauma ahead. "It's not popular to say this, but we may pay a large human price as we gear up to compete not just with the Europeans but the Brazilians, the Koreans, the Caribbeans, and all the -ans," says a corporate doctor. "Like the Japanese, we are learning that negative stress goes along with success."

As a result, companies are being urged to pin-point crucial stress centers in their firms, attempt to eliminate them, and document all their actions—just in case employees lash out with claims and lawsuits.

It appears that few companies and few occupations are immune to stress suits. As a *Harvard Business Review* analysis puts it: "Managers can no longer choose whether to recognize and deal with the symptoms of stress on the job. It has become a legal obligation. . . . Whether they like it or not, managers must learn to deal with stress before they end up having to explain their lack of action in court."

Paul Rosch of the American Institute of Stress says that stress has become yet another "disease of civilization." But he is convinced that companies must do more than they have been doing to establish coping strategies for their employees. "Too many are applying Band-Aids," he says, "rather than devising meaningful stress-awareness and stress-reduction programs."

Though some companies have for years sought ways to help their employees cope with stress, there has recently been a resurgence of interest. More companies now perceive that they have an important stake in preventing mental disabilities that are pushing up corporate health and insurance costs and resulting in lowered productivity.

Some experts, such as Rosch, are worried that growing claims could bankrupt the worker compensation system. But NCCI officials and others believe that with fine-tuning, the current system can cope. They warn that limitations must be placed on stress claims, just as they were on claims for black lung disease. NCCI officials also suggest the use of impartial panels of medical experts to examine mental stress claims, to sort out the legitimate cases from the illegitimate.

Some observers suggest that "stress" has simply become a fashionable buzzword, a kind of primal scream used to express discomfort of all kinds.

William Levasseur, head of an American Bar Association committee on worker's compensation, says that people who once complained that "this job is difficult" are now using the word *stress* to describe their predicament.

"There is no doubt that some people's jobs cause psychological bleeding, even if we can't see the blood," says a Boston-based human resources consultant. "But that's always been true. Stress has become the new chic expression today, and a lot of people wear it like a designer's label. It's my observation that too many people who can't stand the heat are taking jobs in the kitchen and screaming stress when their inadequacies are exposed."

Self-fulfilling Stereotypes

Mark Snyder

This reading emphasizes the pervasiveness with which stereotypes about physical attractiveness, sex, race, and intelligence are used in forming initial impressions of others. A serious consequence of this process is that the stereotyped individuals behave in ways that conform to the stereotypes.

Mark Snyder is a professor of social psychology at the University of Minnesota.

Gordon Allport, the Harvard psychologist who wrote a classic work on the nature of prejudice, told a story about a child who had come to believe that people who lived in Minneapolis were called monopolists. From his father, moreover, he had learned that monopolists were evil folk. It wasn't until many years later, when he discovered his confusion, that his dislike of residents of Minneapolis vanished.

Allport knew, of course, that it was not so easy to wipe out prejudice and erroneous stereotypes. Real prejudice, psychologists like Allport argued, was buried deep in human character, and only a restructuring of education could begin to root it out. Yet many people whom I meet while lecturing seem to believe that stereotypes are simply beliefs or attitudes that change easily with experience. Why do some people express the view that Italians are passionate, blacks are lazy, Jews materialistic, or lesbians mannish in their demeanor? In the popular view, it is because they have not learned enough about the diversity among these groups and have not had enough contact with members of the groups for their stereotypes to be challenged by reality. With more experience, it is presumed, most people of good will are likely to revise their stereotypes.

My research over the past decade convinces me that there is little justification for such optimism—and not only for the reasons given by Allport. While it is true that deep prejudice is often based on the needs of pathological character structure, stereotypes are obviously quite common even among fairly normal individuals. When people first meet others, they cannot help noticing certain highly visible and distinctive characteristics: sex, race, physical appearance, and the like. Despite people's best intentions, their initial impressions of others are shaped by their assumptions about such characteristics.

What is critical, however, is that these assumptions are not merely beliefs or attitudes that exist in a vacuum; they are reinforced by the behavior of both prejudiced people and the targets of their prejudice. In recent years, psychologists

Source: Mark Snyder, "Self-Fulfilling Stereotypes," *Psychology Today* magazine, July, 1982.

have collected considerable laboratory evidence about the processes that strengthen stereotypes and put them beyond the reach of reason and good will.

My own studies initially focused on first encounters between strangers. It did not take long to discover, for example, that people have very different ways of treating those whom they regard as physically attractive and those whom they consider physically unattractive, and that these differences tend to bring out precisely those kinds of behavior that fit with stereotypes about attractiveness.

In an experiment that I conducted with my colleagues Elizabeth Decker Tanke and Ellen Berscheid, pairs of college-age men and women met and became acquainted in telephone conversations. Before the conversations began, each man received a Polaroid snapshot, presumably taken just moments before, of the woman he would soon meet. The photograph, which had actually been prepared before the experiment began, showed either a physically attractive woman or a physically unattractive one. By randomly choosing which picture to use for each conversation, we insured that there was no consistent relationship between the attractiveness of the woman in the picture and the attractiveness of the woman in the conversation.

By questioning the men, we learned that even before the conversations began, stereotypes about physical attractiveness came into play. Men who looked forward to talking with physically attractive women said that they expected to meet decidedly sociable, poised, humorous, and socially adept people, while men who thought that they were about to get acquainted with unattractive women fashioned images of rather unsociable, awkward, serious, and socially inept creatures. Moreover, the men proved to have very different styles of getting acquainted with women whom they thought to be attractive and those whom they believed to be unattractive. Shown a photograph of an attractive woman, they behaved with warmth, friendliness, humor, and animation. However, when the woman in the picture was unattractive, the men were cold, uninteresting, and reserved.

These differences in the men's behavior elicited behavior in the women that was consistent with the men's stereotyped assumptions. Women who were believed (unbeknown to them) to be physically attractive behaved in a friendly, likeable, and sociable manner. In sharp contrast, women who were perceived as physically unattractive adopted a cool, aloof, and distant manner. So striking were the differences in the women's behavior that they could be discerned simply by listening to tape recordings of the women's side of the conversations. Clearly, by acting upon their stereotyped beliefs about the women whom they would be meeting, the men had initiated a chain of events that produced *behavioral confirmation* for their beliefs.

Similarly, Susan Andersen and Sandra Bem have shown in an experiment at Stanford University that when the tables are turned—when it is women who have pictures of men they are to meet on the telephone—many women treat the men according to their presumed physical attractiveness, and by so doing encourage the men to confirm their stereotypes. Little wonder, then, that so many people remain convinced that good looks and appealing personalities go hand in hand.

◆   SEX AND RACE

It is experiments such as these that point to a frequently unnoticed power of stereotypes: the power to influence social relationships in ways that create the illusion of reality. In one study, Berna Skrypnek and I arranged for pairs of previously unacquainted students to interact in a situation that permitted us to control the information that each one received about the apparent sex of the other. The two people were seated in separate rooms so that they could neither see nor hear each other. Using a system of signal lights that they operated with switches, they negotiated a division of labor, deciding which member of the pair would perform each of several tasks that differed in sex-role connotations. The tasks varied along the dimensions of masculinity and femininity: sharpen a hunting knife (masculine), polish a pair of shoes (neutral), iron a shirt (feminine).

One member of the team was led to believe that the other was, in one condition of the experiment, male; in the other, female. As we had predicted, the first member's belief about the sex of the partner influenced the outcome of the pair's negotiations. Women whose partners believed them to be men generally chose stereotypically masculine tasks; in contrast, women whose partners believed that they were women usually chose stereotypically feminine tasks. The experiment thus suggests that much sex-role behavior may be the product of other people's stereotyped and often erroneous beliefs.

In a related study at the University of Waterloo, Carl von Baeyer, Debbie Sherk, and Mark Zanna have shown how stereotypes about sex roles operate in job interviews. The researchers arranged to have men conduct simulated job interviews with women supposedly seeking positions as research assistants. The investigators informed half of the women that the men who would interview them held traditional views about the ideal woman, believing her to be very emotional, deferential to her husband, home-oriented, and passive. The rest of the women were told that their interviewer saw the ideal woman as independent, competitive, ambitious, and dominant. When the women arrived for their interviews, the researchers noticed that most of them had dressed to meet the stereotyped expectations of their prospective interviewers. Women who expected to see a traditional interviewer had chosen very feminine-looking makeup, clothes, and accessories. During the interviews (videotaped through a one-way mirror) these women behaved in traditionally feminine ways and gave traditionally feminine answers to questions such as "Do you have plans to include children and marriage with your career plans?"

Once more, then, we see the self-fulfilling nature of stereotypes. Many sex differences, it appears, may result from the images that people create in their attempts to act out accepted sex roles. The implication is that if stereotyped expectations about sex roles shift, behavior may change, too. In fact, statements by people who have undergone sex-change operations have highlighted the power of such expectations in easing adjustment to a new life. As the writer Jan Morris said in recounting the story of her transition from James to Jan: "The more I was treated as a woman, the more woman I became."

The power of stereotypes to cause people to confirm stereotyped expectations can also be seen in interracial relationships. In the first of two investigations done at Princeton University by Carl Word, Mark Zanna, and Joel Cooper, white undergraduates interviewed both white and black job applicants. The applicants were actually confederates of the experimenters, trained to behave consistently from interview to interview, no matter how the interviewers acted toward them.

To find out whether or not the white interviewers would behave differently toward white and black job applicants, the researchers secretly videotaped each interview and then studied the tapes. From these, it was apparent that there were substantial differences in the treatment accorded blacks and whites. For one thing, the interviewers' speech deteriorated when they talked to blacks, displaying more errors in grammar and pronunciation. For another, the interviewers spent less time with blacks than with whites and showed less "immediacy," as the researchers called it, in their manner. That is, they were less friendly, less outgoing, and more reserved with blacks.

In the second investigation, white confederates were trained to approximate either the immediate or the non-immediate interview styles that had been observed in the first investigation as they interviewed white job applicants. A panel of judges who evaluated the tapes agreed that applicants subjected to the non-immediate styles performed less adequately and were more nervous than job applicants treated in the immediate style. Apparently, then, the blacks in the first study did not have a chance to display their qualifications to the best advantage. Considered together, the two investigations suggest that in interracial encounters, racial stereotypes may constrain behavior in ways that cause both blacks and whites to behave in accordance with those stereotypes.

◆   *REWRITING BIOGRAPHY*

Having adopted stereotyped ways of thinking about another person, people tend to notice and remember the ways in which that person seems to fit the stereotype, while resisting evidence that contradicts the stereotype. In one investigation that I conducted with Seymour Uranowitz, student subjects read a biography of a fictitious woman named Betty K. We constructed the story of her life so that it would fit the stereotyped images of both lesbians and heterosexuals. Betty, we wrote, never had a steady boyfriend in high school, but did go out on dates. And although we gave her a steady boyfriend in college, we specified that he was more of a close friend than anything else. A week after we had distributed this biography, we gave our subjects some new information about Betty. We told some students that she was now living with another woman in a lesbian relationship; we told others that she was living with her husband.

To see what impact stereotypes about sexuality would have on how people remembered the facts of Betty's life, we asked each student to answer a series of questions about her life history. When we examined their answers, we found that the students had reconstructed the events of Betty's past in ways that supported their own stereotyped beliefs about her sexual orientation. Those who believed that Betty was a lesbian remembered that Betty had never had a steady boyfriend in high school, but tended to neglect the fact that she had gone out on many dates in college. Those who believed that Betty was now a heterosexual tended to remember that she had formed a steady relationship with a man in college, but tended to ignore the fact that this relationship was more of a friendship than a romance.

The students showed not only selective memories but also a striking facility for interpreting what they remembered in ways that added fresh support for their stereotypes. One student who accurately remembered that a supposedly lesbian Betty never had a steady boyfriend in high school confidently pointed to that fact as an early sign of her lack of romantic or sexual interest in men. A student who correctly remembered that a purportedly lesbian Betty often went out on dates in college was sure that these dates were signs of Betty's early attempts to mask her lesbian interests.

Clearly, the students had allowed their preconceptions about lesbians and heterosexuals to dictate the way in which they interpreted and reinterpreted the facts of Betty's life. As long as stereotypes make it easy to bring to mind evidence that supports them and difficult to bring to mind evidence that undermines them, people will cling to erroneous beliefs.

◆   *STEREOTYPES IN THE CLASSROOM
AND WORKPLACE*

The power of one person's beliefs to make other people conform to them has been well demonstrated in real life. Back in the 1960s, as most people well remember, Harvard psychologist Robert Rosenthal and his colleague Lenore Jacobson entered elementary-school classrooms and identified one out of every five pupils in each room as a child who could be expected to show dramatic improvement in intellectual achievement during the school year. What the teachers did not know was that the children had been chosen on a random basis. Nevertheless, something happened in the relationships between teachers and their supposedly gifted pupils that led the children to make clear gains in test performance.

It can also do so on the job. Albert King, now a professor of management at Northern Illinois University, told a welding instructor in a vocational training center that five men in his training program had unusually high aptitude. Although these five had been chosen at random and knew nothing of their designation as high-aptitude workers, they showed substantial changes in performance. They were absent less often than were other workers, learned the basics of the welder's trade in about half the usual time, and scored a full 10 points higher than other trainees on a welding test. Their gains were noticed not only by the researcher and by the welding instructor, but also by other trainees, who singled out the five as their preferred co-workers.

Might not other expectations influence the relationships between supervisors and workers? For example, supervisors who believe that men are better suited to some jobs and women to others may treat their workers (wittingly or unwittingly) in ways that encourage them to perform their jobs in accordance with stereotypes about differences between men and women. These same stereotypes may determine who gets which job in the first place. Perhaps some personnel managers allow stereotypes to influence, subtly or not so subtly, the way in which they interview job candidates, making it likely that candidates who fit the stereotypes show up better than job-seekers who do not fit them.

Unfortunately, problems of this kind are compounded by the fact that members of stigmatized groups often subscribe to stereotypes about themselves. That is what Amerigo Farina and his colleagues at the University of Connecticut found when they measured the impact upon mental patients of believing that others knew their psychiatric history. In Farina's study, each mental patient co-operated with another person in a game requiring teamwork. Half of the patients believed that their partners knew they were patients; the other half believed that their partners thought they were nonpatients. In reality, the nonpatients never knew a thing about anyone's psychiatric history. Nevertheless, simply believing that others were aware of their history led the patients to feel less appreciated, to find the task more difficult, and to perform poorly. In addition, objective observers saw them as more tense, more anxious, and more poorly adjusted than patients who believed that their status was not known. Seemingly, the belief that others perceived them as stigmatized caused them to play the role of stigmatized patients.

◆   *CONSEQUENCES FOR SOCIETY*

Apparently, good will and education are not sufficient to subvert the power of stereotypes. If people treat others in such a way as to bring out behavior that supports stereotypes, they may never have an opportunity to discover which of their stereotypes are wrong.

I suspect that even if people were to develop doubts about the accuracy of their stereotypes, chances are they would proceed to test them by gathering precisely the evidence that would appear to confirm them.

The experiments I have described help to explain the persistence of stereotypes. But, as is so often the case, solving one puzzle only creates another. If by acting as if false stereotypes were true, people lead others, too, to act as if they were true, why do the stereotypes not come to *be* true? Why, for example, have researchers found so little evidence that attractive people are generally friendly, sociable, and outgoing and that unattractive people are generally shy and aloof?

I think that the explanation goes something like this: Very few among us have the kind of looks that virtually everyone considers either very attractive or very unattractive. Our looks make us rather attractive to some people but somewhat less attractive to other people. When we spend time with those who find us attractive, they will tend to bring out our more sociable sides, but when we are with those who find us less attractive, they will bring out our less sociable sides. Although our actual physical appearance does not change, we present ourselves quite differently to our admirers and to our detractors. For our admirers we become attractive people, and for our detractors we become unattractive. This mixed pattern of behavior will prevent the development of any consistent relationship between physical attractiveness and personality.

Now that I understand some of the powerful forces that work to perpetuate social stereotypes, I can see a new mission for my research. I hope, on the one hand, to find out how to help people see the flaws in their stereotypes. On the other hand, I would like to help the victims of false stereotypes find ways of liberating themselves from the constraints imposed on them by other members of society.

Is the Work Ethic Dead?

Michael Rozek

This article presents results from national surveys which show that the work ethic is alive and well. Critics argue that employees are not necessarily the ones to be faulted when productivity lags. Rather, management needs to recognize its key role of nurturing positive attitudes in the workplace.

Michael Rozek is a contributor to *Incentive* magazine.

The notions of "America" and "work ethic" have long been entwined. The laboring class, venerated in story and song, made up the backbone of the nation's progress and might. And during World War II, the nation pulled together and worked harder than ever before.

Today, some argue, the spirit's gone: America is full of lazy, unprincipled employees who would rather watch the clock (or TV) than give an honest day's work for an honest day's pay.

Surveys, however, indicate that there's little truth to this. According to a recent story in The Washington Times, a slew of recent opinion polls is consistent in one finding—people like to work, and they like to work hard:

• Surveys by Roper, the National Opinion Research Center and Daniel Yankelovich all indicate that more than 80 percent of Americans are satisfied with their jobs.

• A Yankelovich survey shows that 90 percent of all American workers say it's important to work hard, while 78 percent indicate an inner need to do their very best while on the job. Plus, notes the survey, workers say that work, rather than leisure, can give them what they're looking for: an outlet for self-expression as well as material rewards.

And, in a recent op-ed piece in Newsday, a New York-area daily newspaper, St. Lawrence University assistant professor of government Alan Draper cites even more positive data. "Reports of the work ethic's demise have been greatly exaggerated," he writes. "More Americans go to work than ever. Labor force participation is at a record 61 percent of the eligible work force. According to public opinion surveys, American workers would not exchange reduced work time for a proportionate reduction in their earnings, and, astonishingly, American youth report higher levels of commitment to work than their Japanese counterparts."

Source: Michael Rozek, "Is the Work Ethic Dead?" *Incentive*, New York, October, 1990, pp. 65–66, 68, 222. Reprinted by permission of the publisher.

Add it all up and the message is clear: Neither American workers nor the people who study them think the work ethic is moribund at all. Then why do so many believe it has vanished? Some say it's because the ethic has been stifled by management.

"It's always easy to blame decreased productivity on the death of the work ethic, but that's a cop-out," insists Jerome Rosow, founder and president of the Work in America Institute, a Scarsdale, N.Y.-based think tank that brings together top American managers and labor officials in an effort to advance productivity and the quality of workplace life. "The real issue is that management needs to handle its resources in a way that gets the most productivity out of them. Management gets the kind of work force it deserves—and workers will always outperform management expectations if they're given the chance. To be a productive employee is in any worker's self-interest, out of self-esteem and sheer survival."

Clifford Sellie, chairman of the Niles, Ill.-based company Standards International, a 45-year-old productivity-consulting firm, agrees. "When we hear people mutter, 'The work ethic is dead,' it's just something management trots out about workers when they need an excuse for their own mistakes—or when some human resources guru has their ear," he says. "The truth is, when there are problems, you have to look to management."

Sellie claims that the work ethic hasn't diminished at all since he began his career—in fact, it has improved. "People are actually working harder at their jobs than they used to," he says.

"There are just as many dedicated workers out there today as there always were—but the work ethic is also relative to quality of supervision," says Marshall Dildy, a regional director of human resources for Hardee's, the Atlanta-based fast-food chain.

One way in which management often contributes to a low "work ethic" is by failing to trust employees. An example of such a failure: airlines, where bosses usually monitor reservation personnel for speed. "It's an approach that backfires," says Barbara Otto, director of programs and public affairs for 9to5, a Cleveland-based group that represents office workers. "The workers only end up angry and less committed to their jobs."

When Northwest Airlines recently stopped monitoring its reservationists, productivity reportedly went way up and absenteeism way down. The moral: When left to their own devices, Americans will work as hard as they can. "Where there is trust, there is productivity," Otto says.

Draper provides other management-related theories: "Fewer jobs [today] have career ladders that permit mobility than was true previously. More labor has been de-skilled," he writes. "Job growth in high-income occupations has stalled while low-wage industries proliferate. Consequently, work is no longer the ticket to middle-class respectability that it once was. . . . Employers use smart machines on the shop floor that need only dumb workers to operate them. Managers have imperiously pursued an anti-union policy that only heightens workers' sense of vulnerability."

Nor, says Draper, is the government blameless—it's unable to reduce unemployment but cuts unemployment insurance, and it avoids responsibility for retraining or hiring the unemployed.

In addition to these alleged failures, another reason for the perception of a dying work ethic is that lifestyles have changed. "Today's workers have different experiences and different needs than workers of years past," says James DeSena, a business consultant on the faculty of the Management Institute at New York University. "They want more balance in their lives, and they're more apt to consider how their job relates to them personally. They have other places for their energy—like family, home and leisure pursuits—and a lot of them refuse to work as hard on the job as their parents did. But that doesn't mean they've lost their commitment to the work ethic; it doesn't mean they're lazy or unmotivated."

But Otto believes that worker performance *has* slipped. She points to a good reason, however: low wages and benefits. "People still want to work hard, but the decline of real wages, the increase in contingent work forces and the systematic stripping away of benefits has eroded what people used to call 'the work ethic,' " she believes. Thirty-seven million full-time American workers have no health insurance, she points out. "If their performance is down, is it any surprise?"

Providing low pay and benefits isn't the only way companies save money. They also do it by downsizing their work forces—which comes into conflict with the work ethic. "When you do that, you reduce your employees to working just to get money to buy things, and prizing early retirement as the greatest bonus of all," comments James Green, director of the labor studies program at the University of Massachusetts. "Now, employers are complaining about what they're reaping as a result, and the antagonism between employer and worker is greater here than in any other industrialized country."

Even Draper, who says that today's work ethic is alive, believes that it might be alive for the wrong reasons. The ethic, writes Draper, is one "whose original definition—that work gives meaning to our lives—has been turned on its head. The work ethic that exists today is defensive and without joy. . . . Workers cling to [it] in hopes of staving off disaster rather than finding fulfillment."

What can managers do to correct the situation? The answers will sound familiar: Listen to their workers and recognize them for their accomplishments— advice that certainly turns the attention to the incentive industry.

"If you create a work environment that empowers employees, recognizes their contributions in a positive way and is sensitive to their needs and concerns, and if you demonstrate that through your actions, you'll end up with employees who are totally committed to the work ethic," Dildy says.

Any company that understands how today's worker differs from those of yesteryear can get A-1 performance from its people, making the term "work ethic" a red herring, says DeSena. "Management can do a lot about the way workers feel about a job," he says. "Give employees a feeling of control over their work environment, and they're going to be twice as likely to put out effort. Fifty years ago, workers did what their company told them to, because they assumed it had all the answers. Today's companies have to realize that their workers have a lot of the answers, and they'll be a lot more interested in working hard if they can share in their company's destiny."

"We do not need to lament the passing of the work ethic," writes Draper. "It is alive and well. What we need to do is recover its original, affirming meaning."

PREDICTING THE FUTURE

Is the work ethic dying? If you could ask just one person, you might best turn to Marvin Cetron—an affable, 60-year-old ex-military researcher. For nearly 20 years, through his Arlington, Va.-based company, Forecasting International, Cetron has been predicting society's future. Working with a bank of computers and a staff of two dozen experts in as many different fields, he sifts through the reams of information that chart modern life. Then, he makes predictions—for prestigious clients like NASA, the European Common Market, several Cabinet departments and a host of U.S. corporations, including Apple, Xerox, General Motors and IBM.

Claiming a 95 percent accuracy rate (based on a survey conducted by a group of his clients), he is quick to differentiate what he does from any head-in-the-clouds futurist. "Futurists forecast what they *hope* will happen," he recently told OMNI magazine, "because [their] fantasy scenarios are nice, neat and clear. . . . I deal with facts—with trends—and [use] computers. That's how I make my forecasts."

In his current book, "American Renaissance: Our Life at the Turn of the 21st Century" (with Owen Davies, St. Martin's Press, $19.95), he makes a very specific one about the work ethic. "In the sense we always think about it, it's in decline, and it's going to keep declining," he told **Incentive**. "Tardiness is increasing on the job, sick-leave abuse is common—and meanwhile, job security and high pay are not the motivators they once were."

On the other hand, Cetron agrees with many experts that American workers don't necessarily reject the idea of hard work—one sign that better management could bring out the "work ethic" that may be locked inside them. "Two-thirds of Americans would like to see an increase in the length of the work week rather than shorter hours," he notes. "That may be something for employers to build on."

PART II

Group Processes

Ex-Champion Nailer

Wessel Hyatt Smitter

Ex-Champion Nailer takes place in an automobile factory of the 1930s, when manual labor was more common. Despite the sexist and ethnic slurs, the theme of how an employee is socialized into a work group is still relevant in contemporary organizations. An old hand recounts how he and his fellow workers dealt with a new recruit whose overzealous attitude violated the norms they had established for nailing lids on boxes. The story also provides a glimpse of the adversarial relationship between labor and management that prevailed during that period. It is interesting to recall that, perhaps not coincidentally, the move toward labor unionization in America was underway at the time this story was published in 1934.

Wessel Hyatt Smitter (b. 1894) also wrote the 1938 novel, *F.O.B. Detroit.* The story of life in the Holt automobile assembly plant is told from a worker's perspective.

I can remember as easy as if it was yesterday the first day he came to work in the factory. It was Monday and we still had a few minutes to loaf before it was time for the bell. All of us nailers were sprawled around on the boxes and Alf was telling about a couple of new janes in a joint on Hastings Street, run by Slant-eye Susie, when Big Barney, the straw-boss, comes up with this new fellow looking scared and sort of trailing behind.

"This is Louie," he said. "I want you fellows to break him in on the nailing. The Old Man has been crabbing to beat the band at the way you fellows have been holding up the line lately."

We had him sized up in a minute. A big fellow he was, with clay on his shoes and eyes like those of a cow. His bushy eyebrows, turned white by the sun, made you think of some wild animal, and the smell of the cow stables hung in his clothes like a fog. But most of all we noticed his hands. They were as big as a couple of slab-sides of bacon and the knuckles stood out like rows of big

Source: From *Story* Magazine, Vol. IV, No. 23, June, 1934. Reprinted by permission.

adams-apples. When he picked up his hammer the whole handle just about disappeared out of sight in his fist.

"Do we have to nail the covers on these boxes," he asked, "while they're moving along on this track?"

"Sure," said Alf, "and it's no fair either hitting your thumb." Alf and I worked together.

Toenails, the little Polak, who looked like a walrus, laughed out of his whiskers, and Louie looked him over with a nervous interest.

"Ever work in an automobile factory before?" asked Alf.

"No," said Louie, "I've never even been in one until now."

"Well, there ain't much to it," said Alf, "it's like I told you, the main thing is—don't hit your thumb. All you need on this job is a weak mind and a strong arm. Of course, our job is a little different from other jobs in this department. Our job is harder. This thing that the boxes ride along on is called a conveyor. It's about 800 feet long and is run by a motor with a speed control button up there by the Old Man's desk. At the head of the line the empty boxes are set on the conveyor and all these other fellows—about two hundred and fifty of them—pack in the stuff. When the boxes get down to us each one is packed with four motors and four chassis assemblies. You can figure it out for yourself what kind of a job you got here. Two hundred and fifty fellows to dump the stuff into the boxes and only six of us to nail on the covers. It's a raw deal any way that you look at it and yet, right away the straw-boss tries to give you a bum impression of us by trying to make you think we're loafing."

"What would happen," Louie asked, "if the boxes came through so fast that we couldn't get the covers nailed on?"

"Plenty," said Alf. "You see that bird up there in that little cage underneath the crane. Well, as soon as we get the last nail drove in he hooks onto the box and takes it over to the loading platform. But he can't take 'em until we get finished else all the stuff would spill out. And if the boxes ain't off by the time they get to the end of the conveyor track, everything gets dumped on the floor. Once, a couple of years ago, they had to shut down the line to give us a chance to catch up with our nailing. The Big Boss had a hemorrhage and up in the front office they ain't done talking about it yet."

Louie had a hand full of nails. He was itching to go. There was a box, half nailed up on the line and he started to hammer. At the first blow we all hollered,—"Hey! wait for the bell!"

"What's the matter?" he asked. "Doesn't anyone go to work until it is just the second for starting?"

"Certainly not," said Alf. "If the boss saw you driving nails before the bell rung he'd think you was crazy."

The first day we had more fun than a circus with Louie. By the way he went at his new job you'd think he'd never had a hammer in his hand till that day. Each nail he tried to drive in was a separate struggle. He went at the job like a fellow going into a fight. Once in a while he got a nail into the wood but most of them curled up under the clumsy blows of his hammer as if they were made out of paper. It's no cinch to drive ten-penny wire nails into elm and hard maple, but we didn't know till that day how good we were compared with a greenhorn like Louie. All that day we had fun. He'd watch one of us old-timers sink the long nails into the wood and then he'd go at it again. But always they curled up and bent over under the fierce blows of his hammer. He didn't realize that some of us had been driving nails on the same job four and five years.

"I can't seem to do it," he'd say. He'd be pretty disgusted.

"Maybe there's something wrong with my hammer. Maybe I'm not holding it the same as you fellows."

"The trouble with you is," said Alf, "you're not hitting 'em hard enough. It don't make so much difference if you hit straight; the main thing is to come down on 'em hard." It was all we could do to keep from laughing out loud.

We got behind a couple of times that day just to make the situation look serious and when Louie saw the big hooks from the crane hanging over our heads waiting to pick up the box that we were still working on he broke out in a cold sweat. We had it figured out. We got the last nails in just before the box reached the end of the conveyor.

When the bell rang that night Louie was still having his troubles. "I can't understand it," he said. "When I watch you fellows it looks so easy, and yet I can't get the hang of it. I don't want to give it up and yet it's not right to fall down on a job and get paid just the same. Maybe I ought to talk to the boss. I'm getting paid five dollars a day and I didn't earn fifty cents. It's not right. Maybe he'd let me work for nothing until I get better."

It was silly talk, but that's what he said.

"Listen," said Alf, "you're too serious. What do you care what you're worth. The main thing is to hold your job and get every cent you got coming on Saturday night. The idea is to hold your job and not do any more work than you have to."

Alf wasn't kidding. I guess he was feeling sorry for Louie. But this Louie was funny.

"I guess you and I don't see things in the same way. I wouldn't feel right," he said, "if I took money that I didn't earn honestly." He was a case if there ever was one.

The next morning he was back on the job full of pep and ambition. He could hardly wait to get started. But he still couldn't get the hang of the job. The nails flew from under his hammer and bent double every time he hit them a hard blow. Then he would try to straighten them out, and by the time he got done fooling around with three or four nails the box would be near the end of the conveyor and we would have to jump in and finish his share of the nailing.

In the middle of the forenoon Big Barney came up to Louie.

"Listen, fellow," he said, "you don't seem to be getting on to this job. This is the second day you been here and so far you ain't drove two pounds of nails. I been watching you. You ain't doing anywheres near your share of the work. What's the matter," he said, "don't you know how to use a hammer?"

"I can't get the trick of it," said Louie. "I'm trying as hard as I can, but they bend over. The nails are too thin."

"You're hitting too hard," said Barney. "Take it easy. First learn to hit straight. It's no use hitting 'em so hard if they don't go in."

Big Barney took the hammer from Louie.

"Watch me," he said. "See—give 'em little taps until you get the feel of the hammer. And don't try to straighten them out when they bend over. Yank 'em out and drive in another. Don't fool away any more time than you have to."

When Big Barney walked away Louie looked pretty serious. For the rest of the day he followed Barney's advice so carefully that one or two boards on each box was about all that he was able to get.

And the nails were still bending over. All afternoon Barney watched him out of the corner of his eye as he prowled around between the boxes and when the bell rang that night he came up again. We could see he had his mind made up to do something.

"Well, fellow," he said, "I guess I'll have to lay you off. This job is just naturally too much for you. I been watching you this afternoon and I can see that you can't make the grade."

Right away Louie spoke up. He was serious.

"Listen," he said, "I can learn this job. All I need is a couple days of practice. I never got fired from a job yet and if I get fired from this one it would hurt me—I'd never forget it. I'll work on this job without pay until I learn it."

"It's against the rules," said Barney.

"In that case," said Louie, "give me one more day to make good. If you'd give me a chance I'd be a good nailer some day. I've got the strength. All I need is some practice. Tomorrow night at this time I'll be lots better."

"You want to keep the job pretty bad, don't you?" said Barney.

"I sure do," said Louie.

"All right then," said Barney. "I'll give you one more chance, but if you keep the job you'll have to be lots better tomorrow."

The next morning Louie told us something that gave us a laugh. He told us that he'd spent most of the whole night practicing in the landlady's garage. He'd been driving nails into blocks of wood, doing it on his own time. He even bought nails with his own money.

We kidded him about it, but he didn't understand.

"What's funny about it?" he said. "It's no more than right."

That day he did some pretty fair nailing. He got the feel of his hammer and he learned to hit straighter so the nails didn't bend over so much. In the afternoon he was almost able to keep up with his share of the work.

"I guess you'll make it all right," said Big Barney that night. "Take it easy for another day or two and then see if you can get up a little more speed."

Louie was tickled.

"It won't be long," he said, "until I'm a good nailer. Pretty soon I'll be as good as you fellows."

He was in earnest. He didn't say it to brag.

In those first days we thought we had him figured out. We thought he was working hard so that he wouldn't lose his job or get fired. But that wasn't the case.

After a couple of weeks he was a good nailer. He was as good as any of us old-timers, and some of us had been on the job four or five years. But after he got to be a good nailer he wasn't satisfied with himself. Pretty soon he learned to drive straighter and harder than anyone else on the job. There was no let down to the way he went at it. To look at him you would think that the boss was standing behind his shoulder watching every stroke of his hammer.

With us driving nails was just work—something disagreeable we had to do to earn our five bucks a day. We didn't think about the job any more than we had to, and we never talked about driving nails unless we absolutely couldn't help it. But with him it was different. He got the idea that his job was pretty important, and he was always talking about "being honest" and "doing justice" to something.

"We've got a big responsibility," he would say. "This job that we've got here is the only one in the whole department they can't do with machinery. If we slow up on our job we hold up the work of all the fellows ahead on the line."

It was easy to see that he needed some education and Alf and the rest of us tried to show Louie where he was wrong.

"Listen," said Alf to him one day, "you've got the wrong idea about this job. If you don't watch your step you're going to cook your own goose on this job and ours, too. We're supposed to nail up four hundred boxes a day, and that's what we're doing. We could get out five hundred if we wanted to work our fool heads off but if we did it once they'd expect us to do it every day and we wouldn't get a cent more for doing it. This job that you've got here is a kind of game. All the bosses are lined up on one side and we're lined up on the other. They're doing everything they can to get more work out of us, and we're doing everything we can to hold back."

But this Louie was funny. He didn't get the point.

"When I work I put myself into it," he said. "I put myself into it for all I'm worth. It ain't the bosses I'm afraid of—it's myself. If I didn't give everything I have to this job I wouldn't be honest; I wouldn't have any respect for myself."

Maybe those wasn't the exact words that he used, but that's the way it sounded. The stuff that he told us sometimes didn't hardly make sense.

There was no holding him back and he kept on getting better and better.

He experimented with hammers of different weights and the muscles of his right arm got as big as a stovepipe. He was driving every nail straight and there was all kinds of power in the way he came down with his hammer. He could sink the heads down into the wood.

One day a nail shot out from under his hammer and hit Toenails, the Polak, in the forehead. It laid the skin wide open. The next morning there was a new order up by the time-clock, saying that all the nailers had to wear goggles.

That didn't make us feel any better about Louie. It's a nuisance to have to wear goggles.

Pretty soon Louie was a better nailer than any of us old-timers. He was so fast that he could nail down his share of the boards and have maybe a half a minute to fool around between boxes. When he started doing that we knew that Big Barney would soon sit up and take notice. Alf got an idea.

"Listen," he said to us fellows one night after Louie had gone, "this fellow is going to ruin our job if we don't get a little sense into his head. He's gonna make us look like a bunch of saps if we don't do something and get him lined up. He ain't regular and maybe it's our fault. Tomorrow let's be nice to him. Let's invite him out tomorrow night and show him a good time. We'll get him drunk first then we'll take him over to Slant-eye's place on Hastings Street. Maybe if we treat him like a regular fellow he'll listen to what we say and line up with us on the job."

The next day we asked him, but it didn't work out like we figured.

"I can't make it," he said, "I'm reading a book. Besides I wouldn't care about doing those things."

And then, he turned around and gave us a lecture on how to drive nails. It was lunch time and we were shooting a game of craps on the floor.

"Have you fellows ever noticed how many times you hit a nail to drive it in?" he asked us.

"No," said Alf, "you tell us."

"Six," said Louie—"I've been watching you lately. You give 'em a light tap to start 'em and then you hit each nail five times to drive 'em down."

"What of it?" said Alf. "We're holding our jobs and getting our money every Saturday night, ain't we?"

"Well," said Louie, "I've found out that it's just as easy to drive 'em down with four or five blows. In fact, I think that any one of us could drive one of those nails down with three blows if we practiced a little and really started out to do it."

It had a funny effect on us, what he said. Some of us old-timers had been doing nothing but driving nails for four or five years and yet I don't believe there was a one of us that knew just how many times we were hitting each nail. That afternoon we all watched each other. We didn't say anything but we couldn't help watch the other fellows to see how many times they were hitting each nail. I guess we did it against our wills. Louie was right. He sunk every nail down out of sight with four smacks of the hammer while Alf and the rest of us were hitting six times to each nail. Even Tom Foley, the big buck nigger whose right arm was the size of a man's thigh, didn't do any better and along towards quitting time some of us went up to seven. After that we didn't have any use for Louie. We kidded him every chance we got but his one-track mind stayed just as serious as ever.

One day, Big Barney stopped at our station with a look on his face that was as dark as a thunder-cloud.

"The Old Man," he said, "is crabbing again. He claims its costing too much to get these boxes nailed up. The way you fellows are loafing is awful. If we had a little more speed over here we could be getting out twenty more boxes a day."

It was the same old belly-ache but Louie fell for it.

"I could be doing twice as much as I am doing now," he said. "I could do two-thirds of the nailing on this side of the line if I had to."

Big Barney exploded.

"Well, then why the Hell don't you do it?" he said. "You're the fellow that's doing all the loafing. Half the time I look at you you're standing here with your hands in your pocket playing pool or something. You go into a trance between every box that comes over the line."

"I'm doing my share of the work," said Louie, "and I'm getting it done just as fast and as good as I can. It's not my fault if there's nothing to do between boxes."

Big Barney got sarcastic. He was so mad he was red.

"Oh," he said, "you're trying to make a fool out of me. You're trying to show me up with the boss; you're trying to make me look like a sap, are you? Here the boss is jumping on me because the boxes ain't getting nailed up and you stand there and tell me you're only working half of the time. What are you doing, trying to make me look like a sucker? Trying to get my job away from me?"

It never fazed Louie a bit.

"Give me a raise," he said, "and I'll do the work of two men. I can do it."

"All right," said Barney. "Starting tomorrow you get six-twenty a day and do the work of two nailers. If you fall down on the job it's your own fault."

"Nice pal, you are," said Alf, after Barney went away. "Here one of us is going to lose his job because you got some funny idea. You were a fool for talking like that. Now Barney thinks you are trying to get him in dutch. Your crazy nailing will make the big boss think Barney can't get enough work out of us."

"If someone is going to lose his job," said Louie, "I'm sorry. But in the long run it's better. No one can do anything to hurt anyone else as long as they're honest."

The next morning Toenails was transferred to the salvage department where he got a job sorting screws and washers out of floor sweepings. Louie did the work of two nailers. None of us thought he could do it. It's easy enough to drive nails as fast as you can for an hour or so but to keep it up for a long time throws a strain on your muscles. But he did it. That day we saw some real nailing and along about ten in the morning he got better than ever. He started driving them down with three powerful smacks of his hammer. Yes, sir—that day he started sinking his nails out of sight in the wood with three blows. None of us could hardly believe it. The crane-man stretched his neck out of the cage, looked at us and grinned. Big Barney peeked from behind pillars and boxes and hardly knew how to take it. It made us old nailers look like a bunch of big saps and we got dirty looks from the big boss and Barney.

After that things started happening fast. Right away Louie got the idea that his job was pretty important and that he himself was mighty darn good. And the worst of it was he started talking to us like a preacher trying to make us feel that we were nothing but a bunch of dumb kids.

"You fellows," he would say, looking at us with his cow eyes, "ain't getting the most out of yourselves. On this nailing, for instance—put yourself in it for all you're worth and see what a different feeling it will give you. We've all got it in us to be great. You could all be just as good on this job as I am if you buckled right down to it and gave it all you got."

Then, like as not, he'd start off and tell us about some book he was reading. It got so pretty soon that when he started his talk we wouldn't listen.

Then something happened that none of us ever expected. One afternoon the guide, Cicero, we called him, came into our department with a long string of visitors looking over the sights of the factory. We were used to that, a big string came through twice every day. But this time it was different. He stopped the whole bunch at our station and lined 'em up in a half circle.

"Judast!" said Alf. "What's Cicero gonna pull off here?"

None of us knew. We were all plenty curious. Every man on the line was watching to see what was going to happen.

Cicero waited until the last stragglers came up and then with his big mouth he went into action.

"Ladies and Gentlemen," he started, "I'm going to let you see an exhibition of nailing. This fellow you see here," he said, pointing his cane at Louie, "is our champion nailer. He is the best nailer, not only in this department, but in the whole factory."

Louie was flabbergasted for a minute or so, but pretty soon got the idea and started driving nails for all he was worth. Cicero went ahead with his spiel.

"Where the ordinary nailer," he said, "has to hit a nail four or five times, this man drives 'em down with three swats. Watch 'em go down out of sight— you'd think he was driving nails into cheese instead of into hard wood. Right now he's doing the work of two men and taking it easy. But don't try it yourself; you might hit your thumb."

A couple of good looking dames giggled. Louie was as good as a circus. With his left fist full of nails, all arranged so that the heads were pointing up, he would sort of spin them out between his forefinger and thumb; a light blow would set them and two powerful blows would sink them out of sight in the wood.

"You'll notice," Cicero said, "all the men working around this fellow have to wear goggles, it's orders. If one of those nails should happen to fly out from under his hammer it would go like a bullet. Notice the way his hammer comes down—true as a die. Look at the muscles he's got in his shoulder and the size of that arm. He's what you might call an expert."

At the end of his spiel he had a hard job getting some of the school teachers started again.

That was just the beginning. After that Louie gave his exhibition twice every day, once in the morning and once in the afternoon. It got to be a regular part of the program. And every time that Cicero went over his spiel he improved it. At first he had Louie doing the work of two men and then he raised it to three. A week later he raised it again. Then he started calling Louie "our champion nailer" and used the word "art." Louie fell in with the show. He would let a nail fly out from under his hammer at just the right second and Cicero would end up his spiel with a bunch of statistics. "If all the nails that this fellow drives in one year," he would say, "were laid end to end, they would make a solid line from Detroit to Cleveland, Ohio."

It was rich. It wasn't long until Louie worked up a pretty good opinion of himself. He started wearing silk shirts to work with the sleeves cut off at the shoulder so that everyone could see the size of his muscles. Then, he got dissatisfied with his wages.

"If I'm worth three or four times as much as you fellows," he said, "why don't I get it?"

"That's it exactly," we told him. "Why don't you see the big boss and tell him he's got to give you a raise or you'll quit."

So that's what he did. He asked the big boss for a raise and the boss turned him down. The next day Louie was mad. Mad and disgusted.

"It's a dirty shame," said Alf; "it's a raw deal you're getting. Here, you're worth as much to the company as four or five of us fellows and they'll only give you six-twenty a day." We all talked as if we were terribly sorry for Louie.

Then, one day, a big order came along for Sao Paulo and the big boss tried to speed up the line. Right away, the first thing in the morning, the big boxes started coming through at the rate of about fifty an hour. At nine o'clock there was hardly time to take a deep breath between boxes, and at ten they were piling up against us, pushing us to the end of the line. Half the time the big boss was fooling around with the regulator, speeding it up when we were only just holding our own and slowing it down when it looked like a box would be dumped on the floor before we could get the cover nailed on. Louie was holding his own and the rest of us were working as though we had all suddenly gone crazy, when Barney came up.

"The Old Man is watching you fellows," he said. "You better snap into it. Here everybody else is trying to get this order out on time and you fellows are laying down, holding up everyone else."

We all looked dumb and acted like he'd hurt our feelings and even Louie, for once, had enough sense to keep his mouth shut. For the rest of the day, Big Barney paced up and down like a panther and the boss sat at his desk with hunched shoulders and glared at us underneath the shade of his lamp. At the end of the day, production was only ten more than an average day's run, and we felt that we had more than held our own against the system. As for Louie, he scarcely realized that all day we had been playing a game with the bosses.

One Saturday afternoon a couple of weeks later, three machine flunkeys brought their tools into the shipping department and squatted down against the wall on their heels. When the bell rang Big Barney came up. He had a grin on his face and was sort of sucking in his breath like he does when he has bad news for somebody.

"Well," he said, rubbing his hands, "Monday morning I'm going to have to scatter you fellows around a little bit. Wouldn't be surprised if I had to lay off one or two. We got a nailing machine coming in."

Louie's jaw dropped a foot.

"A nailing machine!" he said "You can't get a machine to nail boxes. There isn't any machine made that will do it. To drive nails into hard wood you have to hit 'em hard and just right. Besides, these boxes are all the time moving."

"This machine is a new one," said Barney. "Our own engineers made it up; you never saw anything like it. It's got an electric motor on top and all the man has to do is press a button. I was gonna give you the job of running it."

"I don't want it," said Louie. "I don't even want to work near it. If I can't keep the job I got now I'll turn in my badge."

"I wanted you to run it," said Barney, "so that you'd be handy in case something went wrong. I'm giving you the first try. Lots of fellows would jump at the chance. You'd be getting the same wages—anyhow for a while."

Louie argued some more and then he changed his mind all of a sudden.

"All right," he said. "I'll take it. But I know it won't do the work."

Monday morning when he got to work they had it set up. The machine flunkeys were still on the job and were breaking it in. Alf and I got the job of laying the boards on top of the boxes. The other fellows were laid off.

It was comical to watch Louie. He walked around the machine and looked it over as though it might take a notion to bite him. He examined the boxes to see if the nails were all the way in.

The machine was perched on four iron legs over the conveyor and there was an electric motor on top. When the boxes got underneath one of the flunkeys pressed a button and a bunch of gears and cams went into motion. It drove sixty-four nails in one crack and there was hardly a sound.

"I didn't think it was possible," said Louie. "If I didn't see it with my own eyes I wouldn't believe it."

"This one is nothing," said one of the flunkeys. "You ought to see the machine we set up in the motor assembly department. It bores forty-eight holes from six different angles at the same time. And in the magneto department we've got one that took the place of twelve men. It can drive screws—sixteen every time you pull down on a lever. There's a machine that's a honey."

When the flunkeys got the nailing machine tuned up, they turned the job over to Louie. It was a cinch and he was lucky to get it. All he had to do was to shovel nails into a hopper that went up and down and every time a box came along he pressed a little black button. That made the thing go into gear and a bunch of spindles came down and pressed the nails into the wood. There was no fuss about it.

When Cicero led his string of sight-seers into the shipping department we expected him to pass through without stopping. But he didn't. He rounded them up about Louie and the nailing machine and got ready to make them a spiel.

We couldn't figure out what he was going to say, Louie no longer being the "Champion Nailer." But Cicero was slick. Not many fellows ever put it over on him.

"I am going to show you," he said, "a little exhibition of mechanical nailing. This machine that you see here is something that was figured out by our own engineers. It does the work of six men without any fuss and in a pinch, when we have to get out a rush order, it can be speeded up fifty per cent."

Cicero looked past Louie in such a way as to make you think there wasn't anyone there. He talked like he owned half the factory, and listening to him you might have thought the nailing machine was his own personal idea.

"Before we got this machine," he said, "we had a man working here who was a pretty good nailer. He had to hit every nail two or three times with a hammer and the best he could do was around twelve thousand a day. This machine drives sixty-four at a crack and it only comes down on 'em once. That's what you call nailing."

Louie looked like he'd turned into rock. His big cow eyes were fastened on Cicero and his mouth was half open.

"And the beauty of it is," Cicero wound up, "a machine like this is always one hundred per cent efficient. It's never late on the job and on Monday mornings it never comes to work with a headache."

A couple of out-of-town Rotary fellows looked at each other and giggled. The whole thing was over in a couple of minutes but it was as good as a circus.

Louie was fairly bristling. Even his eyebrows seemed to stick out more than usual and his eyes looked black against his white face. When he pressed the button he shoved his thumb down on it as if he were trying to push the machine clear out of the factory.

In the afternoon there was an accident. Louie let out a yell and we saw him pull his arm out of the machine. There was a smear of blood on his hand. Alf and I saw right away what had happened. He had tried to jam a piece of wood into the gears of the nailing machine.

Barney came up on the run.

Louie was so mad he was dancing around in a circle. It looked as if he was mad enough to tear something to pieces. He was screaming so that you could have heard him above the noise of the machinery.

"It ain't right," he said, "I won't stand for it. It's got my job away from me and now it's making a fool out of me. It's making a fool out of me, I tell you, and I won't stand for it."

"What's the matter?" said Barney, all excited.

"It's this nailing machine. It's got my job away from me and then it tries to take off my hand. It ain't right. Everybody around here is laughing at me; I'm not going to stand it."

While Barney was trying to calm him down the little motor up on top of the nailing machine was humming along as if nothing had happened. Louie looked at it fiercely.

"Look at that motor," he said, "I'd like to smash it to pieces."

Barney sent Louie to the first-aid to get his hand fixed and when no one was looking Alf knocked the block of wood out of the machine. Nothing was damaged and we figured there was no use letting Barney know how the accident happened.

When Louie got back the safety engineers were already on the job looking things over. They watched Louie work for a while and then they stood around in a huddle talking things over.

"There's no excuse for it," they said, "he must have stuck his hand in there on purpose. The safer we make 'em the dumber it seems to make the fellows that run 'em. We'll get it fixed up tonight," they said.

In the morning they had finished their job. And you had to admit it was a swell piece of work. Instead of one button to press there were two, and they were far enough apart so that Louie had to use both hands at the same time. And they had something else. They had a little steel gate affair that slid up in front of Louie every time he pressed down on the buttons. It came up just before the machine went into gear. After the nails were punched in it dropped down. You had to admit it was good.

When Cicero came through with his bunch of sight-seers and started off on his spiel he was better than ever. Just before he got to the end of his speech he came to a pause. Then he came out with a hot one.

"If all the nails, he said, "that this machine can drive in a year were laid end to end they would reach from here to San Francisco—from Detroit all the way to the Pacific Ocean." That was something. All the school teachers wrote it down in their books.

Then Cicero noticed the double button effect and the little gate that slid up and down.

"You'll notice," he said, "this machine is one hundred per cent fool proof. The operator couldn't get his hands into the wheels if he tried. In order to throw the machine into gear he's got to press two buttons at the same time or else it won't go. But our engineers are not satisfied with making machines one hundred per cent safe. They've got to be safer than that. They've got to be so safe that the fellow that runs 'em couldn't get hurt even if he figured out ways to do it. And that's the reason for the little steel gate that slides up in front of his nose every time he punches the buttons."

We had to laugh. All the fellows had grins on their faces.

After that Louie was different. He was more like he was on the first morning when he came to work in the factory. All the fight was gone out of him and he had that scared look on his face. When Alf said something to him he looked straight at Alf a long time as if it was something terribly serious.

When the bell rang he trailed Alf and me to the tool-crib though he didn't have a single tool to turn in.

"You fellows going out tonight?" he asked us.

"Sure," we said, "it's Saturday night."

"Are you going to Slant-eye's and all those other places you were telling me about once?" he asked.

"Sure," said Alf, "but Saturday night is your night for going down to the library, ain't it?"

"If you don't mind," said Louie, "I'd like to go along with you fellows."

Then he looked at us for maybe a half minute or so.

"If it hadn't been for that little gate," he said—

"Yeah," said Alf, "if it hadn't been for that little gate and the nailing machine you would've been a stick-in-the-mud all the rest of your life. That nailing machine has made a man out of you."

And that's just about the end of the story. We took Louie out with us and showed him a swell time. After that we treated him like one of the fellows, and none of us ever kidded him any more except Alf. Every once in a while Alf calls him the "ex-champion nailer."

◆ DISCUSSION QUESTIONS

1. How do you feel toward Louie: do you admire him, pity him, sympathize with him? Support your answer with material from the story.

2. Use reading 9.1, *The Development and Enforcement of Group Norms,* to analyze the norms in the work group and the organization as follows:
    (a) Describe the norms and their impact on satisfaction and productivity.
    (b) Feldman presents four conditions under which group norms are most likely to be enforced. Identify how these conditions apply to each of the norms in the story.
    (c) Discuss how these norms may have developed according to the four ways described by Feldman.
    (d) How can management foster new norms to improve organizational effectiveness and labor-management relations?

3. How was Louie socialized into the organization? Make recommendations to the management to improve the socialization process [1].

4. Refer to reading 9.2, *Face Your Problem Subordinates Now,* to answer the following questions:
    (a) According to Veiga's classification, what type of subordinates are the workers in the group that Louie joined?
    (b) Draw up a plan for management (based on Veiga's recommendations) to use to improve the employees' attitudes and behavior.

5. The story is told from the point of view of one of the workers. How would the situation have been described if it had been written by Louie? What kind of job do you think Louie will have five years hence and what will be his attitude toward work?

6. This story depicts restriction of output among blue collar workers fifty years

ago. Give examples of this phenomenon in contemporary organizations. Discuss how white collar workers and professionals may engage in restriction of output. What strategies can management use to discourage such behavior?

◆   *REFERENCES*

1. Van Maanen, J. 1978. People Processing: Strategies of organizational socialization. *Organizational Dynamics* 7: 19–36.

Shooting an Elephant

George Orwell

In this essay George Orwell recounts his personal experience as a police officer in Burma under British colonial rule in the 1920s. A crowd of Burmese pressure him to kill a rampaging elephant, against his will. He is faced with the dilemma of compromising his own principles, or looking like a fool for not doing what is expected of him. The story highlights the issues an authority figure must consider in dealing with group pressure.

George Orwell (1903–1950) was born in India to English parents. Following his education in England, he returned to India and Burma to work as a police officer. Many of his literary works deal with the theme of power and authority. Among the most famous are the anti-totalitarian *Animal Farm* and *1984*.

In Moulmein, in lower Burma, I was hated by large numbers of people—the only time in my life that I have been important enough for this to happen to me. I was sub-divisional police officer of the town, and in an aimless, petty kind of way anti-European feeling was very bitter. No one had the guts to raise a riot, but if a European woman went through the bazaars alone somebody would probably spit betel juice over her dress. As a police officer I was an obvious target and was baited whenever it seemed safe to do so. When a nimble Burman tripped me up on the football field and the referee (another Burman) looked the other way, the crowd yelled with hideous laughter. This happened more than once. In the end the sneering yellow faces of young men that met me everywhere, the insults hooted after me when I was at a safe distance, got badly on my nerves. The young Buddhist priests were the worst of all. There were several thousands of them in the town and none of them seemed to have anything to do except stand on street corners and jeer at Europeans.

All this was perplexing and upsetting. For at that time I had already made up my mind that imperialism was an evil thing and the sooner I chucked up my job and got out of it the better. Theoretically—and secretly, of course—I was all for the Burmese and all against their oppressors, the British. As for the job I was doing, I hated it more bitterly than I can perhaps make clear. In a job like that you see the dirty work of Empire at close quarters. The wretched prisoners huddling in the stinking cages of the lock-ups, the grey, cowed faces of the long-

Source: "Shooting an Elephant" from *Shooting an Elephant and Other Essays* by George Orwell, copyright 1950 by Sonia Brownell Orwell and renewed 1978 by Sonia Pitt Rivers, reprinted by permission of Harcourt Brace Jovanovich, Inc.

term convicts, the scarred buttocks of the men who had been flogged with bamboos—all these oppressed me with an intolerable sense of guilt. But I could get nothing into perspective. I was young and ill-educated and I had had to think out my problems in the utter silence that is imposed on every Englishman in the East. I did not even know that the British Empire is dying, still less did I know that it is a great deal better than the younger empires that are going to supplant it. All I knew was that I was stuck between my hatred of the empire I served and my rage against the evil-spirited little beasts who tried to make my job impossible. With one part of my mind I thought of the British Raj as an unbreakable tyranny, as something clamped down, in *saecula saeculorum*, upon the will of prostrate peoples; with another part I thought that the greatest joy in the world would be to drive a bayonet into a Buddhist priest's guts. Feelings like these are the normal by-products of imperialism; ask any Anglo-Indian official, if you can catch him off duty.

One day something happened which in a roundabout way was enlightening. It was a tiny incident in itself, but it gave me a better glimpse than I had had before of the real nature of imperialism—the real motives for which despotic governments act. Early one morning the sub-inspector at a police station the other end of the town rang me up on the phone and said that an elephant was ravaging the bazaar. Would I please come and do something about it? I did not know what I could do, but I wanted to see what was happening and I got on to a pony and started out. I took my rifle, an old .44 Winchester and much too small to kill an elephant, but I thought the noise might be useful *in terrorem*. Various Burmans stopped me on the way and told me about the elephant's doings. It was not, of course, a wild elephant, but a tame one which had gone "must." It had been chained up, as tame elephants always are when their attack of "must" is due, but on the previous night it had broken its chain and escaped. Its mahout, the only person who could manage it when it was in that state, had set out in pursuit, but had taken the wrong direction and was now twelve hours' journey away, and in the morning the elephant had suddenly reappeared in the town. The Burmese population had no weapons and were quite helpless against it. It had already destroyed somebody's bamboo hut, killed a cow, and raided some fruit-stalls and devoured the stock; also it had met the municipal rubbish van and, when the driver jumped out and took to his heels, had turned the van over and inflicted violences upon it.

The Burmese sub-inspector and some Indian constables were waiting for me in the quarter where the elephant had been seen. It was a very poor quarter, a labyrinth of squalid bamboo huts, thatched with palm-leaf, winding all over a steep hillside. I remember that it was a cloudy, stuffy morning at the beginning of the rains. We began questioning the people as to where the elephant had gone and, as usual, failed to get any definite information. That is invariably the case in the East; a story always sounds clear enough at a distance, but the nearer you get to the scene of events the vaguer it becomes. Some of the people said that the elephant had gone in one direction, some said that he had gone in another, some professed not even to have heard of any elephant. I had almost made up my mind that the whole story was a pack of lies, when we heard yells a little distance away. There was a loud, scandalized cry of "Go away, child! Go away this instant!" and an old woman with a switch in her hand came round the corner of a hut, violently shooing away a crowd of naked children. Some more women followed, clicking their tongues and exclaiming; evidently there was something that the children ought not to have seen. I rounded the hut and saw a man's dead body sprawling in the mud. He was an Indian, a black Dravidian coolie, almost naked, and he could not have been dead many minutes. The people said that the elephant had come suddenly upon him round the corner of the hut, caught him with its trunk, put its foot on his back, and ground him into the earth. This was the rainy season and the ground was soft, and his face had scored a trench a foot deep and a couple of yards long. He was lying on his belly with arms crucified and head sharply twisted to one side. His face was coated with mud, the eyes wide open, the teeth bared and grinning with an expression of unendurable agony. (Never tell me, by the way, that the dead look peaceful. Most of the corpses I have seen looked devilish.) The friction of the great beast's foot had stripped the skin from his back as neatly as one skins a rabbit. As soon as I saw the dead man I sent an orderly to a friend's house nearby to borrow an elephant rifle. I had already sent back the pony, not wanting it to go mad with fright and throw me if it smelt the elephant.

The orderly came back in a few minutes with a rifle and five cartridges, and meanwhile some Burmans had arrived and told us that the elephant was in the paddy fields below, only a few hundred yards away. As I started forward practically the whole population of the quarter flocked out of the houses and followed me. They had seen the rifle and were all shouting excitedly that I was going to shoot the elephant. They had not shown much interest in the elephant when he was merely ravaging their homes, but it was different now that he was going to be shot. It was a bit of fun to them, as it would be to an English crowd; besides they wanted the meat. It made me vaguely uneasy. I had no intention of shooting the elephant—I had merely sent for the rifle to defend myself if necessary—and it is always unnerving to have a crowd following you. I marched down the hill, looking and feeling a fool, with the rifle over my shoulder and an ever-growing army of people jostling at my heels. At the bottom, when you got away from the huts, there was a metalled road and beyond that a miry waste of paddy fields a thousand yards across, not yet ploughed but soggy from the first rains and dotted with coarse grass. The elephant was standing eight yards from the road, his left side towards us. He took not the slightest notice of the crowd's approach. He was tearing up bunches of grass, beating them against his knees to clean them and stuffing them into his mouth.

I had halted on the road. As soon as I saw the elephant I knew with perfect certainty that I ought not to shoot him. It is a serious matter to shoot a working elephant—it is comparable to destroying a huge and costly piece of machinery—and obviously one ought not to do it if it can possibly be avoided. And at that distance, peacefully eating, the elephant looked no more dangerous than a cow. I thought then and I think now that his attack of "must" was already passing off; in which case he would merely wander harmlessly about until the mahout came back and caught him. Moreover, I did not in the least want to shoot him. I decided that I would watch him for a little while to make sure that he did not turn savage again, and then go home.

But at that moment I glanced round at the crowd that had followed me. It was an immense crowd, two thousand at the least and growing every minute. It blocked the road for a long distance on either side. I looked at the sea of yellow faces above the garish clothes—faces all happy and excited over this bit of fun, all certain that the elephant was going to be shot. They were watching me as they would watch a conjurer about to perform a trick. They did not like me, but with the magical rifle in my hands I was momentarily worth watching. And suddenly I realized that I should have to shoot the elephant after all. The people expected it of me and I had got to do it; I could feel their two thousand wills pressing me forward, irresistibly. And it was at this moment, as I stood there with the rifle in my hands, that I first grasped the hollowness, the futility of the white man's dominion in the East. Here was I, the white man with his gun, standing in front of the unarmed native crowd—seemingly the leading actor of the piece; but in reality I was only an absurd puppet pushed to and fro by the will of those yellow faces behind. I perceived in this moment that when the white man turns tyrant it is his own freedom that he destroys. He becomes a sort of hollow, posing dummy, the conventionalized figure of a sahib. For it is the condition of his rule that he shall spend his life in trying to impress the "natives," and so in every crisis he has got to do what the "natives" expect of him. He wears a mask, and his face grows to fit it. I had got to shoot the elephant. I had committed myself to doing it when I sent for the rifle. A sahib has got to act like a sahib; he has got to appear resolute, to know his own mind and do definite things. To come all that way, rifle in hand, with two thousand people marching at my heels, and then to trail feebly away, having done nothing—no, that was impossible. The crowd would laugh at me. And my whole life, every white man's life in the East, was one long struggle not to be laughed at.

But I did not want to shoot the elephant. I watched him beating his bunch of grass against his knees, with that preoccupied grandmotherly air that elephants have. It seemed to me that it would be murder to shoot him. At that age I was not squeamish about killing animals, but I had never shot an elephant and never wanted to. (Somehow it always seems worse to kill a *large* animal.) Besides, there was the beast's owner to be considered. Alive, the elephant was worth at least a hundred pounds; dead, he would only be worth the value of his tusks, five pounds, possibly. But I had got to act quickly. I turned to some experienced-looking Burmans who had been there when we arrived, and asked them how the elephant had been behaving. They all said the same thing: he took no notice of you if you left him alone, but he might charge if you went too close to him.

It was perfectly clear to me what I ought to do. I ought to walk up to within, say, twenty-five yards of the elephant and test his behavior. If he charged, I could shoot; if he took no notice of me, it would be safe to leave him until the mahout came back. But also I knew that I was going to do no such thing. I was a poor shot with a rifle and the ground was soft mud into which one would sink at every step. If the elephant charged and I missed him, I should have about as much chance as a toad under a steam-roller. But even then I was not thinking particularly of my own skin, only of the watchful yellow faces behind. For at that moment, with the crowd watching me, I was not afraid in the ordinary sense, as I would have been if I had been alone. A white man mustn't be frightened in front of "natives"; and so, in general, he isn't frightened. The sole thought in my mind was that if anything went wrong those two thousand Burmans would see me pursued, caught, trampled on, and reduced to a grinning corpse like that Indian up the hill. And if that happened it was quite probable that some of them would laugh. That would never do. There was only one alternative. I shoved the cartridges into the magazine and lay down on the road to get a better aim.

The crowd grew very still, and a deep, low, happy sigh, as of people who see the theatre curtain go up at last, breathed from innumerable throats. They were going to have their bit of fun after all. The rifle was a beautiful German thing with cross-hair sights. I did not then know that in shooting an elephant one would shoot to cut an imaginary bar running from ear-hole to ear-hole. I ought, therefore, as the elephant was sideways on, to have aimed straight at his ear-hole; actually I aimed several inches in front of this, thinking the brain would be further forward.

When I pulled the trigger I did not hear the bang or feel the kick—one never does when a shot goes home—but I heard the devilish roar of glee that went up from the crowd. In that instant, in too short a time, one would have thought, even for the bullet to get there, a mysterious, terrible change had come over the elephant. He neither stirred nor fell, but every line of his body had altered. He looked suddenly stricken, shrunken, immensely old, as though the frightful impact of the bullet had paralysed him without knocking him down. At last, after what seemed a long time—it might have been five seconds, I dare say—he sagged flabbily to his knees. His mouth slobbered. An enormous senility seemed to have settled upon him. One could have imagined him thousands of years old. I fired again into the same spot. At the second shot he did not collapse but climbed with desperate slowness to his feet and stood weakly upright, with legs sagging and head drooping. I fired a third time. That was the shot that did for him. You could see the agony of it jolt his whole body and knock the last remnant of strength from his legs. But in falling he seemed for a moment to rise, for as his hind legs collapsed beneath him he seemed to tower upward like a huge rock toppling, his trunk reaching skywards like a tree. He trumpeted, for the first and only time. And then down he came, his belly toward me, with a crash that seemed to shake the ground even where I lay.

I got up. The Burmans were already racing past me across the mud. It was obvious that the elephant would never rise again, but he was not dead. He was breathing very rhythmically with long rattling gasps, his great mound of a side painfully rising and falling. His mouth was wide open—I could see far down into caverns of pale pink throat. I waited a long time for him to die, but his breathing did not weaken. Finally I fired my two remaining shots into the spot where I thought his heart must be. The thick blood welled out of him like red velvet, but still he did not die. His body did not even jerk when the shots hit him, the tortured breathing continued without a pause. He was dying, very slowly and in great agony, but in some world remote from me where not even a bullet could damage him further. I felt that I had got to put an end to that deadful noise. It seemed dreadful to see the great beast lying there, powerless to move and yet powerless to die, and not even to be able to finish him. I sent back for my small rifle and poured shot after shot into his heart and down his throat. They seemed to make no impression. The tortured gasps continued as steadily as the ticking of a clock.

In the end I could not stand it any longer and went away. I heard later that it took him half an hour to die. Burmans were bringing dahs and baskets even before I left, and I was told they had stripped his body almost to the bones by the afternoon.

Afterwards, of course, there were endless discussions about the shooting of the elephant. The owner was furious, but he was only an Indian and could do nothing. Besides, legally I had done the right thing, for a mad elephant has to be killed, like a mad dog, if its owner fails to control it. Among the Europeans opinion was divided. The older men said I was right, the younger men said it was a damn shame to shoot an elephant for killing a coolie, because an elephant was worth more than any damn Coringhee coolie. And afterwards I was very glad that the coolie had been killed; it put me legally in the right and it gave me a sufficient pretext for shooting the elephant. I often wondered whether any of the others grasped that I had done it solely to avoid looking a fool.

◆   *DISCUSSION QUESTIONS*

1. Should Orwell have shot the elephant? If you had been in his place, what would you have done? What alternatives were available to Orwell and what outcomes would they have produced?

2. Orwell yielded to group pressure and killed the elephant. Analyze the incident according to the following factors that have been found to induce conformity to group pressure:
   (a) ambiguous situation.
   (b) interdependent group members.
   (c) personality of the individual being influenced (high authoritarianism, low self-esteem, and low intelligence).
   (d) public commitment of the individual to an attitude or behavior.

3. What kinds of expectations do subordinates have of leaders and how are they formed? Did Orwell himself set up the crowd's expectations for him to shoot the elephant? Did Orwell identify too much with the Burmese?

4. Orwell says that he shot the elephant "solely to avoid looking a fool." Do you agree?

5. Develop a set of recommendations for Orwell to prevent a recurrence of unnecessarily shooting an elephant. Make use of the suggestions about establishing relationships with others presented in reading 9.3, *Influence Without Authority: The Use of Alliances, Reciprocity, and Exchange to Accomplish Work.*

6. Group pressure can be very powerful: "I could feel their two thousand wills pressing me forward, irresistibly." Describe situations in contemporary work settings where a manager might feel pressured to give in to the crowd. What impact does yielding to group pressure have on long-term superior-subordinate relations?

SECTION 7
Power and Communication

The Catbird Seat

James Thurber

In this story Erwin Martin, the loyal and unassuming head of the filing department at F&S Company, concocts an evil plan to eliminate a power hungry new manager who threatens his department. The story examines the problems created by poorly defined power relationships and inadequate communication in an exaggerated and humorous way. It also raises the issue of how to deal with difficult employees and provides one outlandish solution.

James Thurber (1894–1961) is one of America's favorite humorists. For 34 years he was a writer and editor for *The New Yorker*. He also was a playwright and cartoonist. *The Catbird Seat* is one of his most famous works, and Thurber once said he considered it to be his best short story.

Mr. Martin bought the pack of Camels on Monday night in the most crowded cigar store on Broadway. It was theater time and seven or eight men were buying cigarettes. The clerk didn't even glance at Mr. Martin, who put the pack in his overcoat pocket and went out. If any of the staff of F & S has seen him buy the cigarettes, they would have been astonished, for it was generally known that Mr. Martin did not smoke, and never had. No one saw him.

It was just a week to the day since Mr. Martin had decided to rub out Mrs. Ulgine Barrows. The term "rub out" pleased him because it suggested nothing more than the correction of an error—in this case an error of Mr. Fitweiler. Mr. Martin had spent each night of the past week working out his plan and examining it. As he walked home now he went over it again. For the hundredth time he resented the element of imprecision, the margin of guesswork that entered into the business. The project as he had worked it out was casual and bold, the risks were considerable. Something might go wrong anywhere along the line. And therein lay the cunning of his scheme. No one would ever see in it the cautious, painstaking hand of Erwin Martin, head of the filing department of F & S, of whom Mr. Fitweiler had once said, "Man is fallible but Martin isn't." No one would see his hand, that is, unless it were caught in the act.

Sitting in his apartment, drinking a glass of milk, Mr. Martin reviewed his case against Mrs. Ulgine Barrows, as he had every night for seven nights. He began at the beginning. Her quacking voice and braying laugh had first profaned the halls of F & S on March 7, 1941 (Mr. Martin had a head for dates). Old Roberts, the personnel chief, had introduced her as the newly appointed special adviser to the president of the firm, Mr. Fitweiler. The woman had appalled Mr. Martin instantly, but he hadn't shown it. He had given her his dry hand, a look of studious concentration, and a faint smile. "Well," she had said, looking at the papers on his desk, "are you lifting the oxcart out of the ditch?" As Mr. Martin recalled that moment, over his milk, he squirmed slightly. He must keep his mind on her crimes as a special adviser, not on her peccadillos as a personality. This he found difficult to do, in spite of entering an objection and sustaining it. The faults of the woman as a woman kept chattering on in his mind like an unruly witness. She had, for almost two years now, baited him. In the halls, in the elevator, even in his own office, into which she romped now and then like a circus horse, she was constantly shouting these silly questions at him. "Are you lifting the oxcart out of that ditch? Are you tearing up the pea patch? Are you hollering down the rain barrel? Are you scraping around the bottom of the pickle barrel? Are you sitting in the catbird seat?"

It was Joey Hart, one of Mr. Martin's two assistants, who had explained what the gibberish meant. "She must be a Dodger fan," he had said. "Red Barber announces the Dodger games over the radio and he uses those expressions— picked 'em up down South." Joey had gone on to explain one or two. "Tearing up the pea patch" meant going on a rampage; "sitting in the catbird seat" meant sitting pretty, like a batter with three balls and no strikes on him. Mr. Martin dismissed all this with an effort. It had been annoying, it had driven him near to distraction, but he was too solid a man to be moved to murder by anything so childish. It was fortunate, he reflected as he passed on to the important charges against Mrs. Barrows, that he had stood up under it so well. He had maintained always an outward appearance of polite tolerance. "Why, I even believe you like the woman," Miss Paird, his other assistant, had once said to him. He had simply smiled.

A gavel rapped in Mr. Martin's mind and the case proper was resumed. Mrs. Ulgine Barrows stood charged with willful, blatant, and persistent attempts to destroy the efficiency and system of F & S. It was competent, material, and relevant to review her advent and rise to power. Mr. Martin had got the story from Miss Paird, who seemed always able to find things out. According to her,

Mrs. Barrows had met Mr. Fitweiler at a party, where she had rescued him from the embraces of a powerfully built drunken man who had mistaken the president of F & S for a famous retired Middle Western football coach. She had led him to a sofa and somehow worked upon him a monstrous magic. The aging gentleman had jumped to the conclusion there and then that this was a woman of singular attainments, equipped to bring out the best in him and in the firm. A week later he had introduced her into F & S as his special adviser. On that day confusion got its foot in the door. After Miss Tyson, Mr. Brundage, and Mr. Bartlett had been fired and Mr. Munson had taken his hat and stalked out, mailing in his resignation later, old Roberts had been emboldened to speak to Mr. Fitweiler. He mentioned that Mr. Munson's department had been a "little disrupted" and hadn't they perhaps better resume the old system there? Mr. Fitweiler had said certainly not. He had the greatest faith in Mrs. Barrows' ideas. "They require a little seasoning, a little seasoning, is all," he had added. Mr. Roberts had given it up. Mr. Martin reviewed in detail all the changes wrought by Mrs. Barrows. She had begun chipping at the cornices of the firm's edifice and now she was swinging at the foundation stones with a pickaxe.

Mr. Martin came now, in his summing up, to the afternoon of Monday, November 2, 1942—just one week ago. On that day, at 3 P.M., Mrs. Barrows had bounced into his office. "Boo!" she had yelled. "Are you scraping around the bottom of the pickle barrel?" Mr. Martin had looked at her from under his green eyeshade, saying nothing. She had begun to wander about the office, taking it in with her great, popping eyes. "Do you really need *all* these filing cabinets?" she had demanded suddenly. Mr. Martin's heart had jumped. "Each of these files," he had said, keeping his voice even, "plays an indispensable part in the system of F & S." She had brayed at him, "Well, don't tear up the pea patch!" and gone to the door. From there she had bawled, "But you sure have got a lot of fine scrap here!" Mr. Martin could no longer doubt that the finger was on his beloved department. Her pickaxe was on the upswing, poised for the first blow. It had not come yet; he had received no blue memo from the enchanted Mr. Fitweiler bearing nonsensical instructions deriving from the obscene woman. But there was no doubt in Mr. Martin's mind that one would be forthcoming. He must act quickly. Already a precious week had gone by. Mr. Martin stood up in his living room, still holding his milk glass. "Gentlemen of the jury," he said to himself, "I demand the death penalty for this horrible person."

The next day Mr. Martin followed his routine, as usual. He polished his glasses more often and once sharpened an already sharp pencil, but not even Miss Paird noticed. Only once did he catch sight of his victim; she swept past him in the hall with a patronizing "Hi!" At five-thirty he walked home, as usual, and had a glass of milk, as usual. He had never drunk anything stronger in his life—unless you could count ginger ale. The late Sam Schlosser, the S of F & S, had praised Mr. Martin at a staff meeting several years before for his temperate habits. "Our most efficient worker neither drinks nor smokes," he had said. "The results speak for themselves." Mr. Fitweiler had sat by, nodding approval.

Mr. Martin was still thinking about that red-letter day as he walked over to the Schrafft's on Fifth Avenue near Forty-sixth Street. He got there, as he always did, at eight o'clock. He finished his dinner and the financial page of the *Sun* at a quarter to nine, as he always did. It was his custom after dinner to take a walk. This time he walked down Fifth Avenue at a casual pace. His gloved hands felt moist and warm, his forehead cold. He transferred the Camels from his overcoat to a jacket pocket. He wondered, as he did so, if they did not represent an unnecessary note of strain. Mrs. Barrows smoked only Luckies. It was his idea to puff a few puffs on a Camel (after the rubbing-out), stub it out in the ashtray holding her lipstick-stained Luckies, and thus drag a small red herring across the trail. Perhaps it was not a good idea. It would take time. He might even choke, too loudly.

Mr. Martin had never seen the house on West Twelfth Street where Mrs. Barrows lived, but he had a clear enough picture of it. Fortunately, she had bragged to everybody about her ducky first-floor apartment in the perfectly darling three-story red-brick. There would be no doorman or other attendants; just the tenants of the second and third floors. As he walked along, Mr. Martin realized that he would get there before nine-thirty. He had considered walking north on Fifth Avenue from Schrafft's to a point from which it would take him until ten o'clock to reach the house. At that hour people were less likely to be coming in or going out. But the procedure would have made an awkward loop in the straight thread of his casualness, and he had abandoned it. It was impossible to figure when people would be entering or leaving the house, anyway. There was a great risk at any hour. If he ran into anybody, he would simply have to place the rubbing-out of Ulgine Barrows in the inactive file forever. The same thing would hold true if there were someone in her apartment. In that case he would just say that he had been passing by, recognized her charming house and thought to drop in.

It was eighteen minutes after nine when Mr. Martin turned into Twelfth Street. A man passed him, and a man and a woman talking. There was no one within fifty paces when he came to the house, halfway down the block. He was up the steps and in the small vestibule in no time, pressing the bell under the card that said "Mrs. Ulgine Barrows." When the clicking in the lock started, he jumped forward against the door. He got inside fast, closing the door behind him. A bulb in a lantern hung from the hall ceiling on a chain seemed to give a monstrously bright light. There was nobody on the stair, which went up ahead of him along the left wall. A door opened down the hall in the wall on the right. He went toward it swiftly, on tiptoe.

"Well, for God's sake, look who's here!" bawled Mrs. Barrows, and her braying laugh rang out like the report of a shotgun. He rushed past her like a football tackle, bumping her. "Hey, quit shoving!" she said, closing the door behind them. They were in her living room, which seemed to Mr. Martin to be lighted by a hundred lamps. "What's after you?" she said. "You're as jumpy as a goat." He found he was unable to speak. His heart was wheezing in his throat. "I—yes," he finally brought out. She was jabbering and laughing as she started to help him off with his coat. "No, no," he said. "I'll put it here." He took it off and put it on a chair near the door. "Your hat and gloves, too," she said. "You're in a lady's house." He put his hat on top of the coat. Mrs. Barrows seemed larger than he had thought. He kept his gloves on. "I was passing by," he said. "I recognized—is there anyone here?" She laughed louder than ever. "No," she said, "we're all alone. You're as white as a sheet, you funny man. Whatever *has* come over you? I'll mix you a toddy." She started toward a door across the room. "Scotch-and-soda be all right? But say, you don't drink, do you?" She turned and gave him her amused look. Mr. Martin pulled himself together. "Scotch-and-soda will be all right," he heard himself say. He could hear her laughing in the kitchen.

Mr. Martin looked quickly around the living room for the weapon. He had counted on finding one there. There were andirons and a poker and something in a corner that looked like an Indian club. None of them would do. It couldn't be that way. He began to pace around. He came to a desk. On it lay a metal paper knife with an ornate handle. Would it be sharp enough? He reached for it and knocked over a small brass jar. Stamps spilled out of it and it fell to the floor with a clatter. "Hey," Mrs. Barrows yelled from the kitchen, "are you tearing up the pea patch?" Mr. Martin gave a strange laugh. Picking up the knife, he tried its point against his left wrist. It was blunt. It wouldn't do.

When Mrs. Barrows reappeared, carrying two highballs, Mr. Martin, standing there with his gloves on, became acutely conscious of the fantasy he had wrought. Cigarettes in his pocket, a drink prepared for him—it was all too grossly improbable. It was more than that; it was impossible. Somewhere in the back of his mind a vague idea stirred, sprouted. "For heaven's sake, take off those gloves," said Mrs. Barrows. "I always wear them in the house," said Mr. Martin. The idea began to bloom, strange and wonderful. She put the glasses on a coffee table in front of a sofa and sat on the sofa. "Come over here, you odd little man," she said. Mr. Martin went over and sat beside her. It was difficult getting a cigarette out of the pack of Camels, but he managed it. She held a match for him, laughing. "Well," she said, handing him his drink, "this is perfectly marvelous. You with a drink and a cigarette."

Mr. Martin puffed, not too awkwardly, and took a gulp of the highball. "I drink and smoke all the time," he said. He clinked his glass against hers. "Here's nuts to that old windbag, Fitweiler," he said, and gulped again. The stuff tasted awful, but he made no grimace. "Really, Mr. Martin," she said, her voice and posture changing, "you are insulting our employer." Mrs. Barrows was now all special adviser to the president. "I am preparing a bomb," said Mr. Martin, "which will blow the old goat higher than hell." He had only had a little of the drink, which was not strong. It couldn't be that. "Do you take dope or something?" Mrs. Barrows asked coldly. "Heroin," said Mr. Martin. "I'll be coked to the gills when I bump that old buzzard off." "Mr. Martin!" she shouted, getting to her feet. "That will be all of that. You must go at once." Mr. Martin took another swallow of his drink. He tapped his cigarette out in the ashtray and put the pack of Camels on the coffee table. Then he got up. She stood glaring at him. He walked over and put on his hat and coat. "Not a word about this," he said, and laid an index finger against his lips. All Mrs. Barrows could bring out was "Really!" Mr. Martin put his hand on the doorknob. "I'm sitting in the catbird seat," he said. He stuck his tongue out at her and left. Nobody saw him go.

Mr. Martin got to his apartment, walking, well before eleven. No one saw him go in. He had two glasses of milk after brushing his teeth, and he felt elated. It wasn't tipsiness, because he hadn't been tipsy. Anyway, the walk had worn off all effects of the whiskey. He got in bed and read a magazine for a while. He was asleep before midnight.

Mr. Martin got to the office at eight-thirty the next morning, as usual. At a quarter to nine, Ulgine Barrows, who had never before arrived at work before ten, swept into his office. "I'm reporting to Mr. Fitweiler now!" she shouted. "If he turns you over to the police, it's no more than you deserve!" Mr. Martin gave her a look of shocked surprise. "I beg your pardon?" he said. Mrs. Barrows snorted and bounced out of the room, leaving Miss Paird and Joey Hart staring after her. "What's the matter with that old devil now?" asked Miss Paird. "I have no idea," said Mr. Martin, resuming his work. The other two looked at him and then at each other. Miss Paird got up and went out. She walked slowly past the closed door of Mr. Fitweiler's office. Mrs. Barrows was yelling inside, but she was not braying. Miss Paird could not hear what the woman was saying. She went back to her desk.

Forty-five minutes later, Mrs. Barrows left the president's office and went into her own, shutting the door. It wasn't until half an hour later that Mr. Fitweiler sent for Mr. Martin. The head of the filing department, neat, quiet, attentive, stood in front of the old man's desk. Mr. Fitweiler was pale and nervous. He took his glasses off and twiddled them. He made a small, bruffing sound in his throat. "Martin," he said, "you have been with us more than twenty years." "Twenty-two, sir," said Mr. Martin. "In that time," pursued the president, "your work and your—uh—manner have been exemplary." "I trust so, sir," said Mr. Martin. "I have understood, Martin," said Mr. Fitweiler, "that you have never taken a drink or smoked." "That is correct, sir," said Mr. Martin. "Ah, yes." Mr. Fitweiler polished his glasses. "You may describe what you did after leaving the office yesterday, Martin," he said. Mr. Martin allowed less than a second for his bewildered pause. "Certainly sir," he said. "I walked home. Then I went to Schrafft's for dinner. Afterward I walked home again. I went to bed early, sir, and read a magazine for a while. I was asleep before eleven." "Ah, yes," said Mr. Fitweiler again. He was silent for a moment, searching for the proper words to say to the head of the filing department. "Mrs. Barrows," he said finally, "Mrs. Barrows has worked hard, Martin, very hard. It grieves me to report that she has suffered a severe breakdown. It has taken the form of a persecution complex accompanied by distressing hallucinations." "I am very sorry, sir," said Mr. Martin. "Mrs. Barrows is under the delusion," continued Mr. Fitweiler, "that you visited her last evening and behaved yourself in an—uh—unseemly manner." He raised his hand to silence Mr. Martin's little pained outcry. "It is the nature of these psychological diseases," Mr. Fitweiler said, "to fix upon the least likely and most innocent party as the—uh—source of persecution. These matters are not for the lay mind to grasp, Martin, I've just had my psychiatrist, Dr. Fitch, on the phone. He would not, of course, commit himself, but he made enough generalizations to substantiate my suspicions. I suggested to Mrs. Barrows when she had completed her—uh—story to me this morning, that she visit Dr. Fitch, for I suspected a condition at once. She flew, I regret to say, into a rage, and demanded—uh—requested that I call you on the carpet. You may not know, Martin, but Mrs. Barrows had planned a reorganization of your department—subject to my approval, of course, subject to my approval. This brought you, rather than anyone else, to her mind—but again that is a phenomenon for Dr. Fitch and not for us. So, Martin, I am afraid Mrs. Barrows' usefulness here is at an end." "I am dreadfully sorry, sir," said Mr. Martin.

It was at this point that the door to the office blew open with the suddenness of a gas-main explosion and Mrs. Barrows catapulted through it. "Is the little rat denying it?" she screamed. "He can't get away with that!" Mr. Martin got up and moved discreetly to a point beside Mr. Fitweiler's chair. "You drank and smoked at my apartment," she bawled at Mr. Martin, "and you know it! You called Mr. Fitweiler an old windbag and said you were going to blow him up when you got coked to the gills on your heroin!" She stopped yelling to catch her breath and a new glint came into her popping eyes. "If you weren't such a drab, ordinary little man," she said, "I'd think you'd planned it all. Sticking your tongue out, saying you were sitting in the catbird seat, because you thought no one would believe me when I told it! My God, it's really too perfect!" She brayed loudly and hysterically, and the fury was on her again. She glared at Mr. Fitweiler. "Can't you see how he has tricked us, you old fool? Can't you see his little game?" But Mr. Fitweiler had been surreptitiously pressing all the buttons under the top of his desk and employees of F & S began pouring into the room. "Stockton," said Mr. Fitweiler, "you and Fishbein will take Mrs. Barrows to her home. Mrs. Powell, you will go with them." Stockton, who had played a little football in high school, blocked Mrs. Barrows as she made for Mr. Martin. It took him and Fishbein together to force her out of the door into the hall, crowded with stenographers and office boys. She was still screaming imprecations at Mr. Martin, tangled and contradictory imprecations. The hubbub finally died out down the corridor.

"I regret that this has happened," said Mr. Fitweiler. "I shall ask you to dismiss it from your mind, Martin." "Yes, sir," said Mr. Martin, anticipating his chief's "That will be all" by moving to the door. "I will dismiss it." He went out and shut the door, and his step was light and quick in the hall. When he entered his department he had slowed down to his customary gait, and he walked quietly across the room to the W20 file, wearing a look of studious concentration.

♦ *DISCUSSION QUESTIONS*

1. What do you think of Mr. Martin? Is he admirable? despicable? pathetic? Give examples from the story to support your opinion.

2. What kind of person is the president, Mr. Fitweiler? What kind of manager is he? What are the authority and communication relationships between Mr. Fitweiler and his employees? What could have led Mr. Fitweiler to hire Mrs. Barrows as his special adviser?

3. Discuss Mr. Martin's approach to dealing with the problem of Mrs. Barrows. Why was it effective? Think of other strategies he could have used and evaluate the likelihood of their success. If you had a similar problem at work, how would you handle it?

4. How might Mrs. Barrows have modified her attempts at changing the organization to increase the likelihood that they would be accepted by the employees? Refer to the currencies of exchange described in reading 9.3, *Influence Without Authority: The Use of Alliances, Reciprocity, and Exchange to Accomplish Work.*

5. Evaluate Mr. Fitweiler's handling of Mrs. Barrows. Refer to reading 9.2, *Face Your Problem Subordinates Now,* to answer the following questions:
   (a) Why did Mr. Fitweiler avoid dealing with the problem of Mrs. Barrows until the end of the story?
   (b) Give Mr. Fitweiler advice on other ways he could have dealt with the problem of Mrs. Barrows.
   (c) Was Mrs. Barrows a problem employee?

6. What is the theme or meaning of the story?

Bartleby the Scrivener
A Story of Wall Street

Herman Melville

In this story a manager's authority is persistently met with passive resistance by a subordinate. To every request, no matter how legitimate, the law clerk Bartleby replies, "I would prefer not to." The lawyer is frustrated as he attempts to communicate with Bartleby and in his failed use of a variety of power tactics. We begin to realize that the lawyer has somehow come under Bartleby's spell and cannot bring himself to fire the recalcitrant employee. The story brings into focus the nature of the rights and obligations people have in relationships with others: as employers and employees, and as human beings.

Herman Melville (1819-1891) is best known as the author of *Moby Dick*. Although now acknowledged as one of America's greatest writers, he was largely unrecognized for his best works in his own time. For several years he sailed the world on a merchant ship and his experiences formed the basis of many of his stories. For twenty years (1866-1886) he was inspector of customs in New York. Melville's knowledge of the legal profession as demonstrated in *Bartleby* may have come from his uncle who was an attorney.

I am a rather elderly man. The nature of my avocations, for the last thirty years, has brought me into more than ordinary contact with what would seem an interesting and somewhat singular set of men, of whom, as yet, nothing, that I know of, has ever been written—I mean, the law-copyists, or scriveners. I have known very many of them, professionally and privately, and, if I pleased, could relate divers histories, at which good-natured gentlemen might smile, and sentimental souls might weep. But I waive the biographies of all other scriveners, for a few passages in the life of Bartleby, who was a scrivener, the strangest I ever saw, or heard of. While, of other law-copyists, I might write the complete life, of Bartleby nothing of that sort can be done. I believe that no materials exist for a full and satisfactory biography of this man. It is an irreparable loss to literature. Bartleby was one of those beings of whom nothing is ascertainable, except from the original sources, and, in his case, those are very small. What my own astonished eyes saw of Bartleby, *that* is all I know of him, except, indeed, one vague report, which will appear in the sequel.

Ere introducing the scrivener, as he first appeared to me, it is fit I make some mention of myself, my employees, my business, my chambers, and general surroundings; because some such description is indispensable to an adequate understanding of the chief character about to be presented. Imprimis: I am a man who, from his youth upwards, has been filled with a profound conviction that the easiest way of life is the best. Hence, though I belong to a profession proverbially energetic and nervous, even to turbulence, at times, yet nothing of that sort have I ever suffered to invade my peace. I am one of those unambitious lawyers who never addresses a jury, or in any way draws down public applause; but, in the cool tranquillity of a snug retreat, do a snug business among rich men's bonds, and mortgages, and title-deeds. All who know me, consider me an eminently *safe* man. The late John Jacob Astor, a personage little given to poetic enthusiasm, had no hesitation in pronouncing my first grand point to be pru- dence; my next, method. I do not speak it in vanity, but simply record the fact, that I was not unemployed in my profession by the late John Jacob Astor; a name which, I admit, I love to repeat; for it hath a rounded and orbicular sound to it, and rings like unto bullion. I will freely add, that I was not insensible to the late John Jacob Astor's good opinion.

Some time prior to the period at which this little history begins, my avo- cations had been largely increased. The good old office, now extinct in the State of New York, of a Master in Chancery, had been conferred upon me. It was not a very arduous office, but very pleasantly remunerative. I seldom lose my temper; much more seldom indulge in dangerous indignation at wrongs and outrages; but, I must be permitted to be rash here, and declare that I consider the sudden and violent abrogation of the office of Master in Chancery, by the new Consti- tution, as a—premature act; inasmuch as I had counted upon a life-lease of the profits, whereas I only received those of a few short years. But this is by the way.

My chambers were up stairs, at No. __Wall Street. At one end, they looked upon the white wall of the interior of a spacious sky-light shaft, penetrating the building from top to bottom.

This view might have been considered rather tame than otherwise, deficient in what landscape painters call "life." But, if so, the view from the other end of my chambers offered, at least, a contrast, if nothing more. In that direction, my windows commanded an unobstructed view of a lofty brick wall, black by age and everlasting shade; which wall required no spyglass to bring out its lurking beauties, but, for the benefit of all near-sighted spectators, was pushed up to within ten feet of my window panes. Owing to the great height of the surround- ing buildings, and my chambers being on the second floor, the interval between this wall and mine not a little resembled a huge square cistern.

At the period just preceding the advent of Bartleby, I had two persons as copyists in my employment, and a promising lad as an office-boy. First, Turkey; second, Nippers; third, Ginger Nut. These may seem names, the like of which are not usually found in the Directory. In truth, they were nicknames, mutually conferred upon each other by my three clerks, and were deemed expressive of their respective persons or characters. Turkey was a short, pursy Englishman, of about my own age—that is, somewhere not far from sixty. In the morning, one might say, his face was of a fine florid hue, but after twelve o'clock, meridian— his dinner hour—it blazed like a grate full of Christmas coals; and continued blazing—but, as it were, with a gradual wane—till six o'clock P.M., or thereabouts; after which, I saw no more of the proprietor of the face, which, gaining its meridian with the sun, seemed to set with it, to rise, culminate, and decline the following day, with the like regularity and undiminished glory. There are many singular coincidences I have known in the course of my life, not the least among which was the fact, that, exactly when Turkey displayed his fullest beams from his red and radiant countenance, just then, too, at that critical moment, began the daily period when I considered his business capacities as seriously disturbed for the remainder of the twenty-four hours. Not that he was absolutely idle, or averse to business, then; far from it. The difficulty was, he was apt to be altogether too energetic. There was a strange, inflamed, flurried, flighty reck-lessness of activity about him. He would be incautious in dipping his pen into his inkstand. All his blots upon my documents were dropped there after twelve o'clock meridian. Indeed, not only would he be reckless, and sadly given to making blots in the afternoon, but, some days, he went further, and was rather noisy. At such times, too, his face flamed with augmented blazonry, as if cannel coal had been heaped on anthracite. He made an unpleasant racket with his chair; spilled his sand-box; in mending his pens, impatiently split them all to pieces, and threw them on the floor in a sudden passion; stood up, and leaned over his table, boxing his papers about in a most indecorous manner, very sad to behold in an elderly man like him. Nevertheless, as he was in many ways a most valuable person to me, and all the time before twelve o'clock meridian, was the quickest, steadiest creature, too, accomplishing a great deal of work in a style not easily to be matched—for these reasons, I was willing to overlook his eccentricities, though, indeed, occasionally, I remonstrated with him. I did this very gently, however, because, though the civilest, nay, the blandest and most reverential of men in the morning, yet, in the afternoon, he was disposed, upon provocation, to be slightly rash with his tongue—in fact, insolent. Now, valuing his morning services as I did, and resolved not to lose them—yet, at the same time, made uncomfortable by his inflamed ways after twelve o'clock—and being a man of peace, unwilling by my admonitions to call forth unseemly retorts from him, I took upon me, one Saturday noon (he was always worse on Satur-days) to hint to him, very kindly, that, perhaps, now that he was growing old, it might be well to abridge his labors; in short, he need not come to my chambers after twelve o'clock, but, dinner over, had best go home to his lodgings, and rest himself till tea-time. But no; he insisted upon his afternoon devotions. His coun-tenance became intolerably fervid, as he oratorically assured me—gesticulating with a long ruler at the other end of the room—that if his services in the morning were useful, how indispensable, then, in the afternoon?

"With submission, sir," said Turkey, on this occasion, "I consider myself your right-hand man. In the morning I but marshal and deploy my columns; but in the afternoon I put myself at their head, and gallantly charge the foe, thus"— and he made a violent thrust with the ruler.

"But the blots, Turkey," intimated I.

"True; but, with submission, sir, behold these hairs! I am getting old. Surely, sir, a blot or two of a warm afternoon is not to be severely urged against gray hairs. Old age—even if it blot the page—is honorable. With submission, sir, we *both* are getting old."

This appeal to my fellow-feeling was hardly to be resisted. At all events, I saw that go he would not. So, I made up my mind to let him stay, resolving, nevertheless, to see to it that, during the afternoon, he had to do with my less important papers.

Nippers, the second on my list, was a whiskered, sallow, and, upon the whole, rather piratical-looking young man, of about five and twenty. I always deemed him the victim of two evil powers—ambition and indigestion. The ambition was evinced by a certain impatience of the duties of a mere copyist, an unwarrantable usurpation of strictly professional affairs, such as the original drawing up of legal documents. The indigestion seemed betokened in an occasional nervous testiness and grinning irritability, causing the teeth to audibly grind together over mistakes committed in copying; unnecessary maledictions, hissed, rather than spoken, in the heat of business; and especially by a continual discontent with the height of the table where he worked. Though of a very ingenious, mechanical turn, Nippers could never get this table to suit him. He put chips under it, blocks of various sorts, bits of pasteboard, and at last went so far as to attempt an exquisite adjustment, by final pieces of folded blotting-paper. But no invention would answer. If, for the sake of easing his back, he brought the table lid at a sharp angle well up towards his chin, and wrote there like a man using the steep roof of a Dutch house for his desk, then he declared that it stopped the circulation in his arms. If now he lowered the table to his waistbands, and stooped over it in writing, then there was a sore aching in his back. In short, the truth of the matter was, Nippers knew not what he wanted. Or, if he wanted anything, it was to be rid of a scrivener's table altogether. Among the manifestations of his diseased ambition was a fondness he had for receiving visits from certain ambiguous-looking fellows in seedy coats, whom he called his clients. Indeed, I was aware that not only was he, at times, considerable of a ward-politician, but he occasionally did a little business at the Justices' courts, and was not unknown on the steps of the Tombs. I have good reason to believe, however, that one individual who called upon him at my chambers, and who, with a grand air, he insisted was his client, was no other than a dun, and the alleged title-deed, a bill. But, with all his failings, and the annoyances he caused me, Nippers, like his compatriot Turkey, was a very useful man to me; wrote a neat, swift hand; and, when he chose, was not deficient in a gentlemanly sort of deportment. Added to this, he always dressed in a gentlemanly sort of way; and so, incidentally, reflected credit upon my chambers. Whereas, with respect to Turkey, I had much ado to keep him from being a reproach to me. His clothes were apt to look oily, and smell of eating-houses. He wore his pantaloons very loose and baggy in summer. His coats were execrable; his hat not to be handled. But while the hat was a thing of indifference to me, inasmuch as his natural civility and deference, as a dependent Englishman, always led him to doff it the moment he entered the room, yet his coat was another matter. Concerning his coats, I reasoned with him; but with no effect. The truth was, I suppose, that a man with so small an income could not afford to sport such a lustrous face and a lustrous coat at one and the same time. As Nippers once observed, Turkey's money went chiefly for red ink. One winter day, I presented Turkey with a highly respectable-looking coat of my own—a padded gray coat, of a most comfortable warmth, and which buttoned straight up from the knee to the neck. I thought Turkey would appreciate the favor, and abate his rashness and obstreperousness of afternoons. But no; I verily believe that buttoning himself up in so downy and blanket-like a coat had a pernicious effect upon him—upon the same principle that too much oats are bad for horses. In fact, precisely as a rash, restive horse is said to feel his oats, so Turkey felt his coat. It made him insolent. He was a man whom prosperity harmed.

Though, concerning the self-indulgent habits of Turkey, I had my own private surmises, yet, touching Nippers, I was well persuaded that, whatever might be his faults in other respects, he was, at least, a temperate young man. But, indeed, nature herself seemed to have been his vintner, and, at his birth, charged him so thoroughly with an irritable, brandy-like disposition, that all subsequent potations were needless. When I consider how, amid the stillness of my chambers, Nippers would sometimes impatiently rise from his seat, and stooping over his table, spread his arms wide apart, seize the whole desk, and move it, and jerk it, with a grim, grinding motion on the floor, as if the table were a perverse voluntary agent and vexing him, I plainly perceive that, for Nippers, brandy-and-water were altogether superfluous.

It was fortunate for me that, owing to its peculiar cause—indigestion—the irritability and consequent nervousness of Nippers were mainly observable in the morning, while in the afternoon he was comparatively mild. So that, Turkey's paroxysms only coming on about twelve o'clock, I never had to do with their eccentricities at one time. Their fits relieved each other, like guards. When Nippers's was on, Turkey's was off; and *vice versa*. This was a good natural arrangement, under the circumstances.

Ginger Nut, the third on my list, was a lad, some twelve years old. His father was a car-man, ambitious of seeing his son on the bench instead of a cart, before he died. So he sent him to my office, as student at law, errand-boy, cleaner and sweeper, at the rate of one dollar a week. He had a little desk to himself; but he did not use it much. Upon inspection, the drawer exhibited a great array of the shells of various sorts of nuts. Indeed, to this quick-witted youth, the whole noble science of the law was contained in a nutshell. Not the least among the employments of Ginger Nut, as well as one which he discharged with the most alacrity, was his duty as cake and apple purveyor for Turkey and Nippers. Copying law-papers being proverbially a dry, husky sort of business, my two scriveners were fain to moisten their mouths very often with Spitzenbergs, to be had at the numerous stalls nigh the Custom House and Post Office. Also, they sent Ginger Nut very frequently for that peculiar cake—small, flat, round, and very spicy—after which he had been named by them. Of a cold morning, when business was but dull, Turkey would gobble up scores of these cakes, as if they were mere wafers—indeed, they sell them at the rate of six or eight for a penny—

the scrape of his pen blending with the crunching of the crisp particles in his mouth. Rashest of all the fiery afternoon blunders and flurried rashnesses of Turkey, was his once moistening a ginger-cake between his lips, and clapping it on to a mortgage, for a seal. I came within an ace of dismissing him then. But he mollified me by making an oriental bow, and saying—

"With submission, sir, it was generous of me to find you in stationery on my own account."

Now my original business—that of a conveyancer and title hunter, and drawer-up of recondite documents of all sorts—was considerably increased by receiving the master's office. There was now great work for scriveners. Not only must I push the clerks already with me, but I must have additional help.

In answer to my advertisement, a motionless young man one morning stood upon my office threshold, the door being open, for it was summer. I can see that figure now—pallidly neat, pitiably respectable, incurably forlorn! It was Bartleby.

After a few words touching his qualifications, I engaged him, glad to have among my corps of copyists a man of so singularly sedate an aspect, which I thought might operate beneficially upon the flighty temper of Turkey, and the fiery one of Nippers.

I should have stated before that ground glass folding-doors divided my premises into two parts, one of which was occupied by my scriveners, the other by myself. According to my humor, I threw open these doors, or closed them. I resolved to assign Bartleby a corner by the folding-doors, but on my side of them, so as to have this quiet man within easy call, in case any trifling thing was to be done. I placed his desk close up to a small side-window in that part of the room, a window which originally had afforded a lateral view of certain grimy backyards and bricks, but which, owing to subsequent erections, commanded at present no view at all, though it gave some light. Within three feet of the panes was a wall, and the light came down from far above, between two lofty build-ings, as from a very small opening in a dome. Still further to a satisfactory arrangement, I procured a high green folding screen, which might entirely isolate Bartleby from my sight, though not remove him from my voice. And thus, in a manner, privacy and society were conjoined.

At first, Bartleby did an extraordinary quantity of writing. As if long fam-ishing for something to copy, he seemed to gorge himself on my documents. There was no pause for digestion. He ran a day and night line, copying by sun-light and by candle-light. I should have been quite delighted with his application, had he been cheerfully industrious. But he wrote on silently, palely, mechanically.

It is, of course, an indispensable part of a scrivener's business to verify the accuracy of his copy, word by word. Where there are two or more scriveners in an office, they assist each other in this examination, one reading from the copy, the other holding the original. It is a very dull, wearisome, and lethargic affair. I can readily imagine that, to some sanguine temperaments, it would be alto-gether intolerable. For example, I cannot credit that the mettlesome poet, Byron, would have contentedly sat down with Bartleby to examine a law document of, say five hundred pages, closely written in a crimpy hand.

Now and then, in the haste of business, it had been my habit to assist in comparing some brief document myself, calling Turkey or Nippers for this purpose. One object I had, in placing Bartleby so handy to me behind the screen, was to avail myself of his services on such trivial occasions. It was on the third day, I think, of his being with me, and before any necessity had arisen for having his own writing examined, that, being much hurried to complete a small affair I had in hand, I abruptly called to Bartleby. In my haste and natural expectancy of instant compliance, I sat with my head bent over the original on my desk, and my right hand sideways, and somewhat nervously extended with the copy, so that, immediately upon emerging from his retreat, Bartleby might snatch it and proceed to business without the least delay.

In this very attitude did I sit when I called to him, rapidly stating what it was I wanted him to do—namely, to examine a small paper with me. Imagine my surprise, nay, my consternation, when, without moving from his privacy, Bartleby, in a singularly mild, firm voice, replied, "I would prefer not to."

I sat awhile in perfect silence, rallying my stunned faculties. Immediately it occurred to me that my ears had deceived me, or Bartleby had entirely misunderstood my meaning. I repeated my request in the clearest tone I could assume; but in quite as clear a one came the previous reply, "I would prefer not to."

"Prefer not to," echoed I, rising in high excitement, and crossing the room with a stride. "What do you mean? Are you moon-struck? I want you to help me compare this sheet here—take it," and I thrust it towards him.

"I would prefer not to," said he.

I looked at him steadfastly. His face was leanly composed; his gray eye dimly calm. Not a wrinkle of agitation rippled him. Had there been the least uneasiness, anger, impatience, or impertinence in his manner; in other words, had there been any thing ordinarily human about him, doubtless I should have violently dismissed him from the premises. But as it was, I should have as soon thought of turning my pale plaster-of-paris bust of Cicero out of doors. I stood gazing at him awhile, as he went on with his own writing, and then reseated myself at my desk. This is very strange, thought I. What had one best do? But my business hurried me. I concluded to forget the matter for the present, reserving it for my future leisure. So calling Nippers from the other room, the paper was speedily examined.

A few days after this, Bartleby concluded four lengthy documents, being quadruplicates of a week's testimony taken before me in my High Court of Chancery. It became necessary to examine them. It was an important suit, and great accuracy was imperative. Having all things arranged, I called Turkey, Nippers, and Ginger Nut from the next room, meaning to place the four copies in the hands of my four clerks, while I should read from the original. Accordingly, Turkey, Nippers, and Ginger Nut had taken their seats in a row, each with his document in his hand, when I called to Bartleby to join this interesting group.

"Bartleby! quick, I am waiting."

I heard a slow scrape of his chair legs on the uncarpeted floor, and soon he appeared standing at the entrance of his hermitage.

"What is wanted?" said he, mildly.

"The copies, the copies," said I, hurriedly. "We are going to examine them. There—" and I held towards him the fourth quadruplicate.

"I would prefer not to," he said, and gently disappeared behind the screen.

For a few moments I was turned into a pillar of salt, standing at the head of my seated column of clerks. Recovering myself, I advanced towards the screen, and demanded the reason for such extraordinary conduct.

"*Why* do you refuse?"

"I would prefer not to."

With any other man I should have flown outright into a dreadful passion, scorned all further words, and thrust him ignominiously from my presence. But there was something about Bartleby that not only strangely disarmed me, but in a wonderful manner, touched and disconcerted me. I began to reason with him.

"These are your own copies we are about to examine. It is labor saving to you, because one examination will answer for your four papers. It is common usage. Every copyist is bound to help examine his copy. Is it not so? Will you not speak? Answer!"

"I prefer not to," he replied in a flutelike tone. It seemed to me that, while I had been addressing him, he carefully revolved every statement that I made; fully comprehended the meaning; could not gainsay the irresistible conclusion; but, at the same time, some paramount consideration prevailed with him to reply as he did.

"You are decided, then, not to comply with my request—a request made according to common usage and common sense?"

He briefly gave me to understand, that on that point my judgment was sound. Yes: his decision was irreversible.

It is not seldom the case that, when a man is browbeaten in some unprecedented and violently unreasonable way, he begins to stagger in his own plainest faith. He begins, as it were, vaguely to surmise that, wonderful as it may be, all the justice and all the reason is on the other side. Accordingly, if any disinterested persons are present, he turns to them for some reinforcement of his own faltering mind.

"Turkey," said I, "what do you think of this? Am I not right?"

"With submission, sir," said Turkey, in his blandest tone, "I think that you are."

"Nippers," said I, "what do *you* think of it?"

"I think I should kick him out of the office."

(The reader, of nice perceptions, will here perceive that, it being morning, Turkey's answer is couched in polite and tranquil terms, but Nippers replies in ill-tempered ones. Or, to repeat a previous sentence, Nippers's ugly mood was on duty, and Turkey's off.)

"Ginger Nut," said I, willing to enlist the smallest suffrage in my behalf, "what do *you* think of it?"

"I think, sir, he's a little *luny*," replied Ginger Nut, with a grin.

"You hear what they say," said I, turning towards the screen, "come forth and do your duty."

But he vouchsafed no reply. I pondered a moment in sore perplexity. But once more business hurried me. I determined again to postpone the consideration of this dilemma to my future leisure. With a little trouble we made out to examine the papers without Bartleby, though at every page or two Turkey deferentially dropped his opinion, that this proceeding was quite out of the common; while Nippers, twitching in his chair with a dyspeptic nervousness, ground out, between his set teeth, occasional hissing maledictions against the stubborn oaf behind the screen. And for his (Nippers's) part, this was the first and the last time he would do another man's business without pay.

Meanwhile Bartleby sat in his hermitage, oblivious to everything but his own peculiar business there.

Some days passed, the scrivener being employed upon another lengthy work. His late remarkable conduct led me to regard his ways narrowly. I observed that he never went to dinner; indeed, that he never went anywhere. As yet I had never, of my personal knowledge, known him to be outside of my office. He was a perpetual sentry in the corner. At about eleven o'clock though, in the morning, I noticed that Ginger Nut would advance toward the opening in Bartleby's screen, as if silently beckoned thither by a gesture invisible to me where I sat. The boy would then leave the office, jingling a few pence, and reappear with a handful of ginger-nuts, which he delivered in the hermitage, receiving two of the cakes for his trouble.

He lives, then, on ginger-nuts, thought I; never eats a dinner, properly speaking; he must be a vegetarian, then; but no; he never eats even vegetables; he eats nothing but ginger-nuts. My mind then ran on in reveries concerning the probable effects upon the human constitution of living entirely on ginger-nuts. Ginger-nuts are so called, because they contain ginger as one of their peculiar constituents, and the final flavoring one. Now, what was ginger? A hot, spicy thing. Was Bartleby hot and spicy? Not at all. Ginger, then, had no effect upon Bartleby. Probably he preferred it should have none.

Nothing so aggravates an earnest person as a passive resistance. If the individual so resisted be of a not inhumane temper, and the resisting one perfectly harmless in his passivity, then, in the better moods of the former, he will endeavor charitably to construe to his imagination what proves impossible to be solved by his judgment. Even so, for the most part, I regarded Bartleby and his ways. Poor fellow! thought I, he means no mischief; it is plain he intends no insolence; his aspect sufficiently evinces that his eccentricities are involuntary. He is useful to me. I can get along with him. If I turn him away, the chances are he will fall in with some less-indulgent employer, and then he will be rudely treated, and perhaps driven forth miserably to starve. Yes. Here I can cheaply purchase a delicious self-approval. To befriend Bartleby; to humor him in his strange willfulness, will cost me little or nothing, while I lay up in my soul what will eventually prove a sweet morsel for my conscience. But this mood was not invariable with me. The passiveness of Bartleby sometimes irritated me. I felt strangely goaded on to encounter him in new opposition—to elicit some angry spark from him answerable to my own. But, indeed, I might as well have essayed to strike fire with my knuckles against a bit of Windsor soap. But one afternoon the evil impulse in me mastered me, and the following little scene ensued:

"Bartleby," said I, "when those papers are all copied, I will compare them with you."

"I would prefer not to."

"How? Surely you do not mean to persist in that mulish vagary?"

No answer.

I threw open the folding-doors near by, and, turning upon Turkey and Nippers, exclaimed:

"Bartleby a second time says, he won't examine his papers. What do you think of it, Turkey?"

It was afternoon, be it remembered. Turkey sat glowing like a brass boiler; his bald head steaming; his hands reeling among his blotted papers.

"Think of it?" roared Turkey; "I think I'll just step behind his screen, and black his eyes for him!"

So saying, Turkey rose to his feet and threw his arms into a pugilistic position. He was hurrying away to make good his promise, when I detained him, alarmed at the effect of incautiously rousing Turkey's combativeness after dinner.

"Sit down, Turkey," said I, "and hear what Nippers has to say. What do you think of it, Nippers? Would I not be justified in immediately dismissing Bartleby?"

"Excuse me, that is for you to decide, sir. I think his conduct quite unusual, and, indeed, unjust, as regards Turkey and myself. But it may only be a passing whim."

"Ah," exclaimed I, "you have strangely changed your mind, then—you speak very gently of him now."

"All beer," cried Turkey; "gentleness is effects of beer—Nippers and I dined together to-day. You see how gentle *I* am, sir. Shall I go and black his eyes?"

"You refer to Bartleby, I suppose. No, not to-day, Turkey," I replied; "pray, put up your fists."

I closed the doors, and again advanced towards Bartleby. I felt additional incentives tempting me to my fate. I burned to be rebelled against again. I remembered that Bartleby never left the office.

"Bartleby," said I, "Ginger Nut is away; just step around to the Post Office, won't you? (it was but a three minutes' walk), and see if there is anything for me."

"I would prefer not to."

"You *will* not?"

"I *prefer* not."

I staggered to my desk, and sat there in a deep study. My blind inveteracy returned. Was there any other thing in which I could procure myself to be ig-nominiously repulsed by this lean, penniless wight?—my hired clerk? What added thing is there, perfectly reasonable, that he will be sure to refuse to do? "Bartleby!"

No answer.

"Bartleby," in a louder tone.

No answer.

"Bartleby," I roared.

Like a very ghost, agreeably to the laws of magical invocation, at the third summons, he appeared at the entrance of his hermitage.

"Go the next room, and tell Nippers to come to me."

"I prefer not to," he respectfully and slowly said and mildly disappeared.

"Very good, Bartleby," said I, in a quiet sort of serenely-severe, self-pos-sessed tone, intimating the unalterable purpose of some terrible retribution very close at hand. At the moment I half intended something of the kind. But upon the whole, as it was drawing towards my dinner-hour, I thought it best to put on my hat and walk home for the day, suffering much from perplexity and distress of mind.

Shall I acknowledge it? The conclusion of this whole business was, that it soon became a fixed fact of my chambers, that a pale young scrivener, by the name of Bartleby, had a desk there; that he copied for me at the usual rate of four cents a folio (one hundred words); but he was permanently exempt from examining the work done by him, that duty being transferred to Turkey and Nippers, out of compliment, doubtless, to their superior acuteness; moreover, said Bartleby was never, on any account, to be dispatched on the most trivial errand of any sort; and that even if entreated to take upon him such a matter, it was generally understood that he would "prefer not to"—in other words, that he would refuse point-blank.

As days passed on, I became considerably reconciled to Bartleby. His stea-diness, his freedom from all dissipation, his incessant industry (except when he chose to throw himself into a standing revery behind his screen), his great still-ness, his unalterableness of demeanor under all circumstances, made him a valu-able acquisition. One prime thing was this—*he was always there*—first in the morning, continually through the day, and the last at night. I had a singular confidence in his honesty. I felt my most precious papers perfectly safe in his hands. Sometimes, to be sure, I could not, for the very soul of me, avoid falling into sudden spasmodic passions with him. For it was exceedingly difficult to bear in mind all the time those strange peculiarities, privileges, and unheard of exemptions, forming the tacit stipulations on Bartleby's part under which he remained in my office. Now and then, in the eagerness of dispatching pressing business, I would inadvertently summon Bartleby, in a short, rapid tone, to put his finger, say, on the incipient tie of a bit of red tape with which I was about compressing some papers. Of course, from behind the screen the usual answer, "I prefer not to," was sure to come; and then, how could a human creature, with the common infirmities of our nature, refrain from bitterly exclaiming upon such perverseness—such unreasonableness. However, every added repulse of this sort which I received only tended to lessen the probability of my repeating the inadvertence.

Here it must be said, that according to the custom of most legal gentlemen occupying chambers in densely-populated law buildings, there were several keys to my door. One was kept by a woman residing in the attic, which person weekly scrubbed and daily swept and dusted my apartments. Another was kept by Turkey for convenience sake. The third I sometimes carried in my own pocket. The fourth I knew not who had.

Now, one Sunday morning I happened to go to Trinity Church, to hear a celebrated preacher, and finding myself rather early on the ground I thought I would walk around to my chambers for a while. Luckily I had my key with me; but upon applying it to the lock, I found it resisted by something inserted from the inside. Quite surprised, I called out; when to my consternation a key was turned from within; and thrusting his lean visage at me, and holding the door ajar, the apparition of Bartleby appeared, in his shirt sleeves, and otherwise in a strangely tattered *déshabillé*, saying quietly that he was sorry, but he was deeply engaged just then, and—preferred not admitting me at present. In a brief word or two, he moreover added, that perhaps I had better walk around the block two or three times, and by that time he would probably have concluded his affairs.

Now, the utterly unsurmised appearance of Bartleby, tenanting my lawchambers of a Sunday morning, with his cadaverously gentlemanly *nonchalance*, yet withal firm and self-possessed, had such a strange effect upon me, that incontinently I slunk away from my own door, and did as desired. But not without sundry twinges of impotent rebellion against the mild effrontery of this unaccountable scrivener. Indeed, it was his wonderful mildness chiefly, which not only disarmed me, but unmanned me as it were. For I consider that one, for the time, is somehow unmanned when he tranquilly permits his hired clerk to dictate to him, and order him away from his own premises. Furthermore, I was full of uneasiness as to what Bartleby could possibly be doing in my office in his shirt sleeves, and in an otherwise dismantled condition of a Sunday morning. Was anything amiss going on? Nay, that was out of the question. It was not to be thought of for a moment that Bartleby was an immoral person. But what could he be doing there?—copying? Nay again, whatever might be his eccentricities, Bartleby was an eminently decorous person. He would be the last man to sit down to his desk in any state approaching to nudity. Besides, it was Sunday; and there was something about Bartleby that forbade the supposition that he would by any secular occupation violate the proprieties of the day.

Nevertheless, my mind was not pacified; and full of a restless curiosity, at last I returned to the door. Without hindrance I inserted my key, opened it, and entered. Bartleby was not to be seen. I looked round anxiously, peeped behind his screen; but it was very plain that he was gone. Upon more closely examining the place, I surmised that for an indefinite period Bartleby must have eaten, dressed, and slept in my office, and that, too, without plate, mirror, or bed. The cushioned seat of a rickety old sofa in one corner bore the faint impress of a lean, reclining form. Rolled away under his desk, I found a blanket; under the empty grate, a blacking box and brush; on a chair, a tin basin, with soap and a ragged towel; in a newspaper a few crumbs of ginger-nuts and a morsel of cheese. Yes, thought I, it is evident enough that Bartleby has been making his home here, keeping bachelor's hall all by himself. Immediately then the thought came sweeping across me, what miserable friendlessness and loneliness are here revealed! His poverty is great; but his solitude, how horrible! Think of it. Of a Sunday, Wall Street is deserted as Petra; and every night of every day it is an emptiness. This building, too, which of week-days hums with industry and life, at nightfall echoes with sheer vacancy, and all through Sunday is forlorn. And here Bartleby makes his home; sole spectator of a solitude which he has seen all populous—a sort of innocent and transformed Marius brooding among the ruins of Carthage!

For the first time in my life a feeling of over-powering stinging melancholy seized me. Before, I had never experienced aught but a not unpleasing sadness. The bond of a common humanity now drew me irresistibly to gloom. A fraternal melancholy! For both I and Bartleby were sons of Adam. I remembered the bright silks and sparkling faces I had seen that day, in gala trim, swan-like sailing down the Mississippi of Broadway; and I contrasted them with the pallid copyist, and thought to myself, Ah, happiness courts the light, so we deem the world is gay; but misery hides aloof, so we deem that misery there is none. These sad fancyings—chimeras, doubtless, of a sick and silly brain—led on to other and more special thoughts, concerning the eccentricities of Bartleby. Presentiments of strange discoveries hovered round me. The scrivener's pale form appeared to me laid out, among uncaring strangers, in its shivering winding sheet.

Suddenly I was attracted by Bartleby's closed desk, the key in open sight left in the lock.

I mean no mischief, seek the gratification of no heartless curiosity, thought I; besides, the desk is mine, and its contents, too, so I will make bold to look within. Everything was methodically arranged, the papers smoothly placed. The pigeon holes were deep, and removing the files of documents, I groped into their recesses. Presently I felt something there, and dragged it out. It was an old bandanna handkerchief, heavy and knotted. I opened it, and saw it was a savings bank.

I now recalled all the quiet mysteries which I had noted in the man. I remembered that he never spoke but to answer; that, though at intervals he had considerable time to himself, yet I had never seen him reading—no, not even a newspaper; that for long periods he would stand looking out, at his pale window behind the screen, upon the dead brick wall; I was quite sure he never visited any refectory or eating house; while his pale face clearly indicated that he never drank beer like Turkey, or tea and coffee even, like other men; that he never went anywhere in particular that I could learn; never went out for a walk, unless, indeed, that was the case at present; that he had declined telling who he was, or whence he came, or whether he had any relatives in the world; that though so thin and pale, he never complained of ill health. And more than all, I remembered a certain unconscious air of pallid—how shall I call it?—of pallid haughtiness, say, or rather an austere reserve about him, which had positively awed me into my tame compliance with his eccentricities, when I had feared to ask him to do the slightest incidental thing for me, even though I might know, from his long-continued motionlessness, that behind his screen he must be standing in one of those dead-wall reveries of his.

Revolving all these things, and coupling them with the recently discovered fact, that he made my office his constant abiding place and home, and not forgetful of his morbid moodiness; revolving all these things, a prudential feeling began to steal over me. My first emotions had been those of pure melancholy and sincerest pity; but just in proportion as the forlornness of Bartleby grew and grew to my imagination, did that same melancholy merge into fear, that pity into repulsion. So true it is, and so terrible, too, that up to a certain point the thought or sight of misery enlists our best affections; but, in certain special cases, beyond that point it does not. They err who would assert that invariably this is owing to the inherent selfishness of the human heart. It rather proceeds from a certain hopelessness of remedying excessive and organic ill. To a sensitive being, pity is not seldom pain. And when at last it is perceived that such pity cannot lead to effectual succor, common sense bids the soul be rid of it. What I saw that morning persuaded me that the scrivener was the victim of innate and incurable disorder. I might give alms to his body; but his body did not pain him; it was his soul that suffered, and his soul I could not reach.

I did not accomplish the purpose of going to Trinity Church that morning. Somehow, the things I had seen disqualified me for the time from churchgoing. I walked homeward, thinking what I would do with Bartleby. Finally, I resolved upon this—I would put certain calm questions to him the next morning, touching his history, etc., and if he declined to answer them openly and unreservedly (and I supposed he would prefer not), then to give him a twenty dollar bill over and above whatever I might owe him, and tell him his services were no longer required; but that if in any way I could assist him, I would be happy to do so, especially if he desired to return to his native place, wherever that might be, I would willingly help to defray the expenses. Moreover, if, after reaching home, he found himself at any time in want of aid, a letter from him would be sure of a reply.

The next morning came.

"Bartleby," said I, gently calling to him behind his screen.

No reply.

"Bartleby," said I, in a still gentler tone, "come here; I am not going to ask you to do anything you would prefer not to do—I simply wish to speak to you."

Upon this he noiselessly slid into view.

"Will you tell me, Bartleby, where you were born?"

"I would prefer not to."

"Will you tell me *anything* about yourself?"

"I would prefer not to."

"But what reasonable objection can you have to speak to me? I feel friendly towards you."

He did not look at me while I spoke, but kept his glance fixed upon my bust of Cicero, which, as I then sat, was directly behind me, some six inches above my head.

"What is your answer, Bartleby," said I, after waiting a considerable time for a reply, during which his countenance remained immovable, only there was the faintest conceivable tremor of the white attenuated mouth.

"At present I prefer to give no answer," he said, and retired into his hermitage.

It was rather weak in me I confess, but his manner, on this occasion, nettled me. Not only did there seem to lurk in it a certain calm disdain, but his perverseness seemed ungrateful, considering the undeniable good usage and indulgence he had received from me.

Again I sat ruminating what I should do. Mortified as I was at his behavior, and resolved as I had been to dismiss him when I entered my office, nevertheless I strangely felt something superstitious knocking at my heart, and forbidding me to carry out my purpose, and denouncing me for a villain if I dared to breathe one bitter word against this forlornest of mankind. At last, familiarly drawing my chair behind his screen, I sat down and said: "Bartleby, never mind, then, about revealing your history; but let me entreat you, as a friend, to comply as far as may be with the usages of this office. Say now, you will help to examine papers to-morrow or next day: in short, say now, that in a day or two you will begin to be a little reasonable:—say so, Bartleby."

"At present I would prefer not to be a little reasonable," was his mildly cadaverous reply.

Just then the folding-doors opened, and Nippers approached. He seemed suffering from an unusually bad night's rest, induced by severer indigestion than common. He overheard those final words of Bartleby.

"*Prefer not*, eh?" gritted Nippers—"I'd *prefer* him, if I were you, sir," addressing me—"I'd give him preferences, the stubborn mule! What is it, sir, pray, that he *prefers* not to do now?"

Bartleby moved not a limb.

"Mr. Nippers," said I, "I'd prefer that you would withdraw for the present."

Somehow, of late, I had got into the way of involuntarily using this word "prefer" upon all sorts of not exactly suitable occasions. And I trembled to think that my contact with the scrivener had already and seriously affected me in a mental way. And what further and deeper aberration might it not yet produce? This apprehension had not been without efficacy in determining me to summary measures.

As Nippers, looking very sour and sulky, was departing, Turkey blandly and deferentially approached.

"With submission, sir," said he, "yesterday I was thinking about Bartleby here, and I think that if he would but prefer to take a quart of good ale every day, it would do much towards mending him, and enabling him to assist in examining his papers."

"So you have got the word, too," said I, slightly excited.

"With submission, what word, sir," asked Turkey, respectfully crowding himself into the contracted space behind the screen, and by so doing, making me jostle the scrivener. "What word, sir?"

"I would prefer to be left alone here," said Bartleby, as if offended at being mobbed in his privacy.

"That's the word, Turkey," said I—*that's* it."

"Oh, *prefer?* oh yes—queer word. I never use it myself, But, sir, as I was saying, if he would but prefer—"

"Turkey," interrupted I, "you will please withdraw."

"Oh, certainly, sir, if you prefer that I should."

As he opened the folding-door to retire, Nippers at his desk caught a glimpse of me, and asked whether I would prefer to have a certain paper copied on blue paper or white. He did not in the least roguishly accent the word prefer. It was plain that it involuntarily rolled from his tongue. I thought to myself, surely I must get rid of a demented man, who already has in some degree turned the tongues, if not the heads of myself and clerks. But I thought it prudent not to break the dismission at once.

The next day I noticed that Bartleby did nothing but stand at his window in his dead-wall revery. Upon asking him why he did not write, he said that he had decided upon doing no more writing.

"Why, how now? what next?" exclaimed I, "do no more writing?"

"No more."

"And what is the reason?"

"Do you not see the reason for yourself," he indifferently replied.

I looked steadfastly at him, and perceived that his eyes looked dull and glazed. Instantly it occurred to me, that his unexampled diligence in copying by his dim window for the first few weeks of his stay with me might have temporarily impaired his vision.

I was touched. I said something in condolence with him. I hinted that of course he did wisely in abstaining from writing for a while; and urged him to embrace that opportunity of taking wholesome exercise in the open air. This, however, he did not do. A few days after this, my other clerks being absent, and being in a great hurry to dispatch certain letters by the mail, I thought that, having nothing else earthly to do, Bartleby would surely be less inflexible than usual, and carry these letters to the post-office. But he blankly declined. So, much to my inconvenience, I went myself.

Still added days went by. Whether Bartleby's eyes improved or not, I could not say. To all appearance I thought they did. But when I asked him if they did, he vouchsafed no answer. At all events, he would do no copying. At last, in reply to my urgings, he informed me that he had permanently given up copying.

"What!" exclaimed I; "suppose your eyes should get entirely well—better than ever before—would you not copy then?"

"I have given up copying," he answered, and slid aside.

He remained as ever, a fixture in my chamber. Nay—if that were possible—he became still more of a fixture than before. What was to be done? He would do nothing in the office; why should he stay there? In plain fact, he had now become a millstone to me, not only useless as a necklace, but afflictive to bear. Yet I was sorry for him. I speak less than truth when I say that, on his own account, he occasioned me uneasiness. If he would but have named a single relative or friend, I would instantly have written, and urged their taking the poor fellow away to some convenient retreat. But he seemed alone, absolutely alone in the universe. A bit of wreck in the mid Atlantic. At length, necessities connected with my business tyrannized over all other considerations. Decently as I could, I told Bartleby that in six days time he must unconditionally leave the office. I warned him to take measures, in the interval, for procuring some other abode. I offered to assist him in his endeavor, if he himself would but take the first step towards a removal. "And when you finally quit me, Bartleby," added I, "I shall see that you go not away entirely unprovided. Six days from this hour, remember."

At the expiration of that period, I peeped behind the screen, and lo! Bartleby was there.

I buttoned up my coat, balanced myself; advanced slowly towards him, touched his shoulder, and said, "The time has come; you must quit this place; I am sorry for you; here is money; but you must go."

"I would prefer not," he replied, with his back still towards me.

"You *must*."

He remained silent.

Now I had an unbounded confidence in this man's common honesty. He had frequently restored to me sixpences and shillings carelessly dropped upon the floor, for I am apt to be very reckless in such shirt-button affairs. The proceeding, then, which followed will not be deemed extraordinary.

"Bartleby," said I, "I owe you twelve dollars on account; here are thirty-two; the odd twenty are yours—Will you take it?" and I handed the bills towards him.

But he made no motion.

"I will leave them here, then," putting them under a weight on the table. Then taking my hat and cane and going to the door, I tranquilly turned and added—"After you have removed your things from these offices, Bartleby, you will of course lock the door—since every one is now gone for the day but you—and if you please, slip your key underneath the mat, so that I may have it in the morning. I shall not see you again; so good-by to you. If, hereafter, in your new place of abode, I can be of any service to you, do not fail to advise me by letter. Good-by, Bartleby, and fare you well."

But he answered not a word; like the last column of some ruined temple, he remained standing mute and solitary in the middle of the otherwise deserted room.

As I walked home in a pensive mood, my vanity got the better of my pity. I could not but highly plume myself on my masterly management in getting rid of Bartleby. Masterly I call it, and such it must appear to any dispassionate thinker. The beauty of my procedure seemed to consist in its perfect quietness. There was no vulgar bullying, no bravado of any sort, no choleric hectoring, and striding to and fro across the apartment, jerking out vehement commands for Bartleby to bundle himself off with his beggarly traps. Nothing of the kind. Without loudly bidding Bartleby depart—as an inferior genius might have done— I *assumed* the ground that depart he must; and upon that assumption built all I had to say. The more I thought over my procedure, the more I was charmed with it. Nevertheless, next morning, upon awakening, I had my doubts—I had somehow slept off the fumes of vanity. One of the coolest and wisest hours a man has, is just after he awakes in the morning. My procedure seemed as sagacious as ever—but only in theory. How it would prove in practice—there was the rub. It was truly a beautiful thought to have assumed Bartleby's departure; but, after all, that assumption was simply my own, and none of Bartleby's. The great point was, not whether I had assumed that he would quit me, but whether he would prefer so to do. He was more a man of preferences than assumptions.

After breakfast, I walked down town, arguing the probabilities *pro* and *con*. One moment I thought it would prove a miserable failure, and Bartleby would be found all alive at my office as usual; the next moment it seemed certain that I should find his chair empty. And so I kept veering about. At the corner of Broadway and Canal Street, I saw quite an excited group of people standing in earnest conversation.

"I'll take odds he doesn't," said a voice as I passed.

"Doesn't go?—done!" said I; "put up your money."

I was instinctively putting my hand in my pocket to produce my own, when I remembered that this was an election day. The words I had overheard bore no reference to Bartleby, but to the success or non-success of some candidate for the mayoralty. In my intent frame of mind, I had, as it were, imagined that all Broadway shared in my excitement, and were debating the same question with me. I passed on, very thankful that the uproar of the street screened my momentary absent-mindedness.

As I had intended, I was earlier than usual at my office door. I stood listening for a moment. All was still. He must be gone. I tried the knob. The door was locked. Yes, my procedure had worked to a charm; he indeed must be vanished. Yet a certain melancholy mixed with this: I was almost sorry for my brilliant success. I was fumbling under the door mat for key, which Bartleby was to have left there for me, when accidentally my knee knocked against a panel, producing a summoning sound, and in response a voice came to me from within— "Not yet; I am occupied."

It was Bartleby.

I was thunderstruck. For an instant I stood like the man who, pipe in mouth, was killed one cloudless afternoon long ago in Virginia, by summer lightning; at his own warm open window he was killed, and remained leaning out there upon the dreamy afternoon, till some one touched him, when he fell.

"Not gone!" I murmured at last. But again obeying that wondrous ascendancy which the inscrutable scrivener had over me, and from which ascendancy, for all my chafing, I could not completely escape, I slowly went down stairs and out into the street, and while walking round the block, considered what I should next do in this unheard-of perplexity. Turn the man out by an actual thrusting I could not; to drive him away by calling him hard names would not do; calling in the police was an unpleasant idea; and yet, permit him to enjoy his cadaverous triumph over me—this, too, I could not think of. What was to be done? or, if nothing could be done, was there anything further that I could *assume* in the matter? Yes, as before I had prospectively assumed that Bartleby would depart, so now I might retrospectively assume that departed he was. In the legitimate carrying out of this assumption, I might enter my office in a great hurry, and pretending not to see Bartleby at all, walk straight against him as if he were air. Such a proceeding would in a singular degree have the appearance of a home-thrust. It was hardly possible that Bartleby could withstand such an application of the doctrine of assumptions. But upon second thoughts the success of the plan seemed rather dubious. I resolved to argue the matter over with him again.

"Bartleby," said I, entering the office, with a quietly severe expression, "I am seriously displeased. I am pained, Bartleby. I had thought better of you. I had imagined you of such a gentlemanly organization, that in any delicate dilemma a slight hint would suffice—in short, an assumption. But it appears I am deceived. Why," I added, unaffectedly starting, "you have not even touched that money yet," pointing to it, just where I had left it the evening previous.

He answered nothing.

"Will you, or will you not, quit me?" I now demanded in a sudden passion, advancing close to him.

"I would prefer *not* to quit you," he replied, gently emphasizing the *not*.

"What earthly right have you to stay here? Do you pay any rent? Do you pay my taxes? Or is this property yours?"

He answered nothing.

"Are you ready to go on and write now? Are your eyes recovered? Could you copy a small paper for me this morning? or help examine a few lines? or step round to the post-office? In a word, will you do anything at all, to give a coloring to your refusal to depart the premises?"

He silently retired into his hermitage.

I was now in such a state of nervous resentment that I thought it but prudent to check myself at present from further demonstrations. Bartleby and I were alone. I remembered the tragedy of the unfortunate Adams and the still more unfortunate Colt in the solitary office of the latter; and how poor Colt, being dreadfully incensed by Adams, and imprudently permitting himself to get wildly excited, was at unawares hurried into his fatal act—an act which certainly no man could possibly deplore more than the actor himself. Often it had occurred to me in my ponderings upon the subject, that had that altercation taken place in the public street, or at a private residence, it would not have terminated as it did. It was the circumstance of being alone in a solitary office, up stairs, of a building entirely unhallowed by humanizing domestic associations—an uncarpeted office, doubtless, of a dusty, haggard sort of appearance—this it must have been, which greatly helped to enhance the irritable desperation of the hapless Colt.

But when this old Adam of resentment rose in me and tempted me concerning Bartleby, I grappled him and threw him. How? Why, simply by recalling the divine injunction: "A new commandment give I unto you, that ye love one another." Yes, this it was that saved me. Aside from higher considerations, charity often operates as a vastly wise and prudent principle—a great safeguard to its possessor. Men have committed murder for jealousy's sake, and anger's sake, and hatred's sake, and selfishness' sake, and spiritual pride's sake; but no man, that ever I heard of, ever committed a diabolical murder for sweet charity's sake. Mere self-interest, then, if no better motive can be enlisted, should, especially with high-tempered men, prompt all beings to charity and philanthropy. At any rate, upon the occasion in question, I strove to drown my exasperated feelings towards the scrivener by benevolently construing his conduct. Poor fellow, poor fellow! thought I, he don't mean anything; and besides, he has seen hard times, and ought to be indulged.

I endeavored, also, immediately to occupy myself, and at the same time to comfort my despondency. I tried to fancy, that in the course of the morning, at such time as might prove agreeable to him, Bartleby, of his own free accord, would emerge from his hermitage and take up some decided line of march in the direction of the door. But no. Half-past twelve o'clock came; Turkey began to glow in the face, overturn his inkstand, and become generally obstreperous; Nippers abated down into quietude and courtesy; Ginger Nut munched his noon apple; and Bartleby remained standing at his window in one of his profoundest dead-wall reveries. Will it be credited? Ought I to acknowledge it? That afternoon I left the office without saying one further word to him.

Some days now passed during which, at leisure intervals I looked a little into "Edwards on the Will," and "Priestley on Necessity." Under the circumstances, those books induced a salutary feeling. Gradually I slid into the persuasion that these troubles of mine, touching the scrivener, had been all predestinated from eternity, and Bartleby was billeted upon me for some mysterious purpose of an all-wise Providence, which it was not for a mere mortal like me to fathom. Yes, Bartleby, stay there behind your screen, thought I; I shall persecute you no more; you are harmless and noiseless as any of these old chairs; in short, I never feel so private as when I know you are here. At last I see it, I feel it; I penetrate to the predestinated purpose of my life. I am content. Others may have loftier parts to enact; but my mission in this world, Bartleby, is to furnish you with office-room for such period as you may see fit to remain.

I believe that this wise and blessed frame of mind would have continued with me, had it not been for the unsolicited and uncharitable remarks obtruded upon me by my professional friends who visited the rooms. But thus it often is, that the constant friction of illiberal minds wears out at last the best resolves of the more generous. Though to be sure, when I reflected upon it, it was not strange that people entering my office should be struck by the peculiar aspect of the unaccountable Bartleby, and so be tempted to throw out some sinister observations concerning him. Sometimes an attorney, having business with me, and calling at my office, and finding no one but the scrivener there, would undertake to obtain some sort of precise information from him touching my whereabouts; but without heeding his idle talk, Bartleby would remain standing immovable in the middle of the room. So after contemplating him in that position for a time, the attorney would depart, no wiser than he came.

Also, when a reference was going on, and the room full of lawyers and witnesses, and business driving fast, some deeply-occupied legal gentleman present, seeing Bartleby wholly unemployed, would request him to run round to his (the legal gentleman's) office and fetch some papers for him. Thereupon, Bartleby would tranquilly decline, and yet remain idle as before. Then the lawyer would give a great stare, and turn to me. And what could I say? At last I was made aware that all through the circle of my professional acquaintance, a whisper of wonder was running round, having reference to the strange creature I kept at my office. This worried me very much. And as the idea came upon me of his possibly turning out a long-lived man, and keep occupying my chambers, and denying my authority; and perplexing my visitors; and scandalizing my professional reputation; and casting a general gloom over the premises; keeping soul and body together to the last upon his savings (for doubtless he spent but half a dime a day), and in the end perhaps outlive me, and claim possession of my office by right of his perpetual occupancy: as all these dark anticipations crowded upon me more and more, and my friends continually intruded their relentless remarks upon the apparition in my room; a great change was wrought in me. I resolved to gather all my faculties together, and forever rid me of this intolerable incubus.

Ere revolving any complicated project, however, adapted to this end, I first simply suggested to Bartleby the propriety of his permanent departure. In a calm and serious tone, I commended the idea to his careful and mature consideration. But, having taken three days to meditate upon it, he apprised me, that his original determination remained the same; in short, that he still preferred to abide with me.

What shall I do? I now said to myself, buttoning up my coat to the last button. What shall I do? what ought I to do? what does conscience say I *should* do with this man, or, rather, ghost. Rid myself of him, I must; go, he shall. But how? You will not thrust him, the poor, pale, passive mortal—you will not thrust such a helpless creature out of your door? you will not dishonor yourself by such cruelty? No, I will not, I cannot do that. Rather would I let him live and die here, and then mason up his remains in the wall. What, then, will you do? For all your coaxing, he will not budge. Bribes he leaves under your own paper-weight on your table; in short, it is quite plain that he prefers to cling to you.

Then something severe, something unusual must be done, What! surely you will not have him collared by a constable, and commit his innocent pallor to the common jail? And upon what ground could you procure such a thing to be done?—a vagrant, is he? What! he a vagrant, a wanderer, who refuses to budge?

It is because he will *not* be a vagrant, then, that you seek to count him as a vagrant. This is too absurd. No visible means of support: there I have him. Wrong again: for indubitably he *does* support himself, and that is the only un-answerable proof that any man can show of his possessing the means so to do. No more, then. Since he will not quit me, I must quit him. I will change my offices; I will move elsewhere, and give him fair notice, that if I find him on my new premises I will then proceed against him as a common trespasser.

Acting accordingly, next day I thus addressed him: "I find these chambers too far from the City Hall; the air is unwholesome. In a word, I propose to remove my offices next week, and shall no longer require your services. I tell you this now, in order that you may seek another place."

He made no reply; and nothing more was said.

On the appointed day I engaged carts and men, proceeded to my chambers, and, having but little furniture, everything was removed in a few hours. Through-out, the scrivener remained standing behind the screen, which I directed to be removed the last thing. It was withdrawn; and, being folded up like a huge folio, left him the motionless occupant of a naked room. I stood in the entry watching him a moment, while something from within me upbraided me.

I re-entered, with my hand in my pocket—and—and my heart in my mouth.

"Good-by, Bartleby; I am going—good-by, and God some way bless you; and take that," slipping something in his hand. But it dropped upon the floor, and then—strange to say—I tore myself from him whom I had so longed to be rid of.

Established in my new quarters, for a day or two I kept the door locked, and started at every footfall in the passages. When I returned to my rooms, after any little absence, I would pause at the threshold for an instant, and attentively listen, ere applying my key. But these fears were needless. Bartleby never came nigh me.

I thought all was going well, when a perturbed-looking stranger visited me, inquiring whether I was the person who had recently occupied rooms at No. __ Wall Street.

Full of forebodings, I replied that I was.

"Then, sir," said the stranger, who proved a lawyer, "you are responsible for the man you left there. He refuses to do any copying; he refuses to do anything; he says he prefers not to; and he refuses to quit the premises."

"I am very sorry, sir," said I, with assumed tranquillity, but an inward tremor, "but, really, the man you allude to is nothing to me—he is no relation or apprentice of mine, that you should hold me responsible for him."

"In mercy's name, who is he?"

"I certainly cannot inform you. I know nothing about him. Formerly I employed him as a copyist; but he has done nothing for me now for some time past."

"I shall settle him, then—good morning, sir."

Several days passed, and I heard nothing more; and, though I often felt a charitable prompting to call at the place and see poor Bartleby, yet a certain squeamishness, of I know not what, withheld me.

All is over with him, by this time, thought I, at last, when, through another week, no further intelligence reached me. But, coming to my room the day after, I found several persons waiting at my door in a high state of nervous excitement.

"That's the man—here he comes," cried the foremost one, whom I recognized as the lawyer who had previously called upon me alone.

"You must take him away, sir, at once," cried a portly person among them, advancing upon me, and whom I knew to be the landlord of No. __Wall Street. "These gentlemen, my tenants, cannot stand it any longer; Mr. B—," pointing to the lawyer, "has turned him out of his room, and he now persists in haunting the building generally, sitting upon the banisters of the stairs by day, and sleeping in the entry by night. Everybody is concerned; clients are leaving the offices; some fears are entertained of a mob; something you must do, and that without delay."

Aghast at this torrent, I fell back before it, and would fain have locked myself in my new quarters. In vain I persisted that Bartleby was nothing to me—no more than to any one else. In vain—I was the last person known to have anything to do with him, and they held me to the terrible account. Fearful, then, of being exposed in the papers (as one person present obscurely threatened), I considered the matter, and, at length, said, that if the lawyer would give me a confidential interview with the scrivener, in his (the lawyer's) own room, I would, that afternoon, strive my best to rid them of the nuisance they complained of.

Going up stairs to my old haunt, there was Bartleby silently sitting upon the banister at the landing.

"What are you doing here, Bartleby?" said I.

"Sitting upon the banister," he mildly replied.

I motioned him into the lawyer's room, who then left us.

"Bartleby," said I, "are you aware that you are the cause of great tribulation to me, by persisting in occupying the entry after being dismissed from the office?"

No answer.

"Now one of two things must take place. Either you must do something, or something must be done to you. Now what sort of business would you like to engage in? Would you like to re-engage in copying for some one?"

"No; I would prefer not to make any change."

"Would you like a clerkship in a dry-goods store?"

"There is too much confinement about that. No, I would not like a clerkship; but I am not particular."

"Too much confinement," I cried, "why you keep yourself confined all the time!"

"I would prefer not to take a clerkship," he rejoined, as if to settle that little item at once.

"How would a bar-tender's business suit you? There is no trying of the eye-sight in that."

"I would not like it at all; though, as I said before, I am not particular."

His unwonted wordiness inspirited me. I returned to the charge.

"Well, then, would you like to travel through the country collecting bills for the merchants? That would improve your health."

"No, I would prefer to be doing something else."

"How, then, would going as a companion to Europe, to entertain some young gentleman with your conversation—how would that suit you?"

"Not at all. It does not strike me that there is anything definite about that. I like to be stationary. But I am not particular."

"Stationary you shall be, then," I cried, now losing all patience, and, for the first time in all my exasperating connection with him, fairly flying into a passion. "If you do not go away from these premises before night, I shall feel bound—indeed, I *am* bound—to—to—to quit the premises myself!" I rather absurdly concluded, knowing not with what possible threat to try to frighten his immobility into compliance. Despairing of all further efforts, I was precipitately leaving him, when a final thought occurred to me—one which had not been wholly unindulged before.

"Bartleby," said I, in the kindest tone I could assume under such exciting circumstances, "will you go home with me now—not to my office, but my dwelling—and remain there till we can conclude upon some convenient arrangement for you at our leisure? Come, let us start now, right away."

"No: at present I would prefer not to make any change at all."

I answered nothing; but, effectually dodging every one by the suddenness and rapidity of my flight, rushed from the building, ran up Wall Street towards Broadway, and, jumping into the first omnibus, was soon removed from pursuit. As soon as tranquillity returned, I distinctly perceived that I had now done all that I possibly could, both in respect to the demands of the landlord and his tenants, and with regard to my own desire and sense of duty, to benefit Bartleby, and shield him from rude persecution. I now strove to be entirely care-free and quiescent; and my conscience justified me in the attempt; though, indeed, it was not so successful as I could have wished. So fearful was I of being again hunted out by the incensed landlord and his exasperated tenants, that, surrendering my business to Nippers, for a few days, I drove about the upper part of the town and through the suburbs, in my rockaway; crossed over to Jersey City and Hoboken, and paid fugitive visits to Manhattanville and Astoria. In fact, I almost lived in my rockaway for the time.

When again I entered my office, lo, a note from the landlord lay upon the desk. I opened it with trembling hands. It informed me that the writer had sent to the police, and had Bartleby removed to the Tombs as a vagrant. Moreover, since I knew more about him than any one else, he wished me to appear at that place, and make a suitable statement of the facts. These tidings had a conflicting effect upon me. At first I was indignant; but, at last, almost approved. The landlord's energetic, summary disposition, had led him to adopt a procedure which I do not think I would have decided upon myself; and yet, as a last resort, under such peculiar circumstances, it seemed the only plan.

As I afterwards learned, the poor scrivener, when told that he must be conducted to the Tombs, offered not the slightest obstacle, but, in his pale, unmoving way, silently acquiesced.

Some of the compassionate and curious bystanders joined the party; and headed by one of the constables arm in arm with Bartleby, the silent procession filed its way through all the noise, and heat, and joy of the roaring thoroughfares at noon.

The same day I received the note, I went to the Tombs, or, to speak more properly, the Halls of Justice. Seeking the right officer, I stated the purpose of my call, and was informed that the individual I described was, indeed, within. I then assured the functionary that Bartleby was a perfectly honest man, and greatly to be compassionated, however unaccountably eccentric. I narrated all I knew, and closed by suggesting the idea of letting him remain in as indulgent confinement as possible, till something less harsh might be done—though, indeed, I hardly knew what. At all events, if nothing else could be decided upon, the almshouse must receive him. I then begged to have an interview.

Being under no disgraceful charge, and quite serene and harmless in all his ways, they had permitted him freely to wander about the prison, and, especially, in the inclosed grass-platted yards thereof. And so I found him there, standing all alone in the quietest of the yards, his face towards a high wall, while all around, from the narrow slits of the jail windows, I thought I saw peering out upon him the eyes of murderers and thieves.

"Bartleby!"

"I know you," he said, without looking round—"and I want nothing to say to you."

"It was not I that brought you here, Bartleby," said I, keenly pained at his implied suspicion. "And to you, this should not be so vile a place. Nothing reproachful attaches to you by being here. And see, it is not so sad a place as one might think. Look, there is the sky, and here is the grass."

"I know where I am," he replied, but would say nothing more, and so I left him.

As I entered the corridor again, a broad meat-like man, in an apron, accosted me, and, jerking his thumb over his shoulder, said—"Is that your friend?"

"Yes."

"Does he want to starve? If he does, let him live on the prison fare, that's all."

"Who are you?" asked I, not knowing what to make of such an unofficially speaking person in such a place.

"I am the grub-man. Such gentlemen as have friends here, hire me to provide them with something good to eat."

"Is that so?" said I, turning to the turnkey.

He said it was.

"Well, then," said I, slipping some silver into the grub-man's hands (for so they called him), "I want you to give particular attention to my friend there; let him have the best dinner you can get. And you must be as polite to him as possible."

"Introduce me, will you?" said the grub-man, looking at me with an expression which seemed to say he was all impatience for an opportunity to give a specimen of his breeding.

Thinking it would prove of benefit to the scrivener, I acquiesced; and, asking the grub-man his name, went up with him to Bartleby.

"Bartleby, this is a friend; you will find him very useful to you."

"Your sarvant, sir, your sarvant," said the grub-man, making a low salutation behind his apron. "Hope you find it pleasant here, sir; nice grounds—cool apartments—hope you'll stay with us sometime—try to make it agreeable. What will you have for dinner to-day?"

"I prefer not to dine to-day," said Bartleby, turning away. "It would disagree with me; I am unused to dinners." So saying, he slowly moved to the other side of the inclosure, and took up a position fronting the dead-wall.

"How's this?" said the grub-man, addressing me with a stare of astonishment. "He's odd, ain't he?"

"I think he is a little deranged," said I, sadly.

"Deranged? deranged is it? Well, now, upon my word, I thought that friend of yourn was a gentleman forger; they are always pale and genteellike, them forgers. I can't help pity 'em—can't help it, sir. Did you know Monroe Edwards?' he added, touchingly, and paused. Then, laying his hand piteously on my shoulder, sighed, "he died of consumption at Sing-Sing. So you weren't acquainted with Monroe?"

"No, I was never socially acquainted with any forgers. But I cannot stop longer. Look to my friend yonder. You will not lose by it. I will see you again."

Some few days after this, I again obtained admission to the Tombs, and went through the corridors in quest of Bartleby; but without finding him.

"I saw him coming from his cell not long ago," said a turnkey, "may be he's gone to loiter in the yards."

So I went in that direction.

"Are you looking for the silent man?" said another turnkey, passing me. "Yonder he lies—sleeping in the yard there. 'Tis not twenty minutes since I saw him lie down."

The yard was entirely quiet. It was not accessible to the common prisoners. The surrounding walls of amazing thickness, kept off all sounds behind them. The Egyptian character of the masonry weighed upon me with its gloom. But a soft imprisoned turf grew under foot. The heart of the eternal pyramids, it seemed, wherein, by some strange magic, through the clefts, grass-seed, dropped by birds, had sprung.

Strangely huddled at the base of the wall, his knees drawn up, and lying on his side, his head touching the cold stones, I saw the wasted Bartleby. But nothing stirred. I paused; then went close up to him; stooped over, and saw that his dim eyes were open; otherwise he seemed profoundly sleeping. Something prompted me to touch him. I felt his hand, when a tingling shiver ran up my arm and down my spine to my feet.

The round face of the grub-man peered upon me now. "His dinner is ready. Won't he dine to-day either? Or does he live without dining?"

"Lives without dining," said I, and closed the eyes.
"Eh!—He's asleep, ain't he?"
"With kings and counselors," murmured I.

There would seem little need for proceeding further in this history. Imagi-nation will readily supply the meagre recital of poor Bartleby's interment. But, ere parting with the reader, let me say, that if this little narrative has sufficiently interested him, to awaken curiosity as to who Bartleby was, and what manner of life he led prior to the present narrator's making his acquaintance, I can only reply, that in such curiosity I fully share, but am wholly unable to gratify it. Yet here I hardly know whether I should divulge one little item of rumor, which came to my ear a few months after the scrivener's decease. Upon what basis it rested, I could never ascertain; and hence, how true it is I cannot now tell. But, inasmuch as this vague report has not been without a certain suggestive interest to me, however said, it may prove the same with some others; and so I will briefly mention it. The report was this: that Bartleby had been a subordinate clerk in the Dead Letter Office at Washington, from which he had been suddenly removed by a change in the administration. When I think over this rumor, hardly can I express the emotions which seize me. Dead letters! does it not sound like dead men? Conceive a man by nature and misfortune prone to a pallid hope-lessness, can any business seem more fitted to heighten it than that of continually handling these dead letters, and assorting them for the flames? For by the cart-load they are annually burned. Some times from out the folded paper the pale clerk takes a ring—the finger it was meant for, perhaps, moulders in the grave; a bank-note sent in swiftest charity—he whom it would relieve, nor eats nor hungers any more; pardon for those who died despairing; hope for those who died unhoping; good tidings for those who died stifled by unrelieved calamities. On errands of life, these letters speed to death.

Ah, Bartleby! Ah, humanity!

♦ *DISCUSSION QUESTIONS*

1. Trace the evolution of incidents in which Bartleby "prefers not" to comply with his boss's requests (there are more than a dozen). Analyze the six most significant encounters with respect to the following: the nature of the request, type of influence strategy employed by the boss, Bartleby's reaction, and the subsequent impact on the boss. Refer to the commonly traded organizational currencies described in reading 9.3, *Influence Without Authority: The Use of Alliances, Reciprocity, and Exchange to Accomplish Work.*

2. Propose alternative ways of dealing with Bartleby and discuss their likely outcomes.

3. Like Mrs. Barrows in *The Catbird Seat*, Bartleby could be considered a problem employee. Use reading 9.2, *Face Your Problem Subordinates Now*, to answer the following questions:

    (a) Why did the lawyer not simply fire Bartleby? How do the reasons for avoiding problem employees described by Veiga explain the lawyer's conduct?

    (b) Would the strategies recommended by Veiga for dealing with problem employees be effective with Bartleby? Justify your answer.

4. Analyze the leadership style of the lawyer-narrator. Use leadership theories such as the managerial grid [1] and vertical dyad linkage model [2] in your analysis. Support your answer with specific examples from the story.

5. What impact do the boss's interactions with Bartleby have on the other employees?

6. What is the broader meaning of this story? How would you interpret the last sentence of the story: "Ah, Bartleby! Ah, humanity!" It has been said that Bartleby symbolizes Christ or a Christian martyr and that the story has a religious meaning. Find clues in the story to support this argument. Why are there so many references to death?

◆   REFERENCES

1. Blake, R.R., and Mouton, J.S. 1974. *The New Managerial Grid*. Houston: Gulf.

2. Dansereau, F., Graen, G., and Haga, W.J. 1975. A vertical dyad linkage approach to leadership within formal organizations: A longitudinal investigation of the role making process. *Organizational Behavior and Human Performance* 23: 46–78.

Sitting

H.E. Francis

Like *Bartleby the Scrivener, Sitting* is a variation on the theme of passive resistance. A couple began sitting on a stranger's step and refuse to budge despite the attempts of many people to remove them. The story is puzzling and evokes feelings of helplessness and frustration. It questions conventional notions of authority and entitlement.

Herbert Edward Francis, Jr. (b. 1924) has spent his career as a professor of English and Spanish at the University of Alabama, Huntsville. He was born in Rhode Island, and has travelled frequently to Argentina, a country he refers to as his spiritual home [1].

In the morning the man and woman were sitting on his front steps. They sat all day. They would not move.

With metronomic regularity he peered at them through the pane in the front door.

They did not leave at dark. He wondered when they ate or slept or did their duties.

At dawn they were still sitting there. They sat through sun and rain.

At first only the immediate neighbors called: Who are they? What are they doing there?

He did not know.

Then neighbors from farther down the street called. People who passed and saw the couple called.

He never heard the man and woman talk.

When he started getting calls from all over the city, from strangers and city fathers, professionals and clerks, garbage and utilities men, and the postman, who had to walk around them to deliver letters, he had to do something.

He asked them to leave.

They said nothing. They sat. They stared, indifferent.

He said he would call the police.

The police gave them a talking to, explained the limits of their rights, and took them away in the police car.

In the morning they were back.

The next time the police said they would put them in jail if the jails were not so full, though they would have to find a place for them somewhere, if he insisted.

Source: "Sitting," by H.E. Francis, published in *The Mississippi Review*, Spring/Summer, 1981. Reprinted by permission of the publisher.

That is your problem, he said.

No, it is really yours, the police told him, but they removed the pair.

When he looked out the next morning, the man and woman were sitting on the steps.

They sat there every day for years.

Winters he expected them to die from the cold.

But he died.

He had no relatives, so the house went to the city.

The man and woman went on sitting there.

When the city threatened to remove the man and woman, neighbors and citizens brought a suit against the city: after sitting so long, the man and woman deserved the house.

The petitioners won. The man and woman took over the house.

In the morning strange men and women were sitting on front steps all over the city.

♦   *DISCUSSION QUESTIONS*

1. Discuss the similarities and differences between *Sitting* and *Bartleby the Scrivener*.

2. What was the couple trying to prove by sitting on the steps?

3. Why did the home owner allow the couple to sit on his steps for years? What would you have done if you were the home owner?

4. Do you agree with the petitioners who claimed that the man and woman deserved the house?

5. How would you handle the situation of people sitting on front steps all over the city?

6. This story is obviously bizarre. However, think of situations in the workplace and life in general that could be compared to this story.

7. What is the meaning of this story? What message does it convey about the powerful and the powerless? What does it suggest about the notion of entitlement?

♦   *REFERENCE*

1. Metzger, L. (ed.) *Contemporary Authors*. New Revision Series. Detroit: Gale Research Co. Vol. 10.

The King of Jazz

Donald Barthelme

This story depicts the cultural differences in the way an American and a Japanese trombone player strive to be the best in their art. The conflict inherent in their competition is tangible in spite of very little being said.

Donald Barthelme (1931-1989) wrote several volumes of short stories, many of which were published in *The New Yorker*. In addition he worked as a journalist, magazine editor, curator of an art gallery, and a university public relations director. He also served in the United States Army in Japan and Korea. He wrote in a minimalist style in which he used fragments of events and satirized contemporary life.

$\mathbf{W}$ell, I'm the king of jazz now, thought Hokie Mokie to himself as he oiled the slide on his trombone. Hasn't been a 'bone man been king of jazz for many years. But now that Spicy MacLammermoor, the old king, is dead, I guess I'm it. Maybe I better play a few notes out of this window here, to reassure myself.

"Wow!" said somebody standing on the sidewalk. "Did you hear that?"

"I did," said his companion.

"Can you distinguish our great homemade American jazz performers, each from the other?"

"Used to could."

"Then who was that playing?"

"Sounds like Hokie Mokie to me. Those few but perfectly selected notes have the real epiphanic glow."

"The what?"

"The real epiphanic glow, such as is obtained only by artists of the caliber of Hokie Mokie, who's from Pass Christian, Mississippi. He's the king of jazz, now that Spicy MacLammermoor is gone."

Hokie Mokie put his trombone in its trombone case and went to a gig. At the gig everyone fell back before him, bowing.

"Hi Bucky! Hi Zoot! Hi Freddie! Hi George! Hi Thad! Hi Roy! Hi Dexter! Hi Jo! Hi Willie! Hi Greens!"

"What we gonna play, Hokie? You the king of jazz now, you gotta decide."

"How 'bout 'Smoke'?"

"Wow!" everybody said. "Did you hear that? Hokie Mokie can just knock a fella out, just the way he pronounces a word. What a intonation on that boy! God Almighty!"

"I don't want to play 'Smoke,' " somebody said.

"Would you repeat that stranger?"

"I don't want to play 'Smoke.' 'Smoke' is dull. I don't like the changes. I refuse to play 'Smoke.' "

"He refuses to play 'Smoke'! But Hokie Mokie is the king of jazz and he says 'Smoke'!"

"Man, you from outa town or something? What do you mean you refuse to play 'Smoke'? How'd you get on this gig anyhow? Who hired you?"

"I am Hideo Yamaguchi, from Tokyo, Japan."

"Oh, you're one of those Japanese cats, eh?"

"Yes, I'm the top trombone man in all of Japan."

"Well you're welcome here until we hear you play. Tell me, is the Tennessee Tea Room still the top jazz place in Tokyo?"

"No, the top jazz place in Tokyo is the Square Box now."

"That's nice. OK, now we gonna play 'Smoke' just like Hokie said. You ready, Hokie? OK, give you four for nothin'. One! Two! Three! Four!"

The two men who had been standing under Hokie's window had followed him into the club. Now they said:

"Good God!"

"Yes, that's Hokie's famous 'English sunrise' way of playing. Playing with lots of rays coming out of it, some red rays, some blue rays, some green rays, some green stemming from a violet center, some olive stemming from a tan center—"

"That young Japanese fellow is pretty good, too."

"Yes, he is pretty good. And he holds his horn in a peculiar way. That's frequently the mark of a superior player."

"Bent over like that with his head between his knees—good God, he's sensational!"

He's sensational, Hokie thought. Maybe I ought to kill him.

But at that moment somebody came in the door pushing in front of him a four-and-one-half-octave marimba. Yes, it was Fat Man Jones, and he began to play even before he was fully in the door.

"What're we playing?"

" 'Billie's Bounce.' "

"That's what I thought it was. What're we in?"

"F."

"That's what I thought we were in. Didn't you use to play with Maynard?"

"Yeah I was in that band for a while until I was in the hospital."

"What for?"

"I was tired."

"What can we add to Hokie's fantastic playing?"

"How 'bout some rain or stars?"

"Maybe that's presumptuous?"

"Ask him if he'd mind."

"You ask him, I'm scared. You don't fool around with the king of jazz. That young Japanese guy's pretty good, too."

"He's sensational."

"You think he's playing in Japanese?"

"Well I don't think it's English."

This trombone's been makin' my neck green for thirty-five years, Hokie thought. How come I got to stand up to yet another challenge, this late in life?

"Well, Hideo—"

"Yes, Mr. Mokie?"

"You did well on both 'Smoke' and 'Billie's Bounce.' You're just about as good as me, I regret to say. In fact, I've decided you're *better* than me. It's a hideous thing to contemplate, but there it is. I have only been the king of jazz for twenty-four hours, but the unforgiving logic of this art demands we bow to Truth, when we hear it."

"Maybe you're mistaken?"

"No, I got ears. I'm not mistaken. Hideo Yamaguchi is the new king of jazz."

"You want to be king emeritus?"

"No, I'm just going to fold up my horn and steal away. This gig is yours, Hideo. You can pick the next tune."

"How 'bout 'Cream'?"

"OK, you heard what Hideo said, it's 'Cream.' You ready, Hideo?"

"Hokie, you don't have to leave. You can play too. Just move a little over to the side there—"

"Thank you, Hideo, that's very gracious of you. I guess I will play a little, since I'm still here. Sotto voce, of course."

"Hideo is wonderful on 'Cream'!"

"Yes, I imagine it's his best tune."

"What's that sound coming in from the side there?"

"Which side?"

"The left."

"You mean that sound that sounds like the cutting edge of life? That sounds like polar bears crossing Arctic ice pans? That sounds like a herd of musk ox in full flight? That sounds like male walruses diving to the bottom of the sea? That sounds like fumaroles smoking on the slopes of Mt. Katmai? That sounds like the wild turkey walking through the deep, soft forest? That sounds like beavers chewing trees in an Appalachian marsh? That sounds like an oyster fungus growing on an aspen trunk? That sounds like a mule deer wandering a montane of the Sierra Nevada? That sounds like prairie dogs kissing? That sounds like witch grass tumbling or a river meandering? That sounds like manatees munching seaweed at Cape Sable? That sounds like coatimundis moving in packs across the face of Arkansas? That sounds like—"

"Good God, it's Hokie! Even with a cup mute on, he's blowing Hideo right off the stand!"

"Hideo's playing on his knees now! Good God, he's reaching into his belt for a large steel sword—Stop him!"

"Wow! That was the most exciting 'Cream' ever played! Is Hideo all right?"

"Yes, somebody is getting him a glass of water."

"You're my man, Hokie! That was the dadblangedest thing I ever saw!"

"You're the king of jazz once again!"

"Hokie Mokie is the most happening thing there is!"

"Yes, Mr. Hokie sir, I have to admit it, you blew me right off the stand. I see I have many years of work and study before me still."

"That's OK, son. Don't think a thing about it. It happens to the best of us. Or it almost happens to the best of us. Now I want everybody to have a good time because we're gonna play 'Flats.' 'Flats' is next."

"With your permission, sir, I will return to my hotel and pack. I am most grateful for everything I have learned here."

"That's OK, Hideo. Have a nice day. He-he. Now, 'Flats.' "

♦ *DISCUSSION QUESTIONS*

1. Trace the evolution of the competition between Hokie and Hideo. Discuss how Hokie and Hideo feel about themselves, how they feel about each other, how they have communicated, and what they have learned from the competition.

2. What does this story tell us about the way Americans and Japanese deal with competition? How do you react in competitive situations?

3. Consider what the story would have been like according to the following scenarios:
   (a) both trombone players had been American.
   (b) both trombone players had been Japanese.
   (c) the competition had taken place in a Japanese jazz club.
   (d) the story had been told from Hideo's point of view.

4. Predict how Hokie and Hideo will treat each other the next time they meet.

5. What point is Barthelme trying to get across to his American readers?

6. What lessons does this story suggest for business relations between the United States and Japan?

Sunday in the Park

Bel Kaufman

This story starts off quite innocently with two families relaxing in the park. Despite attempts at calm reasoning to solve a minor problem, conflict escalates and emotion overcomes reason. The story gives us pause about the difficulties of keeping aggression in check.

Bel Kaufman wrote this story in the 1940s when she was raising her children. She filed it away in a drawer where it remained for decades. In 1983 she decided to submit it to the Available Press/PEN short story competition and won a prize for it.* Ms. Kaufman also wrote the bestselling novel, *Up the Down Staircase,* which was based on her twenty-years' experience as a New York City high school teacher. The book was made into a feature film.

It was still warm in the late-afternoon sun, and the city noises came muffled through the trees in the park. She put her book down on the bench, removed her sunglasses, and sighed contentedly. Morton was reading the *Times Magazine* section, one arm flung around her shoulder; their three-year-old son, Larry, was playing in the sandbox: a faint breeze fanned her hair softly against her cheek. It was five-thirty of a Sunday afternoon, and the small playground, tucked away in a corner of the park, was all but deserted. The swings and seesaws stood motionless and abandoned, the slides were empty, and only in the sandbox two little boys squatted diligently side by side. *How good this is,* she thought, and almost smiled at her sense of well-being. They must go out in the sun more often; Morton was so city-pale, cooped up all week inside the gray factorylike university. She squeezed his arm affectionately and glanced at Larry, delighting in the pointed little face frowning in concentration over the tunnel he was digging. The other boy suddenly stood up and with a quick, deliberate swing of his chubby arm threw a spadeful of sand at Larry. It just missed his head. Larry continued digging; the boy remained standing, shovel raised, stolid and impassive.

"No, no, little boy." She shook her finger at him, her eyes searching for the child's mother or nurse. "We mustn't throw sand. It may get in someone's eyes and hurt. We must play nicely in the nice sandbox." The boy looked at her in unblinking expectancy. He was about Larry's age but perhaps ten pounds heavier, a husky little boy with none of Larry's quickness and sensitivity in his

Source: Published in *The Available Press/PEN Short Story Collection,* New York, Ballantine, 1985, in cooperation with the PEN Syndicated Fiction Project. Reprinted by permission of the author and publisher.
*Personal communication.

face. Where was his mother? The only other people left in the playground were two women and a little girl on roller skates leaving now through the gate, and a man on a bench a few feet away. He was a big man, and he seemed to be taking up the whole bench as he held the Sunday comics close to his face. She supposed he was the child's father. He did not look up from his comics, but spat once deftly out of the corner of his mouth. She turned her eyes away.

At that moment, as swiftly as before, the fat little boy threw another spadeful of sand at Larry. This time some of it landed on his hair and forehead. Larry looked up at his mother, his mouth tentative; her expression would tell him whether to cry or not.

Her first instinct was to rush to her son, brush the sand out of his hair, and punish the other child, but she controlled it. She always said that she wanted Larry to learn to fight his own battles.

"Don't *do* that, little boy," she said sharply, leaning forward on the bench. "You mustn't throw sand!"

The man on the bench moved his mouth as if to spit again, but instead he spoke. He did not look at her, but at the boy only.

"You go right ahead, Joe," he said loudly. "Throw all you want. This here is a *public* sandbox."

She felt a sudden weakness in her knees as she glanced at Morton. He had become aware of what was happening. He put his *Times* down carefully on his lap and turned his fine, lean face toward the man, smiling the shy, apologetic smile he might have offered a student in pointing out an error in his thinking. When he spoke to the man, it was with his usual reasonableness.

"You're quite right," he said pleasantly, "but just because this is a public place. . . ."

The man lowered his funnies and looked at Morton. He looked at him from head to foot, slowly and deliberately. "Yeah?" His insolent voice was edged with menace. "My kid's got just as good right here as yours, and if he feels like throwing sand, he'll throw it, and if you don't like it, you can take your kid the hell out of here."

The children were listening, their eyes and mouths wide open, their spades forgotten in small fists. She noticed the muscle in Morton's jaw tighten. He was rarely angry; he seldom lost his temper. She was suffused with a tenderness for her husband and an impotent rage against the man for involving him in a situation so alien and so distasteful to him.

"Now, just a minute," Morton said courteously, "you must realize. . . ."

"Aw, shut up," said the man.

Her heart began to pound. Morton half rose; the *Times* slid to the ground. Slowly the other man stood up. He took a couple of steps toward Morton, then stopped. He flexed his great arms, waiting. She pressed her trembling knees together. Would there be violence, fighting? How dreadful, how incredible. . . . She must do something, stop them, call for help. She wanted to put her hand on her husband's sleeve, to pull him down, but for some reason she didn't.

Morton adjusted his glasses. He was very pale. "This is ridiculous," he said unevenly. "I must ask you. . . ."

"Oh, yeah?" said the man. He stood with his legs spread apart, rocking a little, looking at Morton with utter scorn. "You and who else?"

For a moment the two men looked at each other nakedly. Then Morton turned his back on the man and said quietly, "Come on, let's get out of here." He walked awkwardly, almost limping with self-consciousness, to the sandbox. He stooped and lifted Larry and his shovel out.

At once Larry came to life; his face lost its rapt expression and he began to kick and cry. "I don't *want* to go home, I want to play better, I don't *want* any supper, I don't *like* supper. . . ." It became a chant as they walked, pulling their child between them, his feet dragging on the ground. In order to get to the exit gate they had to pass the bench where the man sat sprawling again. She was careful not to look at him. With all the dignity she could summon, she pulled Larry's sandy, perspiring little hand, while Morton pulled the other. Slowly and with head high she walked with her husband and child out of the playground.

Her first feeling was one of relief that a fight had been avoided, that no one was hurt. Yet beneath it there was a layer of something else, something heavy and inescapable. She sensed that it was more than just an unpleasant incident, more than defeat of reason by force. She felt dimly it had something to do with her and Morton, something acutely personal, familiar, and important.

Suddenly Morton spoke. "It wouldn't have proved anything."

"What?" she asked.

"A fight. It wouldn't have proved anything beyond the fact that he's bigger than I am."

"Of course," she said.

"The only possible outcome," he continued reasonably, "would have been— what? My glasses broken, perhaps a tooth or two replaced, a couple of days' work missed—and for what? For justice? For truth?"

"Of course," she repeated. She quickened her step. She wanted only to get home and to busy herself with her familiar tasks; perhaps then the feeling, glued like heavy plaster on her heart, would be gone. *Of all the stupid, despicable bullies,* she thought, pulling harder on Larry's hand. The child was still crying. Always before she had felt a tender pity for his defenseless little body, the frail arms, the narrow shoulders with sharp, winglike shoulder blades, the thin and unsure legs, but now her mouth tightened in resentment.

"Stop crying," she said sharply. "I'm ashamed of you!" She felt as if all three of them were tracking mud along the street. The child cried louder.

If there had been an issue involved, she thought, *if there had been something to fight for. . . . But what else could he possibly have done? Allow himself to be beaten? Attempt to educate the man? Call a policeman? "Officer, there's a man in the park who won't stop his child from throwing sand on mine. . . ."* The whole thing was as silly as that, and not worth thinking about.

"Can't you keep him quiet, for Pete's sake?" Morton asked irritably.

"What do you suppose I've been trying to do?" she said.

Larry pulled back, dragging his feet.

"If you can't discipline this child, I will," Morton snapped, making a move toward the boy.

But her voice stopped him. She was shocked to hear it, thin and cold and penetrating with contempt. "Indeed?" she heard herself say. "You and who else?"

♦ *DISCUSSION QUESTIONS*

1. Trace the stages of conflict in this incident: latent, perceived, felt, manifest, and conflict aftermath or outcomes [1].

2. Describe other ways the conflict could have been handled. Classify them according to the conflict handling styles of competing (forcing), avoiding, accommodating, compromising and collaborating [2]. Include an evaluation of the options that the wife mentioned: let the bully beat her husband, attempt to educate the bully, call a policeman. What solution do you propose? Why?

3. What have each of the characters—the mother, her husband, their son, and the other boy and his father—learned about conflict resolution from this incident?

4. Anticipate the problems the woman, Morton, and Larry may have in their relationship. How should they best deal with them?

5. Describe examples from work organizations and other aspects of life that are similar to this incident. Explain the nature of the conflict, the way the conflict was resolved, and the consequences.

6. Does this story imply that basically we are just animals hiding beneath a veneer of civility? How can we keep aggression in check?

♦ *REFERENCES*

1. Pondy, L.R. 1967. Organizational conflict: Concepts and models. *Administrative Science Quarterly* 12: 296-320.

2. Thomas, K.W. 1976. "Conflict and Conflict Management." *In* M.D. Dunnette ed. *Handbook of Industrial and Organizational Psychology*, Chicago: Rand McNally.

The Development and Enforcement
of Group Norms

Daniel Feldman

This article examines the reasons why groups desire and enforce conformity to the informal rules that comprise norms, and the factors that determine how norms develop in some groups and not in others.

Daniel Feldman is a professor of organizational behavior at the University of South Carolina, Columbia.

Group norms are the informal rules that groups adopt to regulate and regularize group members' behavior. Although these norms are infrequently written down or openly discussed, they often have a powerful, and consistent, influence on group members' behavior [1].

This paper focuses on two frequently overlooked aspects of the group norms literature. First, it examines *why* group norms are enforced. Why do groups desire conformity to these information rules? Second, it examines *how* group norms develop. Why do some norms develop in one group but not in another? Much of what is known about group norms comes from post hoc examination of their impact on outcome variables; much less has been written about how these norms actually develop and why they regulate behavior so strongly.

Understanding how group norms develop and why they are enforced is important for two reasons. First, group norms can play a large role in determining whether the group will be productive or not. If the work group feels that management is supportive, group norms will develop that facilitate—in fact, enhance—group productivity. In contrast, if the work group feels that manage-

Source: Excerpted from Daniel C. Feldman, "The Development and Enforcement of Group Norms," *The Academy of Management Review,* 1984, Vol. 9, No. 1, pp. 47-53. Reprinted by permission of the author and publisher.

ment is antagonistic, group norms that inhibit and impair group performance are much more likely to develop. Second, managers can play a major role in setting and changing group norms. They can use their influence to set task-facilitative norms; they can monitor whether the group's norms are functional; they can explicitly address counterproductive norms with subordinates. By understanding how norms develop and why norms are enforced, managers can better diagnose the underlying tensions and problems their groups are facing, and they can help the group develop more effective behavior patterns.

◆   WHY NORMS ARE ENFORCED

(1) Norms are likely to be enforced if they facilitate group survival. A group will enforce norms that protect it from interference or harassment by members of other groups. For instance, a group might develop a norm not to discuss its salaries with members of other groups in the organization, so that attention will not be brought to pay inequities in its favor. Groups might also have norms about not discussing internal problems with members of other units. Such discussions might boomerang at a later date if other groups use the information to develop a better competitive strategy against the group.

Enforcing group norms also makes clear what the "boundaries" of the group are. As a result of observation of deviant behavior and the consequences that ensue, other group members are reminded of the *range* of behavior that is acceptable to the group [2]. The norms about productivity that frequently develop among piecerate workers are illustrative here. By observing a series of incidents (a person produces 50 widgets and is praised; a person produces 60 widgets and receives sharp teasing; a person produces 70 widgets and is ostracized), group members learn the limits of the group's patience: "This far, and no further." The group is less likely to be "successful" (i.e., continue to sustain the low productivity expectations of management) if it allows its jobs to be reevaluated.

(2) Norms are likely to be enforced if they simplify, or make predictable, what behavior is expected of group members. If each member of the group had to decide individually how to behave in each interaction, much time would be lost performing routine activities. Moreover, individuals would have more trouble predicting the behaviors of others and responding correctly. Norms enable group members to anticipate each other's actions and to prepare the most appropriate response in the most timely manner [3].

For instance, when attending group meetings in which proposals are presented and suggestions are requested, do the presenters really want feedback or are they simply going through the motions? Groups may develop norms that reduce this uncertainty and provide a clearer course of action, for example, make suggestions in small, informal meetings but not in large, formal meetings.

Norms also may reinforce specific individual members' roles. A number of different roles might emerge in groups. These roles are simply expectations that are shared by group members regarding who is to carry out what types of activities under which circumstances [4]. Although groups obviously create pressure toward uniformity among members, there also is a tendency for groups to create and maintain *diversity* among members [1]. For instance, a group might have one person whom others expect to break the tension when tempers become too hot. Another group member might be expected by others to take notes, keep minutes, or maintain files.

None of these roles are *formal* duties; but they are activities that the group needs accomplished and has somehow parcelled out among members. If the role expectations are not met, some important jobs might not get done, or other group members might have to take on additional responsibilities. Moreover, such role assignments reduce individual members' ambiguities about what is expected specifically of them. It is important to note, though, that who takes what role in a group also is highly influenced by individuals' personal needs. The person with a high need for structure often wants to be in the note-taking role to control the structuring activity in the group; the person who breaks the tension might dislike conflict and uses the role to circumvent it.

(3) Norms are likely to be enforced if they help the group avoid embarrassing interpersonal problems. Goffman's work on "facework" gives some insight on this point. Goffman argues that each person in a group has a "face" he or she presents to other members of a group [5]. This "face" is analogous to what one will call "self-image," the person's perceptions of himself or herself and how he or she would like to be seen by others. Groups want to insure that no one's self-image is damaged, called into question, or embarrassed. Consequently, the group will establish norms that discourage topics of conversation or situations in which face is too likely to be inadvertently broken. For instance, groups might develop norms about not discussing romantic involvements (so that differences in moral values do not become salient) or about not getting together socially in people's homes (so that differences in taste or income do not become salient).

(4) Norms are likely to be enforced if they express the central values of the group and clarify what is distinctive about the group's identity. Norms can provide the social justification for group activities to its members [6]. When the production group labels rate-busting deviant, it says: "We care more about maximizing group security than about individual profits." Group norms also convey what is distinctive about the group to outsiders. When an advertising agency labels unstylish clothes deviant, it says: "We think of ourselves, personally and professionally, as trend-setters, and being fashionably dressed conveys that to our clients and our public."

One of the key expressive functions of group norms is to define and legitimate the power of the group itself over individual members [6]. When groups punish norm infraction, they reinforce in the minds of group members the authority of the group.

Finally, this expressive function of group norms can be seen nicely in circumstances in which there is an inconsistency between what group members *say* is the group norm and how people actually *behave*. For instance, sometimes groups will engage in a lot of rhetoric about how much independence its managers are allowed and how much it values entrepreneurial effort; yet the harder data suggest that the more conservative, deferring, or dependent managers get rewarded. Such an inconsistency can reflect conflicts among the group's expressed values. The expressed group norm allows the group members a chance to present a "face" to each other and to outsiders that is more socially desirable than reality.

◆   HOW GROUP NORMS DEVELOP

Most norms develop in one or more of the following four ways: explicit statements by supervisors or co-workers; critical events in the group's history; primacy; and carry-over behaviors from past situations.

(1) Explicit statements by supervisors or co-workers. Norms that facilitate group survival or task success often are set by the leader of the group or powerful members [7]. For instance, a group leader might explicitly set norms about not drinking at lunch because subordinates who have been drinking are more likely to have problems dealing competently with clients and top management or they are more likely to have accidents at work. The group leader might also set norms about lateness, personal phone calls, and long coffee breaks if too much productivity is lost as a result of time away from the work place.

Explicit statements by supervisors also can increase the predictability of group members' behavior. For instance, supervisors might have particular preferences for a way of analyzing problems or presenting reports. Strong norms will be set to ensure compliance with these preferences. Consequently, supervisors will have increased certainty about receiving work in the format requested, so they can plan accordingly; workers will have increased certainty about what is expected, so they will not have to outguess their boss or redo their projects.

Managers or important group members also can define the specific role expectations of individual group members. For instance, a supervisor or a co-worker might go up to a new recruit after a meeting to give the proverbial advice: "New recruits should be seen and not heard." The senior group member might be trying to prevent the new recruit from appearing brash or incompetent or from embarrassing other group members. Such interventions set specific role expectations for the new group member.

Norms that cater to supervisor preferences also are frequently established even if they are not objectively necessary to task accomplishment. For example, although organizational norms may be very democratic in terms of everybody calling each other by their first names, some managers have strong preferences about being called Mr., Ms., or Mrs. Although the form of address used in the work group does not influence group effectiveness, complying with the norm bears little cost to the group member, whereas noncompliance could cause daily friction with the supervisor. Such norms help group members avoid embarrassing interpersonal interactions with their managers.

Fourth, norms set explicitly by the supervisor frequently express the central values of the group. For instance, a dean can set very strong norms about faculty keeping office hours and being on campus daily. Such norms reaffirm to members of the academic community their teaching and service obligations, and they send signals to individuals outside the college about what is valued in faculty behavior or distinctive about the school. Such norms, too, legitimate other types of faculty behavior and send signals to both insiders and outsiders about some central values of the college.

(2) *Critical events in the group's history.* At times there is a critical event in the group's history that establishes an important precedent. For instance, a group member might have discussed hiring plans with members of other units in the organization, and as a result new positions were lost or there was increased competition for good applicants. Such indiscretion can substantially hinder the survival and task success of the group; very likely the offender will be either formally censured or informally rebuked. As a result of such an incident, norms about secrecy might develop that will protect the group in similar situations in the future.

Sometimes group norms can be set by a conscious decision of a group after a particularly good or bad experience the group has had. To illustrate, a group might have had a particularly constructive meeting and be very pleased with how much it accomplished. Several people might say, "I think the reason we got so much accomplished today is that we met really early in the morning before the rest of the staff showed up and the phone started ringing. Let's try to continue to meet at 7:30 A.M." Others might agree, and the norm is set. Such norms develop to facilitate task success and to reduce uncertainty about what is expected for each individual in the group.

Critical events also can identify awkward interpersonal situations that need to be avoided in the future. For instance, a divorce between two people working in the same group might have caused a lot of acrimony and hard feeling in a unit, not only between the husband and wife but also among various other group members who got involved in the marital problems. After the unpleasant divorce, a group might develop a norm about not hiring spouses to avoid having to deal with such interpersonal problems in the future.

Finally, critical events also can give rise to norms that express the central, or distinctive, values of the group. When a peer review panel finds a physician or lawyer guilty of malpractice or malfeasance, first it establishes (or reaffirms) the rights of professionals to evaluate and criticize the professional behavior of their colleagues. Moreover, it clarifies what behaviors are inconsistent with the group's self-image or its values.

(3) *Primacy.* The first behavior pattern that emerges in a group often sets group expectations. If the first group meeting is marked by very formal interaction between supervisors and subordinates, then the group often expects future meetings to be conducted in the same way. Where people sit in meetings or rooms frequently is developed through primacy. People generally continue to sit in the same seats they sat in at their first meeting, even though those original seats are not assigned and people could change where they sit at every meeting.

Most friendship groups of students develop their own "turf" in a lecture hall and are surprised/dismayed when an interloper takes "their" seats.

Norms that develop through primacy often do so to simplify, or make predictable, what behavior is expected of group members. There may be very little task impact from where people sit in meetings or how formal interactions are. However, norms develop about such behaviors to make life much more routine and predictable.

(4) Carry-over behaviors from past situations. Many group norms in organizations emerge because individual group members bring set expectations with them from other work groups in other organizations. Accountants expect to behave towards colleagues at Firm I (e.g., dress code, adherence to statutes) as they behaved towards those at Firm II. In fact, much of what goes on in professional schools is giving new members of the profession the same standards and norms of behavior that practitioners in the field hold.

Such carry-over of individual behaviors from past situations can increase the predictability of group members' behaviors in new settings and facilitate task accomplishment. For instance, students and professors bring with them fairly constant sets of expectations from class to class. As a result, they do not have to relearn continually their roles from class to class. In addition, presumably the most task-successful norms will be the ones carried over from organization to organization.

Moreover, such carry-over norms help avoid embarrassing interpersonal situations. Individuals are more likely to know which conversations and actions provoke annoyance, irritation, or embarrassment to their colleagues. Finally, when groups carry over norms from one organization to another, they also clarify what is distinctive about the occupational or professional role.

♦ **SUMMARY**

Norms generally are enforced only for behaviors that are viewed as important by most group members. Groups do not have the time or energy to regulate each and every action of individual members. Only those behaviors that ensure group survival, facilitate task accomplishment, contribute to group morale, or express the group's central values are likely to be brought under normative control. Norms that reflect these group needs will develop through explicit statements of supervisors, critical events in the group's history, primacy, or carry-over behaviors from past situations.

♦ **REFERENCES**

1. Hackman, J.R. 1976. "Group Influences on Individuals." *In* Dunnette, ed. *Handbook of Industrial and Organizational Psychology*. Chicago: Rand McNally. 1455-1525.

2. Dentler, R.A., and Erikson, K.T. 1959. "The Functions of Deviance in Groups." *Social Problems*, 7: 98-107.

3. Hackman, op. cit. Shaw, M. 1981. *Group Dynamics,* 3rd ed. New York: Harper.

4. Bales, R.F., and Slater, P.E. 1955. "Role Differentiation in Small Groups." *In* T. Parson, R.F. Bales, J. Olds, M. Zelditch, and P.E. Slater eds. *Family Socialization, and Interaction Process.* Glencoe, Ill.: Free Press, 35-131.

5. Goffman, E. 1955. "On Face-work: An Analysis of Ritual Elements in Social Interaction." *Psychiatry,* 18:213-231.

6. Katz, D., and Kahn, R.L. 1978. *The Social Psychology of Organizations,* 2nd ed. New York: Wiley.

7. Whyte, W.F. 1955. *Street Corner Society.* Chicago: University of Chicago Press.

Face Your Problem Subordinates Now

John F. Veiga

This reading explains why managers tend to avoid dealing with problem employees. It then presents a typology of problem subordinates, and offers recommendations for dealing with them.

John F. Veiga is a professor and head of the Department of Management and Organization at the University of Connecticut.

Ask any manager the question, "Do you have problem subordinates?" and the reply is generally an emphatic "Yes!" or a more cynical "You *must* be kidding!" If there is one universal truth about managers, it is that all of them have problem subordinates. If there is a second truth, it is that the stories they have to tell about these subordinates often reflect a good deal of disparagement and despair.

In many cases, problem subordinates are as much a result of mismanagement (or failure to manage) as they are of personal shortcomings. Hence, both parties are victims *and* both are to blame. The tragedy is that because no action is taken—a strategy the vast majority of the executives I surveyed admitted having followed—matters get worse. Clearly, managers at all levels need to examine their role in creating problem subordinates and determine preventive measures to be taken. Senior managers who are derelict must take the lead.

◆ *NAME CALLING IS THE EASY PART*

My research on problem subordinates[1] was limited to those long-term cases that senior executives found exasperating to manage—where tough but seldom-made calls are involved. I omitted cases outside the manager's control, such as alcoholism or drug abuse, where outside help or referral to an employee assistance program is called for, and clear-cut cases of total incompetence or dishonesty, where termination is the only answer.

In gathering the survey data, I asked executives taking part in one of several seminars I conducted to write detailed case histories of problem subordinates who worked for them. As these executives soon found out, describing a problem subordinate turned out to be very difficult. Name-calling was the easy part: "He's an SOB," or "She's a game player." Going beyond the superficial and

Source: Excerpted from John F. Veiga, "Face Your Problem Subordinates Now!" *The Academy of Management EXECUTIVE*, 1988, Vol. II, No. 2, pp. 145-152. Reprinted by permission of the author and publisher.

describing how these people actually behaved proved difficult but enlightening. In some cases, the executives were amazed at how little evidence they could muster. In others, the evidence often involved very subtle behavior; some easy to describe, some not. The initial descriptions were usually based on how the problem subordinates made their bosses feel—"She drives me nuts!"—and not in terms of behaviors that caused the feelings. This exercise illustrated that while problem subordinates are discussed and thought about frequently, such musing rarely produces useful information for providing effective feedback. And operating on pejoratives and half-truths only makes matters worse. In many cases, these executives found themselves in a classic perceptual trap. Using limited and selectively perceived information they focused on a single trait, to the exclusion of many positive attributes the problem subordinates might have had.

♦   WHY ARE PROBLEM SUBORDINATES AVOIDED?

Why do managers from the executive ranks down to first-line supervisors avoid confronting the source of their pain? Could it be that managers, especially top executives, just do not have the guts to talk to their people face to face?[2] Perhaps. However, upon closer examination, I found a variety of reasons for avoidance.

First of all, it is too simplistic to attribute "being chicken" as the primary reason for such avoidance behavior. Certainly, some bosses avoid confrontation because they are afraid that they will jeopardize a long-term friendship—the most common reason given—or they are afraid they might create an even worse relationship: "She's so defensive that if I confront her, she could just get worse or even turn on me." Others experience guilt:

> "Just after Jim's wife died we decided not to promote him as planned. I felt he needed some space to get his life in order. As I look back on it now, it was shortly after these events that Jim's attitude turned sour and I never— well, I never knew how to approach him after he blamed me. . . . I know I should have, but I hoped that time would straighten him out."

In almost all cases, bosses feel frustrated or hopeless. Sometimes bosses are insecure: "She knows more about running this place than I do!"—or are reluctant to "play God"—"I don't want to be the one to push him over the edge. This wouldn't be the first time someone has considered suicide or gone on a rampage after a poor performance review."[3] Avoidance also results from a tendency on the part of managers to want overwhelming proof before taking action against a problem employee—a tendency often reinforced by personnel policies designed to avoid litigation and thus severely restrict managerial response.

♦   TYPES OF PROBLEM SUBORDINATES

In my examination of the case histories of problem subordinates, two recurring themes emerged. The first theme related to job performance: that is, whether or not the individual performed above or below the boss's expectation. The second related to interpersonal skills: that is, whether or not the individual worked effectively with others.[4] Combining these two themes resulted in the grid shown in Exhibit 1.

I also attempted to classify the hundreds of reported cases in the hope of identifying some common ground. Therefore, the most pervasive problem subordinates were classified into three types: the talented but abrasive (cited by 40% of the executives), the charming but unreliable (cited by 33%), and the plateaued but indifferent (cited by 20%). The fourth type on the grid, the ideal subordinate, represents the talent mix that managers desire—one who performs up to expectation and works effectively with others.

Talented but abrasive subordinates were generally described as very bright and gifted performers who were insensitive to others and lacked interpersonal skills. Most were perceived as "superstars" or "comers," and yet because they played solely to their strengths and were either unaware of or ignored their weaknesses, they were eventually labeled everything from "arrogant know-it-alls" and "pushy, unfeeling SOBs" to "smart asses." In some instances their behavior was excused: "She is always willing to take more responsibility" or justified: "We needed some asses kicked, and he was the man for the job." Because abrasive subordinates were usually quite good at their jobs, they tended to become impatient with anyone who could not keep up. In some cases, this impatience showed itself in both verbal and nonverbal behaviors such as the caustic remark or the silent stare. These individuals were also perceived as having a talent for making politically insensitive remarks, which was often further exacerbated by their general unwillingness to concern themselves with issues of political sensitivity. Paradoxically, by trying to avoid encounters or tune out

E X H I B I T 1

How Managers Classify Subordinates

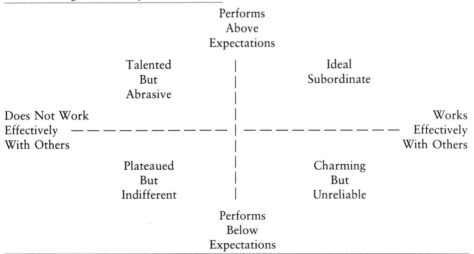

abrasive individuals, bosses and co-workers often unwittingly reinforced such unwanted behavior.

Charming but unreliable subordinates were in many ways the exact opposites of the abrasive individuals. The former were perceived as interpersonally skillful—what one executive called "personality plus"—but their job performance was problematic. Although they were not incompetent, they seemed to have a penchant for not delivering what they promised. Generally, they got the job done, but often it was because others, including their bosses, picked up the pieces or because they were able to talk their way out of doing all that was asked of them. Their bosses often marvelled at their uncanny ability to survive ("He always comes out smelling like a rose" or "She always lands on her feet"). Unfortunately, because the real deficit went unaddressed, their major strength eventually became a liability ("He's nothing but a game player"; "She's a real smoothie—all style and no substance").

Plateaued but indifferent subordinates did not merely combine the flaws of the other two problem types.[5] At some point in their pasts, many of these individuals would have been classified as either talented but abrasive or charming but unreliable—a time when they should have been dealt with. They were typically viewed as interpersonally ineffective because others refused to take them seriously. Traits that at one time would have produced pejoratives were now seen as harmless; e.g., "Her bark is worse than her bite." And while their performance was below expectations, it wasn't because they made promises they couldn't keep; rather, they were perceived as preretirement-aged plodders who either hadn't kept up, or couldn't be counted on because they were past their prime. Because of this "deadwood" status, then, they were generally given unimportant, make-work assignments or expected to do the bare minimum. Their indifference was as much the result of how they were treated as it was a chosen state of mind. Although their co-workers accepted that these individuals were just biding their time until retirement, they were far less forgiving when asked to carry part of what should have been the indifferent subordinate's work load—much to the boss's chagrin.

◆   WHAT'S A BOSS TO DO?

In my consultations with hundreds of managers over the last 10 years, no easy answers have emerged. No one can guide you with complete confidence. One thing is clear, however: There are many alternatives a manager can exercise besides getting rid of a problem subordinate or just doing nothing. Just because certain individuals are talented does not mean you must tolerate abrasiveness or treat such individuals as special; neither is there any reason to avoid straight talk with the unreliable performer, plausible excuses or not.

While the executives I surveyed spoke of many different company-sponsored programs to assist managers in dealing with problem subordinates, they all agreed that ultimate responsibility for initiating action lies squarely on the boss's shoulders. Following are some maxims for dealing with problem subordinates, offered by these executives, which all managers must heed.

Confrontation Must Be Direct

Contrary to the usual prescriptions for helping a person with a problem, most of the executives queried believed that candor promotes credibility and that problematic individuals cannot be handled with kid gloves or in a detached, counseling-like way. This is no time to offer a "positive sandwich"—praise followed by criticism, followed by praise again—because most subordinates are smart enough to perceive its contents as "baloney." The goal is to clarify the unwanted behaviors and the consequences. From the start be prepared to take a tough stand; take the risk of owning up to your position first, then be prepared to be receptive.[6] Blaming and fault finding will not work. Both parties must accept the fact that each is responsible at some level for allowing the situation to continue. Remember that you are dealing with individuals who probably know they disappoint you. Thus, your attempt to unravel this illusion about their performance calls for straight talk. Clear-cut expectations must be established; make clear what is wrong and what you expect to see changed. Offering psychological safety and support to encourage a small but new step is essential. Help these individuals face the central question: Why do they behave as they do? Are they unsure of themselves? Are they having trouble managing their time or establishing priorities? Are there legitimate, personal reasons or priorities that have caused them to behave as they do? Or are they having trouble admitting that they are not well suited to their jobs?

Frozen Evaluations Can Get in the Way

All too often, ability and potential become inextricably tied to past performance. This is especially true when subordinates do not live up to their bosses' expectations. As one executive observed: "In organizations we label people. . . . It's a gradual, insidious kind of process . . . but, over time, labels stick and become well known, unspoken fact." Such labeling gradually reduces the confidence a boss will show in a subordinate and eventually may threaten the subordinate's self-worth. Once this happens, both the charming but unreliable performers and the talented but abrasive individuals are likely to start making extra efforts to prove their value by engaging in activities that place greater emphasis on their strengths—in most cases, whatever they do well they will try to do more of. In turn, the boss will assign them less important projects or compensate by monitoring their work more frequently.

Labeling subordinates based solely on past performance rests on the faulty assumption that people are unable to change over time. Moreover, such unchanged or "frozen evaluations" are unfair and in many cases are merely excuses for the boss to do nothing.[7] Once previously held views are put aside, the potential for new insights can be enormous. As one boss explained:

> "I used to tune this woman out because she grated on me. The more I tuned out, the more she would push her point. Finally, one day I started to listen. As painful as it was, I kept telling myself, 'This woman is bright; just try to see her point of view.' Eventually, I got past my negative reaction and she started to behave less abrasively. What I need to do now is to help her to see

how her desire to be heard and have her ideas appreciated is causing her to
be too pushy and triggering many of the problems she has with others."

Early Warning Signals Are Easily Missed or Ignored

Many problem subordinates start out with great promise. Some are so
likeable that in early career their shortcomings are easily overlooked: "She's so
pleasant to work with I'm sure it's only a matter of time before she comes up
to speed." Others are so talented that a few eccentricities are hardly noticed:
"He's just a little strong willed." Thus, the insidious thing about looking for
warning signs is that they are easily missed or ignored. All too often, bright and/
or charming young subordinates seem to be given a special dispensation by their
seniors. Indeed, many of the problem subordinates described in the survey were
not perceived as problematic until after they turned 40 and took on a major
management responsibility. As one CEO from an electronics firm observed: "What
passes for hard-driving, mover-and-shaker behavior at age 30 is quite often perceived as arrogance and insensitivity at 45." And yet, the prognosis is likely to
be more promising in early career when the individual is the most malleable and
the damage minimal. This is the time when they are most easily turned around
or redirected.

Accept the fact that it is going to be difficult to challenge youthful brash-
ness because such attempts can backfire. If your efforts become too threatening,
you could be faced with a hostile and uncooperative subordinate. You might
also find yourself trying to convince him or her to stay or, worse, you could
stand accused of causing the problem. Don't wait for all the evidence to accu-
mulate before you start a dialogue. When in doubt, trust your instincts. Most
managers have good instincts but often fail to follow them. Early coaching can
make a difference; waiting until the warning signs can no longer be ignored is a
mistake.

There is No Excuse for Continued Neglect

Shelving an individual in midcareer because of shortcomings that should
have been dealt with years before is inexcusable, but continuing to write him or
her off as "deadwood" is also wrong. In many of these cases, an attitude of
"why bother" prevails, leaving both boss and subordinate feeling helpless, believing the situation is outside their control and seeing little hope of escape. Given
the long history of neglect from which such cases have evolved, both parties are
right; little can be done to change what has already happened, and little can be
done at this stage in the individual's career to offer major redirection. But does
that mean that these individuals deserve continued neglect? Hardly.

Often the plateaued but indifferent subordinate has potential and talent;
your job is to identify it. Just as you would be unwilling to drive an automobile
running on fewer than all its cylinders, you should also be unwilling to allow
any human resource to be underutilized. In the beginning, these indifferent individuals must be involved in mainstream activity, no matter how trivial their
part. At a minimum, they should be expected to carry their fair share of the

workload. Find out what interests them and encourage them to follow through. Not all your people have to do the same thing. Try to juggle the workload to match individual interests and talents. (These subordinates may be ideal candidates for retraining or job rotation.) As the following case illustrates, sometimes a small effort, even in late career, can make a difference:

"I manage a group of designers. Many of them love creating new ideas but lack the patience for the detail work after the initial design is accepted. One of my designers, an older woman named Mary, hadn't been assigned any major projects for several years. Mary was considered good in her day but she had not kept pace with the times. Other designers refused to work with her because she was considered a 'nit-picker' and that disturbed their creative flow. As a consequence, I had to assign her to minor projects.

"One day a couple of my best designers approached me with a complaint. . . . They felt it was unfair that they had to do projects that Mary should be doing. They were especially unhappy about doing the additional burdensome detail work. . . . That meeting gave me an idea. I decided to experiment by assigning Mary to do the follow-up detail work on accepted designs. This would free up the other designers to do what they loved to do best. It turned out to be a perfect marriage after some encouraging and nudging on my part. Mary's attention to detail resulted in her finding minor flaws in the accepted designs and saved us production glitches. The other designers began to respect her 'eye for detail' and seek her advice during the preliminary stages of design. This gave Mary a greater sense of ownership in the project."

To be sure, there are also a number of plateaued but indifferent workers who, for whatever reasons—cynicism, despair, or apathy—are less willing to respond to such change attempts. Before you throw in the towel, however, recognize that helplessness conditioned by years of neglect requires a patient response on your part; don't give up too easily.[8] As one executive summed up, "There are no easy answers when you deal with human beings. . . . If there were, we wouldn't need managers."

Own Up to the Part You've Played

Regardless of the type of problem subordinate you face, the place to start is with yourself. How big a part have you played in creating the problem or allowing it to continue? When is the last time you paid attention to a problem subordinate or took the time to find out how he or she feels about the job? In all likelihood, it has been a long time. Sadly, such attempts are frequently affected by a simplistic cost/benefit decision: Managers will invest energy in a subordinate when the payoff is substantial, but are unwilling to do so when it is not. However, writing off another human being as a bad investment is not only a dereliction of a manager's responsibility to develop human resources—it is dehumanizing as well. Although you cannot undo past practices or necessarily fix what is broken, there are many instances where effective interventions have made a difference.

You can also begin by recognizing that the metaphors used to describe problem subordinates often create more hostility and frustration in you than is warranted, and that such metaphors, whether derogatory or despairing, tend to guide and shape how you respond. Recognize, too, that such actions detract from your primary mission of developing productive human beings.

When Don Quixote thrust his lance at "monsters" created out of windmills, it was funny; when managers allow themselves to be hassled by "monstrous" kinds of behavior, some real and some imagined, it is not. Perhaps it is time to recast these metaphors to produce more positive images: A subordinate with a problem, rather than a problem subordinate, could become a potential challenge and not a threat, a mismatch and not a misfit. And perhaps it is time to stop passing the buck, arguing that "It's not my fault, I inherited him (or her)." Managers don't "inherit" people, but they do inherit responsibility for their performance and development, a rule to which most managers subscribe but for which few are willing to foot the bill.

◆   ENDNOTES

1. These findings are based on a formal survey of 150 executives from over 100 firms and on informal surveys of over 2,000 managers who attended my seminars over the past 10 years as well as extensive in-depth, follow-up interviews with 15 executives. The participants in the formal survey averaged 49 years of age and held positions from vice-president to CEO (86% males, 14% females). The typical problem manager averaged 44 years of age; 64% were male, 36% were female. Both sexes were equally scathed by their bosses, except in the choice of adjectives used. Thus, gender per se played no unique role in the name calling.

2. This case was made the strongest in Walter Kiechel III's "No Words From On High," *Fortune*, January 6, 1986. 125–126.

3. The front-page story of the *New York Times* on August 21, 1986, "Oklahoma Letter Carrier Kills 14 and Then Himself," is a chilling reminder to all managers as to what could happen when poor performance is confronted. However, it should be noted that according to the newspaper account, this was a rare case involving an employee with a history of instability *and* a management that allegedly had engaged in verbal abuse of employees and other forms of harassment.

4. These themes are similar to the "technical" and "human skills" discussed in Robert L. Katz's "Skills of an Effective Administrator," *Harvard Business Review*, September-October 1974, 90–102.

5. There is a growing body of research on the nature of the plateaued performer. See especially Thomas P. Ference, James A. F. Stoner, and E. Kirby Warren's "Managing the Career Plateau." *Academy of Management Review*, 1977, 2(4), 602–612, and John F. Veiga's "Plateaued Versus Nonplateaued Managers: Career Patterns, Attitudes, and Path Potential." *Academy of Management Journal*, 1981, 24(3), 566–578.

6. For information on how to coach managers effectively, see Ferdinand F. Fournies' *Coaching for Improved Work Performance*, New York: Van Nostrand Reinhold Company, Inc., 1978; Michael Beer's "Performance Appraisal," in Jay W. Lorsch (Ed.) *Handbook of Organizational Behavior*, Englewood Cliffs, NJ: Prentice-Hall, Inc., 1987; and Charles D. Orth, Harry E. Wilkinson, and Robert C. Benfari's "The Manager's Role as Coach and Mentor." *Organizational Dynamics*, Spring 1987, 66–74.

7. For more information on avoiding "frozen evaluations," see Chapter 13 of William V. Haney's *Communication and Interpersonal Relations: Text and Cases*, 5th Edition, Homewood, IL: Richard D. Irwin, Inc., 1986, pp. 408–432.

8. The consequences of failure to give individuals effective career feedback are clearly highlighted in John F. Veiga's "Do Managers on the Move Get Anywhere?" *Harvard Business Review*, March-April 1981, 20–38, and Jay W. Lorsch and Haruo Takagi's "Keeping Managers Off the Shelf," *Harvard Business Review*, July-August 1986, 60–65.

Influence Without Authority: The Use of Alliances, Reciprocity, and Exchange to Accomplish Work

Allan R. Cohen ♦ *David L. Bradford*

This reading is grounded in the law of reciprocity and the expectation of reciprocal exchanges at work. It uses the metaphor of currencies to conceptualize the types of things that people can trade with each other to accomplish their objectives without the use of formal authority.

Allan R. Cohen is The Walter H. Carpenter Professor of Management at Babson College in Wellesley, Massachusetts. David L. Bradford is a lecturer in organizational behavior at the Graduate School of Business, Stanford University.

Organizational members who want to make things happen, irrespective of whether they are staff or line employees, professionals or managers, find it increasingly necessary to influence colleagues and superiors. These critical others control needed resources, possess required information, set priorities on important activities, and have to agree and cooperate if plans are to be implemented. They cannot be ordered around because they are under another area's control and can legitimately say no because they have many other valid priorities. They respond only when they choose to. Despite the clear need and appropriateness of what is being asked for (certainly as seen by the person who is making the request), compliance may not be forthcoming.

All of this places a large burden on organizational members, who are expected not only to take initiatives but also to respond intelligently to requests made of them by others. Judgment is needed to sort out the value of the many requests made of anyone who has valuable resources to contribute.

A key current problem, then, is finding ways to develop mutual influence without the formal authority to command. A peer cannot "order" a colleague to change priorities, modify an approach, or implement a grand new idea. A staff member cannot "command" his or her supervisor to back a proposal, fight top management for greater resources, or allow more autonomy.

♦ EXCHANGE AND THE LAW OF RECIPROCITY

The way influence is acquired without formal authority is through the "law of reciprocity"—the almost universal belief that people should be paid back for what they do, that one good (or bad) deed deserves another. This belief is held by people in primitive and not-so-primitive societies all around the world, and it serves as the grease that allows the organizational wheels to turn smoothly. Because people expect that their actions will be paid back in one form or another, influence is possible.

It is important to recognize that reciprocity is the basic principle behind all organizational transactions. For example, the basic employment contract is an exchange ("an honest day's work for an honest day's pay").

The expectation of reciprocal exchanges occurs between an employee and his or her supervisor, among peers, with higher-level managers in other parts of the organization, or all of the above. The exchange can be of tangible goods, such as a budget increase, new equipment, or more personnel; of tangible services, such as a faster response time, more information, or public support; or of sentiments, such as gratitude, admiration, or praise. Whatever form exchanges take, unless they are roughly equivalent over time, hard feelings will result.

Exchanges enable people to handle the give-and-take of working together without strong feelings of injustice arising. They are especially important during periods of rapid change because the number of requests that go far beyond the routine tends to escalate. In those situations, exchanges become less predictable, more free-floating, and spontaneous. Nevertheless, people still expect that somehow or other, sooner or later, they will be (roughly) equally compensated for the acts they do above and beyond those that are covered by the formal exchange agreements in their job. Consequently, some kind of "currency" equivalent needs to be worked out, implicitly if not explicitly, to keep the parties in the exchange feeling fairly treated.

◆   CURRENCIES: THE SOURCE OF INFLUENCE

A useful way to think of how the process of exchange actually works in organizations is to use the metaphor of "currencies." This metaphor provides a powerful way to conceptualize what is important to the influencer and the person to be influenced. Just as many types of currencies are traded in the world financial market, many types are "traded" in organizational life.

Some major currencies that are commonly valued and traded in organizations are listed in Exhibit 1. Although not exhaustive, the list makes evident that a person does not have to be at the top of an organization or have hands on the formal levers of power to command multiple resources that others may value.

Part of the usefulness of currencies comes from their flexibility. For example, there are many ways to express gratitude and to give assistance. A manager who most values the currency of appreciation could be paid through verbal thanks, praise, a public statement at a meeting, informal comments to his peers, and/or a note to her boss. However, the same note of thanks seen by one person as a sign of appreciation may be seen by another person as an attempt to brown-nose or by a third person as a cheap way to try to repay extensive favors and

E X H I B I T 1

Commonly Traded Organizational Currencies

Inspiration-Related Currencies

Vision	Being involved in a task that has larger significance for the unit, organization, customers, or society.
Excellence	Having a chance to do important things really well.
Moral/Ethical Correctness	Doing what is "right" by a higher standard than efficiency.

Task-Related Currencies

Resources	Lending or giving money, budget increases, personnel, space, and so forth.
Assistance	Helping with existing projects or undertaking unwanted tasks.
Cooperation	Giving task support, providing quicker response time, approving a project, or aiding implementation.
Information	Providing organizational as well as technical knowledge.

Position-Related Currencies

Advancement	Giving a task or assignment that can aid in promotion.
Recognition	Acknowledging effort, accomplishment, or abilities.
Visibility	Providing chance to be known by higher-ups or significant others in the organization.
Reputation	Enhancing the way a person is seen.
Importance/Insiderness	Offering a sense of importance, of "belonging."
Network/Contacts	Providing opportunities for linking with others.

Relationship-Related Currencies

Acceptance/Inclusion	Providing closeness and friendship.
Personal Support	Giving personal and emotional backing.
Understanding	Listening to others' concerns and issues.

Personal-Related Currencies

Self-Concept	Affirming one's values, self-esteem, and identity.
Challenge/Learning	Sharing tasks that increase skills and abilities.
Ownership/Involvement	Letting others have ownership and influence.
Gratitude	Expressing appreciation or indebtedness.

service. Thus currencies have value not in some abstract sense but as defined by the receiver.

Although we have stressed the interactive nature of exchange, "payments" do not always have to be made by the other person. They can be self-generated to fit beliefs about being virtuous, benevolent, or committed to the organization's welfare. Someone may respond to another person's request because it reinforces cherished values, a sense of identity, or feelings of self-worth.

Of course, the five categories of currencies listed in Exhibit 1 are not mutually exclusive. When the demand from the other person is high, people are likely to pay in several currencies across several categories.

◆ THE PROCESS OF EXCHANGE

To make the exchange process effective, the influencer needs to (1) think about the person to be influenced as a potential ally, not an adversary; (2) know the world of the potential ally, including the pressures as well as the person's needs and goals; (3) be aware of key goals and available resources that may be valued by the potential ally; and (4) understand the exchange transaction itself so that win-win outcomes are achieved. Each of these factors is discussed below.

Potential Ally, Not Adversary

A key to influence is thinking of the other person as a potential ally. Just as many contemporary organizations have discovered the importance of creating strategic alliances with suppliers and customers, employees who want influence within the organization need to create internal allies. Even though each party in an alliance continues to have freedom to pursue its own interests, the goal is to find areas of mutual benefit and develop trusting, sustainable relationships. Similarly, each person whose cooperation is needed inside the organization is a potential ally. Each still has self-interests to pursue, but those self-interests do not preclude searching for and building areas of mutual benefit.

Seeing other organizational members as potential allies decreases the chance that adversarial relationships will develop—an all-too-frequent result when the eager influencer does not quickly get the assistance or cooperation needed. Assuming that even a difficult person is a potential ally makes it easier to understand that person's world and thereby discover what that person values and needs.

The Potential Ally's World

We have stressed the importance of knowing the world of the potential ally. Without awareness of what the ally needs (what currencies are valued), attempts to influence that person can only be haphazard. Although this conclusion may seem self-evident, it is remarkable how often people attempt to influence without adequate information about what is important to the potential ally. Instead, they are driven by their own definition of "what should be" and "what is right" when they should be seeing the world from the other person's perspective.

Several factors can keep the influencer from seeing the potential ally clearly. The frustration of meeting resistance from a potential ally can get in the way of really understanding the other person's world. The desire to influence is so strong that only the need for cooperation is visible to the influencer. As a result of not being understood, the potential ally digs in, making the influencer repeat an inappropriate strategy or back off in frustration.

When a potential ally's behavior is not understandable, the influencer tends to stereotype that person. If early attempts to influence do not work, the influencer is tempted to write the person off as negative, stubborn, selfish, or "just another bean counter/whiz kid/sales-type" or whatever pejorative label is used in that organizational culture to dismiss those organizational members who are different.

Although some stereotypes may have a grain of truth, they generally conceal more than they reveal. The actuary who understands that judgment, not just numbers, is needed to make decisions disappears as an individual when the stereotype of "impersonal, detached number machine" is the filter through which he or she is seen. Once the stereotype is applied, the frustrated influencer is no longer likely to see what currencies that particular potential ally actually values.

Sometimes, the lack of clear understanding about a potential ally stems from the influencer's failure to appreciate the organizational forces acting on the potential ally. To a great extent, a person's behavior is a result of the situation in which that person works (and not just his or her personality). Potential allies are embedded in an organizational culture that shapes their interests and responses. For example, one of the key determinants of anyone's behavior is likely to be the way the person's performance is measured and rewarded. In many instances, what is mistaken for personal orneriness is merely the result of the person's doing something that will be seen as good performance in his or her function.

The salesperson who is furious because the plant manager resists changing priorities for a rush order may not realize that part of the plant manager's bonus depends on holding unit costs down—a task made easier with long production runs. The plant manager's resistance does not necessarily reflect his or her inability to be flexible or lack of concern about pleasing customers or about the company's overall success.

Other organizational forces that can affect the potential ally's behavior include the daily time demands on that person's position; the amount of contact the person has with customers, suppliers, and other outsiders; the organization's information flow (or lack of it); the style of the potential ally's boss; the belief and assumptions held by that person's co-workers; and so forth. Although some of these factors cannot be changed by the influencer, understanding them can be useful in figuring out how to frame and time requests. It also helps the influencer resist the temptation to stereotype the noncooperator.

Self-Awareness of the Influencer

Unfortunately, people desiring influence are not always aware of precisely what they want. Often their requests contain a cluster of needs (a certain product, arranged in a certain way, delivered at a specified time). They fail to think through which aspects are more important and which can be jettisoned if necessary.

Further, there is a tendency to confuse and intermingle the desired end goal with the means of accomplishing it, leading to too many battles over the wrong things.

Sometimes influencers underestimate the range of currencies available for use. They may assume, for example, that just because they are low in the organization they have nothing that others want. Employees who want to influence their boss are especially likely not to realize all of the supervisor's needs that they can fulfill. They become so caught up with their feelings of powerlessness that they fail to see the many ways they can generate valuable currencies.

In other instances, influencers fail to be aware of their preferred style of interaction and its fit with the potential ally's preferred style. Everyone has a way of relating to others to get work done. However, like the fish who is unaware of the water, many people are oblivious of their own style of interaction or see it as the only way to be. Yet interaction style can cause problems with potential allies who are different.

For example, does the influencer tend to socialize first and work later? If so, that style of interaction will distress a potential ally who likes to dig right in to solve the problem at hand and only afterward chat about sports, family, or office politics.

Nature of the Exchange Transaction

Many of the problems that occur in the actual exchange negotiation have their roots in the failure to deal adequately with the first three factors outlined above. Failure to treat other people as potential allies, to understand a potential ally's world, and to be self-aware are all factors that interfere with successful exchange. In addition, some special problems commonly arise when both parties are in the process of working out a mutually satisfactory exchange agreement.

• *Not knowing how to use reciprocity.* Using reciprocity requires stating needs clearly without "crying wolf," being aware of the needs of an ally without being manipulative, and seeking mutual gain rather than playing "winner takes all."

• *Preferring to be right rather than effective.* This problem is especially endemic to professionals of all kinds. Because of their dedication to the "truth" (as their profession defines it), they stubbornly stick to their one right way when trying to line up potential allies instead of thinking about what will work given the audience and conditions. Organizational members with strong technical backgrounds often chorus the equivalent of "I'll be damned if I'm going to sell out and become a phony salesman, trying to get by on a shoeshine and smile." The failure to accommodate to the potential ally's needs and desires often kills otherwise sound ideas.

• *Overusing what has been successful.* When people find that a certain approach is effective in many situations, they often begin to use it in places where it does not fit. By overusing the approach, they block more appropriate methods. For example, the human resources director at a medium-size company often cultivated support for new programs by taking people out to fancy restaurants for an evening of fine food and wine. One time, a new program he wanted to introduce required the agreement of the head of engineering. The engineer saw the attempts at socializing as a sleazy and crude way of trying to soften him up. Thus the HR director lost his opportunity to sell a program that, ironically, the engineering manager would have found valuable had it been implemented.

◆ THE ROLE OF RELATIONSHIPS

All of the preceding discussion needs to be conditioned by one important variable: the nature of the relationship between both parties. The greater the extent to which the influencer has worked with the potential ally and created trust, the easier the exchange process will be. Each party will know the other's desired currencies and situational pressures, and each will have developed a mutually productive interaction style. With trust, less energy will be spent on figuring out the intentions of the ally, and there will be less suspicion about when and how the payback will occur.

A poor relationship (based on previous interactions, on the reputation each party has in the organization, and/or on stereotypes and animosities between the functions or departments that each party represents) will impede an otherwise easy exchange. Distrust of the goodwill, veracity, or reliability of the influencer can lead to the demand for "no credit; cash up front," which constrains the flexibility of both parties.

The nature of the interaction during the influencer process also affects the nature of the relationship between the influencer and the other party. The way that the HR director attempted to relate to the head of engineering not only did not work but also irreparably damaged any future exchanges between them.

Few transactions within organizations are one-time deals. (Who knows when the other person may be needed again or even who may be working for him or her in the future?) Thus in most exchange situations two outcomes matter: success in achieving task goals and success in improving the relationship so that the next interaction will be even more productive. Too often, people who want to be influential focus only on the task and act as if there is no tomorrow. Although both task accomplishment and an improved relationship cannot always be realized at the same time, on some occasions the latter can be more important than the former. Winning the battle but losing the war is an expensive outcome.

◆   *INCONVERTIBLE CURRENCIES*

We have spelled out ways organizational members operate to gain influence for achieving organizational goals. By effectively using exchange, organizational members can achieve their goals and at the same time help others achieve theirs. Exchange permits organizational members to be assertive without being antagonistic by keeping mutual benefit a central outcome.

In many cases, organizational members fail to acquire desired influence because they do not use all of their potential power. However, they sometimes fail because not all situations are amenable to even the best efforts at influencing. Not everything can be translated into compatible currencies. If there are fundamental differences in what is valued by two parties, it may not be possible to find common ground, as illustrated in the example below.

The founder and chairman of a high-technology company and the president he had hired five years previously were constantly displeased with one another. The president was committed to creating maximum shareholder value. Accordingly, he had concluded that the company was in a perfect position to cash in by squeezing expenses to maximize profits and going public. The chairman valued a totally different currency, the fun of technological challenge. An independently wealthy man, the chairman had no interest in realizing the $10 million or so he would get if the company maximized profits by cutting research and selling out. He wanted a place to test his intuitive, creative research hunches, not a source of income.

Thus the president's and chairman's currencies were not convertible into one another at an acceptable exchange rate. After they explored various possibilities but failed to find common ground, they mutually agreed that the president should leave.

Influence is enhanced by using the model of strategic alliances to engage in mutually beneficial exchanges with potential allies. Even though it is not always possible to be successful, the chances of achieving success can be greatly increased. In a period of rapid competitive, technological, regulative, and consumer change, individuals and their organizations need all the help they can get.

◆   *SELECTED BIBLIOGRAPHY*

Some of the classic work on exchange as a process of influence was done by Peter Blau. His book *The Dynamics of Bureaucracy* (University of Chicago Press, 1963) was a landmark study of how tax assessors traded gratitude for expert assistance. When exchange is added to notions about the universality of reciprocity, as outlined by Alvin Gouldner in his pioneering article "The Norm of Reciprocity: A Preliminary Statement" *(American Sociological Review, 25, 1960)*, a powerful way of thinking about influence is created.

David Berlew picked up on these ideas and wrote an interesting piece addressed to people who want more influence: "What You Can Do When Persuasion Doesn't Work" *(NTL Connections,* 1986). He discussed three types of exchange that can be used by those attempting to get things done.

The case for managers needing to build alliances in order to accomplish work was made by Robert Kaplan in his article "Trade Routes: The Manager's Network of Relationships" *(Organizational Dynamics,* 1984). John Kotter found in his study of successful general managers *(The General Managers,* Free Press, 1982) that they had wide networks of contacts in their organizations, which helped them find the right person(s) when trying to make things happen. Rosabeth Moss Kanter's *The Change Masters* (Simon & Schuster, 1983) is the best examination of the ways organization members go about achieving major innovations through alliances. It shows the steps that innovative members go through, including the many ways they use influence to build coalitions and overcome resistance. We have built on her work by looking with a microscope at the mechanisms behind the processes she describes.

Other researchers have explored influence processes from many angles. David Kipnis and his collaborators found that they can categorize influence styles along seven dimensions. In "Patterns of Managerial Influence: Shotgun Managers, Tacticians, and Bystanders" *(Organizational Dynamics,* 1984), they identify the problem of managers who lack organizational power (and by implication what to do about it) and therefore give up attempting to influence. John Kotter addressed ways of increasing influence in *Power in Management: How to Understand, Acquire and Use It,* (AMACOM, 1979). He shows the advantages and disadvantages of different methods.

Our own book *Managing for Excellence: The Guide to High Performance in Contemporary Organizations* (John Wiley & Sons, 1984) addresses influence downward by arguing that shared responsibility is needed with subordinates in order to get the best from them and that treating them as full partners in the unit's management is necessary even though formal authority rests with the manager. We also show that mutual influence is needed to allow both parties to use their full strength. These ideas translate directly into lessons for influence when formal authority is lacking.

Finally, the literature of negotiations has many applications for using exchange for influence. Although there are popular books on negotiating that overlook important issues of trust when relationships are ongoing within the same organization, there is much to be learned from applying negotiating insights. Roger Fisher's and William Ury's book *Getting to Yes* (Houghton Mifflin, 1981) is helpful on ways to approach someone to look for common interests despite having differing specific objectives. An excellent overview of the issues involved in any kind of negotiation can be found in Roy Lewicki and Joseph Litterer's text *Negotiation* (G.D. Irwin, 1985). Their discussion of exchange and equity is particularly relevant to influence as we have described it. In addition, Roy Lewicki's comments on an earlier draft of this article were particularly helpful, and we are grateful for his wisdom and generosity.

PART III

The Organization

SECTION 10

Job Design

Confessions of a Working Stiff

Patrick Fenton

This is an account of what it was like to work as an airline cargo handler in the 1970s. The author, writing from experience, paints a bleak picture of how a job and working conditions can undermine the human spirit. This essay underscores the importance of designing jobs in ways that respect human dignity.

Patrick Fenton (b. 1941) dropped out of school at age sixteen. After working in a New York City factory, he spent two years with the United States army in Germany. He then began writing and working as a cargo handler at Seaboard World Airlines. Eight years later he joined the civil service and continued writing and pursuing a college education.

The Big Ben is hammering out its 5:45 alarm in the half-dark of another Tuesday morning. If I'm lucky, my car down in the street will kick over for me. I don't want to think about that now; all I want to do is roll over into the warm covers that hug my wife. I can hear the wind as it whistles up and down the sides of the building. Tuesday is always the worst day—it's the day the drudgery, boredom, and fatigue start all over again. I'm off from work on Sunday and Monday, so Tuesday is my blue Monday.

I make my living humping cargo for Seaboard World Airlines, one of the big international airlines at Kennedy Airport. They handle strictly all cargo. I was once told that one of the Rockefellers is the major stockholder for the airline, but I don't really think about that too much. I don't get paid to think. The big thing is to beat that race with the time clock every morning of your life so the airline will be happy. The worst thing a man could ever do is to make suggestions about building a better airline. They pay people $40,000 a year to come up with better ideas. It doesn't matter that these ideas never work; it's just that they get

Source: Copyright (c) 1990 News America Publishing Incorporated. All rights reserved. Reprinted with permission of *New York* magazine.

nervous when a guy from South Brooklyn or Ozone Park acts like he actually has a brain.

I throw a Myadec high-potency vitamin into my mouth to ward off one of the ten colds I get every year from humping mailbags out in the cold rain at Kennedy. A huge DC-8 stretch jet waits impatiently for the 8,000 pounds of mail that I will soon feed its empty belly. I wash the Myadec down with some orange juice and grab a brown bag filled with bologna and cheese. Inside the lunch bag there is sometimes a silly note from my wife that says, "I Love You— Guess Who?" It is all that keeps me going to a job that I hate.

I've been going there for seven years now and my job is still the same. It's weary work that makes a man feel used up and worn out. You push and you pull all day long with your back. You tie down pallets loaded with thousands of pounds of freight. You fill igloo-shaped containers with hundreds of boxes that look the same. If you're assigned to work the warehouse, it's really your hard luck. This is the job all the men hate most. You stack box upon box until the pallet resembles the exact shape of the inside of the plane. You get the same monotonous feeling an adult gets when he plays with a child's blocks. When you finish one pallet, you find another and start the whole dull process over again.

The airline pays me $192 a week for this. After they take out taxes and $5.81 for the pension, I go home with $142. Once a month they take out $10 for term life insurance, and $5.50 for union dues. The week they take out the life insurance is always the worst: I go home with $132. My job will never change. I will fill up the same igloos with the same boxes for the next 34 years of my life, I will hump the same mailbags into the belly of the plane, and push the same 8,000-pound pallets with my back. I will have to do this until I'm 65 years old. Then I'll be free, if I don't die of a heart attack before that, and the airline will let me retire.

In winter the warehouse is cold and damp. There is no heat. The large steel doors that line the warehouse walls stay open most of the day. In the cold months, wind, rain and snow blow across the floor. In the summer the warehouse becomes an oven. Dust and sand from the runways mix with the toxic fumes of fork lifts, leaving a dry, stale taste in your mouth. The high windows above the doors are covered with a thick, black dirt that kills the sun. The men work in shadows with the constant roar of jet engines blowing dangerously in their ears.

Working the warehouse is a tedious job that leaves a man's mind empty. If he's smart he will spend his days wool-gathering. He will think about pretty girls that he once knew, or some other daydream of warm, dry places where you never had a chill. The worst thing he can do is to think about his problems. If he starts to think about how he is going to pay the mortgage on the $30,000 home that he can't afford, it will bring him down. He will wonder why he comes to the cargo airline every morning of his life, and even on Christmas Day. He will start to wonder why he has to listen to the deafening sound of the jets as they rev up their engines. He will wonder why he crawls on his hands and knees, breaking his back a little bit more every day.

To keep his kids in that great place in the country in the summer, that great place far away from Brooklyn and the South Bronx, he must work every hour of overtime that the airline offers him. If he never turns down an hour, if he works some 600 hours over, he can make about $15,000. To do this he must turn against himself, he must pray that the phone rings in the middle of the night, even though it's snowing out and he doesn't feel like working. He must hump cargo late into the night, eat meatball heroes for supper, drink coffee that starts to taste like oil, and then hope that his car starts when it's time to go home. If he gets sick—well, he better not think about that.

All over Long Island, Ozone Park, Brooklyn, and as far away as the Bronx, men stir in the early morning hours as a new day begins. Every morning is the same as the last. Some of the men drink beer for breakfast instead of coffee. Way out in Bay Shore a cargoman snaps open a can of Budweiser. It's 6 A.M., and he covers the top of the can with his thumb in order to keep down the loud hiss as the beer escapes. He doesn't want to awaken his children as they dream away the morning in the next room. Soon he will swing his Pinto wagon up onto the crowded Long Island Expressway and start the long ride to the job. As he slips the car out of the driveway he tucks another can of beer between his legs.

All the men have something in common: they hate the work they are doing and they drink a little too much. They come to work only to punch a timecard that has their last name on it. At the end of the week they will pick up a paycheck with their last name on it. They will never receive a bonus for a job well done, or even a party. At Christmastime a card from the president of the airline will arrive at each one of their houses. It will say Merry Christmas and have the president's name printed at the bottom of it. They know that the airline will be there long after they are dead. Nothing stops it. It runs non-stop, without sleep, through Christmas Day, New Year's Eve, Martin Luther King's birthday, even the deaths of Presidents.

It's seven in the morning and the day shift is starting to drift in. Huge tractors are backing up to the big-mouth doors of the warehouse. Cattle trucks bring in tons of beef to feed its insatiable appetite for cargo. Smoke-covered trailers with refrigerated units packed deep with green peppers sit with their diesel engines idling. Names like White, Mack, and Kenworth are welded to the front of their radiators, which hiss and moan from the overload. The men walk through the factory-type gates of the parking lot with their heads bowed, oblivious of the shuddering diesels that await them.

Once inside the warehouse they gather in groups of threes and fours like prisoners in an exercise yard. They stand in front of the two time clocks that hang below a window in the manager's office. They smoke and cough in the early morning hour as they await their work assignments. The manager, a nervous-looking man with a stomach that is starting to push out at his belt, walks out with the pink work sheets in his hand.

Eddie, a young Irishman with a mustache, has just bolted in through the door. The manager has his timecard in his hand, holding it so no one else can hit Eddie in. Eddie is four minutes late by the time clock. His name will now go down in the timekeeper's ledger. The manager hands the card to him with a "you'll be up in the office if you don't straighten out" look. Eddie takes the card, hits it in, and slowly takes his place with the rest of the men. He has been out till four in the morning drinking beer in the bars of Ozone Park; the time clock and the manager could blow up, for all he cares. "Jesus," he says to no one in particular, "I hope to Christ they don't put me in the warehouse this morning."

Over in another group, Kelly, a tall man wearing a navy knit hat, talks to the men. "You know, I almost didn't make it in this morning. I passed this green VW on the Belt Parkway. The girl driving it was singing. Jesus, I thought to myself, it must be great going somewhere at 6:30 in the morning that makes you want to sing." Kelly is smiling as he talks. "I often think, why the hell don't you keep on going, Kelly? Don't get off at the cargo exit, stay on. Go anywhere, even if it's only Brooklyn. Christ, if I was a single man I think I would do just that. Some morning I'd pass this damn place by and drive as far away as Riverhead. I don't know what I'd do when I got there—maybe I'd pick up a pound of beefsteak tomatoes from one of those roadside stands or something."

The men laugh at Kelly but they know he is serious. "I feel the same way sometimes," the man next to him says. "I find myself daydreaming a lot lately; this place drives you to do that. I get up in the morning and I just don't want to come to work. I get sick when I hit that parking lot. If it wasn't for the kids and the house I'd quit." The men then talk about how hard it is to get work on "the outside." They mention "outside" as if they were in a prison.

Each morning there is an Army-type roll call from the leads. The leads are foremen who must keep the men moving; if they don't, it could mean their jobs. At one time they had power over the men but as time went by the company took away their little bit of authority. They also lost the deep interest, even enjoyment, for the hard work they once did. As the cargo airline grew, it beat this out of them, leaving only apathy. The ramp area is located in the backyard of the warehouse. This is where the huge jets park to unload their 70,000-pound payloads. A crew of men fall in behind the ramp lead as he mopes out of the warehouse. His long face shows the hopelessness of another day.

A brutal rain has started to beat down on the oil-covered concrete of the ramp as the 306 screeches in off the runway. Its engines scream as they spit off sheets of rain and oil. Two of the men cover their ears as they run to put up a ladder to the front of the plane. The airline will give them ear covers only if they pay for half of them. A lot of the men never buy them. If they want, the airline will give them two little plugs free. The plugs don't work and hurt the inside of the ears.

The men will spend the rest of the day in the rain. Some of them will set up conveyor belts and trucks to unload the thousands of pounds of cargo that sit in the deep belly of the plane. Then they will feed the awkward bird until it is full and ready to fly again. They will crawl on their hands and knees in its belly, counting and humping hundreds of mailbags. The rest of the men will work up topside on the plane, pushing 8,000-pound pallets with their backs.

Like Egyptians building a pyramid, they will pull and push until the pallet finally gives in and moves like a massive stone sliding through sand. They don't complain too much; they know that when the airline comes up with a better system some of them will go.

The old-timers at the airline can't understand why the younger men stay on. They know what the cargo airline can do to a man. It can work him hard but make him lazy at the same time. The work comes in spurts. Sometimes a man will be pushed for three hours of sweat, other times he will just stand around bored. It's not the hard work that breaks a man at the airline, it's the boredom of doing the same job over and over again.

At the end of the day the men start to move in off the ramp. The rain is still beating down at their backs but they move slowly. Their faces are red and raw from the rain-soaked wind that has been snapping at them for eight hours. The harsh wind moves in from the direction of the city. From the ramp you can see the Manhattan skyline, gray- and blue-looking, as it peeks up from the west wall of the warehouse. There is nothing to block the winter weather as it rolls in like a storm across a prairie. They head down to the locker room, heads bowed, like a football team that never wins.

With the workday almost over, the men move between the narrow, gray rows of lockers. Up on the dirty walls that surround the lockers someone has written a couple of four-letter words. There is no wit to the words; they just say the usual. As they strip off their wet gear the men seem to come alive.

"Hey, Arnie! You want to stay four hours? They're asking for overtime down in Export," one of the men yells over the lockers.

Arnie is sitting about four rows over, taking off his heavy winter clothing. He thinks about this for a second and yells back, "What will we be doing?"

"Working the meat trailer." This means that Arnie will be humping huge sides of beef off rows of hooks for four hours. Blood will drip down onto his clothes as he struggles to the front of the trailer. Like most of the men, he needs the extra money, and knows that he should stay. He has Master Charge, Korvettes, Times Square Stores, and Abraham & Straus to pay.

"Nah, I'm not staying tonight. Not if it's working the meat trailer. Don wanted to stop for a few beers at The Owl; maybe I'll stay tomorrow night."

It's four o'clock in the afternoon now—the men have twelve minutes to go before they punch out. The airline has stopped for a few seconds as the men change shifts. Supervisors move frantically across the floor pushing the fresh lot of new men who have just started to come in. They hand out work sheets and yell orders: "Jack, get your men into their rain gear. Put three men in the bellies to finish off the 300 flight. Get someone on the pepper trailers, they've been here all morning."

The morning shift stands around the time clock with three minutes to go. Someone says that Kevin Delahunty has just been appointed to the Fire Department. Kevin, a young Irishman from Ozone Park, has been working the cargo airline for six years. Like most of the men, he has hated every minute of it. The men are openly proud of him as they reach out to shake his hand. Kevin has found a job on "the outside." "Ah, you'll be leaving soon," he tells Pat. "I never thought I'd get out of here either, but you'll see, you're going to make it."

The manager moves through the crowd handing out timecards and stops when he comes to Kevin. Someone told him Kevin is leaving. "Is that right, Delahunty? Well I guess we won't expect you in tomorrow, will we? Going to become a fireman, eh? That means you'll be jumping out of windows like a crazy man. Don't act like you did around here," he adds as he walks back to his office.

The time clock hits 4:12 and the men pour out of the warehouse. Kevin will never be back, but the rest of them will return in the morning to grind out another eight hours. Some of them will head straight home to the bills, screaming children, and a wife who tries to understand them. They'll have a Schaefer or two, then they'll settle down to a night of television.

Some of them will start to fill up the cargo bars that surround Kennedy Airport. They will head to places like Gaylor's on Rockaway Boulevard or The Dew Drop Inn down near Farmers Boulevard. They will drink deep glasses of whiskey and cold mugs of Budweiser. The Dew Drop has a honky-tonk mood of the Old West to it. The barmaid moves around like a modern-day Katie Elder. Like Brandy, she's a fine girl, but she can out-curse any cargoman. She wears a low-cut blouse that reveals most of her breasts. The jukebox will beat out some Country & Western as she says, "Ah, hell, you played my song." The cargomen will hoot and holler as she substitutes some of her own obscene lyrics.

They will drink late into the night, forgetting time clocks, Master Charge, First National City, Korvettes, mortgages, cars that don't start, and jet engines that hurt their ears. They will forget about damp, cold warehouses, winters that get longer and colder every year, minutes that drift by like hours, supervisors that harass, and the thought of growing old on a job they hate. At midnight they will fall dangerously into their cars and make their way up onto the Southern State Parkway. As they ride into the dark night of Long Island they will forget it all until 5:45 the next morning—when the Big Ben will start up the whole grind all over again.

♦   *DISCUSSION QUESTIONS*

1. Describe the tasks comprising the job of cargo handler and the working conditions and management practices at Seaboard World Airlines. What impact do they have on worker attitudes, behavior, and productivity?

2. Redesign the job of cargo handler according to the following methods of job design, and discuss the advantages and disadvantages of each:
   (a) job specialization [1].
   (b) job enlargement; i.e., horizontal job loading [2].
   (c) job characteristics model of job enrichment [3].

3. Review the ways the cargo handlers cope with the stress of their jobs. Com-

pare the effectiveness of these coping mechanisms with others that could be adopted.

4. Use the concepts from social information processing theory [4] to show how, if possible, the cargo handlers' job attitudes could be improved without redesigning the job.

5. To whom is the author making these "confessions" and why? If he were truly serious about improving the job and the working conditions, what should he do?

◆   REFERENCES

1. Taylor, F.W. 1911. *The Principles of Scientific Management.* New York: Harper & Row.

2. Ford, R.N. January–February 1973. Job enrichment lessons from AT&T. *Harvard Business Review* 96–106.

3. Hackman, J.R., and Oldham, G. 1980. *Work Redesign.* Reading, MA: Addison-Wesley.

4. Salancik, G., and Pfeffer, J. 1978. A social information processing approach to job attitudes and task design. *Administrative Science Quarterly* 23: 224–253.

The Facts in the Great Beef Contract

Mark Twain

In his typical humorous style, Mark Twain presents a satire of the classic bureaucratic runaround. As you follow the persistent narrator through a web of government departments in his quest for payment of a long-overdue bill, think of how organizations can best be structured to accomplish their goals.

Mark Twain (1835–1910) is the pen name of Samuel Clemens. In addition to his famous novels, *Adventures of Huckleberry Finn* and *Adventures of Tom Sawyer,* Clemens was a prolific contributor to newspapers in Buffalo, California, and Nevada.

In as few words as possible I wish to lay before the nation what share, howsoever small, I have had in this matter—this matter which has so exercised the public mind, engendered so much ill-feeling, and so filled the newspapers of both continents with distorted statements and extravagant comments.

The origin of this distressful thing was this—and I assert here that every fact in the following résumé can be amply proved by the official records of the General Government:

John Wilson Mackenzie, of Rotterdam, Chemung County, New Jersey, deceased, contracted with the General Government, on or about the 10th day of October 1861, to furnish to General Sherman the sum total of thirty barrels of beef.

Very well.

He started after Sherman with the beef, but when he got to Washington, Sherman had gone to Manassas; so he took the beef and followed him there, but arrived too late; he followed him to Nashville, and from Nashville to Chattanooga, and from Chattanooga to Atlanta—but he never could overtake him. At Atlanta he took a fresh start and followed him clear through his march to the sea. He arrived too late again by a few days; but hearing that Sherman was going out in the *Quaker City* excursion to the Holy Land, he took shipping for Beirut, calculating to head off the other vessel. When he arrived in Jerusalem with his beef, he learned that Sherman had not sailed in the *Quaker City,* but had gone to the Plains to fight the Indians. He returned to America and started for the Rocky Mountains. After sixty-eight days of arduous travel on the Plains, and when he had got within four miles of Sherman's headquarters, he was tomahawked and scalped, and the Indians got the beef. They got all of it but one barrel. Sherman's army captured that, and so, even in death, the bold navigator partly fulfilled his contract. In his will, which he had kept like a journal, he bequeathed the contract to his son Bartholomew W. Bartholomew W. made out the following bill, and then died:

THE UNITED STATES
    In account with JOHN WILSON MACKENZIE, of New Jersey, deceased   Dr.
To thirty barrels of beef for General Sherman, at $100, $3,000
To traveling expenses and transportation   14,000

                         Total $17,000
                     Rec'd Pay't.

He died then; but he left the contract to Wm. J. Martin, who tried to collect it, but died before he got through. *He* left it to Barker J. Allen, and he tried to collect it also. He did not survive. Barker J. Allen left it to Anson G. Rogers, who attempted to collect it, and got along as far as the Ninth Auditor's Office, when Death, the great Leveler, came all unsummoned, and foreclosed on *him* also. He left the bill to a relative of his in Connecticut, Vengeance Hopkins by name, who lasted four weeks and two days, and made the best time on record, coming within one of reaching the Twelfth Auditor. In his will he gave the contract bill to his uncle, by the name of O-be-joyful Johnson. It was too undermining for Joyful. His last words were: "Weep not for me—*I* am willing to go." And so he was, poor soul. Seven people inherited the contract after that; but they all died. So it came into my hands at last. It fell to me through a relative by the name of Hubbard—Bethlehem Hubbard, of Indiana. He had had a grudge against me for a long time; but in his last moments he sent for me, and forgave me everything, and, weeping, gave me the beef contract.

    This ends the history of it up to the time that I succeeded to the property. I will now endeavor to set myself straight before the nation in everything that concerns my share in the matter. I took this beef contract, and the bill for mileage and transportation, to the President of the United States.

    He said, "Well, sir, what can I do for you?"

    I said, "Sire, on or about the 10th day of October, 1861, John Wilson Mackenzie, of Rotterdam, Chemung County, New Jersey, deceased, contracted with the General Government to furnish to General Sherman the sum total of thirty barrels of beef—"

    He stopped me there, and dismissed me from his presence—kindly, but firmly. The next day I called on the Secretary of State.

    He said, "Well, sir?"

I said, "Your Royal Highness: on or about the 10th day of October, 1861, John Wilson Mackenzie, of Rotterdam, Chemung County, New Jersey, deceased, contracted with the General Government to furnish to General Sherman the sum total of thirty barrels of beef—"

"That will do, sir—that will do; this office has nothing to do with contracts for beef."

I was bowed out. I thought the matter all over, and finally, the following day, I visited the Secretary of the Navy, who said, "Speak quickly, sir; do not keep me waiting."

I said, "Your Royal Highness, on or about the 10th day of October, 1861, John Wilson Mackenzie, of Rotterdam, Chemung County, New Jersey, deceased, contracted with the General Government to furnish to General Sherman the sum total of thirty barrels of beef—"

Well, it was as far as I could get. *He* had nothing to do with beef contracts for General Sherman, either. I began to think it was a curious kind of a government. It looked somewhat as if they wanted to get out of paying for that beef. The following day I went to the Secretary of the Interior.

I said, "Your Imperial Highness, on or about the 10th day of October—"

"That is sufficient, sir. I have heard of you before. Go, take your infamous beef contract out of this establishment. The Interior Department has nothing whatever to do with subsistence for the army."

I went away. But I was exasperated now. I said I would haunt them; I would infest every department of this iniquitous government till that contract business was settled. I would collect that bill, or fall, as fell my predecessors, trying. I assailed the Postmaster-General; I besieged the Agricultural Department; I waylaid the Speaker of the House of Representatives. *They* had nothing to do with army contracts for beef. I moved upon the Commissioner of the Patent Office.

I said, "Your August Excellency, on or about—"

"Perdition! have you got *here* with your incendiary beef contract, at last? We have *nothing* to do with beef contracts for the army, my dear sir."

"Oh, that is all very well—but *somebody* has got to pay for that beef. It has got to be paid *now*, too, or I'll confiscate this old Patent Office and everything in it."

"But, my dear sir—"

"It don't make any difference, sir. The Patent Office is liable for that beef, I reckon; and, liable or not liable, the Patent Office has got to pay for it."

Never mind the details. It ended in a fight. The Patent Office won. But I found out something to my advantage. I was told that the Treasury Department was the proper place for me to go to. I went there. I waited two hours and a half, and then I was admitted to the First Lord of the Treasury.

I said, "Most noble, grave, and reverend Signor, on or about the 10th day of October, 1861, John Wilson Macken—"

"That is sufficient, sir. I have heard of you. Go the First Auditor of the Treasury."

I did so. He sent me to the Second Auditor. The Second Auditor sent me to the Third, and the Third send me to the First Comptroller of the Corn-Beef Division. This began to look like business. He examined his books and all his loose papers, but found no minute of the beef contract. I went to the Second Comptroller of the Corn-Beef Division. He examined his books and his loose papers, but with no success. I was encouraged. During that week I got as far as the Sixth Comptroller in that division; the next week I got through the Claims Department; the third week I began and completed the Mislaid Contracts Department, and got a foothold in the Dead Reckoning Department. I finished that in three days. There was only one place left for it now. I laid siege to the Commissioner of Odds and Ends. To his clerk, rather—he was not there himself. There were sixteen beautiful young ladies in the room, writing in books, and there were seven well-favored young clerks showing them how. The young women smiled up over their shoulders, and the clerks smiled back at them, and all went merry as a marriage bell. Two or three clerks that were reading the newspapers looked at me rather hard, but went on reading, and nobody said anything. However, I had been used to this kind of alacrity from Fourth Assistant Junior Clerks all through my eventful career, from the very day I entered the first office of the Corn-Beef Bureau clear till I passed out of the last one in the Dead Reckoning Division. I had got so accomplished by this time that I could stand on one foot from the moment I entered an office till a clerk spoke to me, without changing more than two, or maybe three, times.

So I stood there till I had changed four different times. Then I said to one of the clerks who was reading:

"Illustrious Vagrant, where is the Grand Turk?"

"What do you mean, sir? whom do you mean? If you mean the Chief of the Bureau, he is out."

"Will he visit the harem to-day?"

The young man glared upon me awhile, and then went on reading his paper. But I knew the ways of those clerks. I knew I was safe if he got through before another New York mailed arrived. He only had two more papers left. After a while he finished them, and then he yawned and asked me what I wanted.

"Renowned and honored Imbecile: on or about—"

"You are the beef-contract man. Give me your papers."

He took them, and for a long time he ransacked his odds and ends. Finally he found the Northwest Passage, as *I* regarded it—he found the long-lost record of that beef contract—he found the rock upon which so many of my ancestors had split before they ever got to it. I was deeply moved. And yet I rejoiced—for I had survived. I said with emotion, "Give it to me. The government will settle now." He waved me back, and said there was something yet to be done first.

"Where is this John Wilson Mackenzie?" said he.

"Dead."

"When did he die?"

"He didn't die at all—he was killed."

"How?"

"Tomahawked."

"Who tomahawked him?"

"Why, an Indian, of course. You didn't suppose it was the superintendent of a Sunday-school, did you?"

"No. An Indian, was it?"

"The same."

"Name of the Indian."

"His name? *I* don't know his name."

"*Must* have his name. Who saw the tomahawking done?"

"I don't know."

"You were not present yourself, then?"

"Which you can see by my hair. I was absent."

"Then how do you know that Mackenzie is dead?"

"Because he certainly died at that time, and I have every reason to believe that he has been dead ever since. I *know* he has, in fact."

"We must have proofs. Have you got the Indian?"

"Of course not."

"Well, you must get him. Have you got the tomahawk?"

"I never thought of such a thing."

"You must get the tomahawk. You must produce the Indian and the tomahawk. If Mackenzie's death can be proven by these, you can then go before the commission appointed to audit claims with some show of getting your bill under such headway that your children may possibly live to receive the money and enjoy it. But that man's death *must* be proven. However, I may as well tell you that the government will never pay that transportation and those traveling expenses of the lamented Mackenzie. It *may* possibly pay for the barrel of beef that Sherman's soldiers captured, if you can get a relief bill through Congress making an appropriation for that purpose; but it will not pay for the twenty-nine barrels the Indians ate."

"Then there is only a hundred dollars due me, and *that* isn't certain! After all Mackenzie's travels in Europe, Asia, and America with that beef; after all his trials and tribulations and transportation; after the slaughter of all those innocents that tried to collect that bill! Young man, why didn't the First Comptroller of the Corn-Beef Division tell me this?"

"He didn't know anything about the genuineness of your claim."

"Why didn't the Second tell me? why didn't the Third? why didn't all those divisions and departments tell me?"

"None of them knew. We do things by routine here. You have followed the routine and found out what you wanted to know. It is the best way. It is the only way. It is very regular, and very slow, but it is very certain."

"Yes, certain death. It has been, to the most of our tribe. I begin to feel that I, too, am called. Young man, you love the bright creature yonder with the gentle blue eyes and the steel pens behind her ears—I see it in your soft glances; you wish to marry her—but you are poor. Here, hold out your hand—here is the beef contract; go, take her and be happy! Heaven bless you, my children!"

This is all I know about the great beef contract that has created so much talk in the community. The clerk to whom I bequeathed it died. I know nothing further about the contract, or any one connected with it. I only know that if a man lives long enough he can trace a thing through the Circumlocution Office at Washington and find out, after much labor and trouble and delay, that which he could have found out on the first day if the business of the Circumlocution Office were as ingeniously systematized as it would be if it were a great private mercantile institution.

♦   *DISCUSSION QUESTIONS*

1. In retrospect, what could Mackenzie have done to avoid his problems?

2. Evaluate the narrator's approach to collecting to bill. What steps did he take? What were his tone and attitude? Why? What other options did he have?

3. Comment on the following remark by a clerk at the Commission of Odds and Ends: "We do things by routine here. You have followed the routine and found out what you wanted to know. It is the best way. It is the only way. It is very regular, and very slow, but it is very certain." In what types of organizations and under what circumstances are these characteristics appropriate and functional?

4. Discuss the origin and mission of The Commission of Odds and Ends.

5. Use reading 13.1, *On the Folly of Rewarding A, While Hoping for B*, as a basis for discussing the following:
   (a) official goals versus operative goals.
   (b) goal displacement.
   (c) the possible causes of the situation at the Commission of Odds and Ends.
   (d) remedies to improve the organization.

6. Imagine you are on a task force to shape up the Commission of Odds and Ends and the departments with which it interacts. Use the following materials to describe the current situation and to suggest recommendations for improvements:
   (a) division of labor: horizontal, vertical, personal, and spatial [1].
   (b) coordination mechanisms: mutual adjustment, direct supervision, standardization of work processes, outputs, and skills [2].
   (c) types of organizational structures: simple, machine bureaucracy, professional bureaucracy, divisionalized form, and adhocracy [3].

7. The last sentence of *The Facts in the Great Beef Contract* suggests that such things do not happen in the private sector. Do you agree? Describe situations from your own experience and explain why they do or do not fall into this pattern.

◆ *REFERENCES*

1. Lawrence, P.R., and Lorsch, J.W. 1967. Differentiation and integration in complex organizations. *Administrative Science Quarterly* 12: 1–47.

2. Mintzberg, H. 1980. *The Structuring of Work*. Englewood Cliffs, NJ: Prentice-Hall.

3. Mintzberg, *op. cit.*

The Inner Circle

James Chposky ♦ *Ted Leonsis*

In contrast to the unwieldly government departments depicted in the previous story, the task force that produced the IBM personal computer is a stellar example of successful organizing and goal accomplishment. This chapter, from *Blue Magic: The Story of the People, the Power and Politics Behind the IBM Personal Computer,* describes the role of the PC development group in achieving IBM's unprecedented goal of designing, developing, and marketing a radically new product within one year. The flexibility of the organizational structure and the special powers granted to the 12 member engineering group are key factors in this success story.

James Chposky is a freelance writer who specializes in business, finance, and marketing. He has written on assignment for IBM, Control Data Corporation, and various computer magazines. Ted Leonsis is a former director of corporate communications at Wang Laboratories and at The Harris Corporation. He is currently the executive publisher of several computer publications.

Saturday mornings in the summer of 1981 at Boca Raton: the streets were quiet, a few lawn sprinklers twirled, a kid here or there on a bike. The pace was so slow. It was the weekend, and a time for rest, or play, or puttering about the house. Even IBMers slept in, then moved leisurely, lazily, through the hazy morning. It was that kind of day in that sort of a place.

But Wilkie was already late, and it was only a few minutes past 8:30. When he pulled his car into the parking lot at Project Chess headquarters, there, side-by-side, were the autos driven by Don Estridge, Bill Sydnes, and Joe Sarubbi. Wilkie yanked the car into the parking space and hurried through the door, into the building, down a corridor and on to the conference room where the others were just getting settled.

After all, it was the weekend, and a time to relax, so here was the unofficial inner circle of Project Chess eagerly engaged in their favorite form of relaxation: Talking about the project and the people and the PC in an easygoing way without phones to answer, problems to resolve, and neckties to wear.

At these gatherings (they weren't really "meetings" or "conferences" in the IBM sense of those terms) Estridge would democratically take care to sit anywhere but at the head of the table. Nobody really "ran" the meetings or called the sessions to order.

Source: From *Blue Magic: The People, the Power and Politics Behind the IBM Personal Computer* by James Chposky and Ted Leonsis. Copyright © 1988 by James Chposky and Ted Leonsis. Reprinted with permission of Facts on File, Inc., New York.

While things would get underway at the office around 8:30 on those Saturday mornings, there was no set time limit; if someone had to leave, they simply did. Around noon or one o'clock, the others would begin to call it a day and rather grumpily head back home to tend to the lawn, go to the hardware store or make the weekly trip to the supermarket.

(Years later, Joe Sarubbi said, "We didn't spend a lot of time at home in those days. Our wives knew we were working on a very exciting and important project and they gave us all the support we needed. Actually, the people on the project didn't see one another socially that much because we spent so much time together otherwise. When I wasn't working, I'd put in time on the beach. That was my social life—I'm a beach bum. One time I asked Estridge to give me an umbrella and a telephone, and I'd work from the beach. Needless to say, he didn't think that was such a good idea.")

The Saturday gatherings proved to be invaluable to the success of the project. During the Monday to Friday workweek, there were just too many interruptions and niggling details that demanded immediate attention. As a result, there was never any time to say, "Stop! Let's take a look at where we are, where we've been and where we're going—especially, where we're going and why."

The weekdays were hectic, so the real critiques and progress reports were held on the weekends.

By mid-summer of 1981, the PC group was going at a fever pitch with scores of critical issues to be resolved daily. When a glitch did develop, this inner circle would quickly gather, sometimes without waiting for all areas of responsibility to get involved. Decisions were made quickly; there was no time for second-guessing. Wrong decisions were redecided. Indecision was never tolerated.

They were, in effect, a tactical unit within the task force. This meant they were also firemen ready to move quickly and focus on a quick solution to a problem. (Reverting to gridiron parlance, Estridge called this team-within-the-team his "downfield blockers.") They were always on duty—Don and Dan and Bill and Joe—and, when trouble arose, Estridge and Wilkie and Sydnes and Sarubbi were the ones the others confidently turned to, especially when confidence in the fate of the project would occasionally waver.

At Microsoft headquarters, confidence was king. Never did Bill Gates doubt his ability and that of his crackerjack programmers to produce a state-of-the-art operating system and BASIC language that would set a standard for the entire personal computing industry.

Privately, though, Gates would concede that his confidence in IBM was less than he wished it would be. Quite frankly, he was always afraid that Big Blue would and could at any time simply cancel Project Chess, pay its bills for work accomplished and head away toward other ventures.

It was common knowledge in the industry that only a fraction of IBM's research projects were ever carried through to product introductions. So Gates, high-strung and nervous by nature, would fret over the worst possible scenario. What other projects were running in tandem with the development of a desktop computer? Were those guys at Boca Raton running around with some half-baked belief that they could keep on managing their own show while they were still on IBM's payroll? What about those persistent rumors that IBM was back to holding secret conversations with Gary Kildall at Digital Research? And then there was the almost-daily speculation in the press about what IBM was up to at Boca Raton. Some of the stories proved to be remarkably accurate, which further upset Gates and caused him to fear that IBM would accuse Microsoft of violating its airtight confidentiality agreement.

Throughout the end of June 1981, the Project Chess team put on their ties and jackets and played host to at least 40 of IBM's top officers, all quite curious to see the midget marvel of a computer which, by now, had seized the imagination of the corporation.

"These reviews by top management were necessary before the machine could be introduced to the public," Joe Sarubbi explained. "We tried to get as many people here at once as we could so we wouldn't have to keep repeating the same information."

Essentially, Estridge and his staff were telling IBM's big brass that they should coordinate their schedules and make an effort to come all at once because there wasn't any time for repetitious private presentations.

Amazingly, management acquiesced. Where, in the past, there would be separate reviews for management at the local, divisional, group and corporate levels, in this case, just one review would have to do. Besides, it gave some of the company's top people their first chance to size up one another face to face without contention.

Contention, often accompanied by confrontation, has been a way of life at IBM since the days of Thomas J. Watson, Sr. For example, a group at one location might be assigned to develop a particular machine, while another group at another site would be working on a somewhat similar project. The choice of which machine gets to market often has very much to do with how persuasive— that is, how "successfully contentious"—one group is at getting its way over the other. This system, obviously, does not always produce the best product, but, at the level of personalities, it most certainly separates the winners from the also-rans within the company.

Like everyone else at IBM, the PC development group was nurtured on the system of contention and confrontation. But there were some subtle differences at Boca Raton. According to Joe Sarubbi:

"There was always the contention of going through corporate procedures, but we were able to re-write most of those rules. When it came to contention within the group, I could hang in with the best of them. But Donnie [Estridge] was uncomfortable with the process, so he would stop everyone and say, 'Wait a minute. What is it we have to do? What do we have to provide?' Then he'd make us stick to the point until we agreed on what we had to do and when we had to do it. The result was that nobody's ego became bigger than the goal of the group, which was, of course, to get that machine out of the shop on time."

By mid-July 1981, the maiden version of the IBM PC was nearly ready for market. All that remained were the myriad final details before the finished product was ready to be unveiled before the Corporate Management Committee (CMC).

During the regular Saturday morning conclave of the inner circle, Estridge took Wilkie aside for a private chat. Wilkie learned that the PC group felt that the nitpickers and detail-compulsives in the systems assurance group had come up with a list of 122 so-called work items that absolutely had to be addressed and corrected before any version of the PC could leave Boca Raton for any purpose whatsoever.

At IBM, the systems assurance people are somewhat akin to in-house censors at a television network. Systems assurance says, "You can't do this" and "You have to do that." They lay down their edicts, then wait for the inevitable onset of contention and confrontation. When the smoke clears, neither systems assurance nor the product designers get everything they want, though each side will always get some concessions. Major points where no compromise is possible are adjudicated before the CMC, which, in such instances, acts as the court of last resort. Although the CMC's decisions are final and binding, conventional wisdom at the company insists that it is never a good idea to get the CMC unnecessarily involved in contentions better confronted and compromised at staff levels.

By now, the PC group and everyone at Boca Raton who had anything to do with the new machine were on a seven-day work schedule. This meant that the systems assurance people were standing by on Saturday when Estridge told Wilkie to solve the list of nits and details.

Looking back to that time, Wilkie said, "We spent about four hours that morning going over every item. When we were done, there was enough paper lying around to cover the walls and floor. Each work item by itself seemed to be a small detail, but when they were considered together . . . well, I agreed with the systems assurance position of nonsupport on releasing the machine for market.

"In one case, there was a problem with the operating manual; another problem had to do with customer service procedures. There were also details we had to clear up with diagnostics, quality checks, and this, that and the other thing."

The biggest problem of all concerned how to work out these items and still keep the PC's introduction on schedule. Here, again, is where the PC group's carte blanche to circumvent corporate protocols and its structured disciplines with demands for checkpoints, reviews and approvals in writing across the chains of command functioned for the common good. Wilkie brought the concerned parties together in small, flexible groups. Specific problems were addressed, trade-offs negotiated and decisions made on the spot. As a result, at least 110 of the 122 work items were fixed within less than a week. The balance were polished off a few days later.

———————

It was almost the end of July 1981 when Microsoft delivered the final version of its disk operating system and BASIC programming language for the PC.

The remaining work items were cleared, the last bolts were tightened on the machine and an IBM logotype was glued to the face of the PC's central processing unit.

The machine was now ready for its preview before the Corporate Management Committee. This was the end of the line; if the CMC was impressed, the wraps would quickly come off the IBM PC, and it could be introduced to the world.

Shuttling from Boca Raton to Armonk was now a routine for Estridge. He'd grab an early flight, land in New York, rent a car, drive to headquarters, tend to business and return to Florida—all in a single day. He would do this at least once and often two and sometimes three times a week. He was not the sort to lay his briefcase on his lap and catch up on work while the plane was airborne. Instead, this was a time to relax, to read a paperback page-turner, or to collect his thoughts out of reach and out of mind from the supercharged atmosphere at Boca Raton.

This time, of course, it was different. Accompanied by Wilkie and other members of the group, Estridge was heading north for the most crucial meeting to date with the CMC. Estridge saw to it that he was well briefed for this meeting. The contents of his flip-charts were committed to memory. In a mock dry run of the session, the PC staff peppered him with what they thought was every conceivable question that could be asked by the members of the CMC.

Estridge would have no more than 45 minutes to explain why the PC was made, what it could do, the markets it would serve and the role it would have in the corporate product mix. He would do this alone, while Wilkie and the others who had come along to lend moral support were told to wait in a room on another floor at corporate headquarters.

As it turned out, Don Estridge tapped his ineffable ability to concoct just the right mixture of charm, tact and sincerity to win the day with the CMC. When his three-quarters of an hour were up, Estridge emerged from the conference room and immediately sought out the PC team. They took one look at that grin and they knew. They knew.

Later, Estridge told them that the toughest question he had to answer was, "Why should IBM risk its name and reputation for customer satisfaction and service by selling this product through non-IBM sales channels?" They also wanted to know how the PC team would assure that customer needs were going to be properly addressed. The queries, pointed as they were, came near the end of

Estridge's presentation. He was taken by surprise because, in all of the prior reviews, these matters never appeared as issues with the CMC. As Wilkie recalled, "Don said the questions were worded in such a way that he felt, 'My God, they are changing their minds!' But Estridge's quick thinking held and he carried the day. So, okay, he had won the battle, but this episode left him clearly aware that the performance of non-IBM delivery channels was an important matter to the CMC. They were satisfied with his answers and so, from that moment, the IBM PC was officially launched."

◆   DISCUSSION QUESTIONS

1. Describe what it was like to work on Project Chess, the personal computer development project. Take into account the team members' personal rewards and sacrifices, the terms they used to describe themselves and their roles, the interpersonal relationships among the team members, and the stressors they experienced. Would you want to be a member of such a team? Explain.

2. Explain why Project Chess was so successful. Take the following factors into account:
   (a) the organizational structure.
   (b) the special powers and privileges granted to the PC development team.
   (c) the personal characteristics of the team members.
   (d) the leadership demonstrated by Don Estridge.
   (e) the nature of the task.

3. The inner circle was an elite subgroup of Project Chess. Identify the benefits that the project accrued because of the existence of this informal group. What problems might a group like this pose for the organization?

4. Describe the relationship between the PC development group and the systems assurance group. How effective is the relationship and why? Propose structural and procedural changes to enhance the effectiveness of the groups' interactions.

5. Discuss the pros and cons of the system of contention and confrontation that is allegedly practiced at IBM to determine which competing group gets approval to develop a product. Propose other ways of fostering new product development and discuss their advantages and disadvantages.

6. The project is over. What should management do to sustain this level of excitement and commitment? How should the team members be rewarded?

The Lottery

Shirley Jackson

This story depicts a horrific annual lottery in which all the residents of an ordinary, peaceful American village participate. As you read the story, think of practices in organizational settings that seem out of place, and suggest what may cause them and perpetuate them.

Shirley Jackson (1919–1965) was born in San Francisco and lived for many years in the small college town of Bennington, Vermont. Many of her works focus on abnormal events occurring in seemingly conventional settings.

The morning of June 27th was clear and sunny, with the fresh warmth of a full-summer day; the flowers were blossoming profusely and the grass was richly green. The people of the village began to gather in the square, between the post office and the bank, around ten o'clock; in some towns there were so many people that the lottery took two days and had to be started on June 26th, but in this village, where there were only about three hundred people, the whole lottery took less than two hours, so it could begin at ten o'clock in the morning and still be through in time to allow the villagers to get home for noon dinner.

The children assembled first, of course. School was recently over for the summer, and the feeling of liberty sat uneasily on most of them; they tended to gather together quietly for a while before they broke into boisterous play, and their talk was still of the classroom and the teacher, of books and reprimands. Bobby Martin had already stuffed his pockets full of stones, and the other boys soon followed his example, selecting the smoothest and roundest stones; Bobby and Harry Jones and Dickie Delacroix—the villagers pronounced his name "Delacroy"—eventually made a great pile of stones in one corner of the square and guarded it against the raids of the other boys. The girls stood aside, talking among themselves, looking over their shoulders at the boys, and very small children rolled in the dust or clung to the hands of their older brothers or sisters.

Soon the men began to gather, surveying their own children, speaking of planting and rain, tractors and taxes. They stood together, away from the pile of stones in the corner, and their jokes were quiet and they smiled rather than laughed. The women, wearing faded house dresses and sweaters, came shortly after their menfolk. They greeted one another and exchanged bits of gossip as they went to join their husbands. Soon the women, standing by their husbands, began to call to their children, and the children came reluctantly, having to be called four or five times. Bobby Martin ducked under his mother's grasping hand and ran, laughing, back to the pile of stones. His father spoke up sharply, and Bobby came quickly and took his place between his father and his oldest brother.

The lottery was conducted—as were the square dances, the teen-age club, the Halloween program—by Mr. Summers, who had time and energy to devote to civic activities. He was a round-faced, jovial man and he ran the coal business, and people were sorry for him, because he had no children and his wife was a scold. When he arrived in the square, carrying the black wooden box, there was a murmur of conversation among the villagers, and he waved and called, "Little late today, folks." The postmaster, Mr. Graves, followed him, carrying a three-legged stool, and the stool was put in the center of the square and Mr. Summers set the black box down on it. The villagers kept their distance, leaving a space between themselves and the stool, and when Mr. Summers said, "Some of you fellows want to give me a hand?" there was a hesitation before two men, Mr. Martin and his oldest son, Baxter, came forward to hold the box steady on the stool while Mr. Summers stirred up the papers inside it.

The original paraphernalia for the lottery had been lost long ago, and the black box now resting on the stool had been put into use even before Old Man Warner, the oldest man in town, was born. Mr. Summers spoke frequently to the villagers about making a new box, but no one liked to upset even as much tradition as was represented by the black box. There was a story that the present box had been made with some pieces of the box that had preceded it, the one that had been constructed when the first people settled down to make a village here. Every year, after the lottery, Mr. Summers began talking again about a new box, but every year the subject was allowed to fade off without anything's being done. The black box grew shabbier each year; by now it was no longer completely black but splintered badly along one side to show the original wood color, and in some places faded or stained.

Mr. Martin and his oldest son, Baxter, held the black box securely on the stool until Mr. Summers had stirred the papers thoroughly with his hand. Because so much of the ritual had been forgotten or discarded, Mr. Summers had been successful in having slips of papers substituted for the chips of wood that had been used for generations. Chips of wood, Mr. Summers had argued, had been all very well when the village was tiny, but now that the population was more than three hundred and likely to keep on growing, it was necessary to use something that would fit more easily into the black box. The night before the lottery, Mr. Summers and Mr. Graves made up the slips of paper and put them in the box, and it was then taken to the safe of Mr. Summers' coal company and locked up until Mr. Summers was ready to take it to the square next morning. The rest of the year, the box was put away, sometimes one place, sometimes another; it had spent one year in Mr. Graves's barn and another year underfoot in the post office, and sometimes it was set on a shelf in the Martin grocery and left there.

There was a great deal of fussing to be done before Mr. Summers declared the lottery open. There were the lists to make up—of heads of families, heads of households in each family, members of each household in each family. There was the proper swearing-in of Mr. Summers by the postmaster, as the official of the lottery; at one time, some people remembered, there had been a recital of some sort, performed by the official of the lottery, a perfunctory, tuneless chant that had been rattled off duly each year; some people believed that the official of the lottery used to stand just so when he said or sang it, others believed that he was supposed to walk among the people, but years and years ago this part of the ritual had been allowed to lapse. There had been, also, a ritual salute, which the official of the lottery had had to use in addressing each person who came up to draw from the box, but this also had changed with time, until now it was felt necessary only for the official to speak to each person approaching. Mr. Summers was very good at all this; in his clean white shirt and blue jeans, with one hand resting carelessly on the black box, he seemed very proper and important as he talked interminably to Mr. Graves and the Martins.

Just as Mr. Summers finally left off talking and turned to the assembled villagers, Mrs. Hutchinson came hurriedly along the path to the square, her sweater thrown over her shoulders, and slid into place in the back of the crowd. "Clean forgot what day it was," she said to Mrs. Delacroix, who stood next to her, and they both laughed softly. "Thought my old man was out back stacking wood," Mrs. Hutchinson went on, "and then I looked out the window and the kids were gone, and then I remembered it was the twenty-seventh and came a-running." She dried her hands on her apron, and Mrs. Delacroix said, "You're in time, though. They're still talking away up there."

Mrs. Hutchinson craned her neck to see through the crowd and found her husband and children standing near the front. She tapped Mrs. Delacroix on the arm as a farewell and began to make her way through the crowd. The people separated good-humoredly to let her through; two or three people said, in voices just loud enough to be heard across the crowd, "here comes your Missus, Hutchinson," and "Bill, she made it after all." Mrs. Hutchinson reached her husband, and Mr. Summers, who had been waiting, said cheerfully, "Thought we were going to have to get on without you, Tessie." Mrs. Hutchinson said, grinning, "Wouldn't have me leave m'dishes in the sink, now, would you, Joe?," and soft laughter ran through the crowd as the people stirred back into position after Mrs. Hutchinson's arrival.

"Well, now," Mr. Summers said soberly, "guess we better get started, get this over with, so's we can go back to work. Anybody ain't here?"

"Dunbar," several people said. "Dunbar, Dunbar."

Mr. Summers consulted his list. "Clyde Dunbar," he said. "That's right. He's broke his leg, hasn't he? Who's drawing for him?"

"Me, I guess," a woman said, and Mr. Summers turned to look at her. "Wife draws for her husband," Mr. Summers said. "Don't you have a grown boy to do it for you, Janey?" Although Mr. Summers and everyone else in the village knew the answer perfectly well, it was the business of the official of the lottery to ask such questions formally. Mr. Summers waited with an expression of polite interest while Mrs. Dunbar answered.

"Horace's not but sixteen yet," Mrs. Dunbar said regretfully. "Guess I gotta fill in for the old man this year."

"Right," Mr. Summers said. He made a note on the list he was holding. Then he asked, "Watson boy drawing this year?"

A tall boy in the crowd raised his hand. "Here," he said. "I'm drawing for m'mother and me." He blinked his eyes nervously and ducked his head as several voices in the crowd said things like "Good fellow, Jack," and "Glad to see your mother's got a man to do it."

"Well," Mr. Summers said, "guess that's everyone. Old Man Warner make it?"

"Here," a voice said, and Mr. Summers nodded.

A sudden hush fell on the crowd as Mr. Summers cleared his throat and looked at the list. "All ready?" he called, "Now, I'll read the names—heads of families first—and the men come up and take a paper out of the box. Keep the paper folded in your hand without looking at it until everyone has had a turn. Everything clear?"

The people had done it so many times that they only half listened to the directions; most of them were quiet, wetting their lips, not looking around. Then Mr. Summers raised one hand high and said, "Adams." A man disengaged himself from the crowd and came forward. "Hi, Steve," Mr. Summers said, and Mr. Adams said, "Hi, Joe." They grinned at one another humorously and nervously. Then Mr. Adams reached into the black box and took out a folded paper. He held it firmly by one corner as he turned and went hastily back to his place in the crowd, where he stood a little apart from his family, not looking down at his hand.

"Allen," Mr. Summers said. "Andrews. . . . Bentham."

"Seems like there's no time at all between lotteries any more," Mrs. Delacroix said to Mrs. Graves in the back row. "Seems like we got through with the last one only last week."

"Time sure goes fast," Mrs. Graves said.

"Clark. . . . Delacroix."

"There goes my old man," Mrs. Delacroix said. She held her breath while her husband went forward.

"Dunbar," Mr. Summers said, and Mrs. Dunbar went steadily to the box while one of the women said, "Go on, Janey," and another said, "There she goes."

"We're next," Mrs. Graves said. She watched while Mr. Graves came around from the side of the box, greeted Mr. Summers gravely, and selected a slip of paper from the box. By now, all through the crowd there were men holding the small folded papers in their large hands, turning them over and over nervously. Mrs. Dunbar and her two sons stood together, Mrs. Dunbar holding the slip of paper.

"Harburt. . . . Hutchinson."

"Get up there, Bill," Mrs. Hutchinson said, and the people near her laughed.

"Jones."

"They do say," Mr. Adams said to Old Man Warner, who stood next to him, "that over in the north village they're talking of giving up the lottery."

Old Man Warner snorted. "Pack of crazy fools," he said. "Listening to the young folks, nothing's good enough for *them*. Next thing you know, they'll be wanting to go back to living in caves, nobody work any more, live *that* way for a while. Used to be a saying about 'Lottery in June, corn be heavy soon.' First thing you know, we'd all be eating stewed chickweed and acorns. There's *always* been a lottery," he added petulantly. "Bad enough to see young Joe Summers up there joking with everybody."

"Some places have already quit lotteries," Mrs. Adams said.

"Nothing but trouble in *that*," Old Man Warner said stoutly. "Pack of young fools."

"Martin." And Bobby Martin watched his father go forward. "Over-dyke. . . . Percy."

"I wish they'd hurry," Mrs. Dunbar said to her older son. "I wish they'd hurry."

"They're almost through," he son said.

"You get ready to run tell Dad," Mrs. Dunbar said.

Mr. Summers called his own name and then stepped forward precisely and selected a slip from the box. Then he called, "Warner."

"Seventy-seventh year I been in the lottery," Old Man Warner said as he went through the crowd. "Seventy-seventh time."

"Watson." The tall boy came awkwardly through the crowd. Someone said, "Don't be nervous, Jack," and Mr. Summers said, "Take you time, son."

"Zanini."

After that, there was a long pause, a breathless pause, until Mr. Summers, holding his slip of paper in the air, said, "All right, fellows." For a minute, no one moved, and then all the slips of paper were opened. Suddenly, all women began to speak at once, saying, "Who is it?," "who's got it?," "Is it the Dunbars?," "Is it the Watsons?" Then the voices began to say, "It's Hutchinson. It's Bill." "Bill Hutchinson got it."

"Go tell your father," Mrs. Dunbar said to her older son.

People began to look around to see the Hutchinsons. Bill Hutchinson was standing quiet, staring down at the paper in his hand. Suddenly, Tessie Hutchinson shouted to Mr. Summers, "You didn't give him time enough to take any paper he wanted. I saw you. It wasn't fair."

"Be a good sport, Tessie," Mrs. Delacroix called, and Mrs. Graves said, "All of us took the same chance."

"Shut up, Tessie," Bill Hutchinson said.

"Well, everyone," Mr. Summers said, "that was done pretty fast, and now we've got to be hurrying a little more to get done in time." He consulted his next list. "Bill," he said, "you draw for the Hutchinson family. You got any other households in the Hutchinsons?"

"There's Don and Eva," Mrs. Hutchinson yelled. "Make *them* take their chance!"

"Daughters draw with their husbands' families, Tessie," Mr. Summers said gently. "You know that as well as anyone else."

"It wasn't *fair*," Tessie said.

"I guess not, Joe." Bill Hutchinson said regretfully. "My daughter draws with her husband's family, that's only fair. And I've got no other family except the kids."

"Then, as far as drawing for families is concerned, it's you," Mr. Summers said in explanation, "and as far as drawing for households is concerned, that's you, too. Right?"

"Right," Bill Hutchinson said.

"How many kids, Bill?" Mr. Summers asked formally.

"Three," Bill Hutchinson said. "There's Bill, Jr., and Nancy, and little Dave. And Tessie and me."

"All right, then," Mr. Summers said. "Harry, you got their tickets back?"

Mr. Graves nodded and held up the slips of paper. "Put them in the box, then," Mr. Summers directed. "Take Bill's and put it in."

"I think we ought to start over," Mrs. Hutchinson said, as quietly as she could. "I tell you it wasn't *fair*. You didn't give him time enough to choose. *Every*body saw that."

Mr. Graves had selected the five slips and put them in the box, and he dropped all the papers but those onto the ground, where the breeze caught them and lifted them off.

"Listen, everybody," Mrs. Hutchinson was saying to the people around her.

"Ready, Bill?" Mr. Summers asked, and Bill Hutchinson, with one quick glance around at his wife and children, nodded.

"Remember," Mr. Summers said, "take the slips and keep them folded until each person has taken one. Harry, you help little Dave." Mr. Graves took the hand of the little boy, who came willingly with him up to the box. "Take a paper out of the box, Davy," Mr. Summers said. Davy put his hand into the box and laughed. "Take just *one* paper," Mr. Summers said. "Harry, you hold it for him." Mr. Graves took the child's hand and removed the folded paper from the tight fist and held it while little Dave stood next to him and looked up at him wonderingly.

"Nancy next," Mr. Summers said. Nancy was twelve, and her school friends breathed heavily as she went forward, switching her skirt, and took a slip daintily from the box. "Bill, Jr.," Mr. Summers said, and Billy, his face red and his feet over-large, nearly knocked the box over as he got a paper out. "Tessie," Mr. Summers said. She hesitated for a minute, looking around defiantly, and then set her lips and went up to the box. She snatched a paper out and held it behind her.

"Bill," Mr. Summers said, and Bill Hutchinson reached into the box and felt around, bringing his hand out at last with the slip of paper in it.

The crowd was quiet. A girl whispered, "I hope it's not Nancy," and the sound of the whisper reached the edges of the crowd.

"It's not the way it used to be," Old Man Warner said clearly. "People ain't the way they used to be."

"All right," Mr. Summers said. "Open the papers. Harry, you open little Dave's."

Mr. Graves opened the slip of paper and there was a general sigh through the crowd as he held it up and everyone could see that it was blank. Nancy and Bill, Jr., opened theirs at the same time, and both beamed and laughed, turning around to the crowd and holding their slips of paper above their heads.

"Tessie," Mr. Summers said. There was a pause, and then Mr. Summers looked at Bill Hutchinson, and Bill unfolded his paper and showed it. It was blank.

"It's Tessie," Mr. Summers said, and his voice was hushed. "Show us her paper, Bill."

Bill Hutchinson went over to his wife and forced the slip of paper out of her hand. It had a black spot on it, the black spot Mr. Summers had made the night before with the heavy pencil in the coal-company office. Bill Hutchinson held it up, and there was a stir in the crowd.

"All right, folks," Mr. Summers said. "Let's finish quickly."

Although the villagers had forgotten the ritual and lost the original black box, they still remembered to use stones. The pile of stones the boys had made earlier was ready; there were stones on the ground with the blowing scraps of paper that had come out of the box. Mrs. Delacroix selected a stone so large she had to pick it up with both hands and turned to Mrs. Dunbar. "Come on," she said. "Hurry up."

Mrs. Dunbar had small stones in both hands, and she said, gasping for breath, "I can't run at all. You'll have to go ahead and I'll catch up with you."

The children had stones already, and someone gave little Davy Hutchinson a few pebbles.

Tessie Hutchinson was in the center of a cleared space by now, and she held her hands out desperately as the villagers moved in on her. "It isn't fair," she said. A stone hit her on the side of the head.

Old Man Warner was saying. "Come on, come on, everyone." Steve Adams was in the front of the crowd of villagers, with Mrs. Graves beside him.

"It isn't fair, it isn't right," Mrs. Hutchinson screamed, and then they were upon her.

◆ DISCUSSION QUESTIONS

1. The annual village lottery is referred to in the story as a ritual (paragraph 6). Does the lottery fit the definition of a ritual provided in reading 13.2, *How an Organization's Rites Reveal its Culture?* What purpose does the lottery

serve? How would you classify it according to Beyer and Trice's typology in Exhibit 3 of their article?

2. Beyer and Trice point out that people may interpret organizational rites as reflecting what management believes in, values, and finds acceptable. These authors argue that managers may promote organizational rites without being fully aware of them or their consequences. Managers may unwittingly convey messages through rites that are inconsistent with the culture they want to create in the organization. What does the lottery say about the culture of the village? Does the lottery fit with other aspects of the culture that you would expect in such a village? Evaluate the village culture based on the following information:
   (a) the tone of the story as conveyed by the words used and the details selected.
   (b) the behavior of the villagers toward each other.
   (c) the topics of conversation.
   (d) the villagers' attitudes toward the lottery.

3. List the procedures involved in running the lottery. What would happen if the procedure were streamlined, and people were simply selected alphabetically, or by age, every year? Think of an organizational example of a rite, and what would happen if it were stripped to the basics.

4. The narrator points out that the villagers had forgotten the origin of the lottery and many of the details of how it was to be conducted. Think of organizational examples that fit this pattern. Why are such practices perpetuated and followed unquestioningly?

5. The story is fictitious. Nevertheless, what organizational equivalents, albeit less horrific, are there to the lottery? What purpose do they serve? How should they be eliminated, and by whom? The lottery had been discontinued in other villages. What would it take to have it eliminated in this village?

6. What does the story suggest about the human capacity for good and evil? Examine in particular the behavior of characters such as Steve Adams, Old Man Warner, and Mrs. Hutchinson and her family.

Memoirs of a Cub

Herbert Hadad

This autobiographical essay describes what it was like to work as a copy boy at *The Boston Globe* newspaper in the 1950s. The author portrays the experience with fondness, and provides rich examples of the organizational culture and socialization processes at *The Globe*.

Herbert Hadad received his liberal arts degree in 1959 from Northeastern University. Through the university's co-operative education program he alternated course work with paid job assignments. In addition to his career as a reporter and writer, Mr. Hadad has been deputy press secretary for the Muskie for President campaign, speech writer for the founder of the children's television program, *Sesame Street,* and chief publicity writer for ABC news.

I never expected anything to come of the co-op job. None of us did that spring of 1955, no matter how interesting our advisers made them sound. Word was out on the freshman grapevine that Northeastern was just trying to find students to fill slots. Only engineering majors were getting jobs in their fields, and because liberal arts types never spoke to engineers, we couldn't even confirm that. The University offered me a choice: insurance clerk or copy boy—whatever that was—copy boy on the night shift.

I showed up at an ancient building in downtown Boston—what a dump!—took the elevator to five and entered a large, disorderly room. The ashtray was the floor. Cackles and shouts bounced off the walls. I asked for the person whose name I had been given. An earnest-looking, unsmiling man appeared and told me the hours were bad and the job had no future. "I'll take it," I said. "You'll work 4:30 until 12:30 in the morning. You'll get Tuesday and Wednesday off. And make sure you arrive on time," he said to me. "Yes, Sir," I answered briskly. He gave me a suspicious look. He seemed to know I would never call him "sir" again.

What the man didn't see behind my eagerness was that I was forced into taking the position by fear of the alternative. It was reasonable for a co-op adviser with a limited range of jobs to offer to place an economics major in a big insurance company. John Hancock was located in one of the most modern buildings in one of the most fashionable parts of the city. But a job there would have been the start of a lifetime of being asked how I came to study economics.

Source: Herbert Hadad, "Memoirs of a Cub," *Northeastern University Magazine*, November, 1990, Vol. 16, No. 2, pp. 11–15. Reprinted by permission of the publisher.

I didn't have an answer. My children ask me now. I still don't know. They've learned that the question puts me in a bad mood.

In addition, the job was a terrible fit for my swaggering if wobbly teenage self-image. Insurance sounded like one long, dismal shuffle to oblivion. Remember, in the movies, how Woody Allen was punished for robbing banks by confinement with a chattering insurance salesman? I don't know what happened to the Northeastern students who took the John Hancock jobs. I suspect some of them are millionaires today summering at Wellfleet.

I showed up early on the appointed afternoon at the building on lower Washington Street that seemed to defy condemnation. I wondered what were the odds of surviving in that place five nights a week for an entire summer. Outside, pressmen in overalls and paper hats copied headlines from a fresh newspaper to a blackboard. The street buzzed with movement and excitement. Gentlemen wearing straw boaters and carrying leather satchels paused to read the latest news posted on the wall. When a woman passed, they tipped their hats. I entered, arrived at the City Room, and began my career at *The Boston Globe.*

I was one of five new copy boys hired that summer. The others were Paul Felt, a veteran with an enigmatic smile that suggested vast worldly experience; Harold Crowley, an unusually agreeable boy who smoked a pipe and sometimes stuttered; Robert Szulkin, a refugee from the war with a wonderful sense of the ridiculous; and Louis Bell, a hypochondriac. Bell believed he contracted every disease featured on a weekly television medical show. He never called in sick. Instead, he brought the illness to work, where no one could convince him his sickness was fanciful. The only cure was the show itself, which led him to exchange one weekly disease for the next.

Coming from the Northeastern "campus," as the Quadrangle was laughingly called in those days, the newspaper was a strange place. A political reporter trying to dodge an especially obsequious politician—having asked everyone to say he was out—was certain to get the phone call. "Hello," a voice said. "This is Senator McGillicuddy and I'm happy to have this opportunity to explain my new legislative package." All around the room jaws grew taut with suppressed laughter. Then the explosion came, as the squirming reporter looked up to see his colleague playing the senator. As he did, someone else administered a hotfoot by lighting a match tucked into his instep. Not knowing what to make of it, I took all of this in.

When the reporters spotted a couple making love in an adjacent office building, someone tracked down the telephone number and dialed. The whole City Room watched as the phone rang and the pair leaped off a desk. "Hello?" said a puzzled voice. "God is watching you," the caller answered. I wondered about the couple for a long time. I bet they fled home and mystified their families and neighbors by resuming regular worship habits.

Yet I noticed that the same men who enjoyed these pranks seemed to take their profession of reporting the news with a gravity that bordered on reverence. Would I want to be one of them one day? It seemed most unlikely.

"No one leaves a staff job at the *Globe,*" we'd been informed. "No one's been hired in five years. No one may be hired in the next 10." We'd been told in a quieter tone, "They don't want Northeastern boys. If a reporter is ever hired, he'll be from Harvard."

Although Northeastern students were welcomed as copy boys, the newspaper, whose upper management was Ivy League, harbored misgivings that it might develop a "Northeastern bias." Not even a college degree, if it was from Northeastern, was enough to land a full-time job there. The idea of being discriminated against because of my university was upsetting, and somewhere inside of me was planted the idea of beating the system simply because the system was wrong.

In 1955, the newspaper, like the country, was undergoing a fundamental change. The era was disappearing when an ambitious youngster could sign on with a firm, serve an apprenticeship, and establish himself in a career. Many of the men in the City Room were ruffians in disguise, street wise but often poorly educated in the formal sense, yet perfectly suited by temperament to cover the daily news. They were to be the last of their breed.

The only figure lower than a copy boy when I arrived was the occasional mouse that skittered across the floor. We were told to sit on an extra metal desk ready to sprint to the first person who hollered, "Copy!" The boy in the wire room ran from one chattering machine to the next, ripping off the news dispatches and delivering them to the appropriate editors. Lagging was impossible, for each story carried the time of transmission. An insistent bell that signalled the wire service was sending a bulletin made the job all the more manic.

Yet even a copy boy's pitiful status carried a modicum of prestige. Unless a boy was entirely obnoxious in his habits or appearance, he was, after a fashion, welcomed into the City Room brotherhood. Some reporters and editors even asked us what we wanted to do when our copy-boy days were over. Even those of us who might have entertained the notion didn't have the audacity to say, "We want to be one of you."

The permanence of the staff was no myth. Many of the reporters looked like old men wearing even older felt hats. Some of the editors looked like a collection of grandfathers. No copy boy that I ever met even thought of becoming an editor—the reporters had all the good times. A reporter who had also become a lawyer refused to give up his newspaper job. We began to feel he was holding onto a position meant for someone new. We wouldn't dare invite him to leave, but perhaps he sensed our resentment. He was a thin man with a bald pate, and every time I passed him, he stared at my black, curly hair and said, "Why don't you get a haircut."

One editor on the copy desk, a tall, emaciated-looking man in a dark suit with a calabash pipe fixed in his mouth, looked so old that someone had posted on his locker, "He fought at Shiloh." When he yelled "Copy!" we moved with extra dispatch, afraid we would be held responsible for his cardiac arrest.

The stories around the City Room were endless. I remember the night when a reporter who had been drinking on his dinner break became very emotional, his shoulders heaving as he said he feared his family life was collapsing. His colleagues held him and spoke soothing words. I had never seen a collection of tough men act so tenderly toward another. I slipped into the bathroom, and when I was certain I was alone, I cried. I wasn't sure why. I saw that reporter at a press conference 15 years later. He stopped what he was doing, walked over, and threw his arms around me. That night had been important to him too.

There was only one woman on the entire floor. Frances Burns, a medical writer. She moved her desk around the corner. When she smiled, it was the gleam of an older sister who had to tolerate the high jinks of a gang of frisky kid brothers.

The ringmaster of this human circus was Alexander J. Haviland, the city editor. He commanded respect and won affection without apparent effort, but I soon saw that he wouldn't tolerate slipshod reporting or writing and would call onto the carpet any reporter suspected of either. As a result, he was both loved and feared. He was of medium height and slim, almost bald and bespectacled, yet extremely handsome. We heard he was a bachelor who lived in a house with a sister in a small town outside of Boston. (No one used the word "suburb" then.) He wore a tweed suit, the jacket of which he removed while presiding over the city desk. He insisted on being called "Al." Invited to call the great Mr. Haviland by his first name, I would never again call the chief copy boy "sir," even though he was an earnest adult with a wife.

Al never seemed to be away from the City Room, spending time at City Hall or the State House or holding clandestine meetings with news sources, activities I imagined necessary to get the good stories. Yet he seemed to know twice as much about the news as his best reporters. I never figured out how he did it. Al, sharpened pencil in hand, went over the story word for word, explaining inconsistencies, suggesting more concise words, challenging interpretations. When it was over, the reporter said, "Thank you, Al," and Al invariably answered, "Not at all."

I watched and listened from my perch on the metal desk. "Not at all," I repeated. What a gracious expression! I began to use it. I use it now, years after Al's death.

"Copy!" one of the gruff editors shouted. Copy! was my first, middle, and last name. "Cream no sugar. And tonight, not tomorrow!" I fetched it from a Howard Johnson's across the street. Placing the coffee on his desk, I expected to be ignored. "Not at all, Harold," I said.

"Copy!" shouted another, flailing the air with a sheaf of papers. I raced about 20 feet, rolled the paper into a cylinder, and tapped it into the pneumatic pipeline for its voyage to the composing room one floor overhead. "Not at all, Warren," I whispered close to his head.

One of the gruffest editors was an assistant to Al, a large, square-jawed man with rimless glasses and a smile that could turn quickly into a snarl. He looked like a humorless priest and he frightened people, but I wasn't the least bit unnerved: I learned from one of the reporters that when he took his wife to the train so she could attend a religious retreat, he ran down the platform, arms outstretched, sobbing like a baby.

It was he who gave me my first "special assignment": making coffee in the house urn, a chore that carried an extra dollar per night. He was a fervent believer that good coffee couldn't be made from the hot tap. It could be made *faster* with hot water, but he convinced me that if I tricked him, he would assign me to hell. "Cold water only," he warned solemnly. People wonder what menial tasks such as making coffee have to do with co-op training. I didn't know it then, but the answer is "a lot" if you were making coffee for those characters in the City Room.

What was drawing me into the business, I realized after some time on the job, was even more compelling than the threat of having to wrestle with economic theory or being turned into an insurance clerk. I was being lured by the increasingly irresistible appeal of the City Room itself. I loved the joy and anarchy that seemed to sprout there with the most meager encouragement. I enjoyed how grown men, men with wives and families, had fun there. I admired that they laughed aloud, played their pranks, swapped jokes and insults, talked with cheerful iconoclasm of the great people of the day, took pleasure in exposing pretense.

"Herbie, you're studying economics, have you decided what you want to be?" my father asked over dinner on one of my nights off. He had been trained as an accountant shortly after arriving in America from the Middle East. My father is a brilliant man, the speaker of almost a dozen languages, but he remained as befuddled as I over the practical applications of economics. I remember staring into the bowl of large purple olives between us. His question made me confess my infatuation. "Dad, I'm going to become a newspaperman," I said.

I returned to the same co-op job twice a year for four years, simultaneously trying to jettison my economics major and take more journalism and English courses. Northeastern was agreeable to the shift, but there was no major in journalism. So my second education commenced in the City Room as my interest in the profession was noticed.

"Write the lead sentence as clearly and as tightly as you can," Al told me one night. "Work on it hard and the rest of the story will fall right into place." It seemed unlikely, no more than an ancient epigram, but I did as instructed. And he was right. When I served for a time as a copy boy for the afternoon paper, Alfred J. Monahan, the day city editor, let his signature cigarette ash fall to his white shirt as he lectured, "The lead on a news story must be a maximum of 16 words, not a word more." I sometimes found this impossible, but it must have sunk in. (The first sentence on this story is 10.)

The reporters added their wisdom. One reached into his breast pocket, removed a few sheets of paper folded into three panels, and pointed to the scribbles on them. I could tell he had been doing this for years. It was as much a part of his ritual as stopping for a beer on the way back from covering a story. "Get the quotes right. The quotes must be absolutely accurate," he said. "The rest of the story you can remember."

Boston at that time had not yet launched into its late-20th century renaissance. The people of the West End were still resisting the bulldozers. A young man could slip into the Old Howard or Casino theaters to enjoy the pleasures of burlesque. The Southeast Expressway existed on a drawing board, if at all. Faneuil Hall was merely Faneuil Hall. It was still a few years before the pile-driving machines moved into the Back Bay rail yards, pounding rhythmically into the ground, and the Prudential Center rose from the ruins. In Copley Square, S.S. Pierce sold quality provisions on Huntington Avenue across the street from the Boston Public Library. Adventurous Northeastern students could find jazz and excitement in the clubs of Columbus Avenue, Boston's Harlem. John F. Kennedy was a United States Senator with a charming wife.

The town, like most towns, was safer then. I lived with my family in an apartment in a racially mixed neighborhood on the Roxbury-Dorchester border called Grove Hall. (No one who lived there knew how it got the name, it containing neither grove nor hall.) Every night I left the newspaper, walked up Washington Street to the subway, and rode on an almost empty train to Dudley Street, where I waited for the trackless trolley to take me the rest of the way home.

I went back to the neighborhood this year with my nine-year-old daughter, Sara. The area showed the wear of shifting populations and the passage of time. Everything looked smaller. It looked like a place in the process of renewal after hostilities. Sara was kind. The worst she said was, "Some buildings could really use a coat of paint." "A lot happened. There was anger here, and it was replaced by hope," I told her. "How do you know?" she asked. "Because my old apartment building has been spruced up. It looks as good as ever. And the firehouse is exactly the same," I said.

It wasn't truly the same, though. The steel shutter over the front doors was new. And around the corner, the pool and billiard room was gone. Unlike a lot of my friends and my younger brother, Alvin, I was not attracted to it as a youth. I thought at the time there was something wrong with me, some genetic deficiency. But I didn't get excited by baseball or Ted Williams either. My father had once taken me to a Red Sox doubleheader and I squirmed most of the afternoon.

Also gone from Grove Hall was the drug store. It had been turned into a diner. It wasn't a hang-out type of drug store, but it was important to me because the assistant druggist had the same last name as I. We were of different religions, brought up in different parts of the city, but I considered him a tie to my ancestry, a brother. He was handsome and gentle and soft-spoken. "You seem like you ought to be a priest," I once told him. "My parents felt the same way," he said, closing the subject.

We copy boys started to go out after work. We drank beers, and on fragrant July nights, we greeted the sunrise bleary-eyed and talked-out at Carson Beach in South Boston or Wollaston Beach in Quincy.

One couldn't be a reporter without certain gear. I went over to Raymond's on Franklin Street—"Where U Bot the Hat" was their slogan—and bought a Panama. I began to smoke cigarettes, as most of the men did, grooming my tough reporter's image long before I was anybody's reporter. I learned how to flip a lighted cigarette into the air and catch it by the cool end in my mouth.

But the Camels and Lucky Strikes were too strong, so I switched to cigars and a pipe. The tobacco was purchased in little packets scooped out of large canisters from Perkins, on Tremont Street. The cigars, known as Rum-Soaked Crooks for their sweet taste and bend in the middle, were available at an Italian smoke shop on Hanover Street in the North End. A more innocuous vice was peanuts. They came roasted from a hot copper box outside a bar on Canal Street. One took the nuts and left the change in a little wooden bowl.

Canal was only a block from Friend Street, where I quietly began to pursue a second career decidedly outside the stewardship of the university. To the consternation of my parents and the amusement of the newspaper reporters, I was training to be a prizefighter. On a typical day, I did morning road work in Franklin Park, boxed afternoons in the Friend Street Gym, then walked to work at the *Globe*. On the night of my first fight, at a stadium near Logan Airport, I was too self-conscious to tell the *Globe* I was fighting (what if I lost?). So I called in sick. I won a three-round fight on a decision. In the locker room afterwards, the promoter gave me $25. The loser got $15.

When I returned to work the next night, the chief copy boy gave me a peculiar greeting: "We're docking you a night's pay." That was a lot of money since the entire week's pay was only about $32. The secret was out. A staff photographer had covered the bouts and returned to the City Room with news of a battling copy boy. I was a momentary celebrity, but I already knew better than to take that status too seriously. I was also upset with the photographer, not because he blew the whistle on me but because he neglected to take a picture of my triumph.

One night shortly later Al summoned me to his desk. "Get to the Parker House. There's a fire alarm in." I began to gush a thank you for this unprecedented opportunity, but his look told me to shut up and run.

I raced across Washington Street and up School Street to the hotel. I saw no smoke or flames or people hanging out of windows. There was no fire apparatus in sight or sounds of sirens. I ran in the side entrance. There was no commotion among the staff.

"I'm here from *The Boston Globe* to cover the fire," I told the clerk at the front desk. He looked dumbfounded. "Get the manager!" I said. I was afraid I might fall over with excitement, but I had to stay cool. The manager appeared and I told him of my mission.

"Yes, an alarm was turned in," he admitted, "but it was inadvertent. One of our guests, perhaps one who had overindulged, pulled an alarm in the hallway in the belief he was summoning room service." I asked him to lead me to the scene. I looked it over. Everything seemed in order, and the manager seemed truthful, so I telephoned a report back to Al. He must have known by then from the fire telegraph system that was monitored in the City Room that the Parker House fire was merely a false alarm. But he said six of the most important words I have ever heard. "Good work. Come on home, son."

My time as a copy boy was coming to an end, and I began to hope for the impossible. I began to hope the *Globe* would truly become my home by giving me a job on the reporting staff. But the information given four years earlier was correct. There would be nothing.

Another ambitious boy arrived from Northeastern, and he too despaired of ever joining the staff. A reporter had given me a silver Fire Department badge that allowed the bearer to cross fire lines. I cherished it and carried it in my wallet at all times. I unpinned it and gave it to him. "Carry this. You'll *feel* like a reporter," I said. Robert J. Anglin did become a reporter and then a City Editor. He was a complex and passionate man. He was a moral nuisance. He became a teacher and an inspiration to aspiring newspaper people for more than 25 years. To me he was also—to use his favorite word—a pal. The *Globe* wrote a column about him when he died.

I walked out in 1959 with a letter of recommendation from one of the senior reporters, Frank P. Harris. The letter said I had "unquestioned integrity." It was far too valuable to send to a prospective employer. I have it in a scrapbook.

The *Globe* built a modern plant on Morrissey Boulevard in Dorchester. I went into the wilds of western New Hampshire to complete my apprenticeship when the *Globe* called and said to return to a job on the reporting staff. So, ultimately, the co-op job provided not only a future, but a way of life. On my co-op job I learned how to write for a newspaper. I learned it was essential to be kind and tender as well as honest and tough. I learned the value of friendship and the folly of vanity. I've held several jobs since, none of which has yet led to a criminal record. And every place I've been, from New Hampshire to Boston, from Washington to New York, I've used the same early lessons of that work experience.

A feeling imposed itself recently, more than three decades after I first entered the ramshackle building on Washington Street. The feeling arrived with a curious force, and it lingered. It was this: had I been able to stay on at the old *Globe,* smiling good evening to Al, greeting my friends and heroes in the City Room and beginning the night's adventures, I would have been happy to show up there every night for the rest of my life.

♦ DISCUSSION QUESTIONS

1. Describe the working conditions at *The Boston Globe* as depicted in this story. What do they suggest about how newspaper reporters viewed their jobs? How have conditions changed? What might be the impact of contemporary working conditions on reporters' attitudes and work behaviors?

2. Herbert Hadad says he never intended to be a reporter. Discuss how the socialization process [1] at *The Boston Globe* influenced him to change his mind. Examine the role models he had and the informal norms that shaped his attitudes. How does this informal process differ from formal training programs?

3. The city editor, Alexander J. Haviland, was described as both loved and

feared by *Globe* employees. Is this a good combination? Refer to reading 14.1 *An Interview with Niccolò Machiavelli,* which discusses these characteristics.

4. Evaluate the way the city editor treated the young copy boy. Why did Hadad say that the editor's words, "Good work. Come on home, son," were "six of the most important words I have ever heard"? What does this incident say about the city editor's leadership style?

5. Identify the rites at *The Globe* according to the typology presented in reading 13.2 *How an Organization's Rites Reveal its Culture.* How effective are rites in shaping attitudes and behaviors at *The Globe?*

6. Organizational culture is often transmitted through stories and anecdotes that are passed down over the years [2]. Which of the stories and anecdotes described in this essay do you think became lore at *The Globe?* What do they reveal about the organizational culture?

◆   REFERENCES

1. Hebden, J.E. Summer 1986. Adopting an organization's culture: The socialization of graduate trainees. *Organizational Dynamics* 54–72.

2. Martin, J. 1982. "Stories and Scripts in Organizational Settings." *In* A. Hastorf and A. Isen eds. *Cognitive Social Psychology.* New York: Elsevier 255–303.

SECTION 13
Management Readings

On the Folly of Rewarding A, While Hoping for B

Steven Kerr

This reading provides examples of misguided rewards that actually reward undesirable behavior but fail to reward desired behavior. The author discusses the consequences of such practices and suggests reasons for their occurrence.

Steven Kerr is a professor of management at the University of Southern California. He is a former president of the Academy of Management.

Whether dealing with monkeys, rats, or human beings, it is hardly controversial to state that most organisms seek information concerning what activities are rewarded, and then seek to do (or at least pretend to do) those things, often to the virtual exclusion of activities not rewarded. The extent to which this occurs of course will depend on the perceived attractiveness of the rewards offered, but neither operant nor expectancy theorists would quarrel with the essence of this notion.

Nevertheless, numerous examples exist of reward systems that are fouled up in that behaviors which are rewarded are those which the rewarder is trying to *discourage,* while the behavior he desires is not being rewarded at all.

In an effort to understand and explain this phenomenon, this paper presents examples from society, from organizations in general, and from profit making firms in particular. Data are examined to demonstrate the consequences of such reward systems for the organizations involved, and possible reasons why such reward systems continue to exist are considered.

Source: Excerpted from Steven Kerr, "On the Folly of Rewarding A, While Hoping for B," *Academy of Management Journal,* 1975, Vol. 18, No. 4, pp. 769–783. Reprinted by permission of the author and the publisher.

◆   *SOCIETAL EXAMPLES*

Politics

Official goals are "purposely vague and general and do not indicate . . . the host of decisions that must be made among alternative ways of achieving official goals and the priority of multiple goals. . ." [1]. They usually may be relied on to offend absolutely no one, and in this sense can be considered high acceptance, low quality goals. An example might be "build better schools." Operative goals are higher in quality but lower in acceptance, since they specify where the money will come from, what alternative goals will be ignored, etc.

The American citizenry supposedly wants its candidates for public office to set forth operative goals, making their proposed programs "perfectly clear," specifying sources and uses of funds, etc. However, since operative goals are lower in acceptance, and since aspirants to public office need acceptance (from at least 50.1 percent of the people), most politicians prefer to speak only of official goals, at least until after the election. They of course would agree to speak at the operative level if "punished" for not doing so. The electorate could do this by refusing to support candidates who do not speak at the operative level.

Instead, however, the American voter typically punishes (withholds support from) candidates who frankly discuss where the money will come from, rewards politicians who speak only of official goals, but hopes that candidates (despite the reward system) will discuss the issues operatively. It is academic whether it was moral for Nixon, for example, to refuse to discuss his 1968 "secret plan" to end the Vietnam war, his 1972 operative goals concerning the lifting of price controls, the reshuffling of his cabinet, etc. The point is that the reward system made such refusal rational.

It seems worth mentioning that no manuscript can adequately define what is "moral" and what is not. However, examination of costs and benefits, combined with knowledge of what motivates a particular individual, often will suffice to determine what for him is "rational."* If the reward system is so designed that it is irrational to be moral, this does not necessarily mean that immorality will result. But is this not asking for trouble?

Medicine

Theoretically, a physician can make either of two types of error, and intuitively one seems as bad as the other. A doctor can pronounce a patient sick when he is actually well, thus causing him needless anxiety and expense, curtailment of enjoyable foods and activities, and even physical danger by subjecting him to needless medication and surgery. Alternatively, a doctor can label a sick

---

*In [2] Simon's (pp. 76–77) terms, a decision is "subjectively rational" if it maximizes an individual's valued outcomes so far as his knowledge permits. A decision is "personally rational" if it is oriented toward the individual's goals.

person well, and thus avoid treating what may be a serious, even fatal ailment. It might be natural to conclude that physicians seek to minimize both types of error.

Such a conclusion would be wrong.* It is estimated that numerous Americans are presently afflicted with iatrogenic (physician *caused*) illnesses [3]. This occurs when the doctor is approached by someone complaining of a few stray symptoms. The doctor classifies and organizes these symptoms, gives them a name, and obligingly tells the patient what further symptoms may be expected. This information often acts as a self-fulfilling prophecy, with the result that from that day on the patient for all practical purposes is sick.

Why does this happen? Why are physicians so reluctant to sustain a type 2 error (pronouncing a sick person well) that they will tolerate many type 1 errors? Again, a look at the reward system is needed. The punishments for a type 2 error are real: guilt, embarrassment, and the threat of lawsuit and scandal. On the other hand, a type 1 error (labeling a well person sick) "is sometimes seen as sound clinical practice, indicating a healthy conservative approach to medicine" [3]. Type 1 errors also are likely to generate increased income and a stream of steady customers who, being well in a limited physiological sense, will not embarrass the doctor by dying abruptly.

Fellow physicians and the general public therefore are really *rewarding* type 1 errors and at the same time *hoping* fervently that doctors will try not to make them.

♦ **GENERAL ORGANIZATIONAL EXAMPLES**

Rehabilitation Centers and Orphanages

In terms of the prime beneficiary classification [4] organizations such as these are supposed to exist for the "public-in-contact," that is, clients. The orphanage therefore theoretically is interested in placing as many children as possible in good homes. However, often orphanages surround themselves with so many rules concerning adoption that it is nearly impossible to pry a child out of the place. Orphanages may deny adoption unless the applicants are a married couple, both of the same religion as the child, without history of emotional or vocational instability, with a specified minimum income, and a private room for the child, etc.

If the primary goal is to place children in good homes, then the rules ought to constitute means toward that goal. Goal displacement results when these "means become ends-in-themselves that displace the original goals" [4].

To some extent these rules are required by law. But the influence of the reward system on the orphanage's management should not be ignored. Consider, for example, that the:

---

*In one study of 14,867 films for signs of tuberculosis, 1,216 positive readings turned out to be clinically negative; only 24 negative readings proved clinically active, a ratio of 50 to 1.

1. Number of children enrolled often is the most important determinant of the size of the allocated budget.
2. Number of children under the director's care also will affect the size of his staff.
3. Total organizational size will determine largely the director's prestige at the annual conventions, in the community, etc.

Therefore, to the extent that staff size, total budget, and personal prestige are valued by the orphanage's executive personnel, it becomes rational for them to make it difficult for children to be adopted. After all, who wants to be the director of the smallest orphanage in the state?

If the reward system errs in the opposite direction, paying off only for placements, extensive goal displacement again is likely to result. A common example of vocational rehabilitation in many states, for example, consists of placing someone in a job for which he has little interest and few qualifications, for two months or so, and then "rehabilitating" him again in another position. Such behavior is quite consistent with the prevailing reward system, which pays off for the number of individuals placed in any position for 60 days or more. Rehabilitation counselors also confess to competing with one another to place relatively skilled clients, sometimes ignoring persons with few skills who would be harder to place. Extensively disabled clients find that counselors often prefer to work with those whose disabilities are less severe.*

Universities

Society *hopes* that teachers will not neglect their teaching responsibilities but *rewards* them almost entirely for research and publications. This is most true at the large and prestigious universities. Cliches such as "good research and good teaching go together" notwithstanding, professors often find that they must choose between teaching and research oriented activities when allocating their time. Rewards for good teaching usually are limited to outstanding teacher awards, which are given to only a small percentage of good teachers and which usually bestow little money and fleeting prestige. Punishments for poor teaching also are rare.

Rewards for research and publications, on the other hand, and punishments for failure to accomplish these, are commonly administered by universities at which teachers are employed. Furthermore, publication oriented resumés usually will be well received at other universities, whereas teaching credentials, harder to document and quantify, are much less transferable. Consequently it is rational for university teachers to concentrate on research, even if to the detriment of teaching and at the expense of their students.

By the same token, it is rational for students to act based upon the goal displacement which has occurred within universities concerning what they are rewarded for. If it is assumed that a primary goal of a university is to transfer

*Personal interviews conducted during 1972–1973.

knowledge from teacher to student, then grades become identifiable as a means toward the goal, serving as motivational, control, and feedback devices to expedite the knowledge transfer. Instead, however, the grades themselves have become much more important for entrance to graduate school, successful employment, tuition refunds, parental respect, etc., than the knowledge or lack of knowledge they are supposed to signify.

It therefore should come as no surprise that information has surfaced in recent years concerning fraternity files for examinations, term paper writing services, organized cheating at the service academies, and the like. Such activities constitute a personally rational response to a reward system which pays off for grades rather than knowledge.

◆ BUSINESS RELATED EXAMPLES

Ecology

Assume that the president of XYZ Corporation is confronted with the following alternatives:

1. Spend $11 million for antipollution equipment to keep from poisoning fish in the river adjacent to the plant; or
2. Do nothing, in violation of the law, and assume a one in ten chance of being caught, with a resultant $1 million fine plus the necessity of buying the equipment.

Under this not unrealistic set of choices it requires no linear program to determine that XYZ Corporation can maximize its probabilities by flouting the law. Add the fact that XYZ's president is probably being rewarded (by creditors, stockholders, and other salient parts of his task environment) according to criteria totally unrelated to the number of fish poisoned, and his probable cause of action becomes clear.

Evaluation of Training

It is axiomatic that those who care about a firm's well-being should insist that the organization get fair value for its expenditures. Yet it is commonly known that firms seldom bother to evaluate a new GRID, MBO, job enrichment program, or whatever, to see if the company is getting its money's worth. Why? Certainly it is not because people have not pointed out that this situation exists; numerous practitioner oriented articles are written each year to just this point.

The individuals (whether in personnel, manpower planning, or wherever) who normally would be responsible for conducting such evaluations are the same ones often charged with introducing the change effort in the first place. Having convinced top management to spend the money, they usually are quite animated afterwards in collecting rigorous vignettes and anecdotes about how successful the program was. The last thing many desire is a formal, systematic, and revealing evaluation. Although members of top management may actually *hope* for such systematic evaluation, their reward systems continue to *reward* ignorance in this area. And if the personnel department abdicates its responsibility, who is to step into the breach? The change agent himself? Hardly! He is likely to be too busy collecting anecdotal "evidence" of his own, for use with his next client.

Miscellaneous

Many additional examples could be cited of systems which in fact are rewarding behaviors other than those supposedly desired by the rewarder. A few of these are described briefly below.

Most coaches disdain to discuss individual accomplishments, preferring to speak of teamwork, proper attitude, and a one-for-all spirit. Usually, however, rewards are distributed according to individual performance. The college basketball player who feeds his teammates instead of shooting will not compile impressive scoring statistics and is less likely to be drafted by the pros. The ballplayer who hits to right field to advance the runners will win neither the batting nor home run titles, and will be offered smaller raises. It therefore is rational for players to think of themselves first, and the team second.

In business organizations where rewards are dispensed for unit performance or for individual goals achieved, without regard for overall effectiveness, similar attitudes often are observed. Under most Management by Objectives (MBO) systems, goals in areas where quantification is difficult often go unspecified. The organization therefore often is in a position where it *hopes* for employee effort in the areas of team building, interpersonal relations, creativity, etc., but it formally *rewards* none of these. In cases where promotions and raises are formally tied to MBO, the system itself contains a paradox in that it "asks employees to set challenging, risky goals, only to face smaller paychecks and possibly damaged careers if these goals are not accomplished" [5].

It is *hoped* that administrators will pay attention to long run costs and opportunities and will institute programs which will bear fruit later on. However, many organizational reward systems pay off for short run sales and earnings only. Under such circumstances it is personally rational for officials to sacrifice long term growth and profit (by selling off equipment and property, or by stifling research and development) for short term advantages. This probably is most pertinent in the public sector, with the result that many public officials are unwilling to implement programs which will not show benefits by election time.

As a final, clear-cut example of a fouled-up reward system, consider the cost-plus contract or its next of kin, the allocation of next year's budget as a direct function of this year's expenditures. It probably is conceivable that those who award such budgets and contracts really hope for economy and prudence in spending. It is obvious, however, that adopting the proverb "to him who spends shall more be given," rewards not economy, but spending itself.

◆   CAUSES

Four general factors may be pertinent to an explanation of why fouled up reward systems seem to be so prevalent.

Fascination with an "Objective" Criterion

It has been mentioned elsewhere that:

Most "objective" measures of productivity are objective only in that their subjective elements are a) determined in advance, rather than coming into play at the time of the formal evaluation, and b) well concealed on the rating instrument itself. Thus industrial firms seeking to devise objective rating systems first decide, in an arbitrary manner, what dimensions are to be rated, . . . usually including some items having little to do with organizational effectiveness while excluding others that do. Only then does Personnel Division churn out official-looking documents on which all dimensions chosen to be rated are assigned point values, categories, or whatever [6].

Nonetheless, many individuals seek to establish simple, quantifiable standards against which to measure and reward performance. Such efforts may be successful in highly predictable areas within an organization, but are likely to cause goal displacement when applied anywhere else. Overconcern with number of people placed in the vocational rehabilitation division may have been largely responsible for the problems described in that organization.

Overemphasis on Highly Visible Behaviors

Difficulties often stem from the fact that some parts of the task are highly visible while other parts are not. For example, publications are easier to demonstrate than teaching, and scoring baskets and hitting home runs are more readily observable than feeding teammates and advancing base runners. Similarly, the adverse consequences of pronouncing a sick person well are more visible than those sustained by labeling a well person sick. Team-building and creativity are other examples of behaviors which may not be rewarded simply because they are hard to observe.

Hypocrisy

In some of the instances described the rewarder may have been getting the desired behavior, notwithstanding claims that the behavior was not desired. This may explain politicians' unwillingness to revise the penalties for disobedience of ecology laws, and the failure of top management to devise reward systems which would cause systematic evaluation of training and development programs.

Emphasis on Morality or Equity Rather than Efficiency

Sometimes consideration of other factors prevents the establishment of a system which rewards behaviors desired by the rewarder. The felt obligation of many Americans to vote for one candidate or another, for example, may impair their ability to withhold support from politicians who refuse to discuss the issues. Similarly, the concern for spreading the risks and costs of wartime military service may outweigh the advantage to be obtained by committing personnel to combat until the war is over.

It should be noted that only with respect to the first two causes are reward systems really paying off for other than desired behaviors. In the case of the third and fourth causes the system *is* rewarding behaviors desired by the rewarder, and the systems are fouled up only from the standpoints of those who believe the rewarder's public statements (cause 3), or those who seek to maximize efficiency rather than other outcomes (cause 4).

♦   CONCLUSIONS

Modern organization theory requires a recognition that the members of organizations and society possess divergent goals and motives. It therefore is unlikely that managers and their subordinates will seek the same outcomes. Three possible remedies for this potential problem are suggested.

Selection

It is theoretically possible for organizations to employ only those individuals whose goals and motives are wholly consonant with those of management. In such cases the same behaviors judged by subordinates to be rational would be perceived by management as desirable. State-of-the-art reviews of selection techniques, however, provide scant grounds for hope that such an approach would be successful [7].

Training

Another theoretical alternative is for the organization to admit those employees whose goals are not consonant with those of management and then, through training, socialization, or whatever, alter employee goals to make them consonant. However, research on the effectiveness of such training programs, though limited, provides further grounds for pessimism [8].

Altering the Reward System

What would have been the result if:

1. Nixon had been assured by his advisors that he could not win reelection except by discussing the issues in detail?
2. Physicians' conduct was subjected to regular examination by review boards for type 1 errors (calling healthy people ill) and to penalties (fines, censure, etc.) for errors of either type?

3. The President of XYZ Corporation had to choose between (a) spending $11 million dollars for antipollution equipment, and (b) incurring a fifty-fifty chance of going to jail for five years?

Managers who complain that their workers are not motivated might do well to consider the possibility that they have installed reward systems which are paying off for behaviors other than those they are seeking. This is what regularly frustrates societal efforts to bring about honest politicians, civic-minded managers, etc.

A first step for such managers might be to find out what behaviors currently are being rewarded. Perhaps an instrument similar to that used in the manufacturing firm could be useful for this purpose. Chances are excellent that these managers will be surprised by what they find—that their firms are not rewarding what they assume they are. In fact, such undesirable behavior by organizational members as they have observed may be explained largely by the reward systems in use.

This is not to say that all organizational behavior is determined by formal rewards and punishments. Certainly it is true that in the absence of formal reinforcement some soldiers will be patriotic, some presidents will be ecology minded, and some orphanage directors will care about children. The point, however, is that in such cases the rewarder is not *causing* the behaviors desired but is only a fortunate bystander. For an organization to *act* upon its members, the formal reward system should positively reinforce desired behaviors, not constitute an obstacle to be overcome.

It might be wise to underscore the obvious fact that there is nothing really new in what has been said. In both theory and practice these matters have been mentioned before. Thus in many states Good Samaritan laws have been installed to protect doctors who stop to assist a stricken motorist. In states without such laws it is commonplace for doctors to refuse to stop, for fear of involvement in a subsequent lawsuit. In college basketball additional penalties have been instituted against players who foul their opponents deliberately. It has long been argued by Milton Friedman and others that penalties should be altered so as to make it irrational to disobey the ecology laws, and so on.

By altering the reward system the organization escapes the necessity of selecting only desirable people or of trying to alter undesirable ones. In Skinnerian terms [9], "As for responsibility and goodness—as commonly defined—no one . . . would want or need them. They refer to a man's behaving well despite the absence of positive reinforcement that is obviously sufficient to explain it. Where such reinforcement exists, 'no one needs goodness.' "

♦ REFERENCES

1. Perrow, C. 1969. The Analysis of Goals in Complex Organizations. *In* A. Etzioni, ed. *Readings on Modern Organizations.* Englewood Cliffs, N.J.: Prentice-Hall.

2. Simon, H.A. 1957. *Administrative Behavior.* New York: Free Press.

3. Scheff, T.J. 1965. Decision Rules, Types of Error, and Their Consequences in Medical Diagnosis. *In* F. Massarik and P. Ratoosh, eds. *Mathematical Explorations in Behavioral Science.* Homewood, Ill.: Irwin.

4. Blau, P.M., and Scott, W.R. 1962. *Formal Organizations.* San Francisco: Chandler.

5. Kerr, S. 1973. Some Modifications in MBO as an OD Strategy. *Academy of Management Proceedings.* 39–42.

6. Kerr, S. 1973. What Price Objectivity? *American Sociologist.* 8:92–93.

7. Webster, E. 1964. *Decision Making in the Employment Interview.* Montreal: Industrial Relations Center, McGill University.

8. Fiedler, F.E. 1972. Predicting the Effects of Leadership Training and Experience from the Contingency Model. *Journal of Applied Psychology,* 56:114–119.

9. Swanson, G.E. 1972. Review Symposium: Beyond Freedom and Dignity. *American Journal of Sociology.* 78:702–705.

How an Organization's Rites Reveal its Culture

Janice M. Beyer ♦ *Harrison M. Trice*

This reading presents a typology of six rites that can be found in organizations. The authors provide vivid examples of each rite and discuss how rites provide a rich outcropping of organizational culture.

Janice M. Beyer is the Rebecca L. Gale Regents Professor in Business at the University of Texas at Austin, and the 1990 president of the Academy of Management. Harrison M. Trice is professor of organizational behavior at the School of Industrial Relations, Cornell University. They are currently preparing a book on organizational culture.

♦ *RITES AS OUTCROPPINGS OF CULTURE*

A rite is a relatively elaborate, dramatic, planned set of activities that combines various forms of cultural expressions and that often has both practical and expressive consequences.

This article deals primarily with organizational rites because, in performing the activities of a rite, people generally use other cultural forms—certain customary language, gestures, ritualized behaviors, artifacts, settings, and other symbols—to heighten the expression of shared understandings appropriate to the occasion. These shared understandings are also frequently conveyed through myths, sagas, legends, or other stories associated with the occasion. Thus rites provide a richer outcropping of cultural understanding than do single cultural forms.

In addition, we focus on rites because they are tangible, accessible, and visible. Identifying the meanings they carry, however, requires interpretive skills not ordinarily taught in business schools or used by practicing managers. We believe, however, that experienced managers are familiar enough with the organizational context to make a working interpretation of organizational rites. We also believe that many managers can learn to interpret their organizations' rites and that the insights they gain in the process will be useful for the enlightened managing and changing of their organizations' cultures.

However, the most important reason for focusing on organizational rites

Source: Excerpted by permission of publisher, from *Organizational Dynamics*, Spring/1987 © 1987. American Management Association, New York. All rights reserved.

is that many managers conduct or sponsor them without being fully aware of it. Many practical managerial activities also act as cultural rites that are interpreted by employees and others as reflecting what management believes in, values, and finds acceptable. Unless expressive consequences are considered, both the activities chosen and the ways of carrying them out may inadvertently convey cultural messages that are consistent with the desired culture.

For example, corporate drug-testing programs that administer reliable tests on an involuntary, random basis might, practically speaking, be very effective in locating drug users, but such "efficient" programs could undermine existing corporate cultures and thus be disastrous in expressive terms. They carry the unmistakable message that all employees are under suspicion; they also cost a lot of money. Thus many managements have decided to employ drug testing only in cases where drug abuse is a suspected cause of poor work performance and to link such testing to employee assistance programs designed to help confirmed abusers rehabilitate themselves. The latter type of program may be relatively "inefficient" in locating drug users in practical terms, but it will probably be effective in expressive terms because it is more consistent with most corporate cultures and with the general values of U.S. workers.

Managers must become sensitive to the possible expressive consequences of their activities; moreover, they must modify those activities to remove culturally inconsistent elements. This is the only way they can ensure that strong cultural messages are being sent about what their organizations stand for. Managers who understand the duality of their actions will be better able to make those actions effective in both practical and cultural terms.

♦   THE SOCIAL CONSEQUENCES OF RITES

Human actions have both practical and expressive consequences at the same time; moreover, people tend to be more aware of some of these consequences than they are of others. Some of the consequences are evident; others may be hidden. As Exhibit 1 shows, a common rite such as training new managers can have four kinds of consequences. In the terminology of cultural anthropology, this program was a rite of passage—a rite whose main cultural function is to ease the transition of people who are moving from one social status to another.

Our research on organizational life suggested that there are other sets of common activities that function as cultural rites but that have different expressive consequences. By comparing anthropological accounts of tribal societies with management writers' descriptions of life in modern organizations, we were able to identify five other common rites that had distinctly different expressive consequences; they are presented in Exhibit 2.

Rites of Passage

In his book *Rites of Passage* (Emil Mourry, 1909), the Dutch scholar Arnold Van Gennep mentioned similarities in many different tribal societies in

E X H I B I T 1

Examples of Four Types of Social Consequences of Rites for Training New Managers

Practical Consequences

Evident   A thorough evaluation of candidates' potential and improvement in their administrative skills so that only the best qualified candidates are promoted to management positions.

Hidden   The relative priorities placed on various areas of performance in the company are communicated and enforced; members of management who act as trainers sharpen and reinforce their own skills; new and old managers size up one another's strengths and weaknesses.

Expressive Consequences

Evident   The transformation of the successful candidate's social identity among people both within and outside of the organization.

Hidden   The enhancement of the prestige of the managerial role within the company; the motivation of nonmanagement personnel to perform according to priorities; the development of social and emotional bonds among managers.

customary behaviors that accompany universal and unavoidable events: pregnancy and childbirth, the onset of sexual maturity, betrothal and marriage, and death. Because such events create marked changes in status for the individuals involved, Van Gennep called their attendant customary behaviors "rites of passage." He grouped these behaviors into three distinct consecutive subsets, which he called rites of separation, rites of transition, and rites of incorporation. The apparently intended consequence of these rites was to restore equilibrium in social relations that had been disturbed by an individual's transition from one social status to another.

Thomas Rohlen observed in his book *For Harmony and Strength: Japanese White Collar Organizations in Anthropological Perspective* (University of California Press, 1974) that managerial trainees in the Japanese banking industry go through intensive rites of passage. Rohlen reported that similar in-company training rites are employed by as many as one-third of all medium-to-large Japanese companies, with apparently successful consequences in terms of employee productivity and commitment. The training he observed at the Uedagin Bank illustrates how elaborate the sequence of events can be. In the rite of separation, trainees and their parents were invited to an entrance ceremony, during which the president of the bank gave a speech congratulating the parents on raising such fine children and reassuring the trainees and their families that taking this job would be like joining a large family that takes good care of its members. The presence of current trainees in uniform, the prominent display of the company logo, the singing of the company song—all symbolized the cohesiveness and continuity of the trainees' new "family."

E X H I B I T   2

A Typology of Rites by Their Evident, Expressive Social Consequences

TYPES OF RITES	EXAMPLE	EVIDENT EXPRESSIVE CONSEQUENCES	EXAMPLES OF POSSIBLE HIDDEN EXPRESSIVE CONSEQUENCES
Rites of passage	Training in Japanese banks	Facilitate transition of persons into social roles and statuses that are new for them.	Minimize changes in ways people carry out social roles. Reestablish equilibrium in ongoing social relations.
Rites of degradation	Firing and replacing top executive	Dissolve social identities and their power.	Publicly acknowledge that problems exist and discuss their details. Defend group boundaries by redefining who belongs and who doesn't. Reaffirm social importance and value of role involved.
Rites of enhancement	Mary Kay seminars	Enhance social identities and their power.	Spread good news about the organization. Provide public recognition of individuals for their accomplishments; motivate others to similar efforts. Enable organizations to take some credit for individual accomplishments. Emphasize social value of performance of social roles.

Rites of renewal	Organizational development activities	Refurbish social structures and improve their functioning.	Reassure members that something is being done about problems. Disguise nature of problems. Defer acknowledgment of problems. Focus attention toward some problems and away from others. Legitimize and reinforce existing systems of power and authority.
Rites of conflict reduction	Collective bargaining	Reduce conflict and aggression.	Deflect attention away from solving problems. Compartmentalize conflict and its disruptive effects. Reestablish equilibrium in disturbed social relations.
Rites of integration	Office Christmas party	Encourage and revive common feelings that bind members together and commit them to a social system.	Permit venting of emotion and temporary loosening of various norms. Reassert and reaffirm, by contrast, moral rightness of usual norms.

The next step in the training program was the successful completion of several rites of transition, each demanding that the trainees submit to new ordeals. The first rite was a two-day trip to a nearby army camp where the trainees were subjected to some of the rigors of basic training; marching under the direction of a sergeant and sweating their way over obstacle courses, they wore castoff army fatigues that symbolized their shared lowly status. They were told that a large company required order and discipline and that military training was the best way to teach these qualities—and they accepted this explanation. They were also taken periodically to a Zen temple for a two-day session in meditation and other Zen practices. At the temple they were subjected to a strict regimen that included eating tasteless gruel and meticulously observing a whole series of rituals.

Perhaps the most arduous ordeal of all was a 25-mile marathon walk held at the end of the training. Trainees were told to walk the first 9 miles together in a single body, the next 9 in designated groups, and the last 7 alone and in silence. Past trainees monitored their conformity to the rules and tempted them with cold drinks, which they were not allowed to accept. The first phase, walking and talking together, was relatively pleasant. During the second phase, intergroup competition emerged, leading the trainees to escalate their pace even though competition had not been encouraged. The result was that many trainees could not stand the pace and had to drop out. The final phase was very painful and difficult, but the trainees who finished took great personal pride in that accomplishment. Rohlen suggests that the marathon walk taught the values of perseverance, self-denial, and rejection of competition as the route to collective accomplishment.

In addition to these ordeals, the trainees were expected to achieve practical expertise; they studied bank operations and pursued a variety of other scheduled activities. Rohlen reports that every day except Sunday was filled with 14 hours of supervised activity. Unfortunately, he did not describe the final phase of these rites—the rite in which the employees were incorporated into the bank.

The rites in the Japanese bank are both powerful and elaborate. They illustrate what rites of passage could be, not what they are currently like in U.S. corporations. Typical U.S. corporate training programs seem pale and ineffectual by comparison.

Powerful, extensive rites of passage do, however, exist in U.S. worklife. They ease the entry into risky occupations such as law enforcement, firefighting, and mining, but they generally occur in educational institutions or through informal socialization by fellow workers on the job rather than in internal management-sponsored programs. Thus managers have little impact on these potent occupational rites in the United States. In the absence of comparable organization-based rites and other cultural forms, U.S. workers often form stronger allegiances to their occupations than they do to their work organizations—an outcome that may be neither desirable nor inevitable.

Rites of Degradation

In his article "Conditions of Successful Degradation Ceremonies" (*American Sociological Review*, March 1956), the sociologist Harold Garfinkel named the next type of rite the degradation ceremony. A vivid example of this rite can be found in a ceremonial practice of the Ashanti, a tribal society in central Ghana in West Africa. The Ashanti chief was placed on an ancestral stool as part of his installment into office; if the tribe decided that it no longer wanted him to be chief, he was "destooled." His sandals were removed so that he had to walk barefoot, and he was placed on the ancestral stool, which was then withdrawn from under him so that his buttocks bumped on the ground. In this way he was reduced to being a commoner.

The procedures used in the rites of degradation that sometimes accompany the removal of high-status officials in modern organizations rarely inflict physical pain, but they can be just as humiliating as the experience of the Ashanti chief. As in rites of passage, the events in rites of degradation seem to fall into stages. First, other organizational members focus attention on the person to be degraded and publicly associate his or her behavior with organizational problems and failures. An important part of this initial stage is the language used by these other organizational members—language that Michael Moch has called "degradation talk" or "chewing ass." Moch observed a production manager being repeatedly degraded by his plant manager's references to difficulties in his private life and by the plant manager's attribution of various problems to the production manager's failures.

Second, the individual is discredited by some supposedly objective report. In the firing of chief executives, consultants are often hired to produce data and analyses documenting that certain detected problems are associated with the CEO. The consultants' status as outsiders and the credentials they possess symbolize their supposed objectivity; their activities are actually rituals designed to produce a necessary artifact—a report that demonstrates to all the erroneous decisions made by those to be deposed.

Third, the person is publicly removed from his or her position. Military organizations provide a telling example: the dramatic cashiering and "drumming out" of officers from the U.S. Marine Corps and similar ceremonies in the other services. Businesses often skip the ceremony and take abrupt action; in one company, some managers came in Monday morning and found that all their furniture, plants, and pictures had been removed over the weekend. At Apple Computer, on the other hand, the recent removal of cofounder Steven Jobs was painfully drawn out. After months of tension and conflict, President John Sculley, backed by the board of directors, first removed Jobs's remaining operating authority as head of the Macintosh Division, then moved his office across the street, and finally announced to the press that there was no role for Jobs in the future of the firm.

In the final step of rites of degradation, a successor is chosen, often with such ceremonial activities as search committees, an extensive search for and wooing of candidates, and the expenditure of much time and effort—all of which symbolize the importance of the position involved.

The evident intended consequences of rites of degradation are to dissolve the social status and associated power of those persons who are subjected to the degradation. In corporations and other modern organizations, these rites occur relatively infrequently; they are usually reserved for the removal of relatively high-status or otherwise influential members. However, with the current rash of hostile takeovers and other mergers, such rites are likely to occur more frequently. Some hidden consequences can be detected from our examples: These rites provide a way to publicly acknowledge problems and to discuss their details; group boundaries are defended by redefining which individuals belong to groups and which do not; and the importance and social value of the role involved are reaffirmed. Of course, the most important practical consequence is that the no-longer-desired leader is forced to leave a position of power.

Rites of Enhancement

We have given the name "rites of enhancement" to ceremonial activities that enhance the personal status and social identities of organizational members. The U.S. presidential inauguration ceremony is one well-known example of rites of enhancement. Other examples include the ceremonious conferral of knighthood in England, the awarding of Nobel prizes to scientists and statesmen in Sweden, and the Oscar and Emmy awards given to U.S. motion picture and television performers.

The Mary Kay Cosmetics Company may provide the best-known examples of the corporate use of rites of enhancement. The plethora of awards and titles given by this company to its high-performing members is clearly intended to enhance the identities of those who receive them. During elaborate meetings called Mary Kay seminars, gold and diamond pins, fur stoles, and the use of pink Cadillacs are awarded to saleswomen who achieve sales quotas. The awards are presented in a setting reminiscent of Miss America pageants; they are held in a large auditorium, on a stage in front of a large, cheering audience, with all the participants dressed in glamorous evening clothes.

Underlying this dramatic rite is the story of how Mary Kay's determination and optimism enabled her to overcome personal hardships and to found her own company. The company's bee-shaped pin is a symbol of Mary Kay's optimistic belief that with help and encouragement everyone can "find their wings and fly." The pink Cadillac is clearly a symbol of exalted status, since Mary Kay herself drives one.

Other corporate examples abound: the awarding of bronze stars at Addison-Wesley Publishing, the "You Want It When?" award at Versatec, special jackets at Diamond International, and so forth. Most companies have some type of award; however, few are bestowed as ceremoniously as the awards at the Mary Kay seminars. All awards are intended to realize the practical consequence of rewarding desired behaviors so that these behaviors will be repeated and emulated by other employees.

These examples also illustrate a hidden expressive consequence of rites of enhancement, a consequence that is diametrically opposed to the consequence of degradation ceremonies: Rites of enhancement spread good news about the organization. Besides providing public recognition of individual accomplishments that all members benefit from, these rites enable the organization to take some share of the credit for these accomplishments. Another hidden consequence of other familiar examples of rites of enhancement, such as the conferral of tenure in academia or the accession of persons to office in associations in general, is the affirmation of the importance of that social role's performance for the organization.

Rites of Renewal

This type of rite includes a variety of elaborate activities intended to strengthen existing social structures and thus improve their functioning. Examples include most organization development (OD) activities: management-by-objectives (MBO) programs, job redesign, team building, quality-of-worklife programs, quality circles, and so forth. These activities tend to fine-tune rather than to fundamentally change organizational systems; they are based on a combination of humanistic and scientific values. For example, team building is justified by the belief that there is a family-life bond within work groups that can be used for the company's benefit. Job design is justified by scientific findings showing that workers' feelings are affected by the nature of their work and by the belief that making constructive changes in that work will result in higher productivity.

Most OD programs use certain standardized sets of techniques; such techniques are rituals in the sense that few have been demonstrated to have intended, practical effects. Team building efforts typically involve a sequence of rituals. The consultant begins by interviewing participants to generate themes for discussion. These interviews are followed by group discussions in which the participants rank and examine problems and then attempt to find and work on solutions and devise steps to realize them. A more extensive intervention called Grid Organization Development has six specific phases, usually lasts for three to five years, and is built around an artifact called the managerial grid, a rather simple two-dimensional scheme for representing the practices of individual managers. Other artifacts commonly used in OD activities include questionnaires and inventories, organizational charts and other diagrams, blackboards and flip charts, and closed-circuit television systems. A large vocabulary of specialized language, including words like "feedback," "behavior mod," and "confrontation," is used by the initiated to describe these activities.

To label these OD activities as rites of renewal is not to deny that they sometimes have important practical consequences. We are suggesting, however, that they seldom drastically alter existing organizations and that many of their important consequences are symbolic and expressive. Some of the possible hidden consequences of such rites of renewal include reassuring members that something is being done about problems, disguising the nature of real problems, deferring the problems' acknowledgment, and focusing attention toward some problems and away from others. In addition, rites of renewal generally reinforce the existing power systems that form the basis for the renewed social arrangements.

Rites of Conflict Reduction

A variety of features in organizational life—hierarchies of formal authority, social stratification, division of labor, differential power and resources of age groups, and all sorts of other differences between persons—tend to produce pervasive conflict and aggressive behavior. Some of the conflicts produced are so pervasive that they give rise to subcultures and even countercultures. Because this kind of conflict and the accompanying aggression are disruptive and potentially damaging to social life, people develop rites to reduce conflicts.

A. R. Radcliffe-Brown's descriptions of the peace-making ceremonies of the North Andamen Islanders in his book *The Andamen Islanders* (New York Free Press, 1964) provide a vivid example. In these ceremonies, dancers from two contending factions mingled randomly to form two groups, each new group consisting of about equal numbers from each faction. One group of dancers then gave outlet to their feelings of aggression by violently shaking the members of the other party. In response, members of the other group showed complete passivity, expressing neither fear nor resentment. In this manner collective anger was appeased, wrongs were forgiven, and peace was temporarily restored.

A familiar example of a rite developed to reduce conflict in modern work organizations is collective bargaining. This rite often begins when union and management present each other with a long, widely divergent list of demands and proposals. Each side prepares these artifacts (1) to disguise its real position and to prepare to explore problems causing conflict and (2) to reassure constituents and other observers that specific complaints will be considered. The lists also symbolically evoke the myth that this rite involves bargaining between equals, as does the setting in which the rites take place. Buried somewhere in the profusion of demands are the realistic outcomes expected by both sides. Both sets of bargainers may have a good idea what the final settlement will be, but union members and many segments of management do not have such inside knowledge. To demonstrate resistance to "unfair" demands to constituents, numerous ritualized "false fights" take place; these fights sometimes last late into the night, symbolizing the tough resistance each side is making to the demands of the other. In reality, these fights involve considerable informal cooperation. For example, when the parties are getting close to tacit agreement, a union representative may become openly hostile, threaten to walk out, and start to leave the bargaining table. Members of management will calm that person down, speak of possible compromises, point to troublesome areas where cooperation is emerging, and generally attempt in ritualistic ways to reduce the union representative's ritualistically generated anger.

Another common conflict-reduction rite in modern organizations is the committee. Organizations form joint labor-management committees, affirmative action committees, and so forth. Widely practiced rituals such as agendas, minutes, and motions provide accepted ways for these committees to proceed. Committees do not need to make substantive changes in order to reduce conflict because their very existence and their activities symbolize the organization's willingness to cope with problems and discontent. The mere holdings of meetings with local managers helped a new manager of General Motors' Chevrolet Division to reduce the fears and hostilities of local managers. In similar ways, the activities of university ombudsmen, committees on judicial ethics in the American Bar Association, consumer affairs departments in retail stores, and faculty senates help to mollify hostile parties.

Conflict-reduction rites often include other important symbols. As taking action symbolizes authorities' willingness to cope with problems, encouraging participation symbolizes their willingness to pay attention to the complaints and ideas of the participants. The settings and procedures used symbolize how far authorities are willing to go in recognizing the claims of participants. Membership alone puts members on a symbolically equal footing. Many techniques such as brainstorming, nominal groups, and the delphi procedure have been developed to facilitate participation from all committee members. Most of the techniques utilize some method that ensures equal participation, and the meetings take place in settings that are designed to symbolize equality. All these symbols help committees realize their major expressive consequences: to minimize and at least temporarily smooth over differences that cause conflict. At a practical level, committees often realize agreement and cooperation in the process.

However, these rites also have a variety of hidden expressive consequences. One such consequence is to divert attention from solving the problems that generated the conflict. Other consequences include containing the conflict and reestablishing social relations that have been disrupted by it.

Rites of Integration

As organizations and other social systems grow larger, they differentiate internally into subgroups. The major evident expressive consequence of rites of integration is the revival of shared feelings that unite subgroups and commit them to the larger system by increasing their interaction. Such ceremonials are consequently very inclusive and public. The mix of participants is especially important; its integrative effects will depend on how successfully a particular rite incorporates members of diverse subgroups. Most large organizations (and all societies) have many rites of integration.

As their businesses grow, exceptional managers seem to recognize the need for rites of integration. One of the many lessons Tom Watson learned from John

H. Patterson, the long-term president of the National Cash Register Company, was the value of bringing far-flung sales staff together for conventions. As Thomas and Maria Belden observed in their book *The Lengthening Shadow: The Life of Thomas J. Watson* (Little, Brown, and Company, 1962), "There were conventions for all of the company salesmen at which bands played, flags flew in the gusty Ohio winds, and men were exhorted to work and to love their work and to know how to work." These conventions not only gave the salesmen valuable information about selling, they "unified the far-flung company, bound it into a family with the factory serving as home and the officers as the center of loyalty. The sales convention was Patterson's . . . way of maintaining unity as the NCR stretched to the far corners of the country, of keeping a small-company spirit along with big-company organization and dividends."

After World War II, when International Business Machines had grown into "gray shapelessness," Watson developed similar but more encompassing rites of integration to unify both field and factory personnel. Huge conventions were held in an elaborate tent city constructed on thirty acres near the IBM factory at Endicott, New York. Paved streets ran between the tents, and terraces planted with flowers surrounded them. Meetings were held in a Barnum and Bailey circus tent. There were many ceremonial events: the group picture, tours of the factory, awards, songs of praise, and visits by distinguished guests. By 1950, however, even with the "tent flaps raised, there was no longer room for the swelling ranks of the company." Thereafter, regional meetings were held and the color and inclusiveness of the Endicott meetings faded. Many companies, of course, have annual conventions of their salespeople; the contents of such rites reflect the cultures of the companies involved.

Christmas parties and annual picnics are other common examples of rites of integration that occur in many organizations. During these rites, managers and nonmanagerial employees interact in settings and activities that lessen the social distance between them. Eating, talking, and drinking together symbolize shared values favoring equality and community. The use of alcohol lowers inhibitions, permitting less guarded interactions than are usual among persons of divergent status. Participants may engage in patting, backslapping, hugging, kissing, and other gestures of affection and approval rarely used in regular work settings. Under such circumstances, they may achieve a temporary sense of closeness. At Christmas parties, some of the rituals and artifacts associated with the Christmas legend are usually included, such as the Christmas tree, traditional food and drink, and the exchange of gifts, often distributed by someone dressed as Santa Claus. Annual picnics often involve ritualized games (like a softball game between different work units or statuses) that act out conflicts from the work setting.

Work-related social gatherings that serve as rites of integration have perhaps the fewest practical consequences of any set of rites; they come closest to being purely cultural or expressive occasions. Even at these events, however, practical matters are often discussed and other business is conducted. Thus while practical consequences are not essential to these rites, they occur nonetheless, making even company parties a mixture of the practical and the expressive.

The annual meetings of corporate boards of directors and of the governing boards of nonprofit organizations provide other examples of rites of integration. These meetings act and preserve the myth of the effective influence of such constituencies. Reports are given by management, tough and embarrassing questions are asked and ritualistically responded to, and votes are taken according to well-established rites. However, the major consequence is expressive: Members of potentially disparate groups are united to voice concern for the prosperity and continuity of the organizations involved.

◆   THE PRACTICAL IMPLICATIONS OF RITES

This analysis is intended as a first step in understanding rites and ceremonials as outcroppings of organizational culture. The six types we have identified are important, widespread, and frequent occurrences in corporations and other organizations. Our types are intended to help managers and other analysts think about these familiar events in new ways and call their attention to important occurrences that they might otherwise have overlooked. Like all pure types, our types will not fit the observed instances perfectly, but they provide useful yard-sticks against which observed events can be compared and assessed. In particular, some events may be a mixture of more than one type of rite. We do not believe that our list of types is exhaustive; it is merely a reasonable starting point for further refinements and additions.

Managing Cultures

Because they communicate and affirm taken-for-granted shared under-standings of an organization's culture, the six types of rites also provide entry points for managing and changing organizational cultures. At the most basic level, managers must learn to assess not only the technical consequences of their own activities and the activities of those they supervise, but also their possible expressive consequences as rites. Managers must know whether the ceremonial, expressive side of their programs reinforces or undermines desired, existing cultural values and beliefs. Because of their intended technical consequences, organizational rites are unfortunately often designed and carried out by technical experts who are unaware of their expressive side. Managers who are less involved with technical details may be better able to detect and assess the cultural messages carried by company programs. Practical, culturally effective alternatives can usually be chosen and implemented.

In addition, research has shown that such familiar activities as training, recruitment and selection, and program evaluation may have expressive consequences that are more important than their technical ones. For example, one study found that the desired technical effects of management training (changes in knowledge and performance) were minimal compared with expressive effects that significantly reduced anxiety about organizational change. In another example, a program evaluation study was responsible not only for goals clarification (an intended technical consequence) but also for generating further negotiation and compromise between subcultures (an expressive conflict-reducing outcome). Managers who are insensitive to the valuable expressive consequences of these rites might discontinue them on technical grounds, thereby unwittingly losing their expressive benefits. Only by becoming sensitive to such expressive consequences of their activities and programs can managers adequately evaluate and manage all aspects of them.

Because rites are important activities in any organization, managers also need to learn and practice ceremonial skills. Some flair for the dramatic and the expressive in speech and action are clear assets for conducting effective rites. For managerial roles with many ceremonial duties, these skills probably should be among the stated qualifications.

Managers must also realize that because rites help maintain the continuity of cultural systems, they may impede organizational adaptability. Managers must consequently pay close attention to managing organizational rites so that they do not dampen or divert change efforts. Existing rites can have unintended, even deleterious consequences for planned change, and may thus need to be modified or supplanted as part of change efforts. Managers should therefore learn how to gauge the extent of both the desired and undesired consequences of rites. An effective manager will be able to make and use such assessments to continue, modify, or terminate ceremonial organizational activities.

One caveat is in order, however: Because rites arise so frequently and universally in human societies, managers probably will not be able to suppress popular rites whenever they want. A better strategy may be to try to "domesticate" such rites—to shape their practice and manage their occurrence so that their conservative consequences can be minimized.

Managers who wish to cultivate change must think creatively in order to modify existing rites or to invent new ones to express new ideas and values. In the process, they will need to find ways to build upon the old rites, for no organization is likely to welcome the wholesale alteration of its culture. Managers will encounter less resistance if they understand and appreciate the existing culture before they try to change it, and then use that understanding and appreciation to affirm and reinforce the direction of the desired change. New beliefs and values can be expressed by adding new forms or changing those used in current popular rites; some of the meanings conveyed by existing rites could be changed simply by changing one or two elements, such as the setting and the performers. For example, the cultural meaning of an internal appeals committee might be changed by moving its deliberations away from the general manager's office to a location on the plant floor, or by including fellow employees as well as members of management in those deliberations. In like manner, the cultural meanings of existing rites of passage could be changed by incorporating previously neglected stories about the organization and its early heroes that reflect desired beliefs and values.

As managers begin to evaluate their activities as rites, they will find that some of these rites are ineffective as cultural forms. Desired cultural values will be absent or compromised to the extent that they convey no consistent messages about the desired culture. In such instances, managers will need to decide whether to create new, more vigorous rites or to try to revive tired old ones. New cultural forms can be added to try to invigorate old rites, but managers may find the gradual replacement of such rites more effective. They should avoid immediate substitutions for or drastic overhauls of such rites; even tired ceremonies may have residual sentiments attached to them, and management may awaken resentment if it callously eliminates them. For example, a new bank president who had tried to reinvigorate a formal company dinner as a meaningful rite of integration felt he was unsuccessful. Instead of recommending that he discontinue the dinner, a consultant suggested that he try instituting a picnic or other informal social event, as well as other activities that would help people lose their awareness of differences in status. If the picnic becomes popular and works better as a rite of integration, he can gradually try again to modify the dinner, or perhaps allow it to wither away by gradually withdrawing financial support.

The cultural forms needed to modify existing rites are occasionally already present in organizational subcultures. If such elements can be incorporated, the modified rites may be more acceptable to the organization's members than rites that are entirely new. As we suggested to the bank manager, managers can also invent and establish new rites that express values consonant with the direction of desired change. If the new rites are successful, the old rites that express old values may lose their appeal and wither away. Rites of passage and enhancement are good places to begin; rites of integration and conflict reduction should be useful in dealing with conflicts that emerge during the change. Rites of degradation are problematic because they provoke resentment and make people feel insecure, but they may be necessary in instances that require drastic change. Existing rites of renewal are dangerous; they should be used only to effect minor cultural change and should be avoided when major change is desired.

♦   *SELECTED BIBLIOGRAPHY*

Readers interested in additional, in-depth examinations of rites and ceremonials in the workplace can find them described in detail in Harrison M. Trice, "Rites and Ceremonials in Organizational Cultures" in *Research in the Sociology of Organizations*, Vol. 4, edited by Sam Bachrach (JAI Press, 1985); in Harrison M. Trice and Janice M. Beyer, "Studying Organizational Cultures through Rites and Ceremonials" (*Academy of Management Review*, October 1984) and in Harrison M. Trice, James Belasco, and Joseph Alutto, "The Role of Ceremonials in Organizational Behavior" (*Industrial and Labor Relations Review*, October 1969).

For a discussion of the twins of "do" and "say" in human actions, see Edmund R. Leach's article "Ritual" in *International Encyclopedia of the Social Sciences,* Vol. 13 (Free Press, 1968). For a definitive statement of manifest and latent consequences, see Robert K. Merton, "The Unintended Consequences of Purposive Social Action" (*American Sociological Review,* December 1936). A fascinating account of rites and ceremonials in a Japanese organization may be found in Thomas P. Rohlen's article "Spiritual Education in a Japanese Bank" (*American Anthropologist,* October 1974) and in his book *For Harmony and Strength: A Japanese White Collar Organization in Anthropological Perspective* (University of California Press, 1974). On the American scene, the following pieces are strongly recommended: Stanley G. Harris and Robert I. Sutton, "Functions of Parting Ceremonies in Dying Organizations" (*Academy of Management Journal,* March 1986) and Albert A. Blum, "Collective Bargaining: Ritual or Reality" (*Harvard Business Review,* November–December 1961). The accounts of events at International Business Machines and the quotations used come from Thomas Graham Belden and Maria Robins Belden, *The Lengthening Shadow: The Life of Thomas J. Watson,* (Little, Brown, and Company, 1962). For a good example of a company picnic as a rite of integration, see R. Richard Ritti and G. Ray Funkhauser, *The Ropes to Skip and the Ropes to Know: Studies in Organizational Behavior* (Grid, 1977); for a dramatic description of a rite of degradation, see N. W. Biggart, "The Creative-Destructive Process of Organizational Change: The Case of the Post Office" (*Administrative Science Quarterly,* September 1977); and for an applied approach to the role of rites in changing cultures, Harrison M. Trice and Janice M. Beyer, "Using Six Organizational Rites to Change Culture" in Ralph H. Kilmann, Mary J. Saxton, and Roy Serpa (Eds.), *Gaining Control of the Corporate Culture* (Jossey Bass, 1985). A very real application to routine worklife can be found in Helen Schwartzman's study of the ubiquitous meeting, "The Meeting as a Neglected Form in Organizational Studies" in Barry M. Staw and L. L. Cummings (Eds.), *Research in Organizational Behavior,* Vol. 8 (JAI Press, 1986). Finally, because these cultural forms carry *meanings,* a reference to the nature of ideologies in organizational behavior is appropriate. Such a reference may be found in Janice M. Beyer, "Ideologies, Values, and Decision Making in Organizations" in Paul C. Nystrom and William H. Starbuck (Eds.), *Handbook of Organizational Design,* Vol. 2 (Oxford University Press, 1981).

PART IV

Cross-Cutting Issues

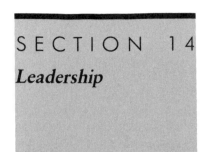

SECTION 14

Leadership

An Interview with Niccolò Machiavelli

Gerald C. Parkhouse

The name Machiavelli often has a negative connotation and has been associated with manipulation and the pursuit of unchecked self-interest and raw power. Through the clever technique of an interview with a fictitious descendant, we learn about Machiavelli's views on leadership and are asked to reassess our opinion of him and the relevance of his views to contemporary management. Judge for yourself.

Gerald C. Parkhouse is the Corning Glass Professor of International Business at Elmira College, Elmira, New York.

Note from Professor Parkhouse: This interview is, of course, imaginary. With the exception of the word substitutions noted below, all the words in quotes in the interview are taken directly from The Prince, *by Niccolò Machiavelli, translated and edited by Robert M. Adams. Copyright 1977 by W.W. Norton & Co. Reprinted with permission. The substitutions include "CEO" for "prince," "management team" for "armies," "Executive Committee Member" for "Minister," "business" for "state," "employees" for "subjects," and "competitive edge" or "restructuring" for "war."*

In existence for well over 100 years, one of Italy's closest-held private corporations deliberately cultivated, until recently, a policy of extreme reticence vis-à-vis the public and the media. Florence-based Industrie dei Principi Spa, better known as IDP, started as a small trading and banking house to serve the needs of merchants in Tuscany and steadily extended its interests. By the beginning of World War II it was a key—but always unobtrusive—enterprise in Italy's economy. After 1945 the company expanded its Italian interests into publishing, engineering, wine production, oil exploration, and marble mining. With the growth of the European Community, IDP gained, by acquisition, substantial

Source: Reprinted from *Business Horizons*, May–June 1990. Copyright 1990 by the Foundation for the School of Business at Indiana University. Used with permission.

interests in Germany and France. By 1985 the company ranked in the top 10 of Italy's industrial corporations.

The big news of 1989 was its abortive bid for Maryland Corporation and its well-publicized plan to build a strong U.S. base in a variety of industries to complement its European activities. IDP's about-face in being open about its business and future plans, which the company says is an adjustment to the present-day business climate and will provide assistance in achieving its objectives, has sparked significant interest in its activities and philosophy.

In an exclusive interview with *Business Horizons*, Harvard Business School-educated Niccolò Machiavelli, great-great-grandson of the company's founder and descendant of the eponymous fifteenth century Italian diplomat and writer, lifts the veil on the management philosophy guiding the fortunes of IDP. Since 1987 the 49-year-old Machiavelli has been chairman of IDPUS, the Stamford, Connecticut-based subsidiary of IDP established in that year. He formerly headed up three of IDP's divisions, spearheaded the move into Germany in 1983, and is currently vice chairman of the holding company in Florence. He is married to the former Jacqueline Wells of the Houston oil family and has two teenage children. He maintains homes in Greenwich and in Vail, in addition to managing the family estate in the medieval town of Fiesole in Tuscany. He is, he says, a passable skier and a collector of fine china. He is also fluent in three languages.

BH: Is there any underlying group of concepts that you would say is the hallmark of IDP's management philosophy? What basic principles have guided decisions about how to survive and grow over such a long period of time?

NM: My ancestor lived at a time of great political change. Italy then still consisted of a number of relatively small nation-states, always at risk from internal squabbles and from invasion by stronger neighbors like the French. He was in the diplomatic service and also advisor to the republican government of Florence until the Medicis came back to power. He put many of his ideas down on paper, and one of his literary efforts, written as long ago as 1516, was a book called, in English, *The Prince*. This was a treatise on how any head of state might best conduct himself to ensure survival for both himself and his state in turbulent times. So the book wasn't about princes as such; it was about leadership and the running of a state. Florence at that time was a thriving commercial city. When my great-great-grandfather founded what is now IDP he adopted many of the precepts of the first Niccolò Machiavelli; these have remained the cornerstone of our family's rules for running our business ever since. Over the centuries poor Niccolò's reputation has been that of an unscrupulous advocate of opportunism, but in reality he was much more shrewd than that. Many writers—philosophers especially—are misunderstood until history puts them in perspective. In Niccolò's case, history is just taking longer than usual to explain his views in a more balanced light. Who knows?

BH: Given IDP's lack of U.S. experience, how do you plan to manage your acquisitions here? Will you impose strict controls, or leave local management basically to its own devices, provided it produces in line with your expectations?

NM: In our view, it is essential to go and live there, as we call it, when you take over a company. "When you are on the spot, you can see troubles getting started, and take care of them right away; when you do not live there, you hear of them only when they have grown great and there is no longer a cure." We don't believe in breaking the company up by liquidating its assets. But on the other hand, for us it's not enough to set goals for local management and simply look for a return on investment in terms of profits as a kind of tribute, to use an old-fashioned term. No. If you're on the spot you can see to it that your ways, and not the old ways, are what count for the future, even if that means being pretty brutal with the inherited management if it doesn't follow your line. "To keep a secure hold [on a newly acquired company/asset] it suffices to have extinguished the 'line' [of succession] of the previous CEO because in other matters, as long as you keep the old way of life and do not change their customs, men will live quietly enough." Also, this way you can better command the loyalty of the new employees you've acquired. "However strong your management team may be, you always need the backing of local people in order to take over a company."

BH: Where does loyalty to the firm come into it in the case of a takeover, in your scheme of things?

NM: I'm afraid you'll think we adopt a rather hard-nosed attitude toward this matter. Of course loyalty is important; those who think otherwise are simply throwing away one of the most valuable assets of a business. But you have to be realistic about it. "All men are ready to change masters in the hope of bettering themselves."

So you have to earn that loyalty, pay for it in some way. One aspect of our philosophy is that you do better with managers who don't particularly like your coming in than with those who feel secure and appear willing to go along with your ideas. "The CEO always gets better service from those who at the beginning of his regime are considered his enemies . . . if they need support to maintain themselves . . . than from men who feel too sure of their jobs."

BH: What do you see as the essential qualities of a successful CEO?

NM: Forgive me for sounding somewhat pretentious, but I could quote a couple of lines from Tacitus: "Nothing is so weak and unstable as a reputation for power not founded on strength of one's own."

Now I'll make myself sound pompous—which I hope I'm really not. To me, "what makes the CEO contemptible is being considered changeable, trifling

. . . . , cowardly, or indecisive; he should avoid this as a pilot does a reef, and make sure that his actions bespeak greatness, courage, seriousness of purpose, and strength." The important thing is to be your own man and to have a very clear concept of what you're trying to accomplish. "A shrewd CEO will lay his foundations on what is under his own control, not on what is controlled by others. Indeed, a CEO will be well thought of when he is a true friend or an honest enemy, that is, when, without any hedging, he takes a stand for one side and against another."

Having said that, I think you've got to be pretty careful. I don't have much time for bosses who are forever going after the big risk as though business was a game of poker. If "a CEO conducts himself with patience and caution, and the times and circumstances are favorable to those qualities, he will flourish; but if times and circumstances change, he will come to ruin when he changes his method of proceeding." A consistent approach, then, is the one that pays off. I don't even mind saying that the CEO can do a lot worse than find a role model in the history of business to set his sights by. "A prudent man should always follow the footsteps of the great and imitate those who have been supreme. His own talent may not come up to theirs, but at least it will have a sniff of it."

Another thing is that I believe the people in your organization like to see you as a kind of figurehead. They want to have confidence in you, even though at times you yourself are not really sure what to do. "Nothing gives a CEO more prestige than undertaking great enterprises and setting a splendid example for his people. It should be a CEO's major concern in everything he does to give the impression of being a great man and of possessing excellent insight." But if you ask me whether I equate caution with an absolute aversion to taking risks, then I have to come down on the side of a well-calculated risk. What's the English expression—nothing ventured, nothing gained? "It is better to be rash than timid." IDP certainly wouldn't be where it is today if we were a timid bunch.

BH: How would you advise a CEO today if he found his authority were being undermined by disaffected senior managers?

NM: Well, you've got to be on your guard. "A CEO should not worry too much about conspiracies, as long as his people are devoted to him; but when they are hostile and feel hatred toward him, he should fear everything and every-body. You should be particularly wary when you notice that your Executive Committee Member is thinking more of himself than of you, and that everything he does serves his own interests, . . . you cannot possibly trust him." Perhaps the main thing is not to let yourself be tempted into relaxing and feeling that you've earned the right to let the reins slip a little. "When CEOs have thought more about the refinements of life than about the competitive edge, they have lost their positions." There's a big graveyard out there of successful people who lost control because they couldn't resist complacency over their own success; either of us could name a dozen instances straight off. This is particularly true of those who've been handed power on a silver plate or who have been born with silver spoons in their mouths. But in my experience, "those men who have become CEOs through their own strength of character may have trouble gaining the power, but they find it easy to hold onto."

BH: How important is it for a CEO to be a leader?

NM: My family's idea of leadership may strike you as being rather old-fashioned. You are a successful leader because you operate from strength, not because you think you have to make your people like you. In IDP we lead—and we have tremendous employee respect and loyalty—but we do so by being recognized for knowing what we're up to. "It is perfectly possible to be feared and not hated." The problem I have with loyalty is how little you can expect from consultants and outside advisors. In the family we call them mercenaries. "Mercenaries and auxiliaries are useless and dangerous. Any man who founds his business on mercenaries can never be safe or secure, because they are disunited, ambitious, undisciplined, and untrustworthy—bold fellows among their friends, but cowardly in the face of the enemy; they have no fear of God, nor loyalty to men." That statement will make the fur fly among your readers!

BH: Does that mean you don't trust your key managers and advisors within your operation?

NM: Not at all. It's just that "a CEO's wisdom does not come from having good policies recommended to him; on the contrary good policy, whoever suggests it, comes from the wisdom of the CEO." If, for some reason, you have to rely on other people's advice, then be sure you listen to one person who knows what he's up to. "A CEO who is not shrewd himself cannot get good counseling, unless he just happens to put himself in the hands of a single able man who makes all the decisions and is very knowing." You see that I'm not a great one for decisions by committee.

BH: So the boss should make the decisions, and to hell with the notion of the corporate responsibility of the Board of Directors?

NM: Yes and no. "A CEO should take counsel when he wants advice, not when others want to give it." On the other hand, "a prudent CEO should ask selected advisors about everything, hear them out, and make his decisions after thinking things over, according to his own style."

BH: With all the current popularity of corporate restructuring, what nuggets of advice would you be willing to offer?

NM: I've already indicated, I think, that I'd rather be respected than conned by sycophants. So I'll again recommend a hard-nosed approach. If you have to be tough, or cruel, to make the business survive, so be it. "Cruelty can be described as well used when it is performed all at once, for reasons of self-preservation; and when the acts are not repeated after that, but rather are turned as much as possible to the advantage of the employees." After all, if you have the power to make the decision, you'd better make it before things go wrong, rather than waiting and hoping that they'll somehow get better. "When misfortune strikes, harsh measures are too late, and the good things you do are not counted to your credit because you seem to have acted under compulsion, and no one will thank you for that." But if you're doing your job right, misfortune shouldn't strike. You should preempt it, and if a major restructuring is the way to avoid disaster, then go to it. "You should never let things get out of hand to avoid a restructuring. You don't avoid such a restructuring, you merely postpone it, to your own disadvantage."

BH: Does it matter to you that you may not be thought of as a nice guy in business?

NM: You already know the answer to that one. "People are less concerned about offending a man who makes himself loved than one who makes himself feared. Is it better to be loved than feared, or vice versa? I don't doubt that every CEO would like to be both; but since it is hard to accommodate these qualities, if you have to make a choice, to be feared is much safer than to be loved."

BH: When a company's survival is at stake, how important is ethical behavior?

NM: Now I'm really going to get into trouble. "It is good to appear merciful, truthful, and humane, sincere, and religious; it is good to be so in reality. But you must keep your mind so disposed that, in case of need, you can turn to the exact contrary." In my estimation, that's what survival is all about. "A CEO who wants to keep his post must learn how not to be good, and use that knowledge, or refrain from using it, as necessity requires."

BH: Well, that's a pretty startling viewpoint. Does luck come into the continued success of a long-surviving business enterprise?

NM: "I think it may be true that Fortune governs half of our actions but that even so she leaves the other half more or less in our power to control." In my view, "how praiseworthy it is for a CEO to keep his word and live with integrity rather than by craftiness, everyone understands; yet we see that those CEOs have accomplished most who paid little heed to keeping their promises, but who knew how . . . to manipulate the minds of men."

BH: Isn't that a scandalously opportunistic view?

NM: Scandalous, no. Opportunistic, yes, if you want to put it that way. I'm sorry, but I'm a realist, and IDP couldn't be where it is today if we'd followed high-sounding principles that didn't work in the rat race of business survival.

BH: To finish, will you share with us your favorite quote from your ancestor's book?

NM: With pleasure. He lived in a simpler world than ours, and I always liked one of his references to the animal kingdom.

> Pick for imitation the fox and the lion. As the lion must protect himself from traps, and the fox cannot defend himself from wolves, you have to be a fox in order to be wary of traps, and a lion to overcome the wolves. Those who try and live by the lion alone are badly mistaken. . . . Thus a prudent man cannot and should not keep his word when to do so would go against his interest.

I don't know what we'd call the lion and the fox today, but to me you have to do what best suits your interests, even if it's not what you planned or even promised. Look at the politicians in Italy, America, or anywhere else, and you'll know what I mean.

♦ *DISCUSSION QUESTIONS*

1. Examine the qualities that Machiavelli considers essential to be a successful CEO. How do they fit with theories of charismatic leadership [1]? Compare these qualities with those of successful contemporary leaders.

2. Machiavelli has two views about CEOs seeking advice. What are the pros and cons of his first view that "a CEO should take counsel when he wants advice, not when others want to give it"? Machiavelli's second view is that a CEO should ask his/her staff for advice and then make decisions after thinking things over. How does this fit with the Vroom-Yetton-Jago model [2] of leadership and decision making?

3. How important are situational factors in Machiavelli's view of leadership? Under what conditions do his principles hold, and when do they not apply? Refer to the path-goal theory of leadership [3].

4. Explain what Machiavelli means in his statement that it is much safer to be feared than loved. Do you agree with him that every CEO wants to be both loved and feared? How would you evaluate Rivière in *Night Flight* (reading 14.2) in this respect?

5. Machiavelli argues that, while it is good to be good, sometimes, in order to survive, one must learn how not to be good. How does this correspond to the position argued in reading 18.2, *Ethical Codes Are Not Enough?* What is your opinion?

6. Refer to the analogy about the fox and the lion. What do the fox and lion stand for? Who or what are the equivalent of traps and wolves in the contemporary business environment?

7. Review the precepts espoused by Machiavelli. Which ones do you agree with, and which ones do you disagree with? What would you suggest in terms of self-development for leaders who subscribe to all of Machiavelli's principles? Refer to reading 18.1, *High Hurdles: The Challenge of Executive Self-Development*. Overall, what is your opinion of Machiavelli?

♦ *REFERENCES*

1. Conger, J.A., Kanungo, R.N. and Associates, eds. 1988. *Charismatic Leadership*. San Francisco: Jossey-Bass.

2. Vroom, V.H., and Jago, A.G. *The New Leadership: Managing Participation in Organizations*. Englewood Cliffs, NJ: Prentice-Hall.

3. House, R.J. September 1971. A path goal theory of leadership effectiveness. *Administrative Science Quarterly*. 321–339.

Night Flight

Antoine de Saint Exupéry

This is an excerpt from the novel by the same name. The story takes place in Argentina during the early years of night mail flights. The main character in the novel is Rivière who is responsible for the airmail service in Argentina, Chile, and Paraguay. He is located in Buenos Aires, where mail is transferred to the postal plane that takes off for Europe around midnight. This excerpt describes how Rivière handles the ill-fated flight by Fabien, the pilot of the Patagonia (a region of Argentina) mail plane, who is lost in a storm.

Antoine de Saint Exupéry (1900–1944), a French writer, has included autobiographical elements in this story. He was a pioneer mail pilot himself and died in a plane crash. Many critics believe that Rivière's character is based on Didier Daurat, the director of the Line in Toulouse, France.

Rivière greeted him.

"That's a nice trick you played on me, your last trip! You turned back though the weather reports were good. You could have pushed through all right. Got the wind up?"

Surprised, the pilot found no answer. He slowly rubbed his hands one on the other. Then, raising his head, he looked Rivière in the eyes.

"Yes," he answered.

Deep in himself Rivière felt sorry for this brave fellow who had been afraid. The pilot tried to explain.

"I couldn't see a thing. No doubt, further on . . . perhaps . . . the radio said. . . . But my lamp was getting weak and I couldn't see my hands. I tried turning on my flying light so as to spot a wing anyhow, but I saw nothing. It was like being at the bottom of a huge pit, and no getting out of it. Then my engine started a rattle."

"No."

"No?"

"No, we had a look at it. In perfect order. But a man always thinks the engine's rattling when he gets the wind up."

"And who wouldn't? The mountains were above me. When I tried to climb I got caught in heavy squalls. When one can't see a damned thing, squalls, you know. . . . Instead of climbing I lost three hundred feet or more. I couldn't even see the gyroscope or the manometers. It struck me that the engine was

Source: Excerpts from *Night Flight* by Antoine de Saint Exupéry, reprinted by permission of Harcourt Brace Jovanovich, Inc.

running badly and heating up, and the oil pressure was going down. And it was dark as a plague of Egypt. Damned glad I was to see the lights of a town again."

"You've too much imagination. That's what it is."

The pilot left him.

Rivière sank back into the armchair and ran his fingers through his grizzled hair.

The pluckiest of my men, he thought. It was a fine thing he did that night, but I've stopped him from being afraid.

He felt a mood of weakness coming over him again.

To make oneself beloved one need only show pity. I show little pity, or I hide it. Sure enough it would be fine to create friendships and human kindness around me. A doctor can enjoy that in the course of his profession. But I'm the servant of events and, to make others serve them too, I've got to temper my men like steel. That dark necessity is with me every night when I read over the flight reports. If I am slack and let events take charge, trusting to routine, always mysteriously something seems to happen. It is as if my will alone forbade the plane in flight from breaking or the storm to hold the mail up. My power sometimes amazes me.

His thoughts flowed on.

Simple enough, perhaps. Like a gardener's endless labor on his lawn; the mere pressure of his hand drives back into the soil the virgin forest which the earth will engender time and time again.

His thoughts turned to the pilot.

I am saving him from fear. I was not attacking *him* but, across him, that stubborn inertia which paralyzes men who face the unknown. If I listen and sympathize, if I take his adventure seriously, he will fancy he is returning from a land of mystery, and mystery alone is at the root of fear. We must do away with mystery. Men who have gone down into the pit of darkness must come up and say—there's nothing in it! This man must enter the inmost heart of night, that clotted darkness, without even his little miner's davy, whose light, falling only on a hand or wing, suffices to push the unknown a shoulder's breath away.

Yet a silent communion, deep within them, united Rivière and his pilots in the battle. All were like shipmates, sharing a common will to victory.

Rivière remembered other battles he had joined to conquer night. In official circles darkness was dreaded as a desert unexplored. The idea of launching a craft at a hundred and fifty miles an hour against the storm and mists and all the solid obstacles night veils in darkness might suit the military arm; you leave on a fine night, drop bombs and return to your starting point. But regular night services were doomed to fail. "It's a matter of life and death," said Rivière, "for the lead we gain by day on ships and railways is lost each night."

Disgusted, he had heard them prate of balance sheets, insurance, and, above all, public opinion. "Public opinion!" he exclaimed. "The public does as it's told!" But it was all waste of time, he was saying to himself. There's something far above all that. A living thing forces its way through, makes its own laws to live and nothing can resist it. Rivière had no notion when or how commercial aviation would tackle the problem of night flying but its inevitable solution must be prepared for.

Those green tablecloths over which he had leaned, his chin propped on his arm, well he remembered them! And his feeling of power as he heard the others' quibbles! Futile these had seemed, doomed from the outset by the force of life. He felt the weight of energy that gathered in him. And I shall win, thought Rivière, for the weight of argument is on my side. That is the natural trend of things. They urged him to propose a utopian scheme, devoid of every risk. "Experience will guide us to the rules," he said. "You can't make rules precede practical experience."

After a hard year's struggles, Rivière got his way. "His faith saw him through," said some, but others: "No, his tenacity. Why, the fellow's as obstinate as a bear!" But Rivière put his success down to the fact that he had lent his weight to the better cause.

Safety first was the obsession of those early days. Planes were to leave only an hour before dawn, to land only an hour after sunset. When Rivière felt surer of his ground, then and only then did he venture to send his planes into the depth of night. And now, with few to back him, disowned by nearly all, he plowed a lonely furrow.

Rivière rang up to learn the latest messages from the planes in flight.

———————

"The Asuncion mail is making good headway; it should be in at about two. The Patagonia mail, however, seems to be in difficulties and we expect it to be much overdue."

"Very good, Monsieur Rivière."

"Quite possibly we won't make the European mail wait for us; as soon as Asuncion's in, come for instructions, please. Hold yourself in readiness."

Rivière read again the weather reports from the northern sectors. "Clear sky; full moon; no wind." The mountains of Brazil were standing stark and clear against the moonlit sky, the tangled tresses of their jet-black forests falling sheer into a silver tracery of sea. Upon those forests the moonbeams played and played in vain, tingeing their blackness with no light. Black, too, as drifting wreckage, the islands flecked the sea. But all the outward air route was flooded by that exhaustless fountain of moonlight.

If Rivière now gave orders for the start, the crew of the Europe mail would enter a stable world, softly illuminated all night long. A land which held no threat for the just balance of light and shade, unruffled by the least caress of those cool winds which, when they freshen, can ruin a whole sky in an hour or two.

Facing this wide radiance, like a prospector eyeing a forbidden gold field, Rivière hesitated. What was happening in the south put Rivière, sole protagonist of night flights, in the wrong. His opponents would make such moral capital out of a disaster in Patagonia that all Rivière's faith would henceforth be unavailing. Not that his faith wavered; if, through a fissure in his work, a tragedy had entered in, well, the tragedy might prove the fissure—but it proved nothing else. Perhaps, he thought, it would be well to have look-out posts in the west. That must be seen to. "After all," he said to himself, "my previous arguments hold good as ever and the possibilities of accident are reduced by one, the one tonight has illustrated." The strong are strengthened by reverses; the trouble is that the true meaning of events scores next to nothing in the match we play with men. Appearances decide our gains or losses and the points are trumpery. And a mere semblance of defeat may hopelessly checkmate us.

He summoned an employee. "Still no radio from Bahia Blanca?"

"No."

"Ring up the station on the phone."

Five minutes later he made further inquiries. "Why don't you pass on the messages?"

"We can't hear the mail."

"He's not sending anything?"

"Can't say. Too many storms. Even if he was sending we shouldn't pick it up."

"Can you get Trelew?"

"We can't hear Trelew."

"Telephone."

"We've tried. The line's broken."

"How's the weather your end?"

"Threatening. Very sultry. Lightning in the west and south."

"Wind?"

"Moderate so far. But in ten minutes the storm will break; the lightning's coming up fast."

Silence.

"Hullo, Bahia Blanca! You hear me? Good. Call me again in ten minutes."

Rivière looked through the telegrams from the southern stations. All alike reported: No message from the plane. Some had ceased by now to answer Buenos Aires and the patch of silent areas was spreading on the map as the cyclone swept upon the little towns and one by one, behind closed doors, each house along the lightless streets grew isolated from the outer world, lonely as a ship on a dark sea. And only dawn would rescue them.

Rivière, poring on the map, still hoped against hope to discover a haven of clear sky, for he had telegraphed to the police at more than thirty upcountry police stations and their replies were coming in. And the radio posts over twelve hundred miles of country had orders to advise Buenos Aires within thirty seconds if any message from the plane was picked up, so that Fabien might learn at once whither to fly for refuge.

The employees had been warned to attend at 1 A.M. and were now at their posts. Somehow, mysteriously, a rumor was gaining ground that perhaps the night flights would be suspended in future and the Europe mail would leave by day. They spoke in whispers of Fabien, the cyclone and, above all, of Rivière whom they pictured near at hand and point by point capitulating to this rebuff the elements had dealt.

Their chatter ceased abruptly; Rivière was standing at his door, his overcoat tight-buttoned across his chest, his hat well down upon his eyes, like the incessant traveler he always seemed. Calmly he approached the head clerk.

"It's one ten. Are the papers for the Europe mail in order?"

"I—I thought—"

"Your business is to carry out orders, not to think."

Slowly turning away, he moved toward an open window, his hands clasped behind his back. A clerk came up to him.

"We have very few replies, sir. We hear that a great many telegraph lines in the interior have been destroyed."

"Right!"

Unmoving, Rivière stared out into the night.

Thus each new message boded new peril for the mail. Each town, when a reply could be sent through before the lines were broken, announced the cyclone on its way, like an invading horde, "It's coming up from the Cordillera, sweeping everything before it, toward the sea."

To Rivière the stars seemed over-bright, the air too moist. Strange night indeed! It was rotting away in patches, like the substance of a shining fruit. The stars, in all their host, still looked down on Buenos Aires—an oasis, and not to last. A haven out of Fabien's range, in any case. A night of menace, touched and tainted by an evil wind. A difficult night to conquer.

Somewhere in its depths an airplane was in peril; here, on the margin, they were fighting to rescue it, in vain.

———————————

Fabien's wife telephoned.

Each night she calculated the progress of the homing Patagonia mail. "He's leaving Trelew now," she murmured. Then went to sleep again. Presently: "He's getting near San Antonio, he has its lights in view." Then she got out of bed, drew back the curtains and summed up the sky. "All those clouds will worry him." Sometimes the moon was wandering like a shepherd and the young wife was heartened by the faithful moon and stars, the thousand presences that watched her husband. Toward one o'clock she felt him near her. "Not far to go, Buenos Aires is in sight." Then she got up again, prepared a meal for him, a nice steaming cup of coffee. "It's so cold up there!" She always welcomed him as if he had just descended from a snow peak. "You *must* be cold!" "Not a bit." "Well, warm yourself anyhow!" She had everything ready at a quarter past one. Then she telephoned. Tonight she asked the usual question.

"Has Fabien landed?"

The clerk at the other end grew flustered. "Who's speaking?"

"Simone Fabien."

"Ah! A moment, please. . . ."

Afraid to answer, he passed the receiver to the head clerk.
"Who's that?"
"Simone Fabien."
"Yes. What can I do for you?"
"Has my husband arrived?"
After a silence which must have baffled her, there came a monosyllable.
"No."
"Is he delayed?"
"Yes."
Another silence. "Yes, he is delayed."
"Ah!"
The cry of a wounded creature. A little delay, that's nothing much, but
when it lasts, when it lasts. . . .
"Yes. And when—when is he expected in?"
"When is he expected? We . . . we don't know exactly . . ."
A solid wall in front of her, a wall of silence, which only gave her back the
echo of her questions.
"Do please tell me, where is he now?"
"Where is he? Wait. . . ."
This suspense was like a torture. Something was happening there, behind
that wall.
At last, a voice! "He left Commodoro at seven thirty this evening."
"Yes? And then?"
"Then—delayed, seriously delayed by stormy weather."
"Ah! A storm!"
The injustice of it, the sly cruelty of that moon up there, that lazing moon
of Buenos Aires! Suddenly she remembered that it took barely two hours to fly
from Commodoro to Trelew.
"He's been six hours on the way to Trelew! But surely you've had messages
from him. What does he say?"
"What does he say? Well, you see, with weather like that . . . it's only
natural . . . we can't hear him."
"Weather like—?"
"You may rest assured, madame, the moment we get news of him, we will
ring you up."
"Ah! You've no news."
"Good night, madame."
"No! No! I want to talk to the director."
"I'm sorry, he's very busy just now; he has a meeting on—"
"I can't help that. That doesn't matter. I insist on speaking to him."
The head clerk mopped his forehead. "A moment, please."
He opened Rivière's door.
"Madame Fabien wants to speak to you, sir."
"Here," thought Rivière, "is what I was dreading." The emotional elements

of the drama were coming into action. His first impulse was to thrust them aside; mothers and women are not allowed in an operating theater. And all emotion is bidden to hold its peace on a ship in peril; it does not help to save the crew. Nevertheless he yielded.

"Switch on to my phone."

No sooner did he hear that far off, quavering voice, than he knew his inability to answer it. It would be futile for both alike, worse than futile, to meet each other.

"Do not be alarmed, madame, I beg you. In our calling it so often happens that a long while passes without news."

He had reached a point where not the problem of a small personal grief but the very will to act was in itself an issue. Not so much Fabien's wife as another theory of life confronted Rivière now. Hearing that timid voice, he could but pity its infinite distress—and know it for an enemy! For action and individual happiness have no truck with each other; they are eternally at war. This woman, too, was championing a self-coherent world with its own rights and duties, that world where a lamp shines at nightfall on the table, flesh calls to mated flesh, a homely world of love and hopes and memories. She stood up for her happiness and she was right. And Rivière, too, was right, yet he found no words to set against this woman's truth. He was discovering the truth within him, his own inhuman and unutterable truth, by an humble light, the lamplight of a little home!

"Madame . . . !"

She did not hear him. Her hands were bruised with beating on the wall and she lay fallen, or so it seemed to him, almost at his feet.

One day an engineer had remarked to Rivière, as they were bending above a wounded man, beside a bridge that was being erected: "Is the bridge worth a man's crushed face?" Not one of the peasants using a road would ever have wished to mutilate this face so hideously just to save the extra walk to the next bridge. "The welfare of the community," the engineer had continued, "is just the sum of individual welfares and has no right to look beyond them." "And yet," Rivière observed on a subsequent occasion, "even though human life may be the most precious thing on earth, we always behave as if there were something of higher value than human life. . . . But what thing?"

Thinking of the lost airmen, Rivière felt his heart sink. All man's activity, even the building of a bridge, involves a toll of suffering and he could no longer evade the issue—"Under what authority?"

These men, he mused, who perhaps are lost, might have led happy lives. He seemed to see as in a golden sanctuary the evening lamplight shine on faces bending side by side. "Under what authority have I taken them from all this?" he wondered. What was his right to rob them of their personal happiness? Did not the highest of all laws ordain that these human joys should be safeguarded? But he destroyed them. And yet one day, inevitably, those golden sanctuaries vanish like mirage. Old age and death, more pitiless than even he, destroy them.

There is, perhaps, some other thing, something more lasting, to be saved; and, perhaps, it was to save this part of man that Rivière was working. Otherwise there could be no defense for action.

To love, only to love, leads nowhere. Rivière knew a dark sense of duty, greater than that of love. And deep within it there might lie another emotion and a tender one, but worlds away from ordinary feelings. He recalled a phrase that he once had read: "The one thing is to make them everlasting. . . . That which you seek within yourself will die." He remembered a temple of the sun god, built by the ancient Incas of Peru. Tall menhirs on a mountain. But for these what would be left of all that mighty civilization which with its massive stones weighs heavy, like a dark regret, on modern man? Under the mandate of what strange love, what ruthlessness, did that primeval leader of men compel his hordes to drag this temple up the mountainside, bidding them raise up their eternity? And now another picture rose in Rivière's mind; the people of the little towns, strolling by nights around their bandstands. That form of happiness, those shackles . . . he thought. The leader of those ancient races may have had scant compassion for man's sufferings, but he had a boundless pity for his death. Not for his personal death, but pity for his race, doomed to be blotted out beneath a sea of sand. And so he bade his folk set up these stones at least, something the desert never would engulf.

◆   DISCUSSION QUESTIONS

1. Describe Rivière's philosophy of life and of management. How does he view his role? What are his values? Is he justified in his views? How ethical is he? Do you agree with him?

2. What kind of leader is Rivière? Analyze his leadership style according to the following theories:
   (a) Blake and Mouton's managerial grid [1].
   (b) McGregor's theory X and theory Y [2].
   (c) Fiedler's contingency theory [3].
   (d) House's path-goal theory [4].
   (e) Hersey and Blanchard's situational leadership [5].
   (f) Conger and Kanungo's charismatic leadership [6].

3. Would you like to work for a Rivière? Are you like Rivière? Under what conditions would he be effective? Ineffective?

4. Use reading 18.1, *High Hurdles: The Challenge of Executive Self-Development,* to answer the following questions:
   (a) How would Rivière benefit from self-development? Evaluate him according to the four major points in the article:

(1) Does the exercise of power prevent Rivière from getting personal criticism that could make him aware of his deficits?

(2) Does Rivière's job prevent him from being introspective?

(3) Does Rivière have difficulty accepting criticism because of a need to appear highly competent?

(4) Does a history of success make it difficult for Rivière to change?

(b) Construct a plan for Rivière's self-development that could be implemented by:

(1) Rivière himself.

(2) the organization.

(3) the people around Rivière—his peers, subordinates, superiors, family.

◆ REFERENCES

1. Blake, R.R., and Mouton, J.S. 1978. *The New Managerial Grid.* Houston: Gulf Publishing Co.

2. McGregor, D. 1961. *The Human Side of Enterprise.* New York: McGraw-Hill.

3. Fiedler, F.E. 1967. *A Theory of Leadership Effectiveness.* New York: McGraw-Hill.

4. House, R.J. September 1971. A path goal theory of leadership effectiveness. *Administrative Science Quarterly.* 321–339.

5. Hersey, P., and Blanchard, K.H. 1982. *Management of Organizational Behavior*, 4th ed. Englewood Cliffs, NJ: Prentice-Hall.

6. Conger, J.A., Kanungo, R.N. and Associates, eds. 1988. *Charismatic Leadership.* San Francisco: Jossey-Bass.

A Day in the Life of the Boss

Hugh Geeslin, Jr.

This is an account of an employee who blows the whistle on an unethical company
practice. The story causes one to wonder how people draw the line between ethical
and unethical behavior, and how they deal with their conscience when they engage in
an unethical act.

He listened a moment at the bathroom door, and being sure finally that neither
Lisa nor Little Mase was there, he entered. Preparing to shave, he gave himself
the musing appraisal in the mirror which was as much a part of the ritual as the
brush or shaving cream.

Staring at himself in the mirror, he saw a narrow face with a sharp nose
and quick, indecisive eyes. He searched himself as he searched an invoice at the
office, quick to seize on the wrong total or the errant shipment. His thin hair
depressed him and he tried unsuccessfully each morning to cover the bald spot.

Applying the lather, he said, "Ugly. Ugly as hell."

There was nothing he could do about the face on which even the beard
was not luxuriant but straggling and growing in patches, and nothing he could
do about the six-feet-three-inch body that was not so much thin as narrow, or
the AAA, size fourteen shoes. These things never entered his morning reverie
because they were impossible to remedy. He could not right them as he did the
mistaken invoice. There was no exchange for Gladstone Mott's self-confidence,
healthy body, and the sense of belonging somewhere in history, and not only
belonging but being of the people who were governors of states and later perhaps
United States senators, of the people who founded businesses, played golf, and
retired early. He couldn't be Gladstone Mott. He could only run his company

for him, standing always at the elbow, sometimes obtrusively (when Gladstone began to make one of his unhinged mistakes), but most often quietly admiring.

He was satisfied, he often told himself during those early morning communions when he had at last wrenched the bathroom from Desiree, his wife, Little Mase, his son, and Lisa, his daughter. But saying this, he knew he lied. Instead he counted the things, the concrete objects which he owned, and which he knew to be important.

There was the house. Brick. Set well back from the street, the quiet dead-end street lined with poplars and pines, where Lisa and Little Mase could play with the other children without danger from passing cars, and lined also with thirty-thousand-dollar houses that were identical to his except for that superficial change that transformed an ell into a front porch and a carport into a brick patio.

("Can't you see they're all alike?" John Shaw used to say before he stopped coming to the house. "Can't you see that they're one and all of that great dead Suburbia where nothing ever happens except promotion, transfer, and death? Can't you see?" John Shaw, who had wanted to be an architect, but had wound up at Mott's instead, had said all this in the living room of the house, leaning toward his host, half drunk on rye highballs.)

There was the house, with the brook running through the front yard, just as it did through the front yards of all of the houses on the street, which offered a rose-covered receptacle to the mailman, who nevertheless called them all mailboxes. There were the house and Desiree and the children. There were two cars in the carport, an old Studebaker which belonged to Desiree and a new Buick which was furnished to him by Mott, Inc., where he was Vice-president and General Sales Manager.

By the time he had seated himself at the breakfast table, his morning reverie was finished. He now devoted himself to arbitrating the contests of Lisa and Little Mase, as they tried to outwit Desiree, or at least perplex her so that she could no longer remember the raincoat—when it rained—or the overcoat—in the winter—or the hundreds of other details which arise from having two children in school and a nine-room house to care for with only a maid and sometimes Willy, the handyman from Mott's, who came when the Motts could spare him from what they assumingly called their estate.

"Why can't I wear high heels, Daddy?" Lisa said. "I'm fourteen and all the girls in my class wear them. Mother says to ask you, Daddy. Why can't I, Daddy?"

He looked at her and was sorry that her eyes were his eyes and that she was positively his daughter and not his wife's. What could he do for her, now or later? Could he change that outer shell of hers, that covering of skin and arrangement of bones which he had never even considered until she was ten or eleven and her classmates at Miss Primrose's school had begun to yell "Ugly-smuggly" at her on the way home in the late afternoons? Could he forestall the anguish that would surely arise from the school proms, swimming parties, and the high school play? What could he do for her?

"Let her wear them, Desiree. I think she's old enough."

"All right, Mason." And then she was herding them through the door and into Miss Primrose's station wagon, which had made itself known by frequent blasts on the horn.

"Mason," Desiree called as he made his way to the carport and the Buick. He stopped at the door and leaning, brushed her cheek with a kiss. "Mason, you shouldn't feel badly about Lisa. She's going to be all right. And so are you, my dear. You're a fine man and she's a wonderful little girl. I'm very proud of both of you."

"Look," he said, already through the door, "I've got a lot of work to do. See you tonight."

The Buick was red-and-white and almost brand new. He had chosen the colors himself and he admired them. The car gave him much satisfaction during the early morning drives through the quiet city streets on his way to work.

He adjusted the wide-brimmed Stetson to the side of his head and settled down to the forty-five-minute drive downtown.

He wanted this time to think, to plan, and to compose himself. It was not fear that he felt rising in his stomach which caused the bitter taste in his mouth. He had not felt real fear since his last trip as navigator for the ATC, during the war. He was confident, as he knew he had a right to be, for he had helped to make the company the largest of its kind in six states. He had brought it almost single-handedly from the lazy little outfit run by old Mr. Mott and his golf-playing son to its present position of authority in the farm equipment industry. He was not afraid but he wanted time to plan his strategy.

John Shaw was resigning today. This he knew. Knowing John Shaw as well as he did after three years of close association, he knew that Shaw was capable of being bitter and accusatory and very likely suffering from a bad hangover. It was never well to leave an accusation unanswered when it was made to Gladstone Mott. Mott had a way of dwelling on events until they were finally resolved, weeks later, and not always in the manner that Mason would have liked. It was always best to end these things before they began.

———————

The Mott, Inc., lot was a choice one on Murphy Avenue. There was one long building, which housed two offices, one the outer office where Mason had his desk along with Jeff Spires, the office clerk, and Chalmers Marchant, the bookkeeper. To the rear were the shops which were headed by Don Swan, who, every day of his working life, ate his lunch at the Vice-president's desk, leaving bits of sandwich and coffee stains on the blotter.

(Leaning over Mason's sofa, holding his fourth drink carelessly, his hair hanging down limp over his face, John Shaw had said: "Why don't you buy him a table if you don't like it? Suppose that he *was* the first man they ever hired. Mott'd understand. Why gripe? Tell him.")

The lot was newly paved and landscaped. Bland gladioli bloomed beneath the office windows and the grass was green and neatly trimmed by Willy, the handyman. Four huge oaks brought shade to the front of the lot and in the rear there were three.

Accelerating the car into the driveway as he always did, Mason smiled. It was always a pleasure to get back to the place. He felt pride of ownership in this place and achievement realized here, as if he had conceived and nurtured it from its founding. He felt joy and anticipation of joy when he thought of the future. Mott would soon be out of it. He never came down to the office more than two or three times a week. He preferred to spend his time at the Crudney Hills Golf Club. Not that the Club wasn't all right. After all, at Gladstone Mott's insistence, he himself was a member. And it had done a lot for him; it had done plenty for him, the associations with really fine fellows, the good exercise, and besides he had met "Hump" Raleigh there and through him had made the arrangements with the Osgood Brothers Implement Company. Of course he got to play on the course only on Thursday afternoon and Saturday and Sunday, and not then if Mott was in a tournament and he had things to do which he couldn't delegate to Jeff Spires or Shaw. Not that he ever got much out of Shaw.

Mason smiled in spite of the taste in his mouth. It was good to get back to the place. He entered the office and sat down at his desk.

The office had been hastily, cheaply, and shoddily built. Loose mortar sifted from between the odd-sized concrete blocks of the walls; celotex panels hung limply from the ceiling where they had been improperly nailed; and the floor slanted crazily toward Mott's office.

The furniture was expensive. There were three desks, matching chairs, and an odd chair, all of which had been selected by Cherie Mott, Gladstone's wife.

John Shaw was sitting aslant in the odd chair at Mason's desk. He swayed front and back, front and back, sometimes glancing at Mason, who was busy at a stack of invoices, and sometimes gazing over the air-conditioning units through the window and into busy Murphy Avenue.

"Morning, Mason-o," he said, grinning. Mason saw that his eyes were clear and alert. Apparently he had had a good night's sleep.

"Hi, John. Say, are you going to take care of this?" He handed John a request from a prospective customer, asking for prices and descriptive literature.

He handed back the letter. "Not today, Mason-o. Today I've got a lot of things to do, but taking care of this guy isn't one of them."

"All right," Mason said, his voice bearing traces of acquiescence and belligerency.

John did not hear Mason's words. He was listening to the tone of his voice. It was the juxtaposition in sound of heroics and cowardice that puzzled him, that manner of speaking which was half plea and half threat, as if Mason stood with an axe in one hand and an olive branch in the other. He could remember talking to Mason on long distance from the territory, and hearing the voice, but after a moment not listening to the words but enjoying the sudden rush of blood to his own face and the tightening of his stomach muscles, momentarily fighting down the rage, and then as Mason's high whine came through over the hundreds of miles of bright wire, dropping reservations and reason and letting the anger take hold completely.

"It's like I wanted to rip the phone off the wall," Shaw would say to Gladstone Mott later, trying to understand Mason, trying to understand him because he wanted to be able to understand him to be able to keep the job. So at last he could keep a job for more than a few months, so he could quit drinking, maybe get married and settle down on a farm somewhere and become the man he secretly believed every man should be, steady and hard-working. He would talk to Mott slowly at first but soon the words would come swiftly and finally cascade, and the only result of them was the reddening of John Shaw's face as he spoke.

Mason was telephoning, and Spires was busy transcribing letters from the dictaphone cylinder. Chalmers was bent slightly over his ledgers, making the neat entries which were automatic and nearly always correct.

Chalmers was small and as neat as his ledgers. His clothes were good and he carried himself confidently. There had always been a haphazard raillery between him and John Shaw. This morning they had said only good morning. Chalmers glanced at his friend now, as he sat negligently in the expensive chair. He felt pity for John, wanted to help him, but knew no way of doing so.

(Over the lunch table, John had once pointed a hard bread stick at Chalmers, underscoring his words. "I don't know about that Mason. I don't know why he rubs me the wrong way. I do know it's becoming a big thing with me. My weekends are ruined. I find myself talking about him to perfect strangers in bars."

"Maybe it's not him at all," Chalmers had said. "Maybe it's you and this town. Maybe you don't belong here."

"Don't talk to me like that." John had grinned, suddenly. "A man like you, a gentleman like you from Blue's Old Stand, Alabama, is simply always a gentleman from Blue's Old Stand, Alabama. Don't talk to me about this city. This is my town, man. It always has been. Other people wanted to go to Paris or Andalusia; I wanted to come here."

"Eat your beef," Chalmers had said.)

Mason was telephoning. Jeff Spires saw John rocking in the window but caught nothing of the tension of which Chalmers and Mason were aware. Spires was small, an inch or two over five feet, made too little money for his wife and two children, and wore clip-on bow ties. He also told jokes.

("Say, Mr. Shaw, did you hear what one psychiatrist said to another one when he passed him on the street one day? Heh. Heh. He said, 'You're all right. How am I?' Heh, hey, Mr. Shaw. He said: 'You're all—' "

"All right, that's one. Two more and you're through for the day. Right?" John said.

"All right." Spires returned to his typing. He was pleased. A careful smile graced his thin, mottled face.)

Listening to Mason on the telephone, John was thinking of Spires and remembering the story that he had told him. After hearing the story, John had defended Spires during an informal meeting between Mason and Cherie, defended him hotly and with enough spirit that the clerk was assured ample time to remedy his overly precise manner when he handled the firm's telephone requests and the few customers who came to the offices.

Weeks before, during an afternoon when Spires and John were alone in the office, John working on an advertising letter and Spires seeming pensive and ill at ease, Spires had begun suddenly to talk about his father: "When I was five or six years old, we lived in a mill town. That was before Daddy and Mother were divorced. Later on they quit and I didn't know why and I still don't. I guess times were hard then. I don't remember anything about that at all. What I remember is Daddy working in a cotton mill and getting off every afternoon at four o'clock and me going down to meet him. I always got there about three-thirty and sat on one of them long wooden benches that the men sat on who were waiting to go to work on the four-o-five shift. I remember it was always smoky and I guess the streets must have been dirty as hell but I don't remember that at all. I'd go down there and sit down on the bench and wait for Daddy to get off from work. And then after a while I'd get up and do a little jig, you know, a buck-and-wing. I always was a dancer. You know I won this cigarette lighter here out in California at the Trianon Ballroom, me and my partner. She got an orchid and a big box of candy. Well, as I was saying, I'd do this little dance for the men there and they must have liked it because every day they'd ask me to dance and pretty soon they began to pitch money on the pavement. I didn't hardly know how to count money, then, but there were nickels and a lot of pennies. Sometimes as much as a quarter. Then the whistle would blow and my daddy would come through the gate and we'd walk home. When we got away from the mill, my daddy would take my arm and say, Give me what you got. And he'd take my money. Every day, he'd take my money."

"Listen, Bishop," Mason was saying into the telephone, "you call up Goode Contracting Company. Yeah, yeah, Goode. Ask for old man Goode. Tell him you heard he wants to buy two tractors in the same class as our LADY. Give him a price of fifty dollars over my price. Yeah, that's right, fifty dollars. In about an hour I'll call him and give him my price and get the business. The next two are yours. Okay? Fine, fine, boy. Goodbye, Harry." Mason was talking, John realized, to Harry Bishop, manager of Standard Tractor, Mott's chief competitor.

John knew what was going on. He knew that Mason had entered into an agreement with Bishop and Standard Tractor, setting the same price for merchandise sold by either company.

"Sewing it up, huh, boy," John said.

"You've got to do it," Mason said.

Don Swan came in from the shops, red-faced and greasy, mumbling and cursing a trunnion shaft. Another day at Mott's, Inc. had begun.

———————————

Gladstone Mott, President and sole owner of Mott Implement Company, sat eating breakfast with his wife Cherie on the terrace overlooking the pool.

He enjoyed his food. Mrs. Knighthammer's biscuits were especially pleasing today, and he wore a gob of butter on his chin, defiantly. The Virginia ham had been prepared just right, and its savor and texture was triumphant. Today he re-examined Mrs. Knighthammer's expertness as he did every day, but his mind strayed unwillingly to the office and the problems which awaited him there. His usually calm face now showed signs of rigid concern.

"What's the matter, Glad?" Cherie searched his tanned face expectantly and lovingly. She knew him well and she was accustomed to his changes of mood and purpose. Almost maternally she considered his open face, the carelessly worn sport shirt for which she had paid twenty dollars, the garbardine slacks which were grease-stained, the bottoms of which were inexactly rolled above his shoes to exhibit red wool golf socks. About money and business he would never know, she realized, and it took nothing from him. The money was hers, and she understood it, just as she understood him. Not perceiving that complex, almost mystic interrelationship of salesman, customer, manufacturer and designer, it was perfectly plain that he commanded a hard and wholly unsolicited and unwanted loyalty from his employees and co-workers. She did not understand why they held in respect and even love his careless gestures of confidence and rare flashes of genuine business acumen. This morning, as on most mornings, she was pleased with him.

"How did you know?" Gladstone said.

"You've only eaten one man's breakfast. Mrs. Knighthammer will think that you're ill."

"I'm not that transparent, I hope. It's a wonder I ever had any business success if my face is such an open book," Gladstone said.

"You forget that I've had years to study it," Cherie said. "It's about Mason and John Shaw, isn't it?"

"Yes, it's been building up a long time. They're both good men. I'd hate for anything to happen now that we've only just got the new line launched."

Cherie lifted her fine head in what could have been an impolite sniff. "Well, you simply can't get along without Mason. Why, he has every part of the business at his fingertips. Where would you find another man who's good at design, better at production and planning, and who's absolutely tops at sales? Where are you going to get a replacement for such a man?"

Gladstone glanced reflectively about the grounds, not admiring the towering maples and spruce, hardly able to identify them, or the thousands of flowers and shrubs, seeing all whole and green, and as a part of the scene. Botany was not one of Gladstone's interests.

"You don't like John Shaw much, do you?" Gladstone said, asking for the judgment which he had come to respect, and to which, in matters of business, he seldom disdained.

"No," her face colored, "he laughs at me. He talks too fast, so many ideas come so swiftly that he wins every argument. He makes me feel like a fool. Now, Mason is a good old boy. Not the best-looking man I ever knew but certainly one of the smartest businessmen."

Gladstone disliked her remarks about Mason's appearance. He knew the depths, almost pathological, of Mason's sensitivity.

"What about the campaign John did on the LADY?" Gladstone said. "We had no hopes at all for that tractor, although we'd been manufacturing it for two years, and along comes John and increases our volume four hundred per cent in a few months."

"The LADY would have sold," Cherie said, vehemently. "Just because that Shaw thought up a few silly slogans, and reorganized the dealer setup, and we got more orders, that doesn't prove much."

"You aren't being fair, Cherie, and you know it. The whole campaign was his, and his alone. We'd sunk plenty into a new design for a small tractor aimed at the do-it-yourself market and they just weren't buying. Remember, John christened the tractor LADY, and he wrote all the advertising."

"Those silly slogans again," Cherie said.

"Maybe . . . maybe they were silly, but they were damned effective. Remember, MRS. HOMEMAKER, IF YOU CAN MAKE A SALAD, YOU CAN OPERATE THE LADY. And, SECRETARIES, IF YOU CAN TYPE, YOU CAN OPERATE THE LADY. We sold tractors and that's always the final test."

Gladstone pushed his chair back and stood up. He kissed his wife on the lips and drove his powder-blue Jaguar to the office.

Driving through the tree-lined streets, Gladstone felt neither resentment nor pleasure at the prospect before him. People and their motives were past his understanding and they had always been. Much better the open fairway and the exultation which came when club connected solidly with ball and he stepped back, knowing the drive good for three hundred yards.

It was almost eleven when he reached the Mott, Inc., offices, as he brought the Jaguar in line with Mason's Buick and extricated himself neatly from it.

At three in the afternoon the Mott offices were just as they had been earlier, except that the afternoon sun had begun to shine into the window above Chalmers' desk with such force that he rose to close the venetian blinds.

As he did so, Gladstone Mott called through the door of his office, "Mason . . . John . . . will you come in here, please?"

Chalmers sat at his desk, fingering a closed ledger. His questions, which had been directed at John Shaw during their lunch together, had brought no confidences or explanations.

As the men entered, Gladstone was seated in what John always called "the throne," a huge upholstered chair which Cherie had ordered from New York. He adjusted the chair to the great desk, much too large for the small cluttered office, and began tentatively to poke into the mass of old memos, letters, invitations to parties, bills from department stores, sales bulletins, catalogues, and old copies of *Sports Illustrated*. He knew that the two men were studying his face, trying to find the answer to what form the conference would take. Purposely Gladstone assumed an introspective demeanor.

"Close the door, men, and take chairs," Gladstone said.

Mason knew instantly that Gladstone was determined to keep the discussion on an unemotional level. Surprisingly, as he admitted to himself, Mason was glad. John was certainly a talker, and in anger he often swayed Gladstone's judgment with sheer eloquence.

John searched the ruined wall for the framed photograph of the LADY. That this photograph hung with the other likenesses of Mott equipment gave him confidence.

"What do you want, Glad?" John said.

Mason admired the opening move. John had achieved his purpose, which was to make Gladstone slightly uneasy.

"That's not the question," Gladstone said. "It's what you want. Mason and I are waiting to hear just what it is that you want."

John flicked his attention from the photograph to the open window and back to Gladstone's face.

"I want to quit. Now. Today," John said.

"That's pretty silly and you know it," Mason said. "You've done all right here. The money has been good and we get along."

"Do we?" John said. "What about the McDarrell deal? Is that an example of how well we get along? What about the Smith deal? Is that another example? And apart from these two, what about 'Hump' Riley and his deal, yes, his deal, his goddamned slimy deal of deals?"

Shaw's face was red, and slowly the crimson spread to his neck.

"Glad approved every one of those deals," Mason said. His voice was high and nervous.

Gladstone laughed jovially, falsely. "Now, fellows, let's not start hollering."

"I can understand the McDarrell deal," John said, "even though I went up there and sold the dealer after first finding him and persuading him to become our dealer, and before that sitting down and deciding what qualifications a good dealer for the LADY would have; and even though I sold him and three days later he called up and Mason answered the phone and went up there and told the man he was Vice-president and got a signed order for fifty machines. I understand that deal, Glad, because Mason, bless his ugly hide, has to have the sales. It keeps him going. It's the one thing that he must have. He's so little like the rest of us, so different and lacking in all those things that you and I and everybody else take for granted, that it was absolutely imperative that he slide up there and steal the order."

Mason's narrow face was pale and quiet.

Gladstone sat behind the mountainous desk, momentarily amazed at the viciousness of Shaw's attack.

"And the Smith deal," John said, rapidly. "I propose that we hereby discuss the Smith deal. Mason, here, is a man who cannot make a mistake. He cannot ever humanly err because to do so would detract an iota from that long glimmering vision he has of himself, that stenciled portrait he carries inside his narrow head, that appears to him inhumanly potent and omniscient. But mistakes become every man and are a part of most of us. Yet when Mason makes one, instead of admitting it, he has to alibi, or blame it on somebody else, or lie out of it."

John half rose from his chair. The room was ringed with the sound of his words.

"Smith bought twenty tractors from me and we didn't have them in stock for immediate delivery. Smith was on his head, so I called Stitch in Chicago and he promised me the machines at a good profit. I remember the day very well. I asked Mason to call Stitch and get a confirming price and also to confirm Smith's arrival to pick up the machines. After all, Mason is supposed to be the Boss. Mason didn't think it necessary to call Stitch. Oh, no. He had to write him an air-mail letter. Smith arrives. Stitch, not hearing from Mason, sells Smith the tractors himself and we're out in the cold completely. Two thousand down the drain. And the air-mail letter. Ah, the letter. It gets to Stitch a day later, after Smith had left Chicago with the machines. Now, here's the topper. That was all right about us losing the money. We could always make more money. But Mason said that he tried to call Stitch and Mason lied. But Mason had to be right. He couldn't make a mistake. The result was that we lost the money, and all the time I spent cultivating Smith was wasted."

"What's the matter with you, John?" Gladstone said. "Are you crazy? Don't you know better than to talk like this?"

"Maybe I am a little nuts, Glad. It's hard to say after three years with Mason. But to enthrone and decorate my insanity: the crowning achievement of Mason's claim to manhood is the agreement he fostered with Hump Riley."

"Glad okayed that deal. Glad wanted to go in with Hump," Mason said, his face ashen, frantically searching Gladstone's appearance for the key to his reactions.

"Sure, Glad wanted the deal. You talked to him night and day for weeks and finally Glad heard so much about it that he thought it was his idea in the first place," John said.

Gladstone said, "I'm that stupid, am I?"

"Not stupidity, Glad," John said. "Just not giving a damn, mostly. Wanting to please Mason because he's a good man and he lives with the business."

"It wasn't a bad deal, really," Gladstone said.

"No. Oh, hell no, it wasn't a bad deal. We had the LADY going like a house afire. We were knocking the hell out of Osgood Brothers Implement Company, and Hump, that noble almost All-American footballer and vaunted sales manager of Osgood Brothers, comes crying to Mason out at dear old Crudney Hills for a combination. 'Let's all get together, Hump,' the hero says. 'Let's Mott and Osgood and Standard Tractor get together and set the price. We don't have any choice, boy. In view of rising labor costs, scarce steel, and skyrocketing freight rates, plus ruinatious competition, we don't have any choice.' Mason listened to Hump and he talked you into it, Glad, whether you'll ever admit it or not."

"What's the matter with the deal?" Mason said.

"In six months, you'll see," John said. "The LADY is such a good little machine that we could have wrapped up the market. Now we're taking thirds. Our volume is bound to drop."

"Bull," Gladstone said, "and Mason didn't talk me into a damned thing." At last he was in perfect control of himself. "We're getting nowhere, John. You'll have to make up your mind to be satisfied. These agreements are the coming thing, old sport. They're what all of us are working toward. Look what's happened in the automobile field, and the paper field, and the metal can field. Some day you'll see these agreements covering every phase of our business, from tractors like the LADY down to our cheapest peanut picker. You wait and see."

"Well, I'll be goddamned." John laughed. "I'll be goddamned if the man isn't sitting there, gazing into the distance, talking about getting together en masse to crooker the customer, and not only talking about it but dreaming about it, as if it were finally a cure for lung cancer or possibly the common cold. Goddammit, Glad, do you know what I'm talking about?"

"I never before realized that you were stupid," Gladstone said quietly. "Here you insult Mason at every turn and question my business sense and all at the top of your voice. You've done good work here, and I'm the first to admit it, but you're through. Where did they dig you up, anyway? What are you, the honor guard of all the fair fair principles? Are you the weeping heart of Murphy Avenue, here to assure all the suckers an even break?"

"It's all in how you see it," John said.

"Well, goddammit, you've got no right to take it out on Mason or Cherie or me. If you want to be a drunk, with all that soul-search mumbling in your beer, all right. That's your business. But you shouldn't cross us in the business." Gladstone's voice was low but his face was slack and disorganized. Perspiration had begun to collect on his forehead.

Getting to his feet, Gladstone said, "Get the hell out of my office, Shaw, before I lose my temper."

John Shaw studied his own hands. They were steady. He lighted a cigarette and strolled through the door, closing it gently behind him.

The late afternoon sunlight made dappled shadows on the walls of Gladstone's office. In the distance, the sound of the homeward bound Murphy Avenue traffic was loud and intermittently raucous. Mason and Gladstone sat in silence.

Finally Mason said, "Where do I stand in all this? You don't blame me, do you? Cherie doesn't blame me?"

"Hell no, Boss. We're old friends. We've been together for a long time," Gladstone said. "I picked you up when you didn't know one fork from another and I taught you how to wear a necktie and run a business. Between us, we've built a big business. Together, we're going to build an even bigger business. We're friends, old sport." Gladstone offered his hand and Mason solemnly shook it.

"One thing, Mason, before you go," Gladstone said. "I've been thinking about your car and I think you should have a new one. Why don't you take it downtown to the dealer's tomorrow and trade for a new one? Or better still, we'll both go. We might be able to work something."

Mason smiled, and the expression erased the strain from his face, and standing on the threshold of Gladstone's office, with the open door before him, he said, "Thanks, Glad. I think I'll get a red one this time, solid red. Thanks very much."

As Mason moved out of the office, Gladstone sat at the prodigious desk, idly studying the photographs which hung on the walls. He knew now that he would soon have to bring in someone to take John Shaw's place. It was true, of course, that no one was going to take Mason's place, no one could for that matter, but Gladstone recognized certain strains of truth in Shaw's accusations. Yes, it would be best to bring in one of those young eastern business school graduates. They always had a lot of new ideas and goodness knows, Gladstone thought, we could always use new ideas.

Mason still smiled as he walked over to the hatrack and donned the wide-brimmed Stetson. He did not appear to notice Chalmers or Jeff Spires as he opened the office door and walked out to his car. Heading into the dense Murphy Avenue traffic, he did not feel his customary annoyance toward the other cars. Today all of them were driven by benign and prosperous strangers.

Accelerating gently so as not to collide with the car ahead, Mason turned on the radio, but did not hear the music. He began to whistle, softly, on key. He was still whistling when he drove into his driveway. He cut the motor and sat quietly, listening. Within the house, he could hear the distant sound of the washing machine motor and in a moment, Desiree's footsteps as she came to meet him.

◆   DISCUSSION QUESTIONS

1. Describe the three main characters: Gladstone Mott, Mason, and John Shaw. What kind of person is each of them? What are their organizational roles? What is the nature of their relationship?

2. Evaluate John Shaw's accusations about the company's business dealings. Was he justified? What motivated him to make the accusations? Do you think Mott or Mason considers the business practice in question unethical? Use the General Ethical Checklist in reading 18.2, *Ethical Codes Are Not Enough,* to evaluate the price-fixing decision. Besides being illegal, which of the six questions did it violate? Why did the company decide to do it anyway?

3. Discuss how each of the three men, Gladstone Mott, Mason, and John Shaw, conducted themselves in their meeting. What other ways could Mott and Mason have handled the meeting, and to what effect?

4. Do you think these are basically honest people? Or is this just the tip of the

iceberg and they engage in other unethical practices at work and in their personal and family lives? How much do you trust Mason and Mott?

5. Write an epilogue to this story that addresses the following issues: Will Gladstone Mott change his attitudes and behavior as a result of John Shaw's outbursts? Will Mason? What predictions do you have for the future of Mott Implement Company? For Mason's career at Mott? Consider the following quotes from reading 18.2, *Ethical Codes Are Not Enough:* "A company is good only if it acts as if it will be around forever," and "A manager is also an ethical link between labor, shareholders, suppliers, and customers."

6. Make suggestions for improving Gladstone Mott's leadership style based on reading 18.1, *High Hurdles: The Challenge of Executive Self-Development.*

This Is My Voice

Jonathan Penner

This is the troubled and emotional testimony of a student who is trying to make sense of why he committed an unethical act. As he reflects about the experience, the student's conscience wrestles with the unethical behavior.

Jonathan Penner (b. 1940) is a professor of English at the University of Arizona. As he did for *This Is My Voice,* he used an academic setting for his 1977 novel, *Going Blind,* the story of a university professor who is gradually losing his eyesight.

Before I speak, can I say one thing? This has all been very upsetting. But I know you've got a job to do, and I know you're extremely intelligent people, and whatever punishment you decide I deserve is fine.

I guess it all began in August, when I first came here. Professor Delavette was still on Martha's Vineyard then. Her boarder got pneumonia and had to be hospitalized. His name was funny, something Saint something.

A saver, this guy was. I found drawers of empty Yoplait containers. He'd wash out the Nine Lives cans after he fed Professor Delavette's cat.

George St. George.

So I was looking for a place to get some writing done before the fall semester began, and the secretary had the keys to Professor Delavette's. St. George had developed something with his liver. He went home to Baltimore, I believe it was.

The secretary phones Professor Delavette and tells her a very large, very young man is available. Extremely, she says, looking up at me. I'm standing there in front of her desk, keeping my arms behind me, because all I did in high school was lift weights. And then I talked, and Professor Delavette said it was fine, so I stayed in her guest house and took care of things.

I have to tell you, and I know Dean Beechel has a meeting. This will be quick. I just have to tell you that Professor Delavette was the main reason I came here in the first place. I consider her one of our finest living writers. You know how informal she is, and the other students call her Gina and so forth, but for me it was thrilling just to cut her grass. Her power mower broke down, so I used a hand one. Once I turned over a wheelbarrow behind the tool shed, and underneath was a footprint in the hardened mud, and every day for the rest of August I came back and looked at it and wondered if it was hers.

I need to explain about me and writing. Too many ideas is what my trouble is. Even for the first word! And the crazy thing, what's so frustrating, is I feel like I already *know* the stories. Is that possible? I could swear they exist, I already know them, somewhere in here, or in here. Writing them down should be so easy, like unwrapping presents, and I'm so amazed when I never can.

Of course I signed up for her workshop. And that's really where I should have begun—I shouldn't have told you about St. George, and the cat, and the secretary. That was a terrible beginning. I signed up for her workshop, and next thing everyone else in the class is handing in stories. She'd get them duplicated and we'd all discuss them.

And what do I know, I'm the last person who should criticize. But I always felt terrible, reading those stories. The characters in them were always learning something important about life—they never just wasted their time, not a minute.

It was enough to make any actual human being feel poor. Is that good writing?

But I couldn't write any stories at all. After three weeks, I showed her a paragraph. Professor Delavette read it fast. Then she gave me a funny look, and sat down and read it slowly, with her finger moving down the margin and stopping sometimes to rub the paper in little circles. Then she hands it back and tells me, "I'm impressed. You have a voice."

Why did she have to say that? I sat and stared at that paragraph. It was something about the vacation I subbed at the post office. It was about carrying mail. It was idiotic, the things I remembered, like my shadow humping over the lawn, and songs I'd hear in my head all day, and places on the route where I could, you know, relieve myself. I tried reading it aloud, alone in my room, and I had to stop in the middle of the first sentence. I think it was right then that I started getting angry at Professor Delavette. When she told me I had a voice. Because it stank, and I'd written it the only way I could.

Whatever punishment you gentlemen decide is okay with me. I'm grateful to you and Professor Delavette for not telling the police. But what I want to emphasize is this. All this time, I was taking care of her place, and all through the semester I tried to do my best.

I swept her steps. I washed her windows inside and out. I kept her grass cut and raked out her hedges. Somehow she got her power mower going again, this old beast of a reel-type. It'd run awhile and stop. I'd pull the cord until my muscles felt like balloons, and take off my shirt and keep yanking, sometimes jerking the whole machine off the ground, until my right hand was cramped into a ball. Then I'd go up to the house, and Professor Delavette would come out and remove the air filter, or clean the plug, or just whack the carburetor, and it would run awhile again. She told me she couldn't afford a new one. Maybe that was my fault, because she'd said I didn't have to pay any rent for the guest house, except the value of my labor.

I guess it actually began when this young kid arrived, the Maharish. His friends call him that now. I don't want to get him mixed up in this. He's from my hometown; I used to baby-sit him and his sister. He quit high school and came to find me at the university, and I was amazed how he's changed. He brought a calendar with scenes of his guru doing yoga between vases of flowers. When I used to take him and his sister to play on the swings, he was a regular kid with a regular name.

Now he wants to be an artist, but he doesn't know how to paint. He doesn't have any paints. He said the first step was getting himself in tune. That's why he came to me, because he thought I was a writer and I'd inspire him. He's been sleeping on my floor in his dhoti. Like a loincloth?

I was afraid to tell Professor Delavette, but I made him phone his parents. He won't eat meat, and I've been trying to get some protein into him. But all he does is read all day, and meditate, and do his tantrum.

Tantrum. You sit a certain way and breathe a certain way.

Well, he saw I wasn't doing any writing, and he gave me some stuff to read. Stories from the Orient. The people in them learned wisdom from locusts and fish.

Next he brought out a magazine, *Ursa Major*. Fantasy. I love that stuff, but it was trash. I assume you gentlemen have all been shown one of those stories, the one where the couple become the slaves of their dog. At the time I just passed over it.

With the Maharish there, things got harder. He never left the room, and I didn't know what to do with him. By this time I'd dropped all my classes except Professor Delavette's, and I'd spend hours every day, sitting with cotton in my ears, staring at my typewriter, until it made me sweat just to roll in a piece of paper, with the Maharish doing his tantrum on the floor behind me. Even with the cotton, I thought I could hear the rhythm of his breathing.

No matter how I tried, I couldn't write a story, and sometimes I felt like I'd kill Professor Delavette, or else the Maharish. The only other thing in the world I could imagine doing was delivering mail again. So I went down to the post office and applied, but I'd gotten a bad report the time I worked for them as a sub.

The postmaster told me forget it. "Trouble with you," he said, "you got an attitude." He looked me up and down, and just from his body type, which was pitiful, I knew what was coming. "Like most jocks," he says, and starts shaking his head. "You think you can get through life on muscles."

No matter how you dress, if you lift too many years, they know. They know from your neck.

In October, there were leaves to rake, and you've heard about the fire. Professor Delavette came out with the garden hose. Then in November a pipe burst in the guest house bathroom. The Maharish discovered it, because he slept on the floor. The next thing I knew he was standing in the middle of my bed, dripping on me.

I pulled on some pants and went outside to shut off the main. Then I looked for a mop, but all there was was a handle with an empty clamp. Professor

Delavette came out and said her water had gone off, and for some reason I felt shy, even though I had my pants on. I leaned around the guest house door and told her the story.

"I've seen a naked man before," she says.

I'm sorry. I shouldn't have told you that.

I finished getting dressed and she gave me her car keys, and I went to the hardware store for a mop. They had mops. They had mops of every kind and size and shape. It was just the same as writing a story. Then I saw a replacement head and I was happy, and I bought it. But when I got it home, I couldn't get it into the clamp on Professor Delavette's old handle. It was too big.

We were on the porch of the guest house, and she stood there watching me. I went and got a hammer. I thought maybe I could just modify the clamp a little. Professor Delavette didn't say anything. She just looked at me so—seriously, or something—that I felt like I'd explode. I was kind of trying to hammer the clamp on my lap, and I could see she was afraid I'd hurt myself, but that she knew I'd be hurt more if she even opened her mouth. Then I did mash myself, a good one on the index finger. "My God," she says, and throws away the hammer. I'm squeezing the finger. "Let me see that," she says, pulling at my wrist.

Just then the Maharish comes out of the guest house. He stands there in the doorway in that loincloth of his, blinking at the daylight. "Something's happened," he tells me. "I'm in tune. I can feel it."

Well, Professor Delavette just looks at him, this practically naked little kid. He smiles at her. "Shanty, shanty, shanty," he says, kind of blessing her with his hand. She nods at him, and says, "Shanty, shanty," herself. Then she says she'll go call the plumber.

I knew what she was thinking, and I followed her up to her door. "He's just this kid," I tell her.

"He's lovely," she says. "Whatever helps. All I want from you is a story."

"I'm having trouble."

"You've got a voice," she says. "Use it." It was a command, like from a queen.

I should have told you that first, because this is when the bad part really began. The Maharish painted all day, except he didn't use paints. He couldn't afford them. He used food. Peanut butter, ketchup, mayonnaise. He used toothpaste and mud. He finger-painted. All this time I was trying to write. Then he said that since I'd helped him, now he was going to help me.

And that's when he came up with the idea for me to hand in that *Ursa Major* story. The one where the couple become the slaves of their dog. Just to get me started, just to get me going. I stood up and I felt like strangling him.

I sat down and tried again to write, and my ideas were like bugs around a streetlamp—all the people I could write about, everything I could make them say and do. And that's when I knew, I really understood for the first time, that there was no way in the world I could write a story.

"Let's see that magazine," I said.

And you know the rest. I stole it.

I was scared to death Professor Delavette would catch me, so you've seen the changes I made. It didn't need to be a couple that got enslaved, so I made it a guy. Instead of a dog, I made it a hobo woman that he befriends. She doesn't exactly enslave him—in fact he makes her hit the road, at the end—but she does, in a way. I thought I better slide in some things, about the job he works at, cleaning up alcoholics—that's where he meets this hobo woman—and about this old Thunderbird his girl friend is after him to buy. It's more confusing than in *Ursa Major*. At least there the story was clear. And in *Ursa Major* they had good writing, all soft and bouncy. Anyone would know I couldn't write that well—the sentences made me think of actual pillows—so I had the guy tell it the way I would, if it were me. If I were him. I titled it "His Master's Voice."

When I finished, my shirt was sticking to me. I didn't know if I could hand that story in. But it was that or give Professor Delavette nothing at all. I knew I couldn't put it in her hands, so I left it in her mailbox at school.

It was almost two weeks after the pipe broke, and we were having Indian summer. The grass needed one more mowing. I started at the back and was working my way forward toward the house, when I saw Professor Delavette coming toward me across the lawn. Right away I was sure she had me. Something was in her hand, and I guessed what it was.

I shut off the lawnmower, and you know how quiet that makes it. She just stood there. There were *tears* in her eyes, and I didn't know exactly what or how, but I knew right then that something terrible was going to happen.

"This is beautiful," she said. "This is wonderful."

She held it out to me and I took it. I just looked at the first page. She'd filled the margins with notes. *Rings true,* and *Captures it,* and *Good!* and *Yes!* all over the place.

I handed it back. "It's garbage," I said. "It isn't even mine." And I told her how I'd gotten the story from that trashy little magazine. But she just kept standing there, smiling and shaking her head.

"This is *yours,*" she says. *This is your voice.*"

Then she must have seen that I was starting to feel pretty bad, because she reached out and touched my arm, and said, "We'll talk about it later. Come up to the house when you're done." She gave the lawnmower a kick. Then she walked away with that awful story in her hand.

Well, I pulled the cord and it started right up. Exercise helps. You go to the weight room all in knots, and come out after your shower all peaceful. I pushed that lawnmower back and forth faster than most people jog.

But it didn't help, not this time. I went roaring past the guest house, where the Maharish was out in front on a blanket, trying for a tan in his loincloth. It was probably the last afternoon of the year that would be warm enough. The guy had inner peace, you've got to give him that. He'd given up his tantrum, and had just told me that morning he didn't need to paint anymore, either. He thought he was about ready to go home to his parents.

He waved his hand at me to slow down, but I couldn't. And the faster I went the worse I felt. And I'm ashamed to admit it, but you know what bothered me? She had no idea who I was. If she really liked me or my writing at all, she should have known that wasn't my work. And you know what else? Not the fact I plagiarized the story, though I'm ashamed of that too. It was the fact that she let herself be fooled. The more I thought about that, the longer I mowed, the more I lost all my respect for Professor Delavette, like I was cutting it down one row at a time.

By the time I finished the lawn it was all gone, and that's the only way I can explain what happened. I was right outside her living room. I shut off the lawnmower, and I knew I would never push that thing again. I felt like throwing it away. I lifted it by the handles, and I never felt so strong in my life.

I began to turn, stepping backward in a circle, leaning against the weight. It's all in the forearms. I got it a few inches off the ground, then higher. I leaned back and got in knee-high, thigh-high, until I could get my legs and shoulders into it, and the lawnmower and I were just whirling each other around, and then I gave it everything I had. It just cleared the sill of her big living room window and went crashing through.

You could hear the thump and clank as it hit the carpet, and the glass tinkling like wind chimes. Then an upstairs window opened, and Professor Delavette leaned her head out.

"What in the world," she says, "was that?"

I tell her, "That was my voice. *That* was my voice."

Well, I know Dean Beechel has to go. I guess all you gentlemen do. I guess I'll be getting a letter after you've decided.

I just wanted you to understand what happened. Naturally, I feel different now. In the last week I've read Professor Delavette's books again, and I can't be angry at her—only grateful. She truly is one of the finest writers alive.

And I realize that's the problem right there. For her, writing is just so easy, it doesn't take any effort at all. She can sit down and write a story anytime she wants to. So how can she understand the fact that I can't?

I know you gentlemen will be writing an official report. I hope you'll say I tried my best. Please put that in my permanent file. But say it was like trying to burn an ice cube.

Say it was like trying to teach a hippo to dance.

Or a sewer to sing.

Then if anybody—some future employer—if anyone ever wants to know about me, they'll simply look it up—I waive my right to privacy—and they'll know. Or the government. They can just read your report, and they'll know the truth. Teachers, in case I ever come back to school—they can look too. I waive my right to privacy—do I have a right to privacy? I don't care who sees it, even Professor Delavette herself, in case someday she needs to put me in a story, and she's trying to get my voice, but all she remembers is a broken window, and the smell of grass coming up her stairs.

♦   *DISCUSSION QUESTIONS*

1. Explain to whom the student/narrator is talking, and why he is telling this story.

2. The student/narrator apparently knew it was wrong to plagiarize, but he went ahead with it anyway. Evaluate all the reasons he claims caused him to plagiarize. What do you think are the real reasons he did it?

3. Reading 18.2, *Ethical Codes Are Not Enough*, argues that people talk themselves into unethical acts because they pretend there are no consequences to suffer; they refuse to think about them, forget about them, or engage in wishful thinking. How does the notion of consequences figure in the student/narrator's thinking?

4. Reading 18.2, *Ethical Codes Are Not Enough*, presents the following contemporary version of the classic Glaucon's challenge: "If a person could lie, cheat, and steal and never be caught, why would he or she ever be honest?" The student/narrator in *This Is My Voice* might never have been caught, yet he turned himself in. Why?

5. Evaluate Professor Delavette's role in the story. What could she have done to help the student? After the student explained how he had gotten the story from the magazine, Professor Delavette said, "This is yours. This is your voice." What did she mean? Did she believe he plagiarized the story?

6. Colleges and universities typically have codes of academic honesty. Reading 18.2, *Ethical Codes Are Not Enough*, suggests that codes are inadequate to ensure ethical behavior. Use the reading and the story as a guide in proposing other measures that academic institutions can implement to foster ethical behavior. Evaluate how well your own college or university promotes an ethical climate for students, faculty, and administrators.

7. Imagine the student a few years later working in an organization. Discuss his strengths and weaknesses in terms of what kind of employee he will make.

READING 16.1

A New Customer

Viktor Slavkin

Anyone who has ever traveled to a foreign country has found themselves in the situation depicted in this story: trying to order a meal in a restaurant. However, this vignette goes beyond the details of filling one's stomach, by satirizing the Soviet work ethic and workers' attitudes toward customer service. The story offers a glimpse of some of the issues western business people must understand before they can expect to do business successfully in another culture.

Viktor Slavkin is a Soviet writer. This story was originally written in Russian and was intended for a Soviet audience.

Around four o'clock, a new customer stepped over the threshold of the second-class restaurant. "Greetings." He crossed the room diagonally and sat down at an empty table.

About twenty minutes passed. Volodia, the waiter, gave his unfinished cigarette to one of his colleagues to hold, with his right hand smoothed over the piece of a Russian folk ornament hanging off his left sleeve, and moved toward the customer. Having approached the table, he silently pointed to a napkin lying in the center of the table, on which was written, "This table is not being served."

The customer looked at the waiter with the eyes of a kind dog who had just heard from its master the words, "Time for a walk."

"Move to a table where there is already someone," Volodia explained patiently. "I won't serve you alone."

"Please do not chase me away," the customer said timidly.

"Don't you understand Russian? I said this table is not set."

"I'll wait."

"As you wish. You'll sit." Volodia lost all interest in the conversation.

Source: From the *Daily Report*, published in Washington by the FBIS.

"I'll sit," said the customer. "Thank you."

"Only there is no need to be rude," the waiter warned.

"I'll sit. Don't worry. It's nothing."

"Besides, how can there be accusations? Just sat down, and already . . ."

"What is your name?" asked the customer.

"Are you going to cause a scene? Watch it."

The other waiters, smoking by the manager's table, felt the trouble brewing. Their loose jackets filled out by young muscles, the lapels flared up.

"I don't want to cause a scene." It seemed as if the customer was about to cry. "I just want an introduction."

Volodia waved his friends off and their jackets loosened up once again.

"Volodia," said he.

"My name might seem strange to you."

"So, what do we want to eat?" asked the waiter and took out his writing pad.

"Don't rush, Volodia. Go, finish your cigarette. Give the other table their bill. Besides, you don't even have a menu with you . . ."

"It's not been printed yet."

"Wonderful. Then I'll just sit. The people who were at this table before me left some bread, there is mustard. What else does one need? After all, it is inconvenient for you to take care of me now."

"Inconvenient," agreed Volodia, but for some strange reason, he did not walk away.

The customer took a piece of bread out of the basket, covered it with a thick layer of mustard, sprinkled it with salt, and bowed his well-groomed head over this dish, deeply inhaled the scent.

"What, you've never seen food?" the waiter snickered.

The customer choked and began coughing. Volodia hit him hard on the back.

"Volodia, I'd like to ask you . . . that is, could you promise me . . . anyway, if I admit something to you, give me your word that your benevolence towards me will not change."

"What are you coming back from, prison?" The waiter guessed.

"I am a . . . foreigner . . ." the customer said quietly. Then in a completely morbid voice he added, "from a capitalist country."

Volodia's Adam's apple bobbed as if he had swallowed an apricot pit, and he asked hoarsely:

"May I be allowed to change the tablecloth?"

"I thought this might happen." The customer hung his head and his thin fingers began running spasmodically over the dirty tablecloth. "This stain reminds me of the shape of my poor country."

Volodia glanced with interest at the stains from the sauce "piquant."

"Gee, I'm not aware of such a country."

"And a good thing it is." The customer covered the stain with his hand. "It is a pygmy country with no particular significance in the world. The name is Grand-Carlo. Have you heard of it?"

"No."

"We're the richest country in the world," the customer said sadly, and bit off another piece of bread.

"But I bet you don't have mustard like this!" Professional pride spoke in the waiter.

"We have everything, except economic problems. Or any problems. None whatsoever."

"Whatever you say," said the waiter somberly. "I have to go to work."

He tried walking away from the table.

The foreigner held him back by his jacket.

"Volodia, my dear! You can't imagine what it's like."

"We can. Saw it in a movie."

"Oh no! What you saw in a movie can not compare to what is happening in our country. It is awful! Awful! Our muscles wither, our brains freeze, our instincts vanish, our immune system disintegrates—the nation is becoming extinct."

Bread trembled in the customer's hand.

"Only here in your country do I feel like a human being." Suddenly the customer smiled. "You know, the moment I crossed the border, I tore off all my clothes and bought clothes made in your country in the nearest Manufactured Goods store. I bought a shirt, shoes, a suit . . . Volodia, buy yourself one like it; there are more. The collar cuts into the neck and under the arms, it pulls in the crotch, the waist is too tight . . . But I feel them. I am in constant contact with them, I fight them! This fills me up with energy and belief in my eventual victory. I know that you dream of getting Cardin clothes. No, Volodia. Don't. Get them only from Manufactured Goods Store."

"Your wealth is making you mad. You know this saying that we have."

"It's not a saying, Volodia, It's a proverb." Once again the customer became sad. "In any case, such is the view of Vladimir Ivanovich Dal'."

"Are your parents Russian?"

"That's another one for you. I am a native Grand-Carlean, but the moment I expressed the desire, our travel agency in two weeks, only two weeks, instilled in me the vocabulary of four volumes of Dal' as well as the total absence of an accent. They have worked out a method. I had to make no effort. But where is the happiness that comes from work, the marvel of comprehending something new? Can one live like that, Volodia?"

"You know what," squinted the waiter, "if you are so sick of it, send all you have in excess to Africa. They'll use it there and you'll be able to relax a bit."

The customer looked at him with respect.

"You have the mind for government, Volodia. But you don't know our immoral industry. We can give away everything. Burn everything. It will all be reproduced immediately, doubled in volume."

"Well, then, I don't know what to tell you." Volodia shrugged his shoulders, and his face showed the utmost concern.

The customer began speaking excitedly.

"This is not my first time in your country. I come here not without reason. Not at all. I walk down the streets, visit stores, cafeterias, other places of communal usage, and everywhere, everywhere I see burning eyes, goal-striving faces, thought-out movements. Life is in full swing, people act, everything around is changing for the better. Man struggles, meaning he exists, damn it! I feel it myself, right now. For example, if I were to walk into one of our Grand-Carlo restaurants, immediately I would be attacked by our service sharks, our courtesy gangsters, our terrorists of communal feeding. In a moment they turn a person into a well-fed satisfied beast. Now let's take your blessed establishment, your soul-saving Greetings. I crossed its threshold experiencing a sharp pang of hunger, a feeling I haven't had in a long time. And you so keenly comprehending my state did not rush over to me. I sat at the table and with nothing to do, my stomach empty, began thinking over my life. The memories came to me by themselves. I remembered how I skinned my knee as a child. I remembered my mother, my father . . . It has been a long time since I've thought of them."

"That's not good," Volodia said strictly. "I personally always bring my mother some goodies once a week."

"And when you came up to me," the customer continued, "you did not spoil my mood. On the contrary, you obliged me with your so pleasant refusal to serve me. Thank you. But how do we teach *our* dummies to do that?"

"That's easy," said the waiter. "How do you say, 'This table is not served' in your language?"

"It's an untranslatable play on words."

"So let your dummy write this play on words on a piece of paper and put it on the table."

"And that's it?"

"That's it."

"But what is the purpose?" It was apparent that the customer had difficulty grasping the novel idea. "After all, the seat is not being used, profits are lost, the earnings . . ." He was reasoning out loud.

"Well, if you think like that, it won't work for sure."

"The kitchen is still preparing food. It must realize . . ."

"So let the kitchen staff consume what they make."

"How's that?"

"Or take it home."

"I don't understand."

"What's there not to understand? Every cook must have a bag with him. He comes in the morning with it empty and goes home with it jammed."

"Jammed? What does 'jammed' mean?"

"So much for your celebrated knowledge of Russian."

The customer's head dropped onto his chest.

"Come, come now. What's the matter? What's with you? . . . Oh come now, stop crying!" Volodia shook the customer by the shoulder, and the customer once again regained control of himself.

"These are not tears my friend. It's a type of contact lenses that we have.

They have neither weight, nor thickness, just sparkle to rejuvenate a person. I am old, Volodia. It is only this physical shape that we are in. Don't believe it, Volodia, don't! I am an old and a sick man. But they, our killers in white coats, they made me young and healthy. I play tennis, I swim. I am loved by young girls. But Volodia, I want to sit in the park with people my age, play chess, stand in line for cottage cheese, and if it's not there or it has run out, to go to another one and another . . . with friends, with a crowd, with company. Or maybe to ride the bus to the other end of town during the traffic hour. How many stories we can tell each other on the way there! All of us together, jointly, all at once, in cohoots, all of us, en masse . . . Do you respect me, Volodia? Do you? Tell me, Volodia, do you respect me?"

"I respect you, pops, I do. But only . . ."

"What!!!" exclaimed the customer tragically. "What!!!"

"Be quiet." Volodia threw a glance around. The restaurant was almost empty. "I'm trying to say that the kitchen is about to close. Nobody here is hired to serve you until all hours of the night."

The customer became depressed.

"Then, Volodia," he said, "I have a last request for you. Bring me something as bad as possible."

"That we'll do." The waiter scribbled something on his pad and started toward the kitchen. He came up to the serving window and shouted:

"Vasia, one burned steak with yesterday's potatoes."

"O.K.," replied Vasia, "O.K.," and carried out the order diligently.

◆ DISCUSSION QUESTIONS

1. The Dutch researcher Geert Hofstede wrote that foreign visitors form impressions of the "national character" of a country, that is, "the cultural mental programming that the people of that country have in common" [1]. From this story what can you say about the "national character" of the Soviet people with respect to the following four dimensions identified by Hofstede: power distance, uncertainty avoidance, masculinity/femininity, and individualism/collectivism?

2. What does this story tell you about the Russian work ethic? Use your knowledge of motivation and reward systems to improve service in this restaurant. What factors would you need to take into account to ensure that your motivational plan would be effective in Russia?

3. Compare your motivational plan with that used by the American fastfood chain, McDonald's, in its Moscow restaurant [2]. The restaurant is run with methods used in the company's American operations. Why is their method successful? McDonald's plans to expand widely throughout Russia. What factors will affect their success?

4. This story was written for a Soviet audience. What message is Slavkin trying to convey to his countrymen? Why does he use a mythical foreigner and satire to convey it?

5. What aspects of the story puzzled or surprised you? What things would you like to learn more about to conduct business effectively in other cultures such as the Soviet culture?

6. Imagine a mythical foreigner visits an American restaurant. What aspects of American business and service culture might be most salient?

◆   REFERENCES

1. Hofstede, G. Summer 1980. Motivation, leadership, and organization: Do American theories apply abroad? *Organizational Dynamics*. 42–63.

2. Hertzfeld, J. January–February 1991. Joint ventures: Saving the Soviets from perestroika. *Harvard Business Review*. 80–91.

"It Got Smashed"

Raymond H. Abbott

This story introduces us to one of the subcultures in the United States—the Sioux Indians. A young man assigned to work on the reservation is baffled by the behavior of an Indian woman. As you read this account, think of the challenges involved in respecting cultural diversity in the workplace and having it enhance organizational effectiveness.

Raymond H. Abbott (b. 1942) was born in Massachusetts, where he worked as a social worker and elementary school teacher. In the mid 1960s he lived on the Rosebud, South Dakota reservation with the Sioux Indians for several years, serving as a Vista volunteer and community development director of the transitional housing program. Several of his stories and novels draw from his life on the reservation. Mr. Abbott says: "I bet a hundred magazines small and large passed on *Smashed.* I was the only believer, at least for a while."* The story won a prize in the PEN syndicated fiction project in 1983.

The Indians carefully looked over the young stranger—the priest they knew well enough by now. But several must have thought it a bit unusual, though, for a Jesuit priest to be going around with a Mormon Elder, for everyone on the reservation knew the Catholics and the Mormons were enemies, since the latter had arrived on the reservation five years earlier and immediately tried to convert long-standing Roman Catholic families to Mormonism.

The priest—Father Keegan was his name—watched with an amused expression as the Indians studied the stranger. He thought, they really must be puzzled as to what he was doing with a Mormon. No one asked, however. The priest was perhaps in his early fifties, thick built, and what hair he had left now, remnants of a once thick head of hair, was on the side of his head near his ears and it was completely white. Little specks of dandruff clung to the hair, eventually landing on his shoulder. The dandruff was very noticeable against the black of his suit, a suit shiny with wear. He didn't seem to notice, however, or if he did he stopped caring about how he looked a long time before. There were other things too about his appearance that said he cared less now, less than he once had. His weight for one thing. He was rapidly putting on pounds, and he slouched as if he were depressed, which he was, but it wasn't something he admitted to even to himself.

Source: Published in *The Available Press/PEN Short Story Collection*, New York, Ballantine, 1985, in cooperation with the PEN Syndicated Fiction Project. Reprinted by permission of the author and publisher.
*Personal communication.

And there had been a time, and it wasn't so long before either, that he cared very much about how he looked, as much as a man might be permitted within the confines of being a Jesuit priest on a rural Indian reservation in South Dakota. After all, he like his fellow priests had taken a vow of poverty when he became a Jesuit Father and came to this reservation many years before.

Just how many years had it been now on this reservation? he thought. Twelve, or was it fourteen? Sometimes he couldn't recall, and there had been other assignments before this one.

The man with Father Keegan was not a Mormon, however. By South Dakota standards he was an easterner. He came from somewhere near Columbus, Ohio, and was on the reservation that week for his first time. He had been there for what seemed to him like the three hottest days he had ever spent anywhere. The temperature so far had been near a hundred degrees every day. Later he was to observe that a Dakota winter—especially when a northwester blew in with the heavy snows—was like nothing he had ever known in Ohio, or even Boston, where he was born and spent ten years before his family moved on to Ohio. He wore a suit and tie and was beginning to feel somewhat silly and damn hot dressed in this way. But he felt he had to do this, for he remembered the words of the tribal Chairman, a man by the name of Amos Featherman, who had said to him and others upon their arrival that he wanted the professional people working for the tribe, and he would be working for the tribe, to look the part— to look like the professionals they were—and that meant wearing ties and jackets at all times. It was Featherman's opinion that appearances and especially the way a man dressed was an example to the Indian people. A goal they might work toward themselves, he said in his little homily that first day they were on the reservation. To John Magley—that was the young man's name—what Featherman said didn't make a hell of a lot of sense. He couldn't see that anyone in this little village of Cut Meat afforded him more respect because of any suit and tie he wore. If anything, he thought they looked at him as if to say, "What a God damn fool that white guy is to wear such uncomfortable clothing on a hot day." Yet he was new to the reservation and didn't wish to violate the instructions of the powerful tribal Chairman, Featherman.

The priest didn't understand either why the young man wore a suit on these hot days. He thought it must simply be a habit, a habit he would soon get out of along with a few others as well, he would guess if he were a guessing man, and he was. Father Keegan was now pointing to land across from where they stood on the steps of the post office in Cut Meat village. It was barren sun-baked land, where only a water windmill stood. The windmill spun rather wildly in the strong wind. Several head of cattle were clustered around the large metal tub that served as a trough. Dust devils scurried across the plowed stretches of a section of land where someone had planned to plant something and never got around to do it. Much of the topsoil had already blown away.

"That's all tribal land," he said with no particular enthusiasm, almost as if he might be pointing at the surface of the moon instead of reservation land. "And we can build the houses there. In a cluster if enough people want to live that way. But these people out here have strange ideas sometimes. They may not go for the cluster idea right away. A lot of people don't like their neighbors and would welcome a chance to move off by themselves. We'll have a time convincing them there is an advantage in living in a cluster—things like sewerage and street-lights and paved streets and a central water system. I guess you can't blame them really—there is so much trouble in these towns on the weekend or whenever a few people have some money for a little booze. Then all kinds of fighting and commotion breaks out; you'll see quick enough."

Father Keegan was talking about a housing project that after years and years of planning—many surveys and countless trips to Washington, D.C., to see the bureaucrats and much, much more—was finally going to happen on this reservation. The funding had already been approved and the young man, John Magley, next to him was the architect who was to design two different houses. Both were supposed to be simple but well-made houses, and for the next year and a half or two years Magley would be returning to the reservation to oversee the construction of the housing units. It was an important project to the young man. Important to his career as an architect and important on a personal level. He very much wished to help poor, downtrodden Indians.

As the priest and the young man stood talking and pointing at the land across the gravel road a squat Indian woman approached. She was of an age difficult to determine—although she had to be beyond thirty and probably older than that. She certainly looked every bit of thirty-five or even forty. She came up to the priest and stood in front of him. She said nothing, waiting until she saw he was done talking with the other white man, the Mormon—that's who she thought John Magley was. It didn't seem at all incongruous to her that the Jesuit priest was with a Mormon. All she saw was his suit and tie, and only Mormons wore those, even on the warmest days.

Father Keegan saw her right away, however, but he continued talking, not paying her any attention at first. Then he spoke to her as if he had seen her for the first time. He spoke in Lakota, giving her a warm greeting, one he had used in a similar situation at least a hundred, no a thousand times before, he thought. He still hadn't got over how indifferent some Indians could be to his efforts to speak their language, especially the women, he had found. They would usually nod or grunt as they might to any white man who spoke to them. There was no acknowledgment that he could determine anyway that even hinted he was some-how different because he spoke their language a little, something most white people were unwilling to try to do.

This day she nodded and sort of smiled, he thought, and answered him in English, using short, clipped sentences to convey what was on her mind. She began to enumerate a few of her recent problems—how difficult life had been for her. Father Keegan knew immediately what this was to lead to—it meant she wanted to borrow two or three dollars until the sudden crisis in her life passed. He had heard it all enough times before to know the signs, but even after a dozen years the use of the word *borrow* still troubled him. He was sure it had to mean something else to Indians, something different at least from what it meant to the white man, because he couldn't remember—with one or two glaring exceptions—when an Indian had ever "borrowed" two dollars and come back with the intention of repaying him.

As he listened to her story he thought that if he gave every person who approached him for money what they asked for he would be without any money at all for anything, so he had learned to anticipate these requests and at times was capable of maneuvering around in such a way as to keep the request from being made. But he seldom did this and when he did it was because he knew the person asking would spend the money on liquor and it wasn't his place to support the liquor industry, and with the requests for cash assistance growing by the month, indeed by the day, he had to be careful, and that meant being selective. He was good at it, although being cunning wasn't something he enjoyed doing.

For some reason he remembered this woman, although she wasn't from his parish. Her name was Gail Yellow Hawk, and he was sure he had seen her a month or two before at the tribal office building or the public health hospital. She had then been late in pregnancy. Now quite obviously she was not pregnant. He wondered what might have happened, for he hadn't heard of her being at the public health hospital to have her baby. It was not so uncommon for women to have their children at home, especially those who lived in remote distant villages, but somehow he didn't think this had happened with Gail.

After a couple of minutes of meaningless chatter he asked what was on his mind. "What happened to your baby, Gail? Did you have it at home?" He almost said again but remembered in time that it was Eileen Two Hawk, not Gail Yellow Hawk, who had had a baby at home last year.

"No, Father," she replied, offering no additional explanation. But he was used to this kind of reply and he also was not timid about getting what he wanted in information, especially if someone was about to borrow money from him.

"So what happened?" he asked. "Where's the baby?"

"It was born in the Valentine Hospital. I was shopping that day when the time came," she said.

"Is it still in the hospital in Valentine?" Valentine, Nebraska, was off the reservation by about sixty miles to the south. It was one of the shopping centers for reservation Indians. It was also a favorite drinking spot for locals.

"No, Father, it died."

John Magley was watching all of this very carefully, as if in what went on between her and priest there might be something he could learn about Sioux Indians. These native people so far were very much a mystery to him. And he wasn't at all sure he would enjoy working on a reservation for two long years with a people who were at times so difficult to understand, and for him to make himself understood too. He had already discovered that when he was talking about one subject, the Indian he spoke to as often as not had not made the transition from the subject that had ended five minutes before. It was frustrating for him, and it was driving him nuts the way everything he said was taken so damn literally.

But when the woman had said her baby died Magley couldn't see any expression of grief on her face, and that puzzled him. She had just said the baby died like she might have said she was going to the market for a loaf of bread.

What an awful thing to have happened, he thought, although he didn't know the circumstances. Still, he knew how he would have felt or, worse yet, how his wife would feel if they lost one of their sons shortly after birth as obviously this woman had.

The priest did not follow through in his questioning and so John Magley did.

"Well, what happened? I mean, how did the baby die?" he asked. He was nervous—this was one of his first conversations with a back-country Indian. So far he had dealt almost entirely with tribal leaders, and many of those seemed to him like white people. Businessmen with a tan, he had heard someone describe them once.

His voice broke a little with emotion as he asked his question, and the voice held all the kindness and sympathy one could bring forth for a near stranger who had recently faced tragedy. But he wasn't prepared for her reply. Then nobody could have been, he thought later, except maybe for the priest. He might have seen the answer coming. And for that reason didn't go on with the questioning.

The woman looked at him, rather sternly he thought, because he was interfering in a way with what she had set out to do that afternoon, and that was to borrow three dollars from the Jesuit priest, Father Keegan. She very much needed three dollars this day. Maybe she felt obligated, but for whatever reasons she answered him again in her abbreviated way of speaking, saying rather matter-of-factly, Magley thought, "It got smashed." That's all she said as she turned back to the priest and asked him for the money she needed.

Magley said nothing, but suddenly he felt keenly aware of the other Indians standing nearby, although it was unlikely they were paying much attention to what the white men and this woman were saying. And why he should care what they thought of him didn't make sense to him either, but he did. It was, after all, a reasonable question to ask considering what had already been said. But he did feel stupid and a bit depressed. And for a moment he wished he weren't standing in this depressing Indian village in South Dakota and was someplace else, like in his air-conditioned office in downtown Columbus.

Father Keegan finally handed the woman one dollar and she walked off toward the shanties behind the post office and country store, and they walked silently toward the car and got in and drove away over the dusty gravel road toward the junction of Route 18, which led into Mission Town twenty miles on down the road. The dust hung heavy behind the car as it moved toward the crossroads. The outline of the village was obscured by the dust.

The priest's eyes twinkled; his depression had lifted somewhat. He had enjoyed watching the exchange between Gail Yellow Hawk and John Magley. He had some difficulty in keeping from laughing, but after a few miles of silence Magley loosened his necktie, looked over to the priest, who was driving, and smiled and said, "Just like that she tells me, 'It got smashed'—that's all, and then she asks you for three dollars. My God!"

The two men then laughed so hard, the priest had to stop the car for fear he would run them off the highway and into a ditch or into an approaching vehicle.

◆ *DISCUSSION QUESTIONS*

1. Discuss John Magley's values and his assumptions about the Sioux nation. What do his lack of preparation for work on the reservation, and the terms he uses to describe the Indians imply about his assumptions and values?

2. What should John Magley have done to prepare for his job as housing director on the Sioux reservation? What aspects of the Sioux culture will be most important for him to learn in order to work effectively in that environment? Refer to the musings and experiences of Father Keenan, and the relationships the whites have with the tribal chiefs and the rest of the Indian community.

3. Examine the interchange between Father Keenan, John Magley, and Gail Yellow Hawk. What do you find puzzling about it? Why did Gail Yellow Hawk address Father Keenan in English? Why did Father Keenan enjoy the exchange between John Magley and Gail Yellow Hawk? What do the Indians think of these men?

4. Suppose individuals from another culture seek employment in mainstream American corporations. According to reading 18.3, *Managing Diversity,* organizations need to learn how to effectively manage minorities, who are becoming a significantly larger portion of the work force. Make recommendations about ways managers can enhance organizational effectiveness by understanding and respecting the cultural diversity of employees. How can special treatment of cultural differences be reconciled with issues of workplace justice and equity?

5. In some companies, according to reading 18.3, *Managing Diversity,* "the corporate culture is not going to change—it's up to the employees themselves whether they want to fit in or not." What are some of the important "ropes to know" in organizations that may be culture-bound [1]? What are the consequences of organizations not adapting to a culturally diverse work force?

◆ *REFERENCES*

1. Adler, N. 1991. *International Dimensions of Organizational Behavior,* 2d ed. Boston: PWS-KENT Publishing Co.

Bureaucrats

Joan Didion

This essay documents the attempts of the California Department of Transportation to change commuting habits in Los Angeles County in the 1970s. The administrators tried to impose change without coming to grips with the fundamental reason why they were encountering strong resistance: America's love affair with the automobile.

Joan Didion (b. 1934) was born in Sacramento and lived for many years in Los Angeles. "For years, Didion's favorite subject was her native California, a state that seemed to supply ample evidence of the disorder of society, confirming her suspicion that 'things fall apart; the center cannot hold,' to quote the poet W.B. Yeats as Didion does. [1]"

◆ ◆ ◆

The closed door upstairs at 120 South Spring Street in downtown Los Angeles is marked OPERATIONS CENTER. In the windowless room beyond the closed door a reverential hush prevails. From six A.M. until seven P.M. in this windowless room men sit at consoles watching a huge board flash colored lights. "There's the heart attack," someone will murmur, or "we're getting the gawk effect." 120 South Spring is the Los Angeles office of Caltrans, or the California Department of Transportation, and the Operations Center is where Caltrans engineers monitor what they call "the 42-Mile Loop." The 42-Mile Loop is simply the rough triangle formed by the intersections of the Santa Monica, the San Diego and the Harbor freeways, and 42 miles represents less than ten per cent of freeway mileage in Los Angeles County alone, but these particular 42 miles are regarded around 120 South Spring with a special veneration. The Loop is a "demonstration system," a phrase much favored by everyone at Caltrans, and is part of a "pilot project," another two words carrying totemic weight on South Spring.

The Loop has electronic sensors embedded every half-mile out there in the pavement itself, each sensor counting the crossing cars every twenty seconds. The Loop has its own mind, a Xerox Sigma V computer which prints out, all day and night, twenty-second readings on what is and is not moving in each of the Loop's eight lanes. It is the Xerox Sigma V that makes the big board flash red when traffic out there drops below fifteen miles an hour. It is the Xerox Sigma V that tells the Operations crew when they have an "incident" out there. An "incident" is the heart attack on the San Diego, the jackknifed truck on the Harbor, the Camaro just now tearing out the Cyclone fence on the Santa Monica. "Out there" is where incidents happen. The windowless room at 120 South Spring is where incidents get "verified." "Incident verification" is turning on the closed-circuit TV on the console and watching the traffic slow down to see (this is "the gawk effect") where the Camaro tore out the fence.

As a matter of fact there is a certain closed-circuit aspect to the entire mood of the Operations Center. "Verifying" the incident does not after all "prevent" the incident, which lends the enterprise a kind of tranced distance, and on the day recently when I visited 120 South Spring it took considerable effort to remember what I had come to talk about, which was that particular part of the Loop called the Santa Monica Freeway. The Santa Monica Freeway is 16.2 miles long, runs from the Pacific Ocean to downtown Los Angeles through what is referred to at Caltrans as "the East-West Corridor," carries more traffic every day than any other freeway in California, has what connoisseurs of freeways concede to be the most beautiful access ramps in the world, and appeared to have been transformed by Caltrans, during the several weeks before I went downtown to talk about it, into a 16.2-mile parking lot.

The problem seemed to be another Caltrans "demonstration," or "pilot," a foray into bureaucratic terrorism they were calling "The Diamond Lane" in their promotional literature and "The Project" among themselves. That the promotional literature consisted largely of schedules for buses (or "Diamond Lane Expresses") and invitations to join a car pool via computer ("Commuter Computer") made clear not only the putative point of The Project, which was to encourage travel by car pool and bus, but also the actual point, which was to eradicate a central Southern California illusion, that of individual mobility, without anyone really noticing. This had not exactly worked out. "FREEWAY FIASCO," the *Los Angeles Times* was headlining page-one stories. "THE DIAMOND LANE: ANOTHER BUST BY CALTRANS." "CALTRANS PILOT EFFORT ANOTHER IN LONG LIST OF FAILURES." "OFFICIAL DIAMOND LANE STANCE: LET THEM HOWL."

All "The Diamond Lane" theoretically involved was reserving the fast inside lanes on the Santa Monica for vehicles carrying three or more people, but in practice this meant that 25 per cent of the freeway was reserved for 3 per cent of the cars, and there were other odd wrinkles here and there suggesting that Caltrans had dedicated itself to making all movement around Los Angeles as arduous as possible. There was for example the matter of surface streets. A "surface street" is anything around Los Angeles that is not a freeway ("going surface" from one part of town to another is generally regarded as idiosyncratic), and surface streets do not fall directly within the Caltrans domain, but now the engineer in charge of surface streets was accusing Caltrans of threatening and intimidating him. It appeared that Caltrans wanted him to create a "confused and congested situation" on his surface streets, so as to force drivers back to the freeway, where they would meet a still more confused and congested situation and decide to stay home, or take a bus. "We are beginning a process of deliberately making it harder for drivers to use freeways," a Caltrans director had in fact said at a transit conference some months before. "We are prepared to endure considerable public outcry in order to pry John Q. Public out of his car. . . . I would emphasize that this is a political decision, and one that can be reversed if the public gets sufficiently enraged to throw us rascals out."

Of course this political decision was in the name of the greater good, was in the interests of "environmental improvement" and "conservation of resources," but even there the figures had about them a certain Caltrans opacity. The Santa Monica normally carried 240,000 cars and trucks every day. These 240,000 cars and trucks normally carried 260,000 people. What Caltrans described as its ultimate goal on the Santa Monica was to carry the same 260,000 people, "but in 7,800 fewer, or 232,000 vehicles." The figure "232,200" had a visionary precision to it that did not automatically create confidence, especially since the only effect so far had been to disrupt traffic throughout the Los Angeles basin, triple the number of daily accidents on the Santa Monica, prompt the initiation of two lawsuits against Caltrans, and cause large numbers of Los Angeles County residents to behave, most uncharacteristically, as an ignited and conscious proletariat. Citizen guerrillas splashed paint and scattered nails in the Diamond Lanes. Diamond Lane maintenance crews expressed fear of hurled objects. Down at 120 South Spring the architects of the Diamond Lane had taken to regarding "the media" as the architects of their embarrassment, and Caltrans statements in the press had been cryptic and contradictory, reminiscent only of old communiqués out of Vietnam.

To understand what was going on it is perhaps necessary to have participated in the freeway experience, which is the only secular communion Los Angeles has. Mere driving on the freeway is in no way the same as participating in it. Anyone can "drive" on the freeway, and many people with no vocation for it do, hesitating here and resisting there, losing the rhythm of the lane change, thinking about where they came from and where they are going. Actual participants think only about where they are. Actual participation requires a total surrender, a concentration so intense as to seem a kind of narcosis, a rapture-of-the-freeway. The mind goes clean. The rhythm takes over. A distortion of time occurs, the same distortion that characterizes the instant before an accident. It takes only a few seconds to get off the Santa Monica Freeway at National-Overland, which is a difficult exit requiring the driver to cross two new lanes of traffic streamed in from the San Diego Freeway, but those few seconds always seem to me the longest part of the trip. The moment is dangerous. The exhilaration is in doing it. "As you acquire the special skills involved," Reyner Banham observed in an extraordinary chapter about the freeways in his 1971 *Los An-*

geles: The Architecture of Four Ecologies, "the freeways become a special way of being alive . . . the extreme concentration required in Los Angeles seems to bring on a state of heightened awareness that some locals find mystical."

Indeed some locals do, and some nonlocals too. Reducing the number of lone souls careering around the East-West Corridor in a state of mechanized rapture may or may not have seemed socially desirable, but what it was definitely not going to seem was easy. "We're only seeing an initial period of unfamiliarity," I was assured the day I visited Caltrans. I was talking to a woman named Eleanor Wood and she was thoroughly and professionally grounded in the diction of "planning" and it did not seem likely that I could interest her in considering the freeway as regional mystery. "Any time you try to rearrange people's daily habits, they're apt to react impetuously. All this project requires is a certain rearrangement of people's daily planning. That's really all we want."

It occurred to me that a certain rearrangement of people's daily planning might seem, in less rarefied air than is breathed at 120 South Spring, rather a great deal to want, but so impenetrable was the sense of higher social purpose there in the Operations Center that I did not express this reservation. Instead I changed the subject, mentioned an earlier "pilot project" on the Santa Monica: the big electronic message boards that Caltrans had installed a year or two before. The idea was that traffic information transmitted from the Santa Monica to the Xerox Sigma V could be translated, here in the Operations Center, into suggestions to the driver, and flashed right back out to the Santa Monica. This operation, in that it involved telling drivers electronically what they already knew empirically, had the rather spectral circularity that seemed to mark a great many Caltrans schemes, and I was interested in how Caltrans thought it worked.

"Actually the message boards were part of a larger pilot project," Mrs. Wood said. "An ongoing project in incident management. With the message boards we hoped to learn if motorists would modify their behavior according to what we told them on the boards."

I asked if the motorists had.

"Actually no," Mrs. Wood said finally. "They didn't react to the signs exactly as we'd hypothesized they would, no. *But.* If we'd *known* what the motorist would do . . . then we wouldn't have needed a pilot project in the first place, would we."

The circle seemed intact. Mrs. Wood and I smiled, and shook hands. I watched the big board until all lights turned green on the Santa Monica and then I left and drove home on it, all 16.2 miles of it. All the way I remembered that I was watched by the Xerox Sigma V. All the way the message boards gave me the number to call for CAR POOL INFO. As I left the freeway it occurred to me that they might have their own rapture down at 120 South Spring, and it could be called Perpetuating the Department. Today the California Highway Patrol reported that, during the first six weeks of the Diamond Lane, accidents on the Santa Monica, which normally range between 49 and 72 during a six-week period, totaled 204. Yesterday plans were announced to extend the Diamond Lane to other freeways at a cost of $42,500,000.

◆ DISCUSSION QUESTIONS

1. Identify the forces pressing for change in the transportation conditions in Los Angeles County.

2. Identify the sources of commuters' resistance to the changes imposed by Caltrans.

3. What does the automobile symbolize to the average American? How should this be taken into account in attempts to change driving habits? Review Didion's description of "participation in the freeway experience."

4. Describe the organizational culture at Caltrans. Examine the atmosphere in the Operations Center. How does this culture affect Caltrans' attitudes towards transportation problems and the assumptions it makes about commuters?

5. Didion claims that Caltrans' actual objective was "to eradicate a central Southern California illusion, that of individual mobility, without anyone really noticing." Compare this assessment with the statements of Caltrans spokesperson, Eleanor Wood. Whose view do you support and why?

6. Evaluate Caltrans' approach to changing the commuting habits of Angelenos. Why did these methods fail? Make recommendations for handling the change process more effectively. Consider methods of overcoming resistance to change [2]. Prepare an action plan to implement and evaluate the proposed changes [3].

◆ REFERENCES

1. Metzger, L. 1981. *Contemporary Authors*. New Revision Series. Detroit: Gale Research Co. Vol. 14.

2. Coch, L. and French, Jr, J. 1984. Overcoming resistance to change. *Human Relations*. 1:512–532.

3. Lewin, K. 1951. *Field Theory in Social Science*. New York: Harper & Row.

Quality

John Galsworthy

The theme of this story is expressed in its title. This 19th century vignette depicts an old world bootmaker who refuses to compromise his ideals by adopting the methods of mass production that are taking business away from him. As you read this touching portrait, think of the reasons why the bootmaker resists changing his ways.

John Galsworthy (1867–1933) was born into a well-to-do, middle-class English family. He graduated from Harrow and Oxford and was trained as a lawyer. Mr. Galsworthy is well known for the novel *The Forsythe Saga*. He received the Nobel Prize for Literature in 1932.

I knew him from the days of my extreme youth, because he made my father's boots; inhabiting with his elder brother two little shops let into one, in a small by-street—now no more, but then most fashionably placed in the West End.

That tenement had a certain quiet distinction; there was no sign upon its face that he made for any of the Royal Family—merely his own German name of Gessler Brothers; and in the window a few pairs of boots. I remember that it always troubled me to account for those unvarying boots in the window, for he made only what was ordered, reaching nothing down, and it seemed so inconceivable that what he made could ever have failed to fit. Had he bought them to put there? That, too, seemed inconceivable. He would never have tolerated in his house leather on which he had not worked himself. Besides, they were too beautiful—the pair of pumps, so inexpressibly slim, the patent leathers with cloth tops, making water come into one's mouth, the tall brown riding-boots with marvelous sooty glow, as if, though new, they had been worn a hundred years. Those pairs could only have been made by one who saw before him the Soul of Boot—so truly were they prototypes incarnating the very spirit of all footgear. These thoughts, of course, came to me later, though even when I was promoted to him, at the age of perhaps fourteen, some inkling haunted me of the dignity of himself and brother. For to make boots—such boots as he made— seemed to me then, and still seems to me, mysterious and wonderful.

I remember well my shy remark, one day, while stretching out to him my youthful foot:

"Isn't it awfully hard to do, Mr. Gessler?"

And his answer, given with a sudden smile from out of the sardonic redness of his beard: "Id is an Ardt!"

Himself, he was a little as if made from leather, with his yellow crinkly face, and crinkly reddish hair and beard, and neat folds slanting down his cheeks to the corners of his mouth, and his guttural and one-toned voice; for leather is a sardonic substance, and stiff and slow of purpose. And that was the character of his face, save that his eyes, which were grey-blue, had in them the simple gravity of one secretly possessed by the Ideal. His elder brother was so very like him—though watery, paler in every way, with a great industry—that sometimes in early days I was not quite sure of him until the interview was over. Then I knew that it was he, if the words, "I will ask my brudder," had not been spoken; and that, if they had, it was his elder brother.

When one grew old and wild and ran up bills, one somehow never ran them up with Gessler Brothers. It would not have seemed becoming to go in there and stretch out one's foot to that blue iron-spectacled glance, owing him for more than—say—two pairs, just the comfortable reassurance that one was still his client.

For it was not possible to go to him very often—his boots lasted terribly, having something beyond the temporary—some, as it were, essence of boot stitched into them.

One went in, not as into most shops, in the mood of: "Please serve me, and let me go!" but restfully, as one enters a church; and, sitting on the single wooden chair, waited—for there was never anybody there. Soon, over the top edge of that sort of well—rather dark, and smelling soothingly of leather—which formed the shop, there would be seen his face, or that of his elder brother, peering down. A guttural sound, and the tip-tap of bast slippers beating the narrow wooden stairs, and he would stand before one without coat, a little bent, in leather apron, with sleeves turned back, blinking—as if awakened from some dream of boots, or like an owl surprised in daylight and annoyed at this interruption.

And I would say: "How do you do, Mr. Gessler? Could you make me a pair of Russia leather boots?"

Without a word he would leave me, retiring whence he came, or into the other portion of the shop, and I would continue to rest in the wooden chair, inhaling the incense of his trade. Soon he would come back, holding in his thin, veined hand a piece of gold-brown leather. With eyes fixed on it, he would remark: "What a beaudiful biece!" When I, too, had admired it, he would speak again. "When do you wand dem?" And I would answer: "Oh! As soon as you conveniently can." And he would say: "To-morrow fordnighd?" Or if he were his elder brother: "I will ask my brudder!"

Then I would murmur: "Thank you! Good-morning, Mr. Gessler." "Goot-morning!" he would reply, still looking at the leather in his hand. And as I moved to the door, I would hear the tip-tap of his bast slippers restoring him, up the stairs, to his dream of boots. But if it were some new kind of footgear that he had not yet made me, then indeed he would observe ceremony—divesting me of my boot and holding it long in his hand, looking at it with eyes at once critical and loving, as if recalling the glow with which he had created it, and rebuking the way in which one had disorganized this masterpiece. Then, placing my foot on a piece of paper, he would two or three times tickle the outer edges with a pencil and pass his nervous fingers over my toes, feeling himself into the heart of my requirements.

I cannot forget that day on which I had occasion to say to him: "Mr. Gessler, that last pair of town walking-boots creaked, you know."

He looked at me for a time without replying, as if expecting me to withdraw or qualify the statement, then said:

"Id shouldn'd 'ave greaked."

"It did, I'm afraid."

"You goddem wed before dey found demselves?"

"I don't think so."

At that he lowered his eyes, as if hunting for memory of those boots, and I felt sorry I had mentioned this grave thing.

"Zend dem back!" he said; "I will look at dem."

A feeling of compassion for my creaking boots surged up in me, so well could I imagine the sorrowful long curiosity of regard which he would bend on them.

"Zome boods," he said slowly, "are bad from birdt. If I can do noding wid dem, I dake dem off your bill."

Once (once only) I went absent-mindedly into his shop in a pair of boots bought in an emergency at some large firm's. He took my order without showing me any leather, and I could feel his eyes penetrating the inferior integument of my foot. At last he said:

"Dose are nod my boods."

The tone was not one of anger, nor of sorrow, not even of contempt, but there was in it something quiet that froze the blood. He put his hand down and pressed a finger on the place where the left boot, endeavoring to be fashionable, was not quite comfortable.

"Id 'urds you dere," he said. "Dose big virms 'ave no self-respect. Drash!" And then, as if something had given way within him, he spoke long and bitterly. It was the only time I ever heard him discuss the conditions and hardships of his trade.

"Dey get id all," he said, "dey get id by advertisement, nod by work. Dey dake it away from us, who lofe our boods. Id gomes to this—bresently I haf no work. Every year id gets less—you will see." And looking at his lined face I saw things I had never noticed before, bitter things and bitter struggle—and what a lot of grey hairs there seemed suddenly in his red beard!

As best I could, I explained the circumstances of the purchase of those ill-omened boots. But his face and voice made so deep an impression that during the next few minutes I ordered many pairs. Nemesis fell! They lasted more terribly than ever. And I was not able conscientiously to go to him for nearly two years.

When at last I went I was surprised to find that outside one of the two little windows of his shop another name was painted, also that of a bootmaker—making, of course, for the Royal Family. The old familiar boots, no longer in

dignified isolation, were huddled in the single window. Inside, the now contracted well of the lone little shop was more scented and darker than ever. And
it was longer than usual, too, before a face peered down, and the tip-tap of the
bast slippers began. At last he stood before me, and gazing through those rusty
iron spectacles, said:

"Mr.—, isn'd it?"

"Ah! Mr. Gessler," I stammered, "but your boots are really *too* good, you
know! See, these are quite decent still!" And I stretched out to him my foot. He
looked at it.

"Yes," he said, "beople do nod wand good boods, id seems."

To get away from his reproachful eyes and voice I hastily remarked: "What
have you done to your shop?"

He answered quietly: Id was too exbensif. Do you wand some boods?"

I ordered three pairs, though I had only wanted two, and quickly left. I
had, I do not know quite what feeling of being part, in his mind, of a conspiracy
against him; or not perhaps so much against him as against his idea of boot.
One does not, I suppose, care to feel like that; for it was again many months
before my next visit to his shop, paid, I remember, with the feeling: "Oh! well,
I can't leave the old boy—so here goes! Perhaps it'll be his elder brother!"

For his elder brother, I knew, had not character enough to reproach me,
even dumbly.

And, to my relief, in the shop there did appear to be his elder brother,
handling a piece of leather.

"Well, Mr. Gessler," I said, "how are you?"

He came close, and peered at me.

"I am breddy well," he said slowly, "but my elder brudder is dead."

And I saw that it was indeed himself—but how aged and wan! And never
before had I heard him mention his brother. Much shocked, I murmured: "Oh!
I am sorry!"

"Yes," he answered, "he was a good man, he made a good bood; but he
is dead." And he touched the top of his head, where the hair had suddenly gone
as thin as it had been on that of his poor brother, to indicate, I suppose, the
cause of death. "He could nod ged over losing de oder shop. Do you wand any
boods?" And he held up the leather in his hand: "Id's a beaudiful biece."

I ordered several pairs. It was very long before they came—but they were
better than ever. One simply could not wear them out. And soon after that I
went abroad.

It was over a year before I was again in London. And the first shop I went
to was my old friend's. I had left a man of sixty, I came back to one of seventy-
five, pinched and worn and tremulous, who genuinely, this time, did not at first
know me.

"Oh! Mr. Gessler," I said, sick at heart; "how splendid your boots are!
See, I've been wearing this pair nearly all the time I've been abroad; and they're
not half worn out, are they?"

He looked long at my boots—a pair of Russia leather, and his face seemed to regain steadiness. Putting his hand on my instep, he said:

"Do day vid you here? I had drouble wid dat bair. I remember."

I assured him that they had fitted beautifully.

"Do you wand any boods?" he said. "I can make dem quickly; id is a slack dime."

I answered: "Please, please! I want boots all round—every kind!"

"I will make a vresh model. Your food must be bigger." And with utter slowness, he traced round my foot, and felt my toes, only once looking up to say:

"Did I dell you my brudder was dead?"

To watch him was painful, so feeble had he grown; I was glad to get away.

I had given those boots up, when one evening they came. Opening the parcel, I set the four pairs out in a row. Then one by one I tried them on. There was no doubt about it. In shape and fit, in finish and quality of leather, they were the best he had ever made me. And in the mouth of one of the town walking-boots I found his bill. The amount was the same as usual, but it gave me quite a shock. He had never before sent it in till quarter day. I flew downstairs and wrote a cheque, and posted it at once with my own hand.

A week later, passing the little street, I thought I would go in and tell him how splendidly the new boots fitted. But when I came to where his shop had been, his name was gone. Still there, in the window, were the slim pumps, the patent leathers with cloth tops, the sooty riding boots.

I went in, very much disturbed. In the two little shops—again made into one—was a young man with an English face.

"Mr. Gessler in?" I said.

He gave me a strange, ingratiating look.

"No, sir," he said, "no. But we can attend to anything with pleasure. We've taken the shop over. You've seen our name, no doubt, next door. We make for some very good people."

"Yes, yes," I said; "but Mr. Gessler?"

"Oh!" he answered; "dead."

"Dead! But I only received these boots from him last Wednesday week."

"Ah!" he said, "a shockin' go. Poor old man starved 'imself."

"Good God!"

"Slow starvation, the doctor called it! You see he went to work in such a way! Would keep the shop on; wouldn't have a soul touch his boots except himself. When he got an order, it took him such a time. People won't wait. He lost everybody. And there he'd sit, goin' on and on—I will say that for him—not a man in London made a better boot! But look at the competition! He never advertised! Would 'ave the best leather, too, and do it all 'imself. Well, there it is. What could you expect with his ideas?"

"But starvation—!"

"That may be a bit flowery, as the sayin' is—but I know myself he was sittin' over his boots day and night, to the very last. You see I used to watch him. Never gave 'imself time to eat; never had a penny in the house. All went in rent and leather. How he lived so long I don't know. He regular let his fire go out. He was a character. But he made good boots."

"Yes," I said, "he made good boots."

◆ *DISCUSSION QUESTIONS*

1. Describe Mr. Gessler's attitude toward his work. What does his work mean to him?

2. Why is Mr. Gessler so resistant to adopting the methods used by the mass production factories that are in competition with him? What is he afraid of losing?

3. This story paints a sympathetic portrait of old-world craftsmanship and condemns mass production. Examine passages in the story that convey this image. What can you say in support of mass production?

4. How can the work values held by craftspeople such as Mr. Gessler be instilled in individuals who work in large, contemporary business organizations? Discuss the forces pushing for change in this direction, and the forces against such change. What types of work design innovations would be appropriate for making this change?

5. The theme of this story is quality. Find passages in the story that suggest that quality refers to more than just workmanship. Also examine the tone with which the narrator refers to Mr. Gessler and his work.

High Hurdles: The Challenge
of Executive Self-Development

*Robert E. Kaplan ♦ Wilfred H. Drath ♦
Joan R. Kofodimos*

This articles probes why executives sometimes have trouble coming to grips with their deficits and offers suggestions for their self-development.

The three authors of this article are employed at the Center for Creative Leadership in Greensboro, North Carolina. Robert E. Kaplan is applications director. Wilfred H. Drath is a research project leader and publications editor. Joan R. Kofodimos is a behavioral scientist.

This paper is about self-development—the efforts of the executive to improve himself or herself, efforts that other people may well aid or hinder. By self-development we mean the conscious, deliberate effort to come to terms with one's limitations. We do not mean the kind of development that springs almost automatically from the new experiences that bring out latent abilities in the executive. We are also not concerned here with the considerable development executives have undergone on their way up.[1] Our interest is in self-aware, self-directed improvement once managers have reached the highest levels.

This paper explores the hypothesis that executives avoid coming to terms with their limitations and that the executive's organization and the people who work directly with the executive shy away from attempts to help. It is based on interviews we conducted with 40 individuals—22 executives and 18 experts on executives, including internal specialists in executive development and external consultants. For this study we defined an executive as an upper-level manager

Source: Excerpted from Robert E. Kaplan, Wilfred H. Drath, and Joan R. Kofodimos, "High Hurdles: The Challenge of Executive Self-Development," *The Academy of Management EXECUTIVE,* 1987, Vol. 1, No. 3, pp. 195–205. Reprinted by permission of the authors and publisher.

in a line position with general management responsibilities, or a high-level head of a function such as chief financial officer or vice-president of administration.[2]

Self-development is important because no executive can escape having deficits and because deficits matter to executives and their organizations.

Self-development is one route for dealing with an executive's deficits. It is a difficult route, one that is underutilized not just by executives but by all humans. Based on our interviews and reading, however, we have come to the conclusion that when people become executives they cross an invisible dividing line that makes self-development significantly more difficult for them. In this paper we will attempt to show just how difficult self-development is, particularly for executives—and how some of those difficulties might be overcome.

Four features stand out as especially affecting the executive's prospects for self-development. For the sake of exposition, we will be treating these features separately, though in reality they act in profound concert. First, we will discuss how the exercise of power keeps executives from getting personal criticism that could lead to the awareness of deficits. Second, we examine how another route to self-awareness—introspection—is blocked by the very nature of the executive job. Third, we'll look at how the ability to accept criticism is limited by the executive's high need to be—and to appear to be—exceptionally competent. Finally, we will discuss how a history of success makes change difficult for executives.

◆   POWER AND GETTING CRITICISM

Executives do not get much feedback from those around them in the organization.

We are not speaking here of the inevitable and frequent criticisms made of the decisions and policies of an executive. These appear regularly in the press and are leveled at executives from many outside interest groups. We are talking about feedback aimed not at what an executive does—the decisions he makes, the policies he formulates—but feedback aimed at how he does his job—his process of making a decision, his way of relating to others, his manner, style, behavior. In short, we are here discussing feedback aimed at the executive's modus operandi, at his managerial character. This is the kind of feedback, we found, that is impeded at the executive level. Our interviews revealed four factors related to the exercise of power that restrict feedback on executive behavior. These interrelated factors are (1) the executive's demeanor, (2) his exaggerated impact, (3) his isolation, and (4) and his relative autonomy.

The Executive's Demeanor

We found that the executive's bearing, his way of behaving around others, can inhibit feedback. This demeanor may stem from his mental acuity, his command of the issues, his history of success, or all three. Whatever its source, the demeanor of people in charge serves a useful—probably indispensable—function. A certain air of authority is no doubt necessary for executives to do their jobs. Yet no matter how necessary it is, an exaggerated, dominating presence often chokes off criticism. Clearly this is not the case with every executive. Some executives openly encourage feedback, though when this is done, the executive may still have problems convincing others of his sincerity.

In general, we found an implicit attitude in the executive's bearing that can discourage others from challenging him—especially about his management style. One executive development specialist put this attitude into words: "It's as if the executive is saying, 'I've made it to the top and one of the characteristics of being here is that the door opens one way; people don't swing my door open and tell me how to do my job.' " In other words, the executive's achievement entitles him to an exemption from advice and criticism.

In extreme cases, an executive's demeanor can cut off information brutally. Although any superior can do this to his or her subordinates, high-level managers have more power and perhaps also a greater need to exercise it. One executive we heard about almost talked in riddles so that not only did he want to control, to do it his way, but often he didn't communicate clearly to subordinates. "I don't understand what you want" was difficult for subordinates to say and even more difficult to repeat.

Such an extreme case illustrates the power of the executive's demeanor, but even in much less obvious cases there can be in the executive's demeanor an implied threat of using his position to a subordinate's disadvantage, which adds fear and resentment to the reasons that lead people to withhold criticism.

Ordinary abrasiveness can also block feedback. According to one of our sources, half the executives identified in his corporation as being "problems" were also considered "abrasive." "Zinging," as one respondent called it, usually destroys any instinct on the part of other people to help the executive with his problems, to give him constructive criticism, or to be a confidante.

To one degree or another, then, the executive's demeanor, which derives from who he is and what he does, affects the willingness of people around the executive to criticize his managerial behavior and character.

The Executive's Impact

One theme we heard again and again in our interviews centered on the executive's extraordinary impact on those around him. A casual comment can reverberate with significance. An executive told us the story of seeing a picture on a subordinate's office wall. He said casually to the subordinate, "Why do you have that picture?" He was only making conversation, or so he thought. The next day when he returned to the subordinate's office he noticed that the picture had been taken away. People hang (or unhang) on every word. Comments become commands; statements become injunctions.[3] This effect can become so pronounced that some executives must guard even the expression on their faces. "If I don't smile," one told us, "people think business is bad."

The problem with this exaggerated impact is that it makes some executives reluctant to speak out at all until they are ready to make a firm decision. They become reluctant to hold casual conversations that may, they fear, turn out later not to have been so casual after all. This tends to add distance to the relationships between an executive and those around him. Keeping one's own counsel, whatever its advantages, has the effect of excluding others from involvement in, say, a decision-making process. This makes for a cooler relationship in which people feel less free to offer criticism—and in which they have less personal contact to use as a basis for criticism.

But what about "insiders," those people with whom the executive feels free to discuss issues openly, with as much speculation and "running things up the flagpole" as he wants? Are they not a valuable source of feedback? For some executives they undoubtedly are. Yet to the extent that these insiders act as "cheerleaders" for the executive, the flow of behavioral information is likely to be retarded. This can happen to any executive, even one who tries to resist it, for the simple reason that such cheerleaders are often acting in their self-interest. They tell the executive what he wants to hear and omit what they do not want him to hear, including news of problems that might reflect badly on them.[4]

As potentially serious as this cheerleading can be, perhaps the most serious form of cheerleading is the unconscious kind, when subordinates don't withhold criticism but instead become blind to any faults in their highly placed superior. This is a form of collusion. Because of their dependency on him, subordinates cooperate with their superior in supporting the image of himself he wishes others to see.[5] By seeing the superior as he wishes to be seen, these subordinates cooperate with their superior in creating a "delusionary system."[6] Such a "delusionary system" is not likely to be fertile ground on which executives can learn and grow.

The Executive's Isolation

Besides this more or less structural isolation of executives, there is an isolation that comes from insulation—the tendency of the organization to protect its executives from the indignities and problems of everyday life. Such insulation can cause the executive to lose touch with the levels below and to become increasingly unaware of much of what is going on in the company.[7]

Isolation takes a toll on communications and criticism upward because the absence of contact guarantees the absence of communication, especially of sensitive information. Moreover, the scant communication that does occur usually takes place on the executive's turf, complete with the trappings of power and the symbols of isolation, all of which can make subordinates uneasy and less comfortable about speaking up.[8]

Executives may need to be somewhat removed to make their jobs feasible. Yet there is the counterbalancing problem: Isolation restricts criticism that an executive could use in an effort to develop and to perform his role even more effectively.

The Executive's Autonomy

Executives who have the autonomy to hire whomever they please can—and some do—often use that autonomy to hire people in their own image, people whose backgrounds, gender, and education make them compatible. Executives who do this are likely to end up with the cheerleaders we mentioned earlier, subordinates who tell them only what they want to hear.[9]

Executives are not likely to get criticism on their behavior by turning to such "mirrors." Performance appraisal is another means by which critical information can be delivered, an institutionalized way in which organizations overcome the disinclination to give feedback about performance. But as DeVries et al. have found in their review of appraisal practices in organizations, formal appraisals thin out at high levels.[10] One consultant described the attitude of executives toward appraisal this way: "You talk about performance appraisal at the executive level? Unh-uh. That's for you folks down there." Executives can, in effect, use their autonomy to exempt themselves from having their performance assessed in this way. When executives put themselves outside the appraisal system, who but the top person is to say otherwise? The personnel executive in charge of the system ordinarily lacks the clout to define it as including the top levels, or to enforce it if the top levels merely go through the motions of participating. In granting such autonomy to its executives, an organization is allowing its executives to grant themselves an immunity to being appraised.

Getting Criticism to the Executive

Though we found that power can and often does impede criticism of the executive's managerial character, we also learned about channels that create a healthier situation for the executive, one in which he receives the critical information he needs to pursue self-development. The solutions can be grouped into those things the organization can do, those things that people around the executive can do, and those things that the executive himself can do.

Organizations can, for example, do a lot to deemphasize power differences. Organizations can reduce the gap between executives and others by making executive offices less impressive and locating those offices closer to those of others.[11] Intel, for example, deliberately avoids separating senior and junior people with perks such as limousines, plush offices, private dining rooms, and other status symbols.[12] If organizations segregate executives less and take away some of the trappings of power, then executives may become more accessible.

Another thing organizations can do is to create mechanisms that generate constructive criticism of executives. Standard practices such as performance appraisal are available; the issue is whether they are applied to executives. Probably the key to whether executives receive appraisals is the top executive and the extent to which that person takes the system seriously and uses it personally.

From our interviews we also learned of other mechanisms the organization can use to encourage constructive criticism. One international financial organization conducts inspections of each major unit of the organization. A member of the board of directors heads a team of three, which goes into a division and conducts confidential interviews, the results of which are channeled to the division's top management. The report includes perceptions of the CEO and the top management team. Another corporation used an outside consultant, who knew the organization and had the respect of many people in it, as a kind of ombudsman. He kept his ear to the ground and regularly fed criticism of top management back to those concerned.

People around the executive also play an important role in freeing the channels for feedback. Although they are in a distinct minority, certain individuals in the executive's world do have the inclination and courage to tell the executive about his shortcomings.

Perhaps the most important factor is the attitude of the executive himself toward being criticized on his managerial behavior. Some executives make it a point to avoid becoming isolated and to solicit reactions to their work. More effective general managers build larger networks and make better, more skillful use of their relationships.[13] One human resources executive we interviewed commented that "the less secure [executives] really hide, but the more secure ones will step out of their offices or go down to the departments, make it a point to stay in touch." Another staff executive reported to us that people two or more levels below would never be open with him in his office, only if he went to them. We also heard from executives that they can learn what their subordinates think of them by paying close attention to cues. As one CEO put it, "You've got to learn how to read very subtle complaints." Furthermore, executives get explicit information about themselves only if they convince others of their desire for it by word and action. A CEO said: "People have to make sure they're being asked honestly, and what they are going to get back is not a 'Louisville slugger.' "

The exercise of power impedes the flow of constructive criticism, yet power must be exercised if executives are to do their jobs. So the issue is not how to reduce the power the executive needs, but how to manage those aspects of its exercise that impede criticism.

◆   THE NATURE OF THE JOB AND INTROSPECTION

Another way for executives to get criticism is from themselves, through introspection. Given the problems just discussed in getting criticism from others, executives may in fact need to rely on introspection more do than lower-ranking managers. Introspection is the process of looking inward, of examining or monitoring ourselves, of trying to understand our behavior, our feelings, our defenses, our effect on others. Introspection is a necessary step in the process of self-development, whether we introspect to gain new insight about ourselves or to make sense of criticism from others. Yet the likelihood that executives will spend time and energy in introspection must be considered in light of the extraordinary demands of their work and the degree to which introspection is immediately relevant to their day-to-day performance.

Most executives are faced with staggering, unremitting demands on their time.

But lack of time is not the whole story.

In part the issue comes down to attitude. Executives may not find the time because introspection is not a high priority. Executives do not value introspection because it is not immediately relevant to the performance of his work. The results an executive is concerned with are external and tangible—turning a plant around, improving profits, boosting productivity. Such results do not manifestly require self-understanding, and therefore do not seem to require introspection. Executives who do not see a connection between introspection and performance are understandably unwilling to give the time and energy that looking inward requires. The issue is not to turn executives into navel gazers, but to help them use introspection to gain information about themselves—their behaviors, their strengths and weaknesses—so that they may develop yet more effective managerial behavior.

◆   THE NEED TO BE COMPETENT AND THE ABILITY TO ACCEPT CRITICISM

We suggest that there is a relationship between the executive's reluctance to accept criticism and the executive's need to be competent. By need to be competent we mean a complex of attributes, including the need to be equal to the demands of the job, to live up to the expectations that come with high positions, and to have a sense of self-worth. A number of the people we interviewed called it "ego," by which they seem to mean pride in one's abilities and position. The need to be competent—to feel good about oneself—is something that all people have. If the executive is different, it is because he carries on this struggle on a larger stage and for higher stakes.

Several factors contribute to the executive's need to be competent. One factor is the set of expectations that come with the territory, a sense that the executive must be almost larger than life. As a highly placed manager who reported to the CEO of a major corporation told us,

> [The CEO] needs to be above everybody. He needs to be smarter than everybody, never wrong. . . . He has to act [as if he were] perfect.

Another factor is that, as holders of great responsibility, executives incur high risks. The high stakes make competent performance vitally important. Millions may be lost, lawsuits may be engendered, careers may be ruined, and jobs lost through the incompetence of a highly placed person.

Executives want to build and maintain their reputations as people who know what they are doing. The opinions they render and the policies they adopt are often highly visible and come under close scrutiny. The need to save face is therefore considerable. If executives make mistakes too often, they erode their confidence in themselves as well as the confidence of others in them. Because of this, some executives learn to be "thick skinned," they learn to protect themselves from criticism. The hitch is that they may learn this lesson too well.

The organization may cap all this by communicating its expectations of competence to the executive in powerful ways. One of the most powerful may be the special treatment that executives are accorded. Executives receive high—even exorbitantly high—salaries, are ensconced in opulent settings, and are afforded every convenience. The executive corridor typically stands as a monument to its occupants' importance.[14] As one executive said, "They sort of handle you like a precious egg." (*New York Times*, November 7, 1982) The implicit message in all of this may be that the executive had better live up to the high expectations of the organization as symbolized by the special treatment. The executive is likely to expect himself to be, and know that others also expect him to be, more than ordinarily competent.

Thus, the executive's expectations of himself and others' expectations of him can subtly—or not so subtly—nudge the executive into an unrealistic sense of his capability and importance—which in turn makes it difficult for him to hear and accept criticism. To the extent that the executive's ambition compensates for underlying doubts about himself, criticism may be unwelcome because it touches off an unconscious feeling of insecurity.

Our interviews provide support for this tendency for some executives to become unduly impressed with their competence and importance and therefore to reject criticism. A staff executive said, "Executives are susceptible to believing in their own infallibility. They think they can do no wrong."

As Hague pointed out,

> [The executive] may get conceited about his successes and blame his failure on external circumstances, but worst of all, he will cease to be self-critical and to learn from his experiences.[15]

Taken to the extreme, this can lead executives to become hypo-critical, and this can be perilous. Thus, confidence turned to arrogance can be the executive's downfall.[16]

What Can Be Done?

We have talked about the tendency for executives to be tempted by an exaggerated sense of their abilities and importance, but there is nothing that says an executive must succumb. Many executives resist this temptation. In fact, their need for competence prompts them to sit tight for criticism precisely because they want to be competent. They realize they must continue learning if they are to remain competent. One executive who made a practice of examining his management style reported that at the end of the day, "I go home to my wife and say, 'I can't be that smart, I can't do everything. . . .'"

By taking himself less seriously, the executive can go a long way toward reducing the loss of confidence that may come with accepting criticism. Yet we should not expect the executive to take himself lightly; he is likely always to feel the sting of criticism especially keenly. As Drucker points out, speaking of political and military leaders, "To be more [than mediocre] requires a man who is conceited enough to believe that the world . . . really needs him and depends on his getting into power."[17]

Good relations with one or more key people can help an executive overcome the temptation to reject criticism. A trusted colleague can help an executive accept negative information because there is an atmosphere of mutual respect.

Finally, if executives are to accept criticism more readily, organizations will probably need to open the way by reducing the link between making mistakes and being judged incompetent.[18] Too often a single mistake, if large enough, brands a manager as being unequal to the task. Yet McCall and Lombardo have shown that successful managers often make many big mistakes, and that the lessons they learn from such mistakes may be critical to their success.[19] Organizations must understand—and encourage their executives to understand—that admitting weakness or ineffectiveness can be the beginning of further development and increased competence.

◆ *SUCCESS AND THE MOTIVATION TO CHANGE*

To become an executive one must succeed, must make the most of ability, connections, and opportunities. Managers who eventually rise to become executives are often highly regarded from the beginning and therefore well situated in the "opportunity structure."[20] These managers usually receive choice assignments in which they distinguish themselves, which leads to further opportunity to advance. This string of success followed by opportunity, opportunity followed by success, stretching over a manager's career, is what Kotter called the "success syndrome."[21] Such a career history may leave a manager well acquainted with his strengths but relatively unacquainted with his weaknesses. More important, the highly successful executive may (with some justification) feel that changing his way of managing, even a little, could hurt his chances for future success.

We found that successful managers instinctively play hands off with their style of managing. It is a conservative, sometimes even superstitious attitude. Successful people see no reason to tamper with a winning formula.

Many successful executives may be worried, perhaps rightly so, about losing their effectiveness if they change. This anxiety may be coupled with a general fear of failure that researchers such as Jennings have noted in executives—an anxiety that they will not accomplish what they want.[22]

Rather than correcting deficiencies, successful executives seem more interested in building on strengths. We interviewed a rising young executive who, for example, excelled at conceptualizing and communicating. But when we asked him whether he tried to develop himself as a manager, the two things he mentioned as developmental targets were analytical ability and communication, just those things he already did well. Although building on strengths can be an effective developmental approach, if it becomes a substitute for correcting deficiencies, if an executive is developmentally satisfied merely to get better at what he or she is already good at, then weaknesses will remain, and they may eventually outweigh the strengths. Building on strengths is the kind of change people generally find comfortable; correcting weaknesses is risky and painful.

Is it success itself that makes change difficult for executives? Isn't the reluctance to change just human nature? Our interviews suggest that success is indeed a significant factor. As one management consultant observed:

> I've worked with people on a lower management rung all the way up to the people at high levels and certainly the people who are lower are much more willing to look at themselves. They're still trying to find their leadership style, define what's going to lead to success in their organizations.

As these managers become more successful, their motivation to change can diminish.

How Do Executives Change?

Executives change for the same reasons that anyone changes—because they want to or have to. The motivation to perform well impels executives to pursue their own development. One group vice-president we heard about started each year by giving his immediate subordinates his agenda for personal change for the coming year. By making his plans public, he committed himself to change.

When the individual executive will not pursue needed change on his own, then an option is for other people to step in and press for change. Alcoholics represent a classic case of executives who have problems that they usually don't solve voluntarily. The task of penetrating these layers of rationalization with which alcoholics surround themselves may require as drastic a step as surprise confrontation.

To overcome stiff resistance to change, it takes manufactured crises like these—or the naturally occurring ones, like actual career failure or life crises, which in one fell swoop can penetrate consciousness, command acceptance, and touch off an effort to change. Even someone else's trouble, when it hits close to home, can encourage learning. One consultant to executives describes a typical reaction to a co-worker being fired: "I thought he was safe and he just got shot down. Am I next? Maybe I'd better not have those blind spots."

◆   CONCLUSION

The best use of self-analysis and self-redirection is in response to a specific need: a setback at work, repeated difficulties at one's job, a career impasse, a transition to radically different responsibilities, a crisis at home, or a build-up of health-threatening stress. Self-development is one effective way to come to terms with transitions, crises, setbacks, or persistent tension from any source. People with a sense of well-being "take time for critical self-reflection only when approaching a tough transition or after making one."[23] Introspection peaks at times of transition and drops to low levels at other times. Executives who react to being plateaued, demoted, or terminated by immediately finding another job and scrupulously avoiding any self-scrutiny are setting themselves up for a repetition of the same problem in their next job.

There is an irony in all of this. The executive whose power, impact, access to resources, experience and skill, and wealth, social position, and success all work to set him above most of his fellow humans and grant him the means to influence and accomplish great things may find more difficulty than most in knowing himself, and he is constrained by his condition from the fullest development of his capabilities. In human, organizational, and societal terms, and despite the obstacles that impede it, self-development for executives is a frontier worth exploring.

◆ ENDNOTES

1. There is a growing body of literature on this subject, including the following: D. W. Bray, R. J. Campbell, and D. L. Grant, *Formative Years in Business: A Long-Term AT&T Study of Managerial Lives.* New York: Wiley-Interscience, 1974; W. Bennis, *The Unconscious Conspiracy: Why Leaders Can't Lead.* New York: AMACOM, 1976; E. H. Schein, *Career Dynamics: Matching Individual and Organizational Needs.* Reading, MA: Addison-Wesley, 1978; and M. M. Lombardo, M. W. McCall, Jr., A. M. Morrison, and R. P. White, "Key Events and Learnings in the Lives of Executives." In M. Lombardo (Chair), "Key Events and Learnings in the Lives of Executives." Symposium presented at the 43rd Annual Meeting of the Academy of Management, Dallas, 1983.

2. All the executives we interviewed and described in the interviews were men. In generalizing from these interviews, we therefore limit our remarks to male executives and use the masculine pronouns exclusively. Also for information regarding this study, a longer version is available from the Center for Creative Leadership, 500 Laurinda Drive, P.O. Box P-1, Greensboro, NC 27402-1660.

3. See R. D. Laing, *Self and Others.* London: Penguin, 1967, for a psychological exposition of this power phenomenon.

4. See, for example, W. H. Read, "Upward Communication in Industrial Hierarchies." *Human Relations* 1962, 15, 3–15; and T. Burns and G. M. Stalker, *The Management of Innovation.* London: Social Science Paperback, Tavistock Publications, 1961.

5. E. Goffman, *The Presentation of Self in Everyday Life.* Garden City, NY: Doubleday, 1959.

6. M. F. R. Kets de Vries, "Managers Can Drive Their Subordinates Mad." *Harvard Business Review* 1979, 57(4), 125–134.

7. For a brief discussion of this "losing touch" behavior, see R. Townsend, "Further Up the Organization." *New Management* 1984, 1(4), 6–11.

8. F. Steele, "The Ecology of Executive Teams: A New View of the Top." *Organizational Dynamics* 1983, 11(4), 65–78.

9. The following authors have highlighted this problem: A. Zaleznik, and M. F. R. Kets de Vries, *Power and the Corporate Mind.* Boston: Houghton Mifflin, 1975; W. Bennis, *The Unconscious Conspiracy: Why Leaders Can't Lead.* New York: AMA-COM, 1976; and R. M. Kanter, *Men and Women of the Corporation.* New York: McGraw-Hill, 1977.

10. D. L. DeVries, A. M. Morrison, M. L. Gerlach, & S. L. Shullman, *Performance Appraisal on the Line.* New York: John Wiley & Sons, 1981.

11. See Steele, Endnote 12.

12. A. S. Grove, "Breaking the Chains of Command (My Turn)." *Newsweek,* October 3, 1983.

13. J. P. Kotter, *The General Managers.* New York: The Free Press, 1982.

14. See, again, Steele, Endnote 8.

15. H. Hague, *Executive Self-Development: Real Learning in Real Situations.* New York: Wiley, 1974.

16. M. W. McCall, Jr. and M. M. Lombardo, *Off the Track: Why and How Successful Executives Get Derailed (Tech. Rep. 21).* Greensboro, N.C.: Center for Creative Leadership, 1983.

17. P. F. Drucker, *The Effective Executive.* New York: Harper & Row, 1966.

18. T. J. Peters and R. H. Waterman, Jr., *In Search of Excellence.* New York: Harper & Row, 1982.

19. See McCall and Lombardo, Endnote 16.

20. See Kanter, Endnote 9.

21. See Kotter, Endnote 13.

22. E. E. Jennings. *The Executive in Crisis.* New York: McGraw-Hill, 1965.

23. G. Sheehy, *Pathfinders.* New York: William Morrow & Co., 1981.

Ethical Codes Are Not Enough

Michael R. Hyman ♦ *Robert Skipper* ♦
Richard Tansey

This article poses the question: "How can a company best train its managers to be moral?" As the title suggests, ethical codes are only part of the solution. The authors present a six-point checklist to evaluate the ethical dimensions of decisions.

Michael R. Hyman is an associate professor of marketing at the University of North Texas, Denton. Robert Skipper is editor for Shepherd Systems, Inc. Richard Tansey is an assistant professor of marketing at the University of Wisconsin—Green Bay.

Many companies have ethical codes, some of which are quite extensive. Some of the best are those of Boeing, GTE, Hewlett-Packard, Johnson & Johnson, and the Norton Company. But ethical codes are usually either too vague or too detailed for practical use. Codes formed of generalizations, according to Donald G. Jones [1], "give people little or no guidance in their day-to-day behavior. Going to the other extreme may be even more dangerous, however. Setting out detailed rules in an attempt to cover all conceivable situations creates . . . a tendency to substitute rules for judgment. The hidden danger is the temptation to use the absence of a direct rule as a reason for plunging ahead even when one's conscience says 'no.' "

♦ GLAUCON AND THE MODERN COMPANY

So exactly what are the hallmarks of good companies? How can a "moral climate" be distinguished from any other climate? From the inside, one can tell good companies by the way they are bound together by mutual trust and co-operation. From the outside, one can spot a good company by the way its actions and advertisements seem to say "we will be around forever." Acting as if one will be around forever is a sign that one is acting ethically.

In *The Republic,* Plato dealt with the key question: Is a just life any better than an unjust one? In that dialogue, the students who had gathered around Socrates ventured several feeble reasons, most of which assumed that justness always led to pleasure, while injustice led to pain. Glaucon, a more cynical character, was not convinced. He asked Socrates to imagine a case in which the results were not so happy. Suppose an unjust man had a magic ring that made him invisible, and a just man had another ring like it. The just man, being modest, would perform good actions and take no credit, whereas the unjust man would do evil with no blame. Glaucon then wondered what would make justice better than injustice, if justness led to poverty while injustice led to riches and pleasure. In modern guise, Glaucon's challenge is: "If a person could lie, cheat, and steal and never be caught, why would he or she ever be honest?"

Glaucon's challenge is faced every day by millions of business people. The argument is very persuasive. In fact, some would say it cannot be refuted without religion. Although we will not answer the challenge, we can make use of it. When people talk themselves into unethical acts, they do so by pretending that there are no consequences to suffer. Some people refuse to even think about the consequences, some conveniently forget them, and some engage in wishful thinking. From nibbling a candy bar to embezzling a million dollars, a temptation is only as great as its cost is small.

When we said that a company is good only if it acts as if it will be around forever, we meant that the actions of a good company clearly show the managers to be always thinking about long-range consequences. In contrast, companies with mistreated workers, bad credit, poor customer service, or environmental problems are usually also companies with no real hopes for the future. The expression "fly-by-night" denotes not only impermanence, but also irresponsibility.

◆   THOUGHTFUL MANAGERS PERSONIFY COMPANY VALUES

"Managers," says Levering [2], "act as *coordinators*—the folks who organize things so that work done by one part of the organization can be used effectively by another part." A manager is also an ethical link between labor, shareholders, suppliers, and customers. Whether meaning to do so or not, each manager sets an example for the rest of the company with his or her every action. The manager, in normal day-to-day activity, indirectly teaches others what is forbidden, what is condoned, and what is required. A manager, therefore, is a showcase for the company.

Recently, business ethics has become a topic of little debate and much concern. Business ethics generates little debate because everyone agrees that business people, like everyone else, should act ethically. Ethics, however, is a topic of much concern, because business people make everyday decisions that are fraught with moral implications.

Yet one question that has resisted easy answers is, "How can a company best train its managers to be moral?" Simply offering a list of rules to memorize will not create moral managers, because no number of rules and policies will add up to a single good act. By the same token, no book of restrictions and guidelines can treat every problem that will arise. Thus, even well-intentioned managers will make mistakes when they confront real problems that are not covered by company policy. Moral action requires a knowledge of all the alternatives, foresight into all the consequences, and two things for which few people have the time: practice and review.

We feel that the keystone to solid moral thinking lies not in having all the answers, but in asking productive questions. According to Tad Tuleja [3], "Human judgment is notoriously unstable, but moral attitude —what some ethicists call 'moral character'—is not. Ethical judgment consists not in getting the right answer all the time, but in consistently asking the right questions." Thus, we suggest that companies interested in the ethical instruction of managers not rely exclusively on general laws engraved in stone tablets, but supplement their rules with a checklist of specific, easy-to-apply questions designed to provoke the type of thinking that usually guides an ethical act.

◆   A CHECKLIST FOR EVALUATING MANAGERIAL DECISIONS

There is no substitute for experience and time. Harried managers, however, must have a way to streamline their ethical thinking. By honestly answering the questions in the figure, managers can bring into relief the underlying moral structure of a decision.

This checklist draws attention to some of the more common causes of unethical decisions. A check in the "yes" column suggests the proposed decision be either changed or discarded. At a minimum, a "yes" means that more care is needed than with decisions scoring all "no"s.

What this checklist does not do is give pat responses to tough problems. Positive solutions always require ingenuity, imagination, and insight. A perfect score will not guarantee the "rightness" of a decision, but it improves the chances of its being ethical. Managers must add their own questions to the list, as their companies, experiences, and personalities dictate.

Bringing the Checklist into Focus

What kinds of productive thoughts might be stimulated by this checklist? Here, in addition to a fuller explanation of what is meant by each checklist question, are some practical examples.

Question #1: "Does my decision treat me, or my company, as an exception to a convention that I must trust others to follow?" If the answer is "yes," there could be ethical problems. Perhaps there are alternatives that do not flout conventions. The smooth functioning of business and society depends on everyone conforming to thousands of rules, both written and unwritten. Diverse examples of conventions are: taking turns, asking permission to smoke in another person's room, being punctual for appointments, parking in proper parking spaces, following through on promises, telling the truth, respecting the property of others, paying taxes, and obeying the law.

FIGURE
GENERAL ETHICAL CHECKLIST

	Yes	No
1. "Does my decision treat me, or my company, as an exception to a convention that I must trust others to follow?"	—	—
2. "Would I repel customers by telling them?"	—	—
3. "Would I repel qualified job applicants by telling them?"	—	—
4. "Have I been cliquish?" (If "Yes," answer questions 4a through 4c. If "No," skip to question 5.)	—	—
4a. "Is my decision partial?"	—	—
4b. "Does it divide the constituencies of the company?"	—	—
4c. "Will I have to pull rank (use coercion) to enact it?"	—	—
5. "Would I prefer to avoid the consequences of this decision?"	—	—
6. "Did I avoid any of the questions by telling myself that I could get away with it?"	—	—

The most common source of unethical acts is the temptation to think of oneself as special. Every wrong can be seen as a case of twisting around a well-known tradition, practice, etiquette, protocol, strategy, technique, rule, or law so that it works against those people who abide by it. For example, only when people form orderly lines can someone gain an advantage by cutting into line. Only if honesty is the norm can lying succeed.

Sam, the president of a small company that develops computer software, is bidding on a contract—a billing program for a local hospital. He faces a choice about timeliness: he could promise a delivery date that is either realistic or overly optimistic. He fears that a realistic promise would lose the contract. He knows that if he overstates and wins, the truth will only come out when it is too late for the hospital to switch to another software company. What should he do? Can he get away with underestimating the time needed to complete the task?

The first question on the checklist would force Sam to think about misrepresenting his service. Truth-telling is perhaps the most commonly assumed convention in the business world. If Sam were to lie, even if he believes that winning the contract is the only way to meet his payroll this month, he would show contempt for business tradition.

Because Sam is the president of his company, his actions set an example for everyone else. If Sam's overstatement is taken to heart by the rest of his company, some people will follow his lead and make their own hyperbolic promises to him. Sam will soon discover that when he exaggerates the already exaggerated claims of others his projections are impossible to fulfill.

Suppose the checklist had made Sam notice that his proposed method of winning the bid was unethical. He might then have realized that his false promises would guarantee customer dissatisfaction. Ethics aside, if he realized how badly this would violate the marketing concept, he might have taken the time to work out another approach. Knowing that few software companies are known for timeliness, he could try to make a name for his company by always delivering a superior product when promised. He could have told the hospital administrators the most probable delivery schedule. If they insisted that he work as fast as one of his competitors claimed to work, he could agree to do so for a premium that would cover the cost of engaging sufficient subcontractors.

Some people feel that the world of business is cutthroat, that what people normally call treachery is nothing more than "business savvy." These people might argue that being deceitful, far from making themselves exceptions to any rule, puts them right in line with standard business practice.

Even if one grants the (false) claim that deceit is rampant in the business world, to argue this way is to confuse a common practice with a convention. There is no convention forcing people to steal, even though theft is common. Bad grammar is the norm; good grammar is the convention. Thus, if one is tempted to avoid the first question by pointing out that "all the others do it," one should ask whether "all the others" are following a rule or breaking one.

Question 2: "Would I repel customers by telling them?" If the answer is "yes"—that is, if a news story exposing the decision would lower profits—it is appropriate to rethink the decision. One should always be suspicious of any act that must be kept quiet. The impending danger is not the obvious consequence that the secret might leak out, but rather the easy-to-ignore consequences of secrecy becoming standard.

This checklist question is similar to but goes far beyond the marketing concept. The marketing concept tells us that the consumer is king: every decision must be made with the goal of profitably satisfying the needs of the consumer in mind. The marketing concept, unfortunately, does not say anything about decisions that may be hidden from the consumer.

Many consumers of foodstuffs are just as concerned with the social history as with the physical chemistry of the product. For example, among many Californians, the demand for some produce varies with the working conditions of the migrant farm hands. For another example, many vegetarians, while having no general qualms about eating flesh, nonetheless boycott commercial meats in protest of the treatment livestock typically suffers in the cote and the abattoir. These examples, and others like them, show that manufacturers must sometimes think of ethics as an additive.

Many times, the answer to Question #2 will be: "I'm not ashamed of the decision. In fact, it saves the customers money. But, because some people might take it the wrong way, I would hate to see it splashed across the front page of the *New York Times*."

If a manager answers in this way, perhaps the decision needs more thought. If only the cleverest and subtlest arguments can salvage a decision, the arguments against it are probably far stronger.

Question #3: "Would I repel qualified job applicants by telling them?" If the answer is "yes," the decision may be unethical. Decisions that would repel the best workers are decisions that hurt the company. For example, conscientious cooks would be wary of working in a restaurant where the manager recently fired a waiter for telling the local press about major health violations.

Betsy manages the field service for a marketing research firm. She must decide whether to enact the following policy: all interviewers, to increase the response rates, are to represent themselves as college students working on a class project. This technique would be very effective, she reasons. It would save money. It might not lose any clients, even if they knew about it (Question #2). Furthermore, by encouraging her interviewers to lie, she herself would not be lying (Question #1).

Question #3 would make Betsy realize that many interviewers would turn down work under those terms. Honesty is a vital trait for interviewers, and the best job applicants would refuse to lie. Betsy understands that if they would be willing to lie to the respondent in order to get his or her cooperation, they cannot be trusted to turn in accurate data to Betsy.

Question #4: "Have I been cliquish?" If the answer is "yes," the manager may not have a broad enough perspective to make an ethical choice. How many opinions are enough? It depends. In a small research firm, five opinions may be more than enough; in a large chemical company, a thousand opinions may be far from enough. Just as the definition of cliquish will differ from one company to another, so too will the methods of obtaining feedback. However Question #4 is best phrased for a particular company, the guiding principle is clear: when fewer people are involved, important issues are more likely to be overlooked.

Says a manager at Mattel Toys, "Ours is a very open company. The most ethical decisions at Mattel are the ones that make the rounds of the whole firm. Decisions directly vary in quality with the number of people involved in making them. When enough people set their minds to work, many bad decisions—what you might call the 'unethical' ones—get weeded out, not so much for moral reasons (at least not on the surface), but because there is always an economically better way."

The reason it works this way is simple. When one person does something for the good of a group, we say he or she is acting morally. But when many people elect to do the same something for themselves, we say they are acting solely in their own self-interest. Thus, any action undertaken by a manager with the approval of a large enough group is automatically moral.

When Dillard's of Arkansas bought Joske's of Texas, Dillard's made no apparent effort to learn from Joske's. Dillard dismissed all the top levels of management and revamped the stores. One major decision was to dismiss all security guards and to remove the bullet-proof glass in the cash offices. Such a decision might have been appropriate for Arkansas, which reported in 1986 an average of 79.7 robberies for every 100,000 people, but it was not appropriate for Texas, which reported a rate in excess of three times that of Arkansas during the same year (239.9 robberies per 100,000 people).

There are two times when company-wide input is impossible or impractical. First, emergencies, as a general rule, must be dealt with at once, by a handful of people, and with little debate. For example, the Tylenol deaths forced a quick, responsible answer from James Burke, chairman of Johnson & Johnson. If the issues had been discussed too long, any well-intentioned action (such as a total product recall or the initiation of a tamper-proof packaging system) may have come too late. Although true emergencies are a good excuse for failing to consult with others, they are just that—an excuse. Any excuse, when overused, becomes feeble. Even in emergencies, there is almost always time to solicit input from a few others. For example, when hurricane Gilbert threatened the Gulf Coast in 1988, Douglas W. Matthews, Galveston's city manager, claimed to have consulted eight department heads before ordering an evacuation.

Second, the need for secrecy may limit the size of a decision-making group. For example, in testing product ideas that cannot be patented, small groups must operate in isolation from the rest of the company.

Emergencies and espionage are two good reasons for confining certain decisions to small, isolated groups. But these are the exceptions, not the norm. Normal, daily business activity is not filled with emergencies and espionage. If it is, something has gone very wrong with the climate. Suppose, however, that good reasons exist for making a cliquish decision. Questions 4a–4c are intended to partly mimic the broadened perspective that other viewpoints could have provided.

Question #4a: "Is my decision partial?" Partiality concerns the unfair distribution of advantages and disadvantages. Does the decision seem to benefit one person or one group without benefiting others? Does the decision make one person or group bear the brunt of a setback while the rest of the company remains untouched? Worst of all, does the decision take away from one group and at the same time benefit another? If the answer is "yes," the decision is partial and could be bettered by one that distributes the benefits or hardships more equitably.

In their effort to acknowledge the value of workers, many companies are committed to job security. For example, Johnson Wax, Hallmark Cards, Hewlett-Packard, DEC, and IBM all have no-layoff policies. There are other ways of showing fairness to employees. Federal Express has a Guaranteed Fair Treatment program that encourages employees who have had problems with supervisors to talk with managers higher in the organization. Levering observes that "good workplaces typically have a variety of *practices that reduce class distinctions*" [4]. He points out that hardly any of the best 100 companies to work for have executive dining rooms that are off-limits to other employees. All employees at Marion Laboratories get stock options. Some companies, like Advanced Micro Devices, have taken the egalitarian spirit into the streets by eliminating executive parking lots.

Question #4b: "Does it divide the constituencies of the company?" This question is closely tied to the previous one, because partial decisions, by treating different groups differently, often split companies into warring factions. Of course, every company has some conflict between goals, but managers need not act in ways that heighten the clash.

Traditionally, labor and management have goals that mix about as well as oil and water. These two groups spoke to each other only in the language of power. Recently, however, various techniques of wedding labor's interest to those of management have been tried. ESOPs were obvious peace offerings. Flex plans, like that of Steelcase, have also been tried. Some companies, such as Volvo, are using other techniques, such as automatic guided vehicles (AGVs).

Question #4c: "Will I have to pull rank (use coercion) to enact it?" If the answer is "yes," perhaps another decision can be found that will sell itself. If a decision is not popular with everyone, only a threat will make it work. But threats are always unwise, because they teach the wrong lessons and they cause more problems than they solve.

People don't like being monitored for productivity any more than they like being treated as if they are thieves; they often take a productivity score to be both an insult and a dare. Foley's of Houston keeps tabs on certain office people by counting the number of customer calls they take. Because "taking a call" is measured by counting the number of times an employee disconnects, customers may call several times before their complaints are processed. Occidental Petroleum measures the productivity of its programmers by counting keystrokes at a computer terminal. This rewards sloppy programming. Cashier productivity, at scanner-equipped grocery stores, may be measured in "dollars per minute" while the cashier is actively signed onto the register. Under this system, cashiers can improve their productivity figures, without increasing dollars checked, simply by ignoring the smaller orders and checking only larger ones. Managers who harp on these dollars-per-minute figures are, in effect, lowering real productivity.

To monitor employees and tell them how they are being evaluated is to redirect their energy into trying to outsmart the system. If one lazy employee learns how, all the others are soon made to look bad. One by one, they all give up trying to be really productive and start working on higher productivity scores.

Question #5: "Would I prefer avoiding the consequences of this decision?" This question is intended to make sure that an imminent promotion, transfer, or retirement is not coloring the decision. If a manager is counting on being absent for the repercussions of a decision, he or she might need to look more carefully at those repercussions. In the zeal to make the current quarterly report the best possible, the future may be forgotten. Aided by fast promotions and frequent transfers, many managers may outrun the real consequences of their decisions for a long time. Question #5 simply draws attention to this possible source of nearsightedness.

Companies, like people, are born and die within a span of time. Companies and people have histories, some that are sources of pride, some of shame. Companies and people have futures they can either worry about or look forward to.

When a rational person thinks about his or her choices and their effects, the value of today's self is no greater than that of tomorrow's self, or that of the day after, or that of 20 years from now. But an irresponsible person values today above all others and acts as if there will be no tomorrow. Clearly, because the rational person takes steps to prolong and enrich his or her life, this normally means outliving the reckless, careless person by many happy years. So too with companies. A history of bare, quarter-to-quarter survival, where any setback would have proven catastrophic, is not reassuring to employees, managers, or investors.

Question #6: "Did I avoid any of the questions by telling myself that I could get away with it?" In a sense, this is the most important question of all. It is an honesty check, ensuring that the real issues have been looked at. The very things managers think they can get away with are probably the same things their staffs are already getting away with. If not, by adopting such decisions, managers teach their staffs how.

For example, if the answer to Question #1 was, "I can get away with it, the customers will never know," the question was brushed off. The very idea of "getting away" with something means the decision is questionable—whether from a practical, a cultural, an economic, a technological, or a moral standpoint. Businesses that thrive on "getting away" with things do not get away with much for long.

◆ REFERENCES

1. Jones, D.G. 1982. *Doing Ethics in Business: New Ventures in Management Development*. Cambridge, MA: Oelgeschlager, Gunn & Hain.

2. Levering, R. 1988. *A Great Place to Work: What Makes Some Employers So Good (And Most So Bad)*. New York: Random House.

3. Tuleja, T. 1985. *Beyond the Bottom Line: How Business Leaders Are Turning Principles into Profits*. New York: Facts on File.

4. Op. cit Levering, R. 1988.

◆ ADDITIONAL REFERENCES

Cohn, B. August 1, 1988. A Glimpse of 'Flex' Future. *Newsweek*. 38–39.

Guzman, W. April 25, 1986. Big Can Still Be Beautiful. *Fortune*. 25–28.

Keogh, J. ed., 1988. *Corporate Ethics: A Prime Business Asset—A Report on Policy and Practice in Company Conduct.* New York: The Business Roundtable.

Parker, M., and Slaughter, J. October 1988. Management by Stress. *Technology Review.* 38–44.

Managing Diversity

Gretchen Haight

This article presents demographic evidence that organizations need to learn how to manage an increasingly diverse work force. Obstacles to understanding people from other backgrounds are explored, and the results of corporate training programs on the management of diversity are featured.

Gretchen Haight is a Los Angeles freelance writer and former managing editor of *Across the Board.*

No one yet knows how to manage a diverse workforce, says Theodore E. Payne, a manager in the corporate affirmative action and equal opportunity department at Xerox Corporation, a company that has been in the forefront of affirmative action efforts ever since civil rights legislation passed in the '60s. "We set goals for each group and try to make managers accountable, but we haven't begun to manage differently. It's still white males telling white males how to manage women and minorities.

"Managing diversity is not natural," explains Payne, who is black. "There's a synergy among likes. Lots of things go unsaid. There's a breakdown in synergy when people are unlike. Even at the top levels, there's something missing when people are unlike. Of 250 vice presidents and directors at Xerox, 42 are minorities and 12 are women, but there's something missing. It's difficult to identify exactly what. In fact, that's probably the major challenge in managing diversity." Payne believes that managers need to be more sensitive to communications difficulties within work groups that include minorities. The diversity of the workforce, which can act as a drag on productivity, can also be turned into an asset, he feels.

During the Reagan years, companies were under less pressure to hire and promote minorities. Many companies saw this as a message that they didn't have to bother—and they didn't. They hired minorities in compliance with the law, but let it go at that. Managers made few minority promotions. Turnover was high, and resentment dragged down worker morale.

Then, in 1987, the Labor Department released its *Workforce 2000* report, which catalyzed renewed efforts toward affirmative action. The report's detailed demographic forecast made it clear that women and minorities, well-adapted to

Source: Excerpted from Gretchen Haight, "Managing Diversity," reprinted from *Across the Board: The Conference Board*, 845 Third Avenue, New York, NY 10022. March, 1990, pp. 22–29. Reprinted by permission of the author and publisher.

corporate life or not, couldn't be ignored. By the year 2000, it said, they would make up 85 percent of the net increase in the national workforce.

Companies concerned by this have been turning to consultants who offer "managing-diversity" training. Such training is available in a variety of forms—one-, two-, and three-day courses, videotapes, seminars, and private consultations. Its objective is two-fold: for managers to learn how to work with people different from themselves, and for underutilized employees to become better adjusted to corporate culture.

The training relies on a basic premise: The problems we have in communicating with people different from ourselves reflect previous experience—or lack of experience—with difference. Often we're not even aware of how we're reacting to others or don't understand how our reactions appear. When our intentions are good but we are told our behavior is racist or sexist, we find the indictment too harsh. But psychologists urge us to look again. A recent article in *The New York Times* provides partial insight into the problem: "The growing consensus from psychological experiments is that racial and ethnic prejudices are an unfortunate byproduct of the way the mind categorizes all experience. Essentially, the mind seeks to simplify the chaos of the world by fitting all perceptions into categories. Thus it fits different kinds of people into pigeonholes, just as it does with restaurants or television programs."

Most of today's training in managing diversity helps individuals to confront their pigeonholes—to better understand their prejudices and those of the people they work with. A corollary to this is that we can't treat everybody the same, as we used to believe. People are different and, as *The New York Times* article points out, "when people try to act color-blind, as though there were no racial or ethnic differences, it backfires." It isn't even enough to treat people as individuals. Part of each person's individuality is his background, which must be understood in order to best manage him.

Companies have different reasons for calling in managing-diversity consultants. Some, such as Xerox, do so because affirmative action is already part of their corporate culture. "When Reagan came into office," says Theodore Payne, "a lot of people at Xerox were relieved—until they got a letter from David Kearns, Xerox's chairman and CEO, saying that it doesn't matter, Xerox is still supporting affirmative action."

Other companies use consultants because they fear affirmative action may not be part of their culture. When Hughes Aircraft Company was undergoing the equal opportunity compliance review three years ago that led to its testifying before the House of Representatives' Subcommittee on Employment Opportunities, it recruited Price Cobbs, one of the most sought-after figures in the managing-diversity business, to help improve its affirmative action program. Though Hughes was not found to have violated any affirmative action law, the company asked Cobbs to continue holding counseling sessions.

A black psychiatrist who switched to management consulting 25 years ago, Cobbs meets with managers and minority employees at Hughes, sometimes together, sometimes separately, and asks such fundamental questions as: "When did you first become aware of difference?" This results in some pretty candid answers according to Terian C. Day, a black who is director of human resources for the space and communications group at Hughes. A white male manager frankly told how his father, a member of the police force of a small Southern California town in the '50s, had been responsible for running Hispanics and blacks out of town. Of course that man will have trouble seeing blacks and Hispanics as intellectual equals, says Day. "Cobbs tells people, 'Don't beat up on yourself about it, but know your own baggage.' "

In a similarly disconcerting exercise, Cobbs asks people to make a list of characteristics following the heading "Blacks are . . ." White managers usually don't want to put anything on the list, says Day. But coaxed by Cobbs, with reassurances that they're not bad or racist, they typically fill in "aggressive, lazy, sexual." Cobbs also asks blacks to list the stereotypical ways in which they are often viewed. "Blacks know their own stereotypes better than whites," Day says. "Their lists are usually not much different from those of the white managers."

When Day first met Cobbs, he thought Cobb's exercise was designed to show that there is something wrong with blacks. He didn't like that. Then he found there really was something that had to be fixed: attitude. "That doesn't include 100 percent of blacks," Day says, "but usually if there are 15 people they'll all have it. It's the idea that 'All I have to do is sit at that desk and do my job. I'm not going to play politics, go to lunch with people just to get ahead, play up to my boss.' "

Over the past two years, Day has set up three career development classes for minority employees with high potential. One class is all black, the other two, black and Hispanic. Because Hughes is satisfied with its representation of women and Asians in its professional and management categories, there has been no such program set up for them.

The question of whether to segregate groups or have one group for all qualified minority employees is a sensitive one. Many employees are insulted when placed in segregated groups; they feel they're being given remedial help. But mixed groups frequently just don't work. Day, who didn't think his company could handle the idea of separate groups, included white women, blacks, and Hispanics in his first career development class. "It was a nightmare," he says. "The blacks were more emotional, more verbal, more firm in it being a bad place to be. Women felt they had their own issues. The Hispanics were passive." Some companies start out with separate groups and work toward integrating them, which, after all, is the point of the sessions. But when problems are being addressed for the first time, separate career development groups are almost always necessary.

Day is pleased with the results of the classes, which have met quarterly for the past two years. He says of the participants. "They can't see how far they've come. But the rage is down. They're not complaining about having to go to lunch with the boss. They see how important it is to develop the nontechnical side of their jobs, to fit in, to network. The corporate culture is not going to change—it's up to the employees themselves whether they want to fit in or not.

The people who have been successful have mastered that environment." He adds proudly that at least half of the members of his groups have received promotions so far.

Security Pacific Corporation has been in the business of managing diversity for as long as anybody. "Nine years ago," says Jackie Hempstead, a black woman who is vice president of human resources, "Dr. Cobbs came in and met with Security Pacific's senior management. He got out on the table their unconscious prejudices, but we think we're past a lot of that."

Cobbs's involvement with Security Pacific began as an outgrowth of a report from the company's black officer task force which had formed in the late '70s. The report was a long laundry list of suggestions for improving relations with minority employees, including recommendations that senior officers become more visibly involved in affirmative action and that training sessions be offered for middle and senior level managers to improve their ability to manage minority employees.

Cobbs was brought in to conduct some of the initial training; now Security Pacific has another system for coaching and supporting minority employees. A program called the minority officers network is made up of chapters located in each of the bank's geographic regions. These chapters encourage the formation of separate ethnic support groups for black, Hispanic, and Asian managers. If there is not sufficient interest for separate groups, a multicultural group may be formed. Anyone is welcome to join any group, which eases fears about what groups may be talking about. "There are whites who have belonged to the black managers' group for years," Hempstead says. More than a dozen network members are selected each year to attend quarterly dinners with Robert H. Smith, Security Pacific's president, to air minority problems and suggest possible solutions.

Another minority effort at Security Pacific is a program in which employees are assigned mentors from the area of banking they are interested in. Ethnic or gender likeness is not a criterion in the selection of the mentor, as minority network members said they felt they already received that kind of support from their network groups.

Not every minority employee chooses to participate in these programs, "We don't force them on anyone," explains Hempstead. "It's not for everybody. Lots of people don't want to be bothered, or don't want to give up part of an evening," she says. "Also, many people will complain until they know there's a resource, then they become silent."

Day of Hughes Aircraft says he concentrates more on career training for minority employees than on teaching managers how to manage diversity. "We're much more successful with them [minorities] than we are with upper management. It's difficult to keep any issue a high priority with management when it is a nonoperating issue.

"What has to happen is that each manager must say when there is a job to be filled, 'Go find me a woman or a minority as one of the candidates.' The usual answer is: 'But I thought you wanted me to find the best person.' " Such unconscious devaluing of minority intellect starts before an individual has even been hired. When Day went through 1,500 blue sheets for interviews, he found that black job applicants were given three or four times as many interviews as white applicants. And he discovered that in the space reserved for interviewer comments it usually said "affirmative action hire" for blacks and Hispanics, rather than some color-blind judgment.

"The hardest part of all this," Day says, "is that when managers make decisions they think they're making fair, objective evaluations. But the ratings for blacks are always lower. Hispanics' are low, too, but the blacks' are worse. The Hughes population is big enough that minority ratings should have a normal evaluation curve." Day suggests to managers: "If you think you're being fair, see if the data support fairness." By data he means the manager's written evaluations of employees: Are his evaluations of blacks always lower than his evaluations of whites? Likewise, in evaluating women, managers should always think twice if they have written "too aggressive."

Numbers tell the story, says David R. Barclay, vice president of human resources at Hughes' corporate headquarters. "Measurement in other areas isn't based on how one feels, but on how many missiles are sent out the back door," he says. When he came to Hughes 18 years ago, Barclay says, 11 percent of the workforce was made up of women and minorities; today it's 31 percent. In 1987 Barclay became the first black vice president in the company. Currently, among the 95 vice presidents, there are three Hispanics, two blacks, one Asian, and two women. Minority employees are not yet evenly dispersed among different divisions; at present, blacks and Hispanics are most prevalent in manufacturing. Management slots are still slow to be filled by blacks and Hispanics because, in many cases, candidates still lack adequate science background. This reflects a nationwide shortage of blacks and Hispanics with a science or engineering background.

The problem of making managers responsible for promoting minorities haunts many companies. Xerox, in its original 1972 affirmative action plan, adopted an innovative program to promote minority employees to top management levels. Key jobs in each area of the company that had once been held by the company's senior leaders were identified. In sales, for example, the position of sales manager was recognized as a key job to have en route to the top. The five regional vice presidents, each with approximately 100 sales managers, were then told to have a certain percentage of minorities promoted each year to that position. "It was a way to prime the pump," says Theodore Payne. "In the beginning we had very tough conversations, but after two or three years, if managers hadn't gone along with the program, they were moved aside. We don't have to do that anymore, but it took 10 years."

At Security Pacific, affirmative action is now a category for evaluation in a manager's job review. He is judged on his attitude rather than by any specific criteria. At Hughes, managers' bonus reviews include a grade for affirmative action performance, but how that grade is weighed relative to other aspects of a manager's job varies from case to case. It is a perplexing problem: How does a company justify taking away part of someone's bonus for underperforming in affirmative action when he has produced outstanding profits for the company? It's not a popular idea.

One obstacle to minority support programs has been that it is difficult to explain what is gained by managing for diversity. There is, of course, the honorable reason—"it's the right thing to do" but that holds little water when a company is eyeing its profit margin. Some argue that companies are more creative when they have input from all kinds of people, but there's scant evidence to prove it. Companies do lose the cost of their investment in training when disenchanted minority employees leave, but, besides that, there has been little clear bottom-line motivation for getting along better with those who are different. Companies have begun to realize, however, that the statistics in the *Workforce 2000* report give them bottom-line numbers. To be competitive in the coming years with the coming labor force, they will have to make managing diversity a strategic priority.